THE GACACA COURTS, POST-GENOCIDE JUSTICE AND RECONCILIATION IN RWANDA

Since 2001, the gacaca community courts have been the centrepiece of Rwanda's justice and reconciliation programme. Nearly every adult Rwandan has participated in the trials, principally by providing eye-witness testimony concerning genocide crimes. Lawyers are banned from any official involvement, an issue that has generated sustained criticism from human-rights organisations and international scepticism regarding gacaca's efficacy.

Drawing on more than seven years of fieldwork in Rwanda and nearly 500 interviews with participants in trials, this in-depth ethnographic investigation of a complex transitional justice institution explores the ways in which Rwandans interpret gacaca. Its conclusions provide indispensable insight into post-genocide justice and reconciliation, as well as the population's views on the future of Rwanda itself.

PHIL CLARK is a research fellow in courts and public policy at the Centre for Socio-Legal Studies, University of Oxford, and a convenor for Oxford Transitional Justice Research. He has used his experience and knowledge of conflict issues in Africa and elsewhere to provide policy advice to a wide range of government and non-government actors.

CAMBRIDGE STUDIES IN LAW AND SOCIETY

Cambridge Studies in Law and Society aims to publish the best scholarly work on legal discourse and practice in its social and institutional contexts, combining theoretical insights and empirical research.

The fields that it covers are: studies of law in action; the sociology of law; the anthropology of law; cultural studies of law, including the role of legal discourses in social formations; law and economics; law and politics; and studies of governance. The books consider all forms of legal discourse across societies, rather than being limited to lawyers' discourses alone.

The series editors come from a range of disciplines: academic law, socio-legal studies, sociology and anthropology. All have been actively involved in teaching and writing about law in context.

Series editors

Chris Arup *Monash University, Victoria*

Martin Chanock *La Trobe University, Melbourne*

Pat O'Malley *University of Sydney*

Sally Engle Merry *New York University*

Susan Silbey *Massachusetts Institute of Technology*

Books in the series

Diseases of the Will
Mariana Valverde

The Politics of Truth and Reconciliation in South Africa: Legitimizing the Post-Apartheid State
Richard A. Wilson

Modernism and the Grounds of Law
Peter Fitzpatrick

Unemployment and Government: Genealogies of the Social
William Walters

Autonomy and Ethnicity: Negotiating Competing Claims in Multi-Ethnic States
Yash Ghai

Constituting Democracy: Law, Globalism and South Africa's Political Reconstruction
Heinz Klug

The Ritual of Rights in Japan: Law, Society, and Health Policy
Eric A. Feldman

The Invention of the Passport: Surveillance, Citizenship and the State
John Torpey

THE GACACA COURTS, POST-GENOCIDE JUSTICE AND RECONCILIATION IN RWANDA

Justice without Lawyers

Phil Clark

CAMBRIDGE UNIVERSITY PRESS
Cambridge, New York, Melbourne, Madrid, Cape Town,
Singapore, São Paulo, Delhi, Tokyo, Mexico City

Cambridge University Press
The Edinburgh Building, Cambridge CB2 8RU, UK

Published in the United States of America by Cambridge University Press, New York

www.cambridge.org
Information on this title: www.cambridge.org/9781107404106

First published 2010
Fourth printing 2011
First paperback edition 2011

A catalogue record for this publication is available from the British Library

Library of Congress Cataloguing in Publication data
Clark, Phil, 1979–
  The Gacaca courts, post-genocide justice and reconciliation in Rwanda : justice
  without lawyers / Phil Clark.
  p. cm. – (Cambridge studies in law and society)
  Includes bibliographical references and index.
  ISBN 978-0-521-19348-1
  1. Gacaca court system. 2. Genocide–Rwanda. 3. Restorative justice–Rwanda.
  I. Title. II. Series.
  KTD454 .C57
  364.15′10967571–dc22
  2010021886

ISBN 978-0-521-19348-1 Hardback
ISBN 978-1-107-40410-6 Paperback

CONTENTS

ACKNOWLEDGEMENTS

This book is the result of nine years of research, beginning as a doctoral thesis at the University of Oxford between 2001 and 2005 and continuing as a postdoctoral project until 2010. It therefore draws on the support and advice of more people than can be reasonably thanked here.

I am deeply indebted to my DPhil supervisors, Professor Henry Shue and Professor David M. Anderson, for their engagement with this project over many years and their constant encouragement and insight.

Since 2001, I have received generous financial and other assistance from a range of institutions, including the Rhodes Trust, Balliol College, Brasenose College, the Department of Politics and International Relations, the Foundation for Law, Justice and Society, the Centre for Socio-Legal Studies and the Faculty of Law at the University of Oxford, the Open Society Justice Initiative in New York, and the Transitional Justice Institute at the University of Ulster. These institutions enabled the fieldwork and the space to think and write that made this book possible.

My family has provided constant love and humour throughout this project, especially the Clark clan (Mum, Dad, Dan, Dave and Steve) in Adelaide and Darwin, Lis and Norm in Adelaide and Belfast, and John and Sandi in Melbourne.

I have benefited enormously from discussions about Rwanda with Zachary Kaufman, Solomon Nsabiyera, Maria Warren, Levi Ochieng, Mark Drumbl, Lars Waldorf, Mauro De Lorenzo, Bruno Versailles and Harry Verhoeven, whose comments and suggestions have constantly sharpened my thinking. Also vital in this regard has been the feedback from lectures and seminars that I delivered at the Kigali Institute of Science and Technology, the Kigali Institute of Health, the National Service of Gacaca Jurisdictions, and the Rotary Club of Kigali-Virunga.

In Oxford and Belfast, an incredible group of friends and colleagues has always taken a keen interest in my research. I am particularly grateful to Clinton Free, Len Epp, Niall Maclean, John and Jo Pickhaver, Ian Macauslan, Anamitra Deb, Jan Strugnell, Chloe Lamb, Nick Gallus,

Tony Buti, Alex Wyatt, Kirk Simpson, Michael Hamilton, Jérémie Gilbert, Shane Darcy, Sara Templer, James Hickling, Steve Allender, Megan Claringbold, Charlie and Gill Foster, Steve and Marj Daley, Luke Jones and Greg O'Mahoney.

Some very special characters outside of Oxford have supported me throughout the writing of this book, particularly Kym, Dianne, Liz and Amanda Boxall, Bill and Sue Bonney, Robyn George, Phil Gregory, Mark Bahlin, Matt Skopal, Brett Stanford, Josh Couts, Paul Eagleton, Jenny Loken and Nate Keidel.

Finally, for her ceaseless love, care, humour, inspiration and passionate insight into Rwanda, I can't give enough thanks to Nikki. I am sure we have many more gloriously winding Great Lakes roads ahead of us.

ABBREVIATIONS

AI	Amnesty International
ASF	Avocats Sans Frontières
BBC	British Broadcasting Corporation
CNDH	National Human Rights Commission
CTV	Canada Television
DCHR	Danish Centre for Human Rights
DDR	Disarmament, Demobilisation and Reintegration
DRC	Democratic Republic of Congo
EU	European Union
FAR	Forces Armées Rwandaises
FDLR	Forces Démocratiques de Libération du Rwanda
FRELIMO	Frente de Libertação de Moçambique
GSF	Genocide Survivors' Fund
HRW	Human Rights Watch
ICC	International Criminal Court
ICG	International Crisis Group
ICTR	International Criminal Tribunal for Rwanda
ICTY	International Criminal Tribunal for the former Yugoslavia
IRDP	Institut de Recherche et de Dialogue pour la Paix
IRIN	Integrated Regional Information Networks
LC	Local council
LIPRODHOR	Ligue Rwandaise pour la Promotion et la Défense des Droits de l'Homme
LRA	Lord's Resistance Army
MDR	Mouvement Démocratique Républican
MINIJUST	Ministry of Justice
MINISANTE	Ministry of Health
MINITER	Ministry of the Interior
MRND	Mouvement Révolutionnaire National pour le Développement

NSGJ	National Service of Gacaca Jurisdictions
NGO	Non-Governmental Organisation
NHCHR	Norwegian Helsinki Committee for Human Rights
NPI	Newark Park Initiative
NRM	National Resistance Movement
NURC	National Unity and Reconciliation Commission
OAU	Organisation of African Unity
PARMEHUTU	Parti du Mouvement de l'Emancipation des Bahutu
PFR	Prison Fellowship Rwanda
PRI	Penal Reform International
RC	Resistance council
RCD	Rally for Congolese Democracy
RPF	Rwandan Patriotic Front
RTLM	Radio-Télévision Libre des Mille Collines
TIG	Travaux d'Intérêts Généraux
TRC	Truth and Reconciliation Commission
UPC	Union de Patriotes Congolais
UN	United Nations
UNAMIR	United Nations Assistance Mission for Rwanda
UNESCO	United Nations Educational, Scientific and Cultural Organisation
UNHCR	United Nations High Commissioner for Refugees
UNOMUR	United Nations Observer Mission Uganda-Rwanda
UK	United Kingdom
US	United States
USAID	United States Agency for International Developmentw

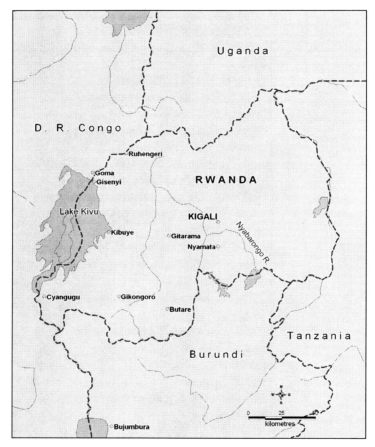

Map of Rwanda

INTRODUCTION

INTRODUCING GACACA

In a Rwandan village near the Burundi border, a crowd chatters impatiently beneath a tattered blue tarpaulin shielding them from the midday sun. Before them on a long, wooden bench sit nine elders, mostly middle-aged men and women, led by a young man – the president of the panel – who stands and addresses the gathering. The president explains that in their midst today is a prisoner, released from jail a week ago, who has confessed to committing crimes during the 1994 Rwandan genocide, which in a little over three months claimed the lives of between 500,000 and 1 million Tutsi and their perceived Hutu and Twa sympathisers.[1] The task of this gathering, the president explains, is to listen to anyone from the village who saw what this prisoner did, to hear from the victims' families of their pain after losing loved ones during the genocide, and for the nine judges – who have been elected by the community for their wisdom, love of truth and justice and dedication to the well-being of the village – to decide the case of the accused. The president calls for a minute's silence in memory of those killed during the genocide and then,

---

[1] There is significant debate over exactly how many Tutsi were killed between April and July 1994. In her comprehensive analysis of the Rwandan genocide, Alison Des Forges estimates that 500,000 Tutsi were murdered (A. Des Forges, *Leave None to Tell the Story: Genocide in Rwanda*, New York: Human Rights Watch, 1999, pp.15–16). Eminent historian Gérard Prunier, however, calculates 'the least bad possible' number of deaths to be 850,000 (G. Prunier, *The Rwanda Crisis: History of a Genocide*, London: Hurst & Co., 1998, p.265). Most writers estimate the number of Tutsi deaths during the genocide to be in the range of 500,000 to 1 million. The exact numbers, however, are not crucial to this book.

after reading a list of procedures that will guide the running of today's meeting, he motions the prisoner forward to address the assembly.

A murmur goes through the gathering as the prisoner walks to the front, standing between the crowd and the line of judges. He mumbles and the president tells him to speak up. The man, with head bowed, explains that he has come to confess that he killed the wife of his neighbour in the first week of May 1994. He found the woman hiding in bushes as gangs of killers walked the paths of the village searching for Tutsi. When he found her, she was crying, screaming at him to let her go. He pulled her out of the bushes and threw her to the ground, then slashed his machete once across her neck, then again, and left her to die. The prisoner, head still bowed, says that he has come today to apologise for what he did. When he was in jail, he had many years to think about his actions, and his conscience was so heavy that he confessed his crimes to the authorities.

A pause, and then the president asks the assembly if this man's testimony is true and complete. The crowd remains silent. Eventually one man at the back stands and says that, yes, it is true that this prisoner killed the woman. But what he has not told the assembly is that the following day he also killed the woman's son with a machete and threw the body in a pit latrine. Another woman stands and says that she too saw the prisoner kill the boy. The president asks the prisoner to respond to these new accusations. The man raises his head slightly and says that it is not true that he killed his neighbour's son; when he received word that the boy was dead he himself was miles away on the road to Kigali, where he had fled in shame after murdering his neighbour's wife. Voices clamour in the crowd: 'He's lying – I saw him in the village on the day the boy was killed.' 'I saw him too – he spoke to my wife in the courtyard that afternoon'. 'And he killed others – more than the woman and the boy.'

The president asks for calm and for each person in the assembly who wishes to speak to do so one at a time. People start to cry. The judges seated on the bench scrawl in the notepads on their laps. In one week they will have to decide what crimes the man committed during the genocide and what punishment he should receive. When this case is decided, there will be more cases, more stories of pain and loss, more claims and counter-claims, more details to verify, more decisions.

This hearing took place in the Bugesera region of Kigali Ngali province in 2003 and represents a common scene from thousands of towns and villages across Rwanda that since 2002 have been participating in a revolutionary court system known as 'gacaca'.[2] Derived from the Kinyarwanda word meaning 'the lawn' or 'the grass'[3] – in reference to the conducting of hearings in open spaces in full view of the community – gacaca is a traditional Rwandan method of conflict resolution that has been controversially revived and transformed to meet the perceived needs of the post-genocide environment.[4] Gacaca gives respected individuals elected by the local population the duty of prosecuting cases and excludes professional judges and lawyers from participating in any official capacity. In 2001, more than 250,000 gacaca judges were elected by their communities in 11,000 jurisdictions.[5] Broadly speaking, the dual aims of gacaca are to prosecute genocide suspects – approximately 120,000 of whom had already been detained in jails around the country when gacaca was inaugurated – and to begin a process of reconstructing the damaged social fabric.[6]

In the face of extreme individual and social devastation, gacaca represents an ambitious attempt to involve the entire population in the processes of justice, reconciliation and post-genocide reconstruction. Among transitional justice institutions around the world, gacaca is unique in its mass involvement of the population that experienced mass conflict firsthand. Today, a huge percentage of Rwandan adults have participated in gacaca in some way, including hundreds of thousands who have been judges or testified during hearings. As Peter Uvin, a Belgian specialist on Rwanda, argues, 'Politically, [gacaca is] a brilliant piece of work. It offers something to all groups – prisoners, survivors – it offers them all hope, and a reason to participate.'[7] As we will see later, however, many critics, particularly human-rights observers, argue that gacaca constitutes an illegitimate form of popular justice that will violate individual rights, especially those of genocide suspects.

The purpose of this book is to explore the nature of gacaca as an institution, to identify its objectives and to judge its effectiveness in

---

[2] Author's gacaca observations, Kigali Ngali, Bugesera, 19 May 2003.

[3] F. Reyntjens, 'Le Gacaca ou la Justice du Gazon au Rwanda', Politique Africaine, December 1990, p.32.

[4] In the remainder of this book, I refer to the historical form of gacaca as 'traditional gacaca' and the modern, genocide-focused version (which the government has termed either the Kinyarwanda phrase 'inkiko gacaca' or the 'juridictions gacaca') as simply 'gacaca'.

[5] African Rights, 'Gacaca Justice: A Shared Responsibility', Kigali: African Rights, January 2003, p.2.

[6] Ibid., p.1.

[7] P. Uvin, quoted in G. Packer, 'Justice on a Hill: Genocide Trials in Rwanda', Dissent, 49, 2, spring 2002, www.dissentmagazine.org/archives/2002/sp02/packer.shtml.

responding to the legacies of the genocide. Different sources, whether among the Rwandan government, the population or observers, interpret gacaca and its aims in various ways and inevitably differ in their views of gacaca's efficacy. One main aim of this book is to more clearly analyse what gacaca is designed to achieve than most observers – and many participants in gacaca – have done so far. At the time of writing, gacaca was nearing completion, having tried hundreds of thousands of genocide suspects. This book explores gacaca's objectives, which will then allow us to more carefully analyse its practice and long-term impact.

ANALYSES OF GACACA TO DATE AND OVERLOOKED ISSUES

The literature on gacaca has mushroomed in recent years, especially after gacaca was extended from a pilot phase in select communities to nationwide operation in early 2005. Analyses of gacaca can be divided roughly into three camps, which are discussed in greater detail later in this book: first, the dominant view of gacaca comes from human rights and legal commentators, either observers from international non-governmental organisations (NGOs) such as Human Rights Watch (HRW) and Amnesty International (AI) or non-Rwandan academic observers. These commentators interpret gacaca primarily as a judicial institution that can be analysed through its governing legal documents and are highly critical of the process. They argue that gacaca's primary objective is the punishment of genocide perpetrators, which they generally claim should help deter future criminals.[8] The second group of commentators, which has emerged more recently, comprises a small number of non-Rwandan academics, including Bert Ingelaere and Lars Waldorf, who have conducted extensive fieldwork into gacaca and criticise various aspects of its practice, particularly what they perceive as the Rwandan state's coercion of popular involvement in gacaca and interference during hearings in order to collectivise the guilt of

---

[8] For an example of HRW's analysis of gacaca, see A. Des Forges and K. Roth, 'Justice or Therapy? A Discussion on Helena Cobban's Essay on Crime and Punishment in Rwanda', *Boston Review*, summer 2002, www.bostonreview.net/BR27.3/rothdesForges.html. See also AI, 'Rwanda – Gacaca: A Question of Justice', AI Doc. AFR 47/007/2002, December 2002. For two key examples of the strictly legal interpretation of gacaca by academic authors, see J. Sarkin, 'The Tension between Justice and Reconciliation in Rwanda: Politics, Human Rights, Due Process and the Role of the Gacaca Courts in Dealing with the Genocide', *Journal of African Law*, 45, 2, 2001, pp.143–72; A. Corey and S. Joireman, 'Retributive Justice: The Gacaca Courts in Rwanda', *African Affairs*, 103, 2004, pp.73–89. I provide a fuller analysis of the range of sources in this first group of observers in Chapters 2 and 10.

all Hutu.[9] Finally, a third group of commentators includes several Rwandan and non-Rwandan observers (of whom Alice Karekezi, Simon Gasibirege and Mark Drumbl are among the main proponents) who argue that gacaca aims to punish *génocidaires* but also contributes (to varying degrees) to other post-genocide objectives, particularly reconciliation.[10] These observers highlight, often implicitly, the need to analyse gacaca both as a set of legal statutes and as a socio-legal practice, in which participants' involvement in, and interpretations of, gacaca are important for understanding and critiquing the institution as a whole.

The analysis of gacaca in this book falls in the third category of interpretation, focusing on a wide range of legal and non-legal objectives, while employing the detailed fieldwork and observations of gacaca hearings that are central to the second category. However, this book seeks to overcome deficiencies in all three groups of analysis. While this book concurs with the second and third groups of commentators that the first view misrepresents gacaca by failing to interpret the institution as an evolving socio-legal practice, the second and third perspectives are also largely inadequate for two main reasons. First, they do not directly counter the deficient analysis of gacaca offered by human rights commentators. In particular, the second and third groups of commentators fail to explain why it is necessary to analyse gacaca on the basis of the population's views and participation during hearings. In response to this shortcoming, this book offers for the first time a detailed critique of the dominant discourse on gacaca and more clearly justifies the need to analyse gacaca as a dynamic, lived socio-legal institution. Furthermore, the

[9] See, for example, B. Ingelaere, 'The Gacaca Courts in Rwanda', in L. Huyse and M. Salter (eds.), *Traditional Justice and Reconciliation after Violent Conflict: Learning from African Experiences*, Stockholm: IDEA, 2008, pp.24–59; B. Ingelaere, '"Does the Truth Pass across the Fire without Burning?" Transitional Justice and its Discontents in Rwanda's Gacaca Courts', Institute of Development Policy and Management Discussion Paper, University of Antwerp, November 2007; L. Waldorf, 'Mass Justice for Mass Atrocity: Rethinking Local Justice as Transitional Justice', *Temple Law Review*, 79, spring 2006, pp.1–92.

[10] See, for example, A. Karekezi, 'Juridictions gacaca: lutte contre l'impunité et promotion de la réconciliation nationale', in E. Ntaganda (ed.), *Les Juridictions gacaca et les processus de réconciliation nationale*, Cahiers de Centre de Gestion des Conflits (no. 3), Butare: Université Nationale du Rwanda, May 2001, pp.9–96; S. Gasibirege, 'L'Élection des juges *Inyangamugayo*: rupture ou continuité?' in E. Ntaganda (ed.), *De la paix à la justice: les enjeux de la réconciliation nationale*, Cahiers de Centre de Gestion des Conflits (no. 6), Butare: Université Nationale du Rwanda, November 2002, pp.93–127; M. Drumbl, 'Punishment, Postgenocide: From Guilt to Shame to Civis in Rwanda', *New York University Law Review*, 75, November 2000, pp.1221–326. I provide a fuller analysis of the range of sources in this second group of observers in Chapters 5–9.

book seeks to overcome a perceived weakness in the second category of analysis, namely the authors' tendency to overstate the role of the Rwandan government in controlling gacaca to the detriment of a finer-grained analysis of popular participation in, and shaping of, gacaca. This book therefore focuses strongly on the agency of everyday Rwandans, while also recognising the crucial national socio-political context within which gacaca operates.

Second, most commentators who imply that an appropriate analysis of gacaca requires close empirical consideration of how gacaca functions have not yet observed and analysed gacaca in this way. What unites the first and third camps of observers is a lack of first-hand observations of gacaca hearings, which would enable an examination of the practice – and not only the potential – of gacaca. Because gacaca is a deeply personal and inter-personal experience for those who participate in it, we require a detailed understanding of people's actions and interactions during hearings and their long-term effects.

This book represents one of the first detailed qualitative accounts of how gacaca operates on a day-to-day basis, based on my personal observations of gacaca hearings, focusing on the population's active involvement in the institution and the key external social, cultural, legal and political factors that influence this. Crucially, this book constitutes the first academic analysis of the entirety of the gacaca process, as my desk research commenced in October 2001, several months after the start of pre-gacaca hearings, and my fieldwork spanned the period from January 2003, when the first genocide suspects began returning from prison to their home communities to await gacaca trials, until April 2010, as gacaca was completing its final cases. This book also draws on 459 interviews with all relevant categories of actors in gacaca, from the officials who created the institution in the late 1990s to academic and NGO observers to everyday citizens who today participate in it, thus combining 'high' and 'low' investigations (including multiple interviews with many of the same individuals over more than seven years) to provide a comprehensive popular and political view on the intentions, modalities and outcomes of gacaca.

METHODOLOGICAL ISSUES

While Chapter 3 outlines in greater detail the analytical rationale for interpreting and critiquing gacaca in this book, it is necessary here to outline some key issues concerning the adopted research methodology, beginning with my main approaches to fieldwork and ending with a brief consideration of some of the research problems encountered. This book focuses on popular understandings of gacaca, interpreted on the basis of 356 interviews that I conducted during fifteen months of fieldwork between January 2003 and April 2010 with genocide suspects, survivors, gacaca judges and the general population, especially in rural communities, and from first-hand observations of sixty-seven gacaca hearings in eleven communities in five provinces. Many current analyses of gacaca take a detached view, interpreting it solely on the basis of its governing legal statutes. The aim of this book is to view gacaca close-up, to analyse what Rwandans in different regions say about gacaca and crucially how they participate in it and live through it, thus treating gacaca as a kinetic social institution that is shaped heavily by the population's perceptions and actions.

Broadly speaking, my fieldwork comprised two phases, which are reflected in the structure of Chapters 6–10: first, I conducted semi-structured, qualitative interviews with official, popular and observer sources regarding the objectives that they associated with gacaca. These interviews involved open-ended, non-leading questions designed to allow respondents to discuss gacaca in their own terms. On the basis of those interviews, I designed the conceptual framework of gacaca's nine objectives detailed later in this book, within which I undertook the second phase of this research, namely the empirical analysis of gacaca's practical operation in communities across Rwanda. The purpose of this approach was to develop a conceptual framework that derived from the perspectives of the parties who in various ways were intimately connected to gacaca, rather than adopting a free-standing conceptual apparatus that would bear little resemblance to how people personally engaged in gacaca have understood the institution.

My general fieldwork method was first to conduct interviews in 2003 with confessed *génocidaires* in four *ingando* or 'solidarity camps', which constitute civic education centres for various groups in Rwanda, principally provisionally released genocide detainees: in Kinyinya (Kigali Ville province), Gashora (Kigali Ngali), Butare Ville (Butare) and Ruhengeri Ville (Ruhengeri).[11] In each camp, I distributed around 200 questionnaires, requesting detainees' personal information, such as name, sex,

---

[11] The Rwandan government and population often use the terms 'ingando' and 'solidarity camps' interchangeably. Given that the former term has predominated in Rwandan discussions in recent years, I use it throughout the remainder of this book.

age, birthplace, the category of the genocide crimes to which they had confessed, level of education and religion.[12] These questionnaires gave crucial insights into the background of genocide suspects in each camp and provided a snapshot of the overall population of suspects imprisoned across Rwanda. Detainees either completed the questionnaires themselves or, if they were illiterate, had a friend complete them on their behalf. On the basis of their responses, I selected approximately twenty detainees in each camp from as wide a range of backgrounds as possible to interview individually.

These interviews with genocide suspects, which typically lasted between forty-five minutes and one hour but sometimes up to two hours, covered a broad range of topics, including the respondents' experiences of the genocide, prison and ingando; their interpretations and expectations of gacaca; and their views on the future. I conducted interviews alone if respondents spoke English or French or, if they spoke only Kinyarwanda, I interviewed them through an interpreter who came from the province where the ingando was located. Between 2003 and 2010, I regularly attended gacaca hearings in communities in the same provinces as the initial ingando interviews, to compare the views of participants in gacaca and the nature of their involvement during hearings with the views of suspects. Finally, I interviewed survivors and the general population in communities near these gacaca jurisdictions, to better understand the key local factors influencing gacaca.

The purpose of this empirical approach was to record the broadest possible spectrum of interpretations by interviewing individuals within all social groups who are directly involved in gacaca, particularly suspects, survivors and gacaca judges. It was also important to interview the general population, who in many cases comprised relatives of genocide suspects. I interviewed the population in a wide range of communities across Rwanda, in both urban and rural areas, but particularly in the latter as communities outside of Kigali are often overlooked in postgenocide research. Like my ingando interviews, these semi-structured interviews in the community covered various themes concerning people's personal experiences of the genocide and its aftermath, which provided a clearer sense of their current circumstances, as well as their perceptions of gacaca.

---

[12] All genocide crimes are divided into three categories, according to their severity. I explain the nature of these categories in greater detail in the 'Mechanics of Gacaca' section in Chapter 2.

In several communities, I stayed in the homes of local families or in a tent nearby when the relevant landowners consented, to be as close as possible to the people whom I was interviewing. At the beginning of my fieldwork and later, between visits to each ingando and the surrounding communities, I conducted 103 interviews with government officials (including Rwandan President Paul Kagame and various cabinet ministers) and NGO personnel, usually in Kigali. I also made one visit to Butare Central Prison in 2003 to interview suspects, gaining a government permit to the prison by accompanying a World Vision team that conducted a healing and reconciliation workshop with detainees, and later visits to Kigali Central Prison and Rilima Prison. Finally, I travelled twice to Arusha, Tanzania, to observe hearings at the International Criminal Tribunal for Rwanda (ICTR) and to interview tribunal personnel about issues of justice and reconciliation in Rwanda, including their views on gacaca.

A central component of the research contained in this book is a series of longitudinal interviews conducted with confessed *génocidaires* at all stages of their journey towards their appearance at gacaca, alongside interviews with survivors and the general population in the same locations and during the same phases. This process began with suspects in prison and continued through their provisional release into ingando, following their return to the same communities where they confessed to committing crimes during the genocide, and during and after their trials at gacaca. I personally witnessed each wave of the 'gacaca journey', beginning with the provisional release of genocide detainees in January 2003 and culminating in the post-trial period in 2008 and 2009. I discuss ingando and the gacaca journey as a whole in greater detail in Chapter 4. The journey is ongoing as subsequent groups of detainees have been released, in preparation for their appearance at gacaca, including the release of approximately 36,000 detainees – the largest group so far – on 29 July 2005 and additional liberations since then.[13] My interviews and observations along the gacaca journey give crucial insights into perpetrators' – and the overall population's – changing attitudes over time towards gacaca and key themes such as justice and reconciliation. By interviewing confessed perpetrators at different junctures, I isolated key cultural, social, economic and political factors that influenced their perceptions of gacaca and issues concerning justice and reconciliation generally. It

[13] IRIN News, 'Rwanda: Release of Thousands of Prisoners Begins', 1 August 2005, www.irinnews. org/report.asp?ReportID=48373&SelectRegion=Great_Lakes&SelectCountry=RWANDA.

was also possible to build greater trust and understanding with the interviewees and their families over this seven-year period, thus deepening our conversations. This approach fills another major gap in the existing literature on gacaca, namely the need to analyse gacaca in a wider social, cultural and political context and over a significant period.

Given the sensitivity of the fieldwork questions, I tape-recorded only a small number of interviews, usually with government officials, and took detailed notes during the remaining interviews, which I double-checked with my interpreter at the end of each day. Throughout this book, I employ pseudonyms for all genocide suspects, survivors, gacaca judges and members of the general population and provide only broad descriptions of their locations (usually the name of the province and district), for legal and security reasons. I discuss many suspects' and survivors' personal experiences of the genocide and its aftermath and their views on gacaca, which in some instances refer to potentially volatile issues in local communities or to evidence bearing upon gacaca trials. Naming these individuals and their specific locations may jeopardise their own or others' safety and may negatively influence legal cases being heard at gacaca. Regarding my first-hand observations of gacaca hearings, because the government forbids tape-recording, filming or photography at gacaca, my analysis draws on notes taken during hearings, with the aid of the same Kinyarwanda interpreters mentioned above.

I end this section by outlining some of the key methodological quandaries encountered during the fieldwork which impinge on the analysis in this book. Overall, two principal challenges to this fieldwork comprised the need to build trust with interviewees and to navigate the unavoidable biases of respondents. In a post-conflict setting such as Rwanda, many people are understandably sceptical or distrustful of outsiders, especially those who ask difficult questions about traumatic events. Given that this research occurred as gacaca trials were under way, there was great sensitivity to legal matters and reluctance among many interviewees to discuss issues that might impinge on genocide cases. Furthermore, during interviews with government officials, it was necessary to remain cautious about exaggerated, self-aggrandising or misleading claims. In all of these situations, a key principle of my research was triangulation, seeking multiple sources to verify the information gathered. One boon in seeking to overcome issues of distrust and suspicion was the ability to return to Rwanda to speak to the same individuals many times over several years, building rapport with respondents and thus encouraging them to speak more openly and honestly about complex issues concerning gacaca.

Regarding practical challenges, during interviews in ingando, I was often interrupted by camp officials, whose presence significantly affected the tone and depth of interviewees' discussions. On most occasions, I was able to explain to the officials the importance of a private space for conducting interviews, but some officials returned later in the day, standing within earshot of the interviews, and had to be asked again to leave. Officials in each camp I visited also refused to let me view the civic education materials used to teach the detainees. Instead, I used the notes of a small number of detainees, who had kept particularly detailed records of the camp lessons, as a basis for my analysis of the camp pedagogy, until the official ingando curriculum became available much later.

Finally, it must be recognised that any study of gacaca is inherently limited by the sheer scale of the institution in terms of the number of jurisdictions and participants, geographical diffusion and the timescale of proceedings, which in some communities have taken place once a week for eight years. Gacaca is too large and too changeable for any single researcher or group of researchers to capture fully. A gacaca jurisdiction in one village may differ in key respects from another less than a kilometre away, and the character of both jurisdictions may evolve substantially over time, depending on how participants engage in the process and subsequently alter their expectations and behaviour. During my fieldwork, I attempted to address this issue by observing gacaca hearings and interviewing participants in a wide range of locations and over many years. This methodology provides a deep insight into the experience of gacaca in eleven communities in five provinces, embedded in a broader context of provincial, national and regional dynamics, and constitutes a more comprehensive approach to analysing gacaca than most published analyses. By comparing the findings from this research with those from other observers operating in different parts of Rwanda and during different periods, it is possible to construct an analysis that gets closer to a comprehensive view and identifies trends that are likely to pertain in all locations across Rwanda. Nevertheless, local influences on gacaca are crucial to any understanding of the process, including discrete social and cultural norms and the role of micro-politics in shaping participants' views on and behaviour during gacaca. We must recognise the substantial limitations of any analysis of gacaca, while also underscoring the enormous virtues of an in-depth exploration of discrete communities that are embedded in a wider socio-political framework and examined over a lengthy period.

HISTORY OF THE RWANDAN GENOCIDE

To understand some of the issues to which gacaca must respond, it is necessary to briefly explore the key historical events preceding and during the genocide, focusing on the origins of violence in Rwanda. Much has been written about the events and causes of the genocide, spawning what René Lemarchand, discussing violence in Burundi, calls a 'meta-conflict'; a conflict about how and why conflict occurred.[14] This section does not engage substantially in the meta-conflict concerning the Rwandan genocide but highlights only the elements of the genocide narrative that are most salient for the later analysis of gacaca. This section begins by describing the events of the genocide and ends with an exploration of the key historical forces that fuelled them.

Between April and July 1994, Rwanda experienced one of the most devastating waves of mass killing in modern history. In around 100 days, nearly three-quarters of the total Tutsi population (which constituted around 11 per cent of the overall population of Rwanda in 1994, while Hutu constituted nearly 84 per cent) were murdered and hundreds of thousands more exiled to neighbouring countries.[15] What distinguishes the Rwandan genocide from other cases of mass murder in the twentieth century, and in particular from the genocide of Jews during the Second World War, is the use of low-technology weaponry, the mass involvement of the Hutu population in the killings, the social and cultural similarities of the perpetrators and victims, and the astonishing speed of the genocide. The majority of murders were carried out brutally with basic instruments such as machetes, spears and spiked clubs and often near victims' homes.[16]

Events in the early 1990s are important for our understanding of the genocide.[17] On 1 October 1990, the Rwandan Patriotic Front (RPF), comprising many descendants of Tutsi refugees who fled Hutu violence in

[14] R. Lemarchand, *Burundi: Ethnic Conflict and Genocide*, New York: Wilson Center, 1996, p.17.
[15] Prunier, *The Rwanda Crisis*, pp.264–8.
[16] See, for example, Des Forges, *Leave None to Tell the Story*, pp.209–12; African Rights, *Rwanda: Death, Despair and Defiance* (revised edition), London: African Rights, 1995, ch. 9; R. Dallaire, *Shake Hands with the Devil: The Failure of Humanity in Rwanda*, Toronto: Random House, 2003, ch. 11.
[17] For a useful account of the flurry of key events in 1990, see P. Uvin, *Aiding Violence: The Development Enterprise in Rwanda*, West Hartford, Conn.: Kumarian Press, 1998, pp. 60–5.

the 1960s, invaded Rwanda from Uganda.[18] Government forces repelled the RPF and a guerrilla war broke out in the north-east of the country. After nearly three years of fighting, the government and the RPF signed the UN-brokered Arusha Peace Accords in August 1993. On 5 October 1993, the UN Security Council authorised the establishment of the United Nations Assistance Mission for Rwanda (UNAMIR), led by Canadian Lieutenant-General Roméo Dallaire and mandated to support the implementation of the Accords.[19] UNAMIR was given a six-month mandate to oversee a transition towards power sharing between Hutu and Tutsi in the Rwandan military and government.[20]

Events both within and outside of Rwanda exacerbated ethnic tensions during this period. The assassination on 21 October 1993 of Burundian President Melchior Ndadaye, a Hutu, by members of the Tutsi-led army, led to mass killings of Burundian Hutu and the exodus of thousands of refugees to Rwanda, sparking fears among Rwandan Hutu that the violence would spill across the border. Many Hutu politicians – aided by extremist media sources such as the Hutu newspaper *Kangura* and the country's largest radio station Radio-Télévision Libre des Mille Collines (RTLM) – used the violence in Burundi as justification to call for greater suppression of Tutsi in Rwanda.[21] Meanwhile, Rwandan President Juvénal Habyarimana, supported by the French government,[22] was training Hutu youth militias called *interahamwe* – Kinyarwanda for 'those who stand together' or 'those who fight together' – in order to attack Tutsi.[23] As Alison Des Forges from HRW explains, before the genocide '[m]assacres of Tutsis and other crimes by the Interahamwe went unpunished, as did some attacks by other groups thus fostering a sense that violence for political ends was "normal"'.[24]

---

[18] Prunier, *The Rwanda Crisis*, p.72 and ch. 3.

[19] Dallaire has become a colossal figure in many accounts of the genocide, largely because of his perceived heroism in commanding UNAMIR throughout the killing spree. Dallaire lobbied his UN superiors to do more to intervene to halt the killings, despite calls from, among others, the USA, France and Belgium to disband UNAMIR after the peacekeeping force suffered casualties in the first weeks of April 1994. (See a brief description of these incidents later in this section.)

[20] Dallaire, *Shake Hands with the Devil*, pp.96–101.

[21] See, for example, African Rights, *Death, Despair and Defiance*, pp.36–45; J.-P. Chrétien, 'Un génocide africain: de l'idéologie à la propagande', in R. Verdier, E. Decaux and J.-P. Chrétien (eds.), *Rwanda: un génocide du XXème siècle*, Paris: L'Harmattan, 1995, pp.45–55.

[22] A. Wallis, *Silent Accomplice: The Untold Story of France's Role in the Rwandan Genocide*, London: I.B. Tauris, 2007, pp.51–78.

[23] Des Forges, *Leave None to Tell the Story*, p.4.

[24] *Ibid.*, p.4.

On the night of 6 April 1994, President Habyarimana and Burundian President Cyprien Ntaryamira were returning from regional talks in Tanzania. At around 8.30 p.m., as their plane neared Kayibanda Airport in Kigali, two missiles fired from near the airport's perimeter struck the aircraft, which crashed into the garden of the presidential palace, killing everyone onboard. Within an hour of the crash, government roadblocks were set up across Kigali and troops and interahamwe began stopping vehicles and checking identity papers. Shots rang out across the city as killings began at the roadblocks and presidential guards and militiamen went from house to house, killing Tutsi and Hutu accused of collaborating with Tutsi.[25]

The killing spree spread rapidly beyond Kigali into towns and villages across Rwanda. In the following weeks, government leaders fanned out from the capital to incite the entire Hutu population to murder Tutsi, backed by messages of hate on RTLM. By most estimates, around 250,000 Tutsi were killed in the first two weeks of the genocide.[26]

The killing of Tutsi was far from spontaneous or indiscriminate and not, as the government tried to tell foreign diplomats and the international media both at the time and after the genocide, merely a proportional military response to the RPF invasion.[27] The violence was the result of long-term planning and systematic implementation by the Hutu regime. One source of evidence of the planning behind the government's campaign of violence was the extent to which the orchestrators of the genocide targeted key Tutsi and Hutu moderate political leaders in the immediate aftermath of Habyarimana's death. Their aim was to wipe out any semblance of political opposition before launching wider attacks against Tutsi.[28] At around 11 a.m. on 7 April, government troops stormed the house of Prime Minister Agathe Uwilingiyimana who had called on the protection of ten Belgian UNAMIR soldiers. When the government troops ordered the peacekeepers to lay down their weapons, UNAMIR's mandate gave the Belgians no choice but to disarm, at which point the

---

[25] Dallaire, *Shake Hands with the Devil*, ch. 10.

[26] African Rights, *Death, Despair and Defiance*, p.258; Des Forges, *Leave None to Tell the Story*, p.770; A. Kuperman, *The Limits of Humanitarian Intervention: Genocide in Rwanda*, Washington, DC: Brookings Institution Press, 2001, p.16.

[27] L. Melvern, *A People Betrayed: The Role of the West in Rwanda's Genocide*, London: Zed Books, 2000, chs. 11–13; L. Melvern, *Conspiracy to Murder: The Rwandan Genocide*, New York: Verso, 2004, ch. 10.

[28] African Rights, *Death, Despair and Defiance*, p. 177.

militiamen carried the peacekeepers away to be slaughtered and killed the defenceless Prime Minister in her front yard.[29]

The murder of the Belgians had an instant effect on the UN mission. The Belgian government called for the immediate withdrawal of all its personnel and for the complete abandonment of UNAMIR, finding an ardent ally in the USA, the largest UN donor country.[30] Dallaire meanwhile called for more peacekeepers to be sent to Rwanda to bring an end to the killings. He watched horrified as Western nations sent troops and aircraft to evacuate foreign nationals while offering no assistance to UNAMIR's attempts to contain the violence.[31] On 21 April, with the Belgian contingent already gone, the UN Security Council determined that the rapidly deteriorating situation posed a major threat to its personnel on the ground. It passed a resolution to reduce the number of UNAMIR troops from approximately 2,000 to 270.[32] While the UN debated the nature of its intervention in the genocide, the RPF swept through the countryside, capturing Kigali on 4 July. Two weeks later, the RPF gained control of the entire country, in the process halting the genocide. Thousands of predominantly Hutu refugees fled into Zaire, among them many of the main organisers of the genocide.[33]

To comprehend how the genocide was possible, we must explore key features of Rwandan history, particularly the nature of divisions between Hutu and Tutsi. Understanding these features will become important for later discussions concerning gacaca, as effectively rebuilding Rwandan society requires confronting the fundamental causes of violence. First, an examination of the pre-colonial era in Rwanda shows that a longlasting hierarchy between different groups emerged gradually. The Twa, a pygmoid race of hunter-gatherers who today make up about 1 per cent of the Rwandan population, probably arrived around AD 1000, followed soon after by the Bantu-speaking Hutu, who were predominantly pastoralists from the east. Tutsi herdsmen, most likely from southern Ethiopia, settled in Rwanda some time in the sixteenth century. The Tutsi arrived in Rwanda armed and well organised for military purposes, and soon

---

[29] *Ibid.*, pp.187–8.

[30] Dallaire, *Shake Hands with the Devil*, pp.293–327.

[31] *Ibid.*, pp.286–7.

[32] UN, 'Security Council Resolution Adjusting UNAMIR's Mandate and Authorizing a Reduction in its Strength', UN Doc. S/RES/912, 21 April 1994.

[33] G. Prunier, 'Opération Turquoise: A Humanitarian Escape from a Political Dead End', in H. Adelman and A. Suhrke (eds.), *The Path of a Genocide: The Rwanda Crisis from Uganda to Zaire*, New Brunswick, NJ: Transaction Publishers, 1999, pp.294–301.

conquered much of central Rwanda. Tutsi clans established territories ruled by a king or *mwami*, a figure that – as the Twa, Hutu and Tutsi evolved a common language and religion – came to be seen as a divine monarch with absolute power.[34]

As the structure of the state became more clearly defined in the eighteenth century, Rwandans began to measure their power by the number of subjects under their control and their wealth in terms of head of cattle.[35] During this period, the word 'Tutsi' came to describe someone with many subjects or a large number of cattle, while 'Hutu' meant a subordinate.[36] Identities on this basis were permeable: people initially labelled 'Hutu' could become 'Tutsi' if they acquired a certain level of prestige or wealth. During this period, however, Tutsi also began capturing land and cattle from Hutu; soon a Tutsi aristocracy emerged that ruled Rwanda by force, establishing a near-feudal class system, in which Tutsi came to dominate all facets of Rwandan life and many Hutu were plunged into abject poverty.[37] Although these socio-economic divisions caused much resentment among Hutu, there is no record of violence between Hutu and Tutsi in the pre-colonial era. In fact, most commentators argue that Rwandan society during this period displayed a remarkable culture of peaceful obedience toward the mwami and his court.[38]

The nature of Hutu–Tutsi relations changed drastically under colonialism, beginning with the arrival of the Germans in Rwanda in 1894. The German colonists immediately forged strong relationships with the ruling Tutsi, whom they perceived – on the basis of social Darwinist ideology – as the natural leaders of Rwanda. The Germans consequently chose to control Rwanda indirectly through the mwami and his circle of Tutsi administrators, thus continuing the 'pre-colonial transformation towards more centralisation … and increase in Tutsi chiefly powers'.[39]

In 1919, Belgium gained control of Rwanda under a League of Nations mandate, and, like the Germans, initially favoured the Tutsi in socio-political terms. The Belgians established a nationwide system of

---

[34] Prunier, *The Rwanda Crisis*, pp.10–20.

[35] Des Forges, *Leave None to Tell the Story*, p.31.

[36] *Ibid.*, p.32.

[37] C. Newbury, *The Cohesion of Oppression: Clientship and Ethnicity in Rwanda, 1860–1960*, New York: Columbia University Press, 1988, pp.140–1.

[38] See, for example, Prunier, *The Rwanda Crisis*, pp.16–23; F. Rutembesa, 'Ruptures culturelles et génocide au Rwanda', in J.-P. Kimonyo (ed.), *Ruptures socioculturelles et conflit au Rwanda*, Cahiers du Centre de Gestion des Conflits (no. 2), Butare: Université Nationale du Rwanda, April 2001, pp.99–105.

[39] Prunier, *The Rwanda Crisis*, p.25.

forced labour in which every man had to contribute a certain amount of time each month to government-sanctioned projects. As Philip Gourevitch argues, '[n]othing so vividly defined the divide [between Hutu and Tutsi] as the Belgian regime of forced labor, which required armies of Hutus to toil en masse … and placed Tutsis over them as taskmasters.'[40]

The most significant contribution by the Belgians to the widening social, cultural and economic divide between Hutu and Tutsi, however, was the introduction of ethnic identity cards in 1933. The Belgians issued an identity card to every Rwandan man and woman that indicated whether he or she was a Hutu, Tutsi or Twa. Numerous factors determined an individual's ethnic categorisation,[41] including his or her ownership of cattle. Individuals with ten or more head of cattle were classified as Tutsi, along with their offspring; those with fewer than ten were classified as Hutu. After 1933 people received their ethnic classification according to their father's line.[42] This system continued throughout the twentieth century until it was abolished after the genocide. It was often on the basis of identity cards that Hutu killers identified Tutsi whom they massacred in 1994.[43]

For more than twenty years, Belgian colonial policy in Rwanda reinforced perceptions of Tutsi superiority and Hutu subjugation. After the Second World War, however, the Belgian colonial administration in Rwanda was placed under a UN trusteeship, which – in the era of growing African nationalism – was designed to move the country towards independence. The Belgians recognised that the Hutu majority would inevitably dominate the nation socio-politically during any transition towards democratic government. To ensure a smooth transfer of power, the colonial administrators gradually began to shift allegiances to the Hutu, offering them jobs in the civil service and promoting them to other positions of influence.[44] The result was a growing sense of Hutu empowerment. As Prunier explains, 'in various parts of the country, the

[40] P. Gourevitch, *We Wish to Inform You that Tomorrow We Will be Killed with Our Families: Stories from Rwanda*, New York: Farrar, Straus, & Giroux, 1998, p.57.
[41] For a longer discussion of the different features according to which the Belgian regime assigned individuals' ethnicity, see N. Eltringham, *Accounting for Horror: Post-Genocide Debates in Rwanda*, London: Pluto Press, 2004, pp.18–19.
[42] J.-P. Chrétien, J.-F. Dupaquier, M. Kabanda and J. Ngarame (eds.), *Rwanda: les médias du génocide*, Paris: Éditions Karthala, 1995, p.161.
[43] Eltringham, *Accounting for Horror*, pp.25–7.
[44] Prunier, *The Rwanda Crisis*, pp.41–53.

Hutu ... started to organize, creating mutual security societies, cultural associations and ... clan organizations.[45]

As Hutu gained control of the primary levers of power in Rwandan society, the years immediately preceding independence in 1962 and the rest of the 1960s were characterised by the first recorded instances of mass violence between Hutu and Tutsi. In 1959 the newly formed Hutu political party, the Parti du Mouvement de l'Emancipation des Bahutu (PARMEHUTU), mounted a successful revolt against the Tutsi mwami. Beginning in 1959 and continuing into the early 1960s, PARMEHUTU characterised all Tutsi as lapdogs of the colonial powers and oppressors of Hutu, and incited mass killings of Tutsi.[46] After independence, violent crackdowns by Hutu leaders on those viewed as subversives created a culture of fear and stymied open debate and criticism of the state. In turn, government impunity became the rule as few Rwandans were willing to confront the violent and near-absolute authority of the Hutu leadership. In the political realm, the new Hutu hierarchy built upon the country's existing, highly centralised administrative structure, establishing the pattern for Rwandan bureaucracies over the next four decades. As Prunier argues, the Hutu government's demand for 'unquestioning obedience was to play a tragic and absolutely central role in the unfolding of the 1994 genocide'.[47]

Three elements of the genocide narrative above are particularly important for the discussion of gacaca in this book. First, 'ethnic' identities in Rwanda derive from permeable socio-economic divisions that became fixed under Belgian colonial rule and were subsequently manipulated by Hutu governments to shore up Hutu control and to subjugate Tutsi. Divisions between Hutu and Tutsi are neither primordial nor static, but rather relatively recent, dynamic socio-political constructs, often manipulated for the sake of dividing the population to maintain control by certain political elites. Second, the Rwandan political realm has often been characterised by highly centralised government, initially in the form of the mwami's court and later by Hutu administrations. Historians have regularly observed unusual and destructive levels of popular obedience towards social and political leaders in Rwanda;[48]

---

[45] *Ibid.*, p.45.

[46] See, for example, C. Overdulve, *Rwanda: un peuple avec une histoire*, Paris: Harmattan, 1997, pp.98–111.

[47] Prunier, *The Rwanda Crisis*, p.57.

[48] See, for example, *ibid.*, pp.54–61; Rutembesa, 'Ruptures culturelles et génocide au Rwanda', pp.96–105.

some argue that this culture of obedience was vital in the government's ability to incite the Hutu population to perpetrate the genocide in 1994.[49] Finally, a culture of impunity permitted the mass murder of Tutsi in 1959 and the early 1960s. Numerous commentators argue that the lack of accountability for crimes committed by these Hutu leaders in part afforded license to those who planned, incited and perpetrated the genocide in 1994.[50]

POST-GENOCIDE LEGAL, MILITARY AND POLITICAL CONTEXT

In the sixteen years since the genocide, the Rwandan legal, military and political landscape has witnessed severe upheaval that greatly influences gacaca's operation and justice and reconciliation processes more generally. In particular, the political transformation involving the RPF's gaining control of the Rwandan government after its victory over the genocidal forces in 1994, before embarking on a period of transition leading to presidential and parliamentary elections in 2003, and beyond, has created a volatile environment that has affected all phases of gacaca. It is necessary here to briefly explore the wider social, legal and political context in which gacaca operates, focusing on three main themes: legal developments involving the government's attempts to capture, detain and prosecute genocide suspects and the evolution of the national courts and the ICTR; national political developments, especially moves by the RPF to shore up power across the country; and violence and social and political instability in the Great Lakes region, in which Rwanda has been a key participant, particularly resulting from military involvement in ex-Zaire, now the Democratic Republic of Congo (DRC). As argued in later chapters, feelings of fear and uncertainty which this social, legal and political environment instils in the population greatly affect popular involvement in gacaca and justice and reconciliation processes more broadly.

---

[49] Des Forges, *Leave None to Tell the Story*, pp.44–7; Gourevitch, *We Wish to Inform You*, pp.23–5. For a critique of the 'culture of obedience' thesis, see J.-P. Kimonyo, *Revue critique des interprétations du conflit Rwandais*, Cahiers du Centre de Gestion des Conflits (no. 1), Butare: Université Nationale du Rwanda, 2000, pp.48–9.

[50] See, for example, A. Des Forges, 'The Ideology of Genocide', *ISSUE: A Journal of Opinion*, 23, 2, 1995, pp.45–6; F. Reyntjens, 'Rwanda, Ten Years On: From Genocide to Dictatorship', *African Affairs*, 103, 2004, pp.208–10; W. Schabas, 'Le Rwanda, le Burundi, et la maladie d'impunité', in Verdier *et al.*, *Rwanda: un génocide du XXème siècle*, pp.115–23.

After coming to power following the genocide, the RPF faced immense challenges in dealing with genocide suspects. The national judiciary had been almost entirely destroyed: most of Rwanda's judges and lawyers had been killed and the judicial infrastructure was decimated. In the direct aftermath of the genocide, the RPF rounded up tens of thousands of genocide suspects and transported them to prisons around Rwanda. In late 1994 and early 1995, the RPF executed large numbers of suspects and carried out revenge massacres of Hutu civilians, most notably in the Kibeho camp for internally displaced Hutu, where some observers allege that on 22 April 1995 between 2,000 and 8,000 civilians were killed.[51] An investigative team from the United Nations High Commissioner for Refugees (UNHCR) concluded in late 1994 that in the months directly following the genocide, the RPF killed 'thousands of civilians per month'.[52] The atmosphere of violent retribution created by the massacres lingers in the current context, causing many genocide suspects to fear the prospect of a return to their home communities where they will face gacaca and creating unease among the general Hutu population.

Between mid-1994 and 1996, two key developments shaped the post-genocide legal landscape. On 8 November 1994, the UN Security Council authorised the establishment of the ICTR to prosecute the primary orchestrators and most serious perpetrators of the genocide. Modelled partly on the International Criminal Tribunal for the former Yugoslavia (ICTY), the ICTR was intended to help end impunity in Rwanda by prosecuting the leaders of the genocide, while leaving lower-level perpetrators to the Rwandan national courts.[53] The ICTR raised the ire of the RPF when, in December 2000, Chief Prosecutor Carla del Ponte announced that she had opened investigations into crimes committed by the RPF during and after the genocide.[54] In 2002, del Ponte complained that since the announcement of investigations into RPF crimes, the Rwandan government had deliberately impeded the progress of the ICTR, for example by banning the travel of tribunal witnesses

---

[51] See, for example, AI, 'Rwanda: Two Years after the Genocide – Rights in the Balance (Open Letter to President Pasteur Bizimungu)', AI Index Africa 47/02/96, 4 April 1996.

[52] UNHCR memo, quoted in Des Forges, *Leave None to Tell the Story*, p.728.

[53] United Nations, 'Security Council Resolution 955 Establishing the International Criminal Tribunal for Rwanda', UN Doc. S/RES/955, 8 November 1994.

[54] IRIN News, 'Rwanda: Del Ponte Addresses Alleged RPF Massacres with Kagame', 14 December 2000, www.irinnews.org/report.asp?ReportID=7752&SelectRegion=Great_Lakes&SelectCountry=RWANDA.

from Rwanda to hearings in Arusha.[55] Bad blood between the government and the ICTR continued to hamper the Tribunal's progress, until the appointment of a new Chief Prosecutor, Hassan Bubacar Jallow, in 2003, a move that appears to have improved relations between the two bodies and increased the efficacy of the ICTR. The inevitably political nature of post-genocide justice in Rwanda continues to shape the running of all the institutions designed to prosecute genocide suspects.

In 1996, with the assistance of the UN, foreign governments and NGOs, the Rwandan government began a massive overhaul of the national judiciary, training new judges and lawyers and establishing new courts across the country to begin dealing with the immense backlog of genocide cases. The national courts were initially slow in hearing the cases of genocide suspects. However, over time, the courts became more efficient and were praised, albeit reservedly, by some international monitors for their speed and improved legal standards.[56]

Second, the post-genocide period in Rwanda has been characterised by immense political upheaval. After gaining control of the country in July 1994, the RPF quickly set about centralising and monopolising power in Rwanda. As Filip Reyntjens observes, the RPF 'introduced a strong executive presidency, imposed the dominance of the RPF in the government, and redrew the composition of parliament'.[57] The rapid growth in RPF power and suppression of dissent led in August 1995 to the resignation of Prime Minister Faustin Twagiramungu, a Hutu, and four Hutu cabinet ministers, who upon finding refuge overseas detailed abuses of power and violations of human rights committed by the RPF.[58] For the next decade, human rights groups reported the arbitrary arrests and 'disappearances' of dissident politicians, journalists and community leaders, including prominent members of the RPF and well-known genocide survivors, such as Bosco Rutagengwa, who founded the survivors' group Ibuka (the Kinyarwanda word for 'remember').[59]

In the midst of acute RPF suppression of dissident parliamentarians in 2000, President Pasteur Bizimungu resigned 'for personal reasons'

---

[55] IRIN News, 'Rwanda: ICTR Preparing to Indict First Tutsis', 12 April 2002, www.irinnews. org/report.asp?ReportID=27252&SelectRegion=Great_Lakes&SelectCountry=RWANDA; V. Peskin, *International Justice in Rwanda and the Balkans: Virtual Trials and the Struggle for State Cooperation*, Cambridge University Press, 2008, pp.207–31.

[56] See, for example, AI, 'Rwanda: The Troubled Course of Justice', AI Index AFR 47/10/00, April 2000, pp.3–6.

[57] Reyntjens, 'Rwanda, Ten Years On', p.178.

[58] *Ibid.*, p.180.

[59] *Ibid.*, p.182.

but, unlike most government leaders who openly opposed the RPF, he remained in the country. Bizimungu was arrested in 2001 for attempting to create a new political party and was imprisoned until he received a presidential pardon in April 2007.[60] The year 2001 marked the beginning of a nationwide 'democratisation process', involving local elections in all communities across Rwanda. Many observers questioned the validity of these elections, citing intimidation by RPF officials and a lack of secrecy in voting procedures.[61]

At the end of the post-genocide transitional period in 2003, the government held a constitutional referendum and prepared the country for the first presidential and parliamentary elections since the genocide. In the lead-up to the elections, the government banned the Mouvement Démocratique Républicain (MDR), the largest Hutu opposition party and effectively the only significant Hutu voice in the Rwandan parliament, on the grounds of 'divisionism' or what the government claimed were attempts to spread 'genocidal ideology'.[62] The same allegations were levelled against the Ligue Rwandaise pour la Promotion de la Défense des Droits de l'Homme (LIPRODHOR), Rwanda's largest human rights organisation, which the government dissolved in January 2005.[63]

The post-genocide period has thus witnessed the rapid emergence and consolidation of an RPF monopoly over the entire Rwandan political system. An issue of great importance later in this book will be the role of the state in the creation and daily operation of gacaca, an institution founded on principles of popular ownership and open dialogue. The sustained rhetoric of openness and public participation that much of the government employs when discussing gacaca may seem incongruous, even disingenuous, alongside the RPF's attempts to shore up political control over the country and to stymie public debate. Certainly there is good reason to be sceptical of much of the state's discourse regarding popular ownership over gacaca. Nevertheless, one important explanation for these seemingly contradictory messages, later chapters will contend, is the existence of different ideological factions within the government,

---

[60] *Ibid.*, p.181.
[61] See, for example, International Crisis Group (ICG), '"Consensual Democracy in Post Genocide Rwanda": Evaluating the March 2001 District Elections', Nairobi/Brussels: ICG, 9 October 2001.
[62] For a thorough discussion of the plans in 2003 to ban MDR, see, HRW, 'Preparing for Elections: Tightening Control in the Name of Unity', HRW Briefing Paper, Kigali: HRW, May 2003.
[63] AI, 'Rwanda: Human Rights Organisation Forced to Close Down', AI Index AFR 47/001/2005, 10 January 2005.

with some leaders, particularly those who have only recently returned to Rwanda from the Tutsi diaspora, and not having lived through the genocide, expressing greater enthusiasm than others for gacaca's ethos of dialogue and communal ownership. As argued later in this book, a lack of coordination – even conflict – between different government departments characterises much of the running of gacaca; this partly explains the apparent disjunct between the RPF's attempts to quash dissent and the government's emphasis on gacaca's encouraging public dialogue and participation.

Finally, violence throughout the Great Lakes region, particularly in the DRC, has had significant repercussions for the political and social landscape in Rwanda. For our purposes here, violence in the region can be divided roughly into three periods: the first Congo war of 1996–7; the second war of 1998–9 and ongoing violence in the Kivu provinces; and ethnic violence in Ituri province of the DRC since 2002. First, war broke out in the former Zaire in 1996 when Rwanda, Uganda and Burundi supported rebels led by Laurent Desirée Kabila to topple the dictator Mobutu Sese Seko, then President of Zaire. In response, Mobutu called on military allies in Angola, Namibia and Zimbabwe. All of the countries involved in this pan-African conflict, whether fighting for Kabila's Alliance or defending Mobutu's crumbling dictatorship, fought to attain their own short- and long-term strategic objectives, turning Zaire into a battleground for a host of competing foreign interests.[64]

The key external players in the conflict were Rwanda and Uganda. Rwanda's involvement stemmed directly from the 1994 genocide: in the aftermath of the killing spree, around 1.5 million Hutu refugees, including many of the orchestrators of the genocide, poured into Zaire at the border crossing at Goma, fleeing the advance of the RPF. After the genocide, members of the interahamwe, fed and clothed unwittingly by Western aid organisations, continued to train in the refugee camps and made several incursions into Rwanda, threatening to 'finish the job' of killing all Rwandan Tutsi.[65] Kabila's Alliance eventually prevailed in May 1997, forcing Mobutu into exile, ensconcing Kabila as President and

---

[64] For an analysis of the role of the different governments and rebel groups in the 1996–7 war in the DRC, see HRW, 'What Kabila is Hiding: Civilian Killings and Impunity in Congo', New York: HRW, October 1997.

[65] See, for example, K. Halvorsen, 'Protection and Humanitarian Assistance in the Refugee Camps in Zaire: The Problem of Security' in Adelman and Suhrke, *The Path of a Genocide*, pp. 307–20.

scattering the interahamwe and Mobutu-backed militias throughout the eastern DRC.

The region was plunged into a second Congo war in 1998 and 1999 as Kabila's Alliance quickly disintegrated. Kabila was angered by the refusal of Rwanda, Burundi and Uganda to leave the eastern DRC. These countries stayed and pillaged the region's gold, diamonds and coltan (a rare mineral used in the manufacture of mobile phones) through military proxies such as the Rwandan-backed Rally for Congolese Democracy (RCD). Kabila turned against his former benefactors and began arming the interahamwe and local militias known as Mai Mai in an attempt to drive the foreign forces, their proxies and Congolese Tutsi out of the DRC.[66] The Rwandan government responded by attacking Goma, Bukavu and Uvira in North and South Kivu in August 1998. Kabila called on the governments of Angola and Zimbabwe to help repel Rwandan, Burundian and Ugandan forces in exchange for a small share of the DRC's mining riches. Between August 1998 and August 2000, as Hutu–Tutsi animosity and a desire for control over DRC's mineral wealth kept the conflict raging, nearly 2 million people died in the eastern DRC either as a direct result of violence or through related disease and deprivation.[67] Violence in the Kivus, which can be traced back to the conflicts of the 1990s, has continued to the present day, causing the deaths of around 4 million civilians and displacing the same number.[68]

The third and most recent period of violence in the DRC centres on the north-eastern province of Ituri and violence between local Hema and Lendu ethnic groups. Traditionally, the Hema, like the Tutsi in Rwanda and Burundi, are pastoralists and the Lendu, like the Hutu, are cultivators. In 1999, a land dispute in the Djugu district of Ituri sparked a violent confrontation between Hema and Lendu which, stoked by Ugandan support for the Hema, flared into widespread conflict. Uganda has long employed the Hema as business partners in the plunder of natural resources from Ituri. In August 2002, Hema combatants and their

---

[66] For the most thorough analysis available of the second war in the DRC in 1998–9, see ICG, 'Scramble for the Congo: Anatomy of an Ugly War', New York: ICG, 20 December 2000.

[67] *Ibid.*, p.6.

[68] International Rescue Committee, 'Mortality in the Democratic Republic of the Congo', New York: IRC, December 2004. The IRC statistics were confirmed in B. Coghlan, R. Brennan, *et al.*, 'Mortality in the Democratic Republic of Congo: A Nationwide Survey', *The Lancet*, 367, 7 January 2006, pp.44–51.

Ugandan allies attacked Lendu militias and civilians in Bunia, the biggest town in Ituri, massacring hundreds and inciting revenge killings by Lendu militias. During an escalation in the Ituri conflict in May 2003, human rights groups accused both sides of committing genocide.[69]

The regional dimension of the Great Lakes conflict is apparent in Ituri, as Uganda helped create the rebel group, the Union de Patriotes Congolais (UPC), only to see the UPC switch allegiances to Rwanda. Rwanda's primary objective was to defeat Uganda for a greater share of Ituri's wealth of gold, diamonds and oil. The conflict in Ituri therefore follows the pattern of other recent conflicts in the DRC, involving rapidly changing alliances between rebel groups supported by regional governments, with ethnicity, greed and power the protagonists' primary motivations. Rwanda's ongoing involvement in conflict in the DRC underlines the extent to which, sixteen years after the genocide, it is still a heavily militarised state. Much of Rwanda's continued military activity in the region stems directly from the genocide, particularly the perceived need to contain interahamwe and other Hutu rebels in the DRC. For many Rwandans, particularly those affected by violence in, or the threat of rebel incursions from, the eastern DRC, the reality of the genocide persists in daily life. The Rwandan government invokes the threat of a second genocide to justify its military presence in the DRC and many of the heavy-handed policies discussed above.[70]

As argued later in this book, these policies run counter to gacaca's ethos of popular participation and open dialogue and have the potential to seriously damage the entire gacaca process. The cacophony of legal, political and military events, within Rwanda and in the wider region, has had a marked effect on a Rwandan population already coming to terms with the legacies of the genocide. Gacaca as an institution designed to deal with many of these legacies is inevitably embedded in the wider context of these national and regional developments. Because gacaca relies so heavily on the population's active participation, predicated on its sense of security and well-being, much of gacaca's success depends on the population's reactions to the prevailing legal, political and military landscape.

[69] HRW, 'Ituri "Covered in Blood": Ethnically Targeted Violence in Northeastern DR Congo', Washington, DC: HRW, April 2003, p.14; ICG, 'Congo Crisis: Military Intervention in Ituri', ICG, 13 June 2003, p.3.
[70] A. Smith, 'Rwanda Warns of Hutus Preparing Second Genocide', Independent, 4 August 2001, p.13.

STRUCTURE AND ARGUMENT

This book is structured in the following way: Chapter 1 situates the analysis of gacaca within the broader study of transitional justice, focusing on a range of key terms, including 'justice and reconciliation', which constitute the potential aims of gacaca expressed by the sources analysed in this book and explored in later chapters. Chapter 2 describes the history of gacaca, tracing its evolution from an ad hoc institution of low-level conflict resolution through various phases of debate and reform to the modernised version designed to deal with genocide cases. This chapter then describes the mechanics of gacaca, including guidelines for how hearings proceed and for gacaca's plea-bargaining scheme. Chapter 3 explores the nature of the current confusion and controversy surrounding gacaca, which necessitates the careful analysis of its objectives and the critique of its success provided in this book. Chapter 3 also establishes the rationale for focusing on popular interpretations in the overall analysis of gacaca and outlines the dominant discourse on gacaca, propagated by human-rights critics. Much of the analysis in Chapters 5–11 is designed to counter the prevailing discourse and in particular its failure to account for popular understandings of gacaca. The purpose of Chapter 4 is to provide a narrative of the gacaca journey outlined above, based on first-hand observations. In particular, this chapter focuses on the personal experiences of three confessed *génocidaires*, whom I interviewed between 2003 and 2009 at all stages along their journey towards gacaca and beyond.

Chapters 5–10 represent a normative and empirical analysis of gacaca's objectives and methods, exploring side by side official, popular and critical interpretations of its aims, highlighting the most compelling, and analysing how effectively gacaca has pursued those aims in practice. While Chapter 5 refers to the modus operandi of gacaca (popular participation in every facet of its daily operation), the remaining chapters consider individual objectives, which the participatory approach is supposed to help facilitate. Chapter 6 explores what I call 'pragmatic' objectives, namely helping overcome two problems regarding Rwanda's massively overcrowded genocide prisons – processing the backlog of genocide cases and improving living conditions in the jails – and facilitating economic development. Chapters 7–10 consider a range of 'profound' objectives – truth (Chapter 7), peace and justice (Chapter 8), healing and forgiveness (Chapter 9) and reconciliation (Chapter 10) – which respond to the population's social, emotional, psychological and psychosocial needs after the genocide, focusing on issues of rebuilding relations between previous antagonists. Finally, on the basis of this interpretation of gacaca's aims and analysis of its practical efficacy, Chapter 11 summarises the key findings of the book. This final chapter also includes a detailed critique of the dominant discourse on gacaca and a summary of the key implications of the findings in terms of other societies that adopt community-based approaches to transitional justice and for the future of Rwanda.

This book constructs five main arguments: first, gacaca is historically and currently a highly dynamic socio-legal institution and not, as some commentators have described it, a static, traditional structure readily comprehensible, and acceptable, to all Rwandans. Gacaca is the product of a complex social, cultural and legal evolution during the twentieth century – including crucial political compromises during negotiations over Rwanda's broad justice and reconciliation strategy – and of the population's proclivity to shape gacaca in its own image, often contrary to the original intentions of gacaca's creators. Thus, gacaca displays what I term 'internal hybridity', as manifested in its traditional-modern features and its combination of legal and non-legal objectives and methods.

Second, we require a more appropriate methodology for interpreting and critiquing gacaca than the current literature employs. In particular, we require a methodology that accounts for the ever-evolving nature of gacaca and for the population's shifting interpretations of, and participation in, it. Gacaca operates very differently in practice from how it appears in its governing legal documents. In particular, given that the modus operandi of gacaca is popular participation, involving the community in all facets of the daily running of the institution, it is necessary to account for gacaca's popular ethos and dynamism in daily operation.

Third, gacaca represents a holistic response to the legacies of the genocide, pursuing via popular participation both pragmatic and profound objectives, which refer to interlocking personal, communal and national aims, seeking to rebuild Rwandan society from the level of the individual and local community upward, in concert with more nationwide processes. Gacaca responds to a range of both legal and non-legal concerns. Some of its aims are more feasible than others: one aim explored in this book – facilitating economic development – is not a feasible objective of gacaca, while gacaca displays a variable capacity to facilitate the remaining eight objectives, depending largely on community-specific conditions.

Fourth, a more nuanced interpretation of gacaca's objectives highlights crucial flaws in the methodology employed by proponents of the dominant discourse on gacaca and in their proposed alternative approach to post-conflict reconstruction, which focuses solely on punishing perpetrators and deterring potential criminals. Human-rights critics generally analyse gacaca solely on the basis of its legal documents and therefore neglect the importance of popular ownership over, and evolving interpretations of, gacaca for understanding its objectives and appropriately assessing its success in achieving them. Consequently, these critics provide an extremely narrow view of gacaca and, in the main, criticise it for failing to achieve ends for which it was never, or at least only partially, intended.

Finally, while it is possible to defend gacaca against most human-rights criticisms, gacaca nonetheless displays significant problems in its daily practice. In particular, gacaca has suffered from difficulties in motivating an often confused, fearful population to engage in an institution whose lifeblood is popular participation. Further challenges to gacaca in many communities include difficulties in recovering the truth about the past, perceptions that gacaca delivers one-sided justice given the absence of prosecutions for RPF crimes, and further traumatisation of many participants because of the highly emotive and divisive nature of testimony during hearings. Gacaca, I contend, overall has been a remarkable success, according to the objectives expressed by the sources analysed here, but it has also created major problems in many communities that will require systemic remedies long after gacaca has completed its work.

CHAPTER 1

FRAMING GACACA: SIX TRANSITIONAL JUSTICE THEMES

INTRODUCTION

Exploring how the Rwandan government and population have responded to the genocide, particularly through their creation of and involvement in gacaca, this book investigates concepts that fit broadly into the field of transitional justice.[1] Transitional justice encompasses a multitude of discrete, though overlapping, and often conflicting themes that concern how societies address periods of conflict and/or repressive rule. At the heart of discussions of transitional justice are questions of what reconstructive objectives such societies should pursue and how they should pursue them. While much transitional justice literature focuses on questions surrounding institutions and processes – often advocating templates, toolkits and menus of options based on historical responses to mass atrocity and presupposing the central aims and actors – this book begins with questions of objectives.[2] In the context of gacaca, it is crucial that we understand how participants in the process interpret its aims, what they expect it to achieve or not achieve, and generally on what basis they determine its success. The purpose of this chapter is to provide some theoretical background to the key concepts that the sources analysed in this book identify as gacaca's objectives.

---

[1] For an expansive discussion of the key concepts and issues considered within transitional justice, see D. Crocker, 'Transitional Justice and International Civil Society: Toward a Normative Framework', *Constellations*, 5, 4, 1998, pp.492–517.

[2] For an example of a model that tends towards this template approach, see International Center for Transitional Justice, 'What is Transitional Justice?', www.ictj.org/en/tj.

Given the complexity of issues surrounding rebuilding societies after mass violence, immense contestation over what transitional justice entails is inevitable. Different transitional societies choose different objectives, and often pursue them in very different ways, usually because of political, social, economic and legal constraints after conflict. The truth commissions of Central and South America in the 1980s and 1990s, for example, sought to establish the truth about crimes committed by political and social elites and, in most instances, offered these individuals amnesty in exchange for the truth.[3] The South African Truth and Reconciliation Commission (TRC) similarly offered amnesty to apartheid leaders in exchange for disclosure about their crimes against the black majority. The TRC differed from previous truth commissions, however, by enshrining reconciliation as a key objective. This policy represented a turning point in the ideas and practices of transitional justice globally. The TRC in South Africa has since served as a touchstone for other post-conflict institutions, inspiring in many cases (usually implicitly) the expressed pursuit of reconciliation, for example in Kenya, Nigeria, Sierra Leone and Timor-Leste. Even the Statute of the UN ICTR – an institution designed primarily to prosecute and punish the main orchestrators of the Rwandan genocide – states that 'prosecution ... would ... contribute to the process of national reconciliation and to the restoration and maintenance of peace'.[4]

Out of the central question of transitional justice – what reconstructive objectives should post-conflict societies pursue? – two specific questions emerge consistently: is it necessary and feasible to punish the perpetrators of mass crimes, and, if so, what is punishment designed to achieve: to fulfil a moral obligation to bring the guilty to account, to deter future perpetrators, or to contribute to wider objectives such as reconciliation? No post-conflict society can avoid addressing these questions. The creators of the Central and South American truth commissions argued that it was not feasible to punish perpetrators if they were to persuade perpetrators to tell the truth about their crimes.[5] The South African TRC held that punishing apartheid leaders was likely to foment civil conflict, and therefore a political compromise – trading amnesty for

[3] P. Hayner, 'Fifteen Truth Commissions: 1974–1994 – A Comparative Study', *Human Rights Quarterly*, 16, 4, November 1994, pp.613–14, 621–3, 628–9, 653–5.

[4] United Nations, 'Statute of the International Criminal Tribunal for Rwanda', www.un.org/ictr/statute.html.

[5] Hayner, 'Fifteen Truth Commissions', pp.613–14, 621–3, 628–9, 653–5.

the truth about crimes and for national reconciliation – was more appropriate.[6] A key sticking point during the Ugandan peace negotiations between 2006 and 2008 was whether rebels from the Lord's Resistance Army would benefit from the national Amnesty Act, which has been in force since 2000, or face prosecution through the International Criminal Court (ICC) or some other punitive mechanism.[7] Meanwhile, the ICTR holds that it is necessary to punish perpetrators, in order not only to fulfil a moral obligation to bring them to account, but also to contribute to national peace and reconciliation. In the South African case, punishment and reconciliation were deemed to be contradictory objectives. The ICTR, however, holds that punishment is a prerequisite of peace and reconciliation.

What these examples show is that not only do different post-conflict institutions explicitly aim for different political, social or legal outcomes, but even in cases where they claim to pursue the same objectives – as in the South African TRC's and the ICTR's claimed pursuit of reconciliation – they often define the same aims, or the methods for achieving them, in very different ways. In the case of the ICTR, the reference to 'national reconciliation' cited above is the sole occurrence of this term in the Tribunal's statute, with no attempt to more clearly define it or to describe how punishing *génocidaires* might contribute to it. Serious questions therefore remain over whether the ICTR genuinely views reconciliation as a key objective and whether, and how, it actively pursues it. These examples highlight that it is not only vital to isolate the purported objectives of particular transitional justice institutions but also to robustly interrogate and interpret their meaning.

This book interprets gacaca's aims and methods on the basis of a range of official, popular and critical sources, focusing on quotidian interpretations of gacaca. This current chapter defines and distinguishes the six key terms that these sources identify as the 'profound' aims of gacaca: truth, peace, justice, healing, forgiveness and reconciliation. The aim in employing these terms when interpreting gacaca's aims and methods is not to impose an external theoretical framework on gacaca, drawing on some universal menu of transitional justice options, but

---

[6] For a useful discussion of the political and social compromises behind the South African TRC, and their often problematic outcomes, see J. Sarkin, 'The Trials and Tribulations of South Africa's Truth and Reconciliation Commission', *South African Journal on Human Rights*, 12, 4, 1996, pp. 617–40.

[7] For a lengthy discussion of these themes, see N. Waddell and P. Clark (eds.), *Courting Conflict: Justice, Peace and the ICC in Africa*, London: Royal African Society, 2008.

rather to analyse these terms in so far as my sources, especially within the Rwandan population, deploy them when discussing gacaca.

The purpose of this current chapter is to introduce the theoretical concepts that my sources define and debate in significantly more detail in later chapters. The role of theory in this book is fundamentally inter-pretive, employing the conceptual and philosophical literature on the six key themes to better interpret my sources' statements regarding gacaca. Their discussions of these themes are inevitably contextual; how they perceive the meaning of terms such as justice and reconciliation gener-ally and how they discern it in gacaca's operation, for example, depend vitally on local values and conditions and the intricacies of the post-genocide setting. Local interpretations also often change substantially over time, as people's circumstances evolve. Highlighting the importance of local context for my sources' interpretations of gacaca, its objectives and methods does not amount to an unquestioning relativism regarding their views. Sometimes, as we will see later, my sources offer contradict-ory or purely self-serving accounts of what concepts such as justice and reconciliation may entail, in which case I highlight the problems with such accounts.

Later chapters argue that the six themes explored here represent gacaca's *profound* objectives, which relate to complex issues of rebuild-ing relationships between parties previously in conflict. Alongside these profound aims, this book argues that gacaca feasibly pursues the first and second of three *pragmatic* objectives, with which my sources asso-ciate it: first, processing the massive backlog of genocide cases; second, improving living conditions in the jails; and third, facilitating eco-nomic development. This current chapter is concerned only with tra-cing the contours of gacaca's profound aims, broadly defining each term and, where necessary, distinguishing them from one another. The task of delineating these six objectives is important because, as will become apparent later, numerous sources analysed in this book conflate several of these terms, for example by equating peace or healing with reconcili-ation. As gacaca's three pragmatic objectives do not manifest the same potential for conflation either with each other or with any of the pro-found objectives, I do not define them in this chapter.

As we will see later, gacaca connects each of the six profound object-ives, and the groups of profound and pragmatic objectives, in particu-lar ways. Gacaca's simultaneous pursuit of profound and pragmatic aims represents a holistic approach to transitional justice, aiming to rebuild individual and communal lives and to contribute to reconstruction in both the short and long term. In the context of transitional justice, holism refers to the need to rebuild the entire society, responding to the various needs of individuals and groups after conflict. A key question in later chapters will be the extent to which gacaca can effectively combine multiple objectives and thus respond holistically to the legacies of the genocide.

This chapter draws the broad outlines of terms to which my sources' discussions add vital substance and nuance. Consequently, the reader may find that such local interpretations of these key themes aid a more general theory of these concepts; in other words, the lived experience of concepts such as justice and reconciliation in the context of gacaca, how people interpret and practise processes concerning these themes in their daily lives, may highlight tensions within such concepts and therefore aid how we understand them theoretically. While this book focuses on interpreting the ideas behind, and the practices of, gacaca, rather than on theoretical understandings of the themes of transitional justice, the detailed analysis of gacaca's objectives in later chapters may offer insights into the theoretical connections between the concepts analysed here.

TRUTH

The theme of truth, its discovery, propagation, and the extent to which it should be pursued along with other objectives in the post-conflict environment, is a perennial consideration in transitional societies. Victims of violence often seek the truth of who organised, perpetrated and covered up crimes, and how they were able to do so. From the perspective of policy-makers, a key reason why questions over truth arise so regularly is that the debate in many post-conflict societies is framed as a stark choice between pursuing justice or pursuing truth.[8] Specifically, policy-makers are often faced with deciding between establishing some sort of judicial structure, whether domestic, international, or some combination, which may try an individual without establishing a full account of the past, or creating some type of truth commission, which often incorporates a promise of amnesty in exchange for full disclosure of the truth.

---

[8] For further discussion of the tensions between truth and justice, see A. Gutmann and D. Thompson, 'The Moral Foundations of Truth Commissions', in R. Rotberg and D. Thompson (eds.), *Truth v. Justice: The Morality of Truth Commissions*, Princeton, NJ: Princeton University Press, 2000, pp.22–44.

What does 'truth' entail in the context of post-conflict societies? Generally, truth after conflict concerns people's understandings of what occurred in the past. As Robert Rotberg argues, 'if societies are to prevent recurrence of past atrocities and to cleanse themselves of the corrosive enduring effects of massive injuries to individuals and whole groups, societies must understand – at the deepest possible levels – what occurred and why.'[9] Truth can be achieved through various means, for example, a legal process, if it involves the provision and weighing of evidence regarding crimes, or an emotional process, when it concerns personal experiences of conflict. A controversial feature of the truth commissions established in South and Central America was their attempts to construct an 'official' version of the truth by producing reports that synthesised evidence gathered from thousands of citizens who had experienced, or witnessed, alleged atrocities.[10] Individuals' and groups' recollections of the past often clash, and may be expressed for various well-intentioned or cynically instrumentalist reasons. Therefore, attempts to produce an account of the past that will adequately represent, and be acceptable to, all individuals and groups who engage in the post-conflict truth process are inherently limited and likely to prove acrimonious.

Despite these caveats, three processes related to uncovering truth after conflict can be distinguished: what I term 'truth-telling', 'truth-hearing' and 'truth-shaping'. First, truth-telling concerns parties' public articulation of the truth, for example with the aim of providing legal evidence at a war-crimes tribunal, or in pursuit of some form of catharsis through emotional expression in front of a truth commission. In these instances, legal evidence that leads to the conviction and sentencing of perpetrators exemplifies how truth can constitute a means towards certain forms of justice; in the case of emotional discourse, truth may help facilitate healing.

Second, truth-hearing entails the reception of truth-telling, focusing on the ways in which different audiences respond to evidence or emotional expressions. Truth-telling and truth-hearing constitute halves of a post-conflict dialogue; in the case of legal settings, this dialogue is less pronounced, as truth-hearers are usually judges who engage in dialogue only in so far as they ask questions of those providing evidence. In

---

[9] R. Rotberg, 'Truth Commissions and the Provision of Truth, Justice and Reconciliation', in Rotberg and Thompson, *Truth v. Justice*, p.3.

[10] See, for example, D. Bronkhorst, *Truth and Reconciliation: Obstacles and Opportunities for Human Rights*, Amsterdam: AI, 1995, pp.15–28, 74–6.

more negotiated settings, such as truth and reconciliation commissions, there is a greater sense of dialogue, as perpetrators and victims are often encouraged to speak face to face.

Third, truth-shaping concerns the ways in which parties external to the initial truth-telling and truth-hearing receive and re-mould evidence to serve purposes for which the original participants may not have intended their discourse. For example, historians and political leaders engage in truth-shaping when they use evidence gleaned from transitional institutions to serve wider social or political purposes, such as to reinterpret historical events or to teach the population moral lessons. This phenomenon can be abused, for example when elites manipulate evidence to serve self-interested, even corrupt, purposes, such as purging history of their own crimes.

One source of complexity and controversy in the TRC in South Africa was that all three truth processes – truth-telling, truth-hearing and truth-shaping – occurred within the same institution. Individual perpetrators and victims sometimes engaged in face-to-face dialogue, and their discussions were recorded, debated and interpreted by a range of external parties, not least by the commissioners of the TRC tasked with producing the Commission's Final Report, which was supposed to provide a basis for post-apartheid nation-building.[11] That the truth concerning past crimes emanates from many different sources and is expressed, and subsequently deployed, for many different reasons ensures that the three processes of truth often intersect and are invariably contentious.

PEACE

Post-conflict institutions, particularly those like gacaca or the ICTR, that pursue justice in some form, are usually connected to the objective of peace through the idea of deterrence. If we punish the orchestrators and perpetrators of mass violence, the argument goes, then we will send a clear message that future criminals will also be punished, thus dissuading them from committing atrocities. As explored in the Introduction to this book, one of the root causes of the genocide in Rwanda was a culture of impunity, as political leaders were rarely held accountable for

---

[11] For a detailed discussion of the role of the Final Report of the TRC in South African nation-building, see J. Cronin, 'A Luta Dis-Continue: The TRC Final Report and the Nation Building Project', paper delivered at the University of the Witwatersrand, Johannesburg, June 1999, www.trcresearch.org.za/papers99/cronin.pdf.

their crimes, thus encouraging them to continue orchestrating violence and creating the conditions whereby mass crimes such as genocide were possible. Eradicating the culture of impunity, by punishing those responsible for serious crimes, is therefore seen as vital for restoring stability in post-conflict societies and for replacing a culture of violence with a culture of peace.

On the basis of notions of deterrence, transitional institutions are regularly viewed as tools of peacebuilding. The Report of the Panel on United Nations Peace Operations, for example, defines peacebuilding as 'activities undertaken on the far side of conflict to reassemble the foundations of peace and provide the tools for building on those foundations something that is more than just the absence of war', including, 'promoting conflict resolution and reconciliation techniques'.[12] Furthermore, the UN states that peacebuilding entails 'in the aftermath of conflict ... identifying and supporting measures and structures which will solidify peace and build trust and interaction among former enemies, in order to avoid a relapse into conflict'.[13] This definition of peacebuilding contains two aspects of 'peace': a negative component, in which peace (usually defined as the absence of conflict) has already been achieved but must now be solidified in the immediate aftermath of violence; and a positive component, in which peace is a long-term condition that must be facilitated for the future, through building trust and encouraging greater interaction between previously antagonistic parties.

Each of these components comprises an interpretation of the timeframe and the necessary measures to bring about peace. In the negative version, peace involves short-term maintenance that shores up a recently achieved situation of non-violence. In the positive component, peace constitutes a long-term process that requires fostering deeper norms and mechanisms in a community to ensure that combatants do not return to conflict. Positive peace seeks to overcome what David Crocker describes as the 'temptation in post-conflict or post-authoritarian societies ... to permit euphoria (which comes from the cessation of hostilities ...) to pre-empt the hard work needed to remove the fundamental causes of injustice and guard against their repetition'.[14] Negative peace

---

[12] UN, 'Report of the Panel on United Nations Peace Operations', UN Doc. A/55/305-S/2000/809, 21 August 2000, p.3.
[13] UN, 'Glossary of UN Peacekeeping Terms', www.un.org/en/peacekeeping/sites/glossary/p.htm.
[14] D. Crocker, 'Truth Commissions, Transitional Justice and Civil Society', in Rotberg and Thompson, Truth v. Justice, p.107.

requires simply that the parties involved maintain security and stability and no longer act violently towards one another. Such processes constitute forms of peacekeeping or peace enforcement, which are the stated purview of armed bodies such as UNAMIR. Positive peace, meanwhile, entails deeper engagement between previous antagonists, requiring new conflict-resolution methods to safeguard against violence in the long term. Negative peace is generally interpreted as a prerequisite of positive peace, as security and stability are necessary for the parties involved to begin constructing safeguards against future conflict. Both components of peace should be viewed as prerequisites of reconciliation, as negative peace helps facilitate positive peace, which, in turn, may help parties to resolve their conflicts more effectively in the future and therefore build stronger, longer-lasting relationships.

JUSTICE

A primary question for many transitional institutions – whether and why it is necessary to punish perpetrators of mass crimes (and the connected question, whether amnesty rather than punishment may ultimately better facilitate peace, reconciliation, truth or some other goal) – highlights the centrality of justice in this context. The regularity of considerations of justice in post-conflict situations, however, has rarely led to clear or comprehensive concepts or methods of justice. In particular, it is not always clear *why* certain institutions pursue justice after mass violence. This uncertainty may stem from what Ruti Teitel describes as the paradox of legal responses to mass crimes.

> Law is between the past and the future ... between retrospective and prospective. Transitions imply paradigm shifts in the conception of justice; thus, law's function is inherently paradoxical. In its ordinary social function, law provides order and stability, but in extraordinary periods of political upheaval, law maintains order, even as it enables transformation.[15]

Post-conflict legal institutions such as the ICTR are trapped uncomfortably between backward- and forward-looking pursuits, punishing perpetrators of past crimes while claiming – though usually failing to articulate precisely how – that punishment will contribute to reconstruction or

---

[15] R. Teitel, 'Transitional Jurisprudence: The Role of Law in Political Transformation', *Yale Law Journal*, 106, 7, May 1997, p.2014.

reconciliation. In order to more clearly explore justice as it manifests in gacaca and other post-conflict justice institutions, I outline the contours of justice here.

First, models of justice in the transitional setting can be divided into three broad categories: retributive, deterrent and restorative. Retributive justice holds that perpetrators must be punished, to bring them to account and to give them what they supposedly 'deserve'. Some authors argue that retributive justice is also necessary for states to adhere to international legal conventions.[16] The deterrent view of justice meanwhile holds that punishment is necessary, not simply because perpetrators deserve it but because it should help discourage a convicted perpetrator from committing another crime, for fear of receiving punishment, as he or she has in the past, and also to dissuade current or potential criminals from continuing or initiating offences, lest they also receive punishment. Finally, a restorative conception of justice differs from the retributive or deterrent models, by holding that punishment alone is insufficient; punishment of criminals is necessary but should be facilitated in ways that allow perpetrators and victims to rebuild relationships, for example by requiring perpetrators to compensate victims or provide reparations, which may contribute to restoring fractured relations. Gerry Johnstone describes restorative justice as a new approach to criminality that

> revolves around the idea that crime is, in essence, a violation of a person by another person (rather than a violation of legal rules); that in responding to a crime our primary concerns should be to make offenders aware of the harm they have caused, to get them to understand and meet their liability to repair such harm, and to ensure that further offences are prevented; that the form and amount of reparation from the offender to the victim and the measures to be taken to prevent re-offending should be decided collectively by offenders, victims and members of their communities through constructive dialogue in an informal and consensual process; and that efforts should be made to improve the relationship between the offender and victim and to reintegrate the offender into the law-abiding community.[17]

In the case of mass crimes such as genocide, restorative justice views the reconciliation of individual perpetrators and survivors and of entire communities as the ultimate objective. Restorative justice therefore attempts

---

[16] See, for example, D. Orentlicher, 'Settling Accounts: The Duty to Prosecute Human Rights Violations of a Prior Regime', *New York Law Journal*, 100, 8, June 1991, pp.2562–8.

[17] G. Johnstone, *Restorative Justice: Ideas, Values, Debates*, Uffculme: Willan Publishing, 2002, p.ix.

to further explain the sorts of conceptual relationships suggested in the clichéd refrain of many commentators on post-conflict societies, that 'no reconciliation is possible ... without justice.'[18]

Second, methods of justice can be divided into two broad categories: formal and negotiated. In the formal interpretation, post-conflict institutions arrive at justice via predetermined (usually legal) statutes and procedures. Due process during criminal hearings constitutes a key component of most formal models. In the negotiated interpretation, institutions achieve justice predominantly through communal discussions of evidence concerning mass crimes. Negotiated justice meanwhile emphasises the role of the community in discussing and debating different versions of the truth about the past and the responses that truth requires, for example, whether perpetrators should be punished and what form of punishment they should receive. These two broad methods of justice – formal and negotiated – are not mutually exclusive. An institution could, theoretically, rely on very broad legal statutes that permit a large degree of communal negotiation within those formal boundaries. I argue in later chapters that gacaca operates on precisely this hybrid basis of formal legal constraints upon the community's negotiation of evidence presented during hearings.

At the theoretical level, formal and negotiated methods may lead to some combination of retributive, deterrent or restorative outcomes. For example, retributive or deterrent justice may be achieved via both formal or negotiated means: in the first instance, independent judges operating in the controlled environment of a conventional courtroom, adhering strictly to predetermined legal statutes governing the running and the range of judicial outcomes of hearings, may punish perpetrators in a fashion consistent with the requirements of retributive or deterrent justice. These requirements could also be fulfilled via a negotiated process that affords the community a central role in debating and judging cases, but that still punishes perpetrators. Similarly, restorative justice could theoretically be achieved by either formal or negotiated means. The formal requirements of a judicial process, for example, could dictate that punishment be systematically directed towards rebuilding relationships between parties, or in the case of negotiated processes, if the very nature of the participatory methods employed were viewed as a means towards restorative ends.

---

[18] Institute for Contextual Theology, 'The Kairos Document: Challenge to the Church', 1985, www.bethel.edu/~letnie/AfricanChristianity/SAKairos.html.

On this basis, we should view Johnstone's account of restorative justice above – with its emphasis on restorative punishment as necessarily 'decided collectively … through constructive dialogue in an informal and consensual process' – as normative, rather than strictly definitional. In a theoretical sense, we can conceive of ways to achieve restorative justice other than through collective deliberation, although Johnstone may be right to argue that, in practice, communal negotiation is the most justifiable and effective means to restoration. No prima-facie reason exists to assume that one particular method of justice will lead automatically to one particular justice outcome, nor that transitional institutions should be limited to employing either a formal or a negotiated method, rather than a hybrid of these approaches.

HEALING

It is impossible to overstate the extent to which severe physical, emotional and psychological trauma characterises many post-conflict communities. In the case of Rwanda, nearly every citizen has been affected individually by violence, whether from direct involvement in perpetrating crimes, from personal injury, or from the injury or death of loved ones.[19] Trauma manifests in numerous ways in post-conflict societies, from individuals' feelings of helplessness and an inability to engage with others, to expressions of mistrust, paranoia, anger and vengefulness, and even to suicide.[20] In the face of such immense and various needs, concepts and processes of healing centre on helping individuals regain a sense of psychological or emotional wholeness that conflict has shattered. Individuals' trauma is not, however, necessarily the result only of physically, psychologically or emotionally damaging experiences such as mass violence. Trauma may also stem from material deprivation, resulting either from conflict or from later disasters, including famine, which may be natural or a consequence of conflict. For this reason, healing must take a holistic approach. In the context of post-conflict healing, holism refers to the need to rebuild the whole or complete person. If we identify the causes of trauma as a combination of psychological,

---

[19] L.A. Pearlman, 'Psychological Trauma', lecture for 'Healing, Forgiving, and Reconciliation' project, John Templeton Foundation, West Conshohocken, Pennsylvania, 13 March 2000, copy on file with author; N. Munyandamutsa, *Question du sens et des repères dans le traumatisme psychique: réflexions autour de l'observation clinique d'enfants et d'adolescents survivants du génocide Rwandais de 1994*, Geneva: Editions Médecine et Hygiène, 2001.

[20] Pearlman, 'Psychological Trauma'.

emotional, material and other factors, then healing must incorporate holistic methods that seek effective responses to this range of causes. Because these causes often compound one another – for example when a lack of food and adequate shelter exacerbates a victim's sense of loss after the murder of a loved one – then methods of healing must respond simultaneously, and in an integrated manner, to all the identifiable causes of trauma.

The concept of healing has only recently become associated with the field of transitional justice. In recent years, greater attention has been paid to issues of psychosocial healing after conflict or periods of repressive rule, largely as a result of the South African TRC, where Archbishop Desmond Tutu in particular emphasised the importance of truth, forgiveness and communal healing in the daily running of the TRC.[21] Where post-conflict reconstruction was once solely the domain of politicians and legal experts, trauma counsellors and other psychological experts now play a greater role in helping individuals come to terms with their personal experiences of conflict. Underlying this shift towards a greater consideration of psychosocial issues is a recognition that conflict not only damages entire nations or cultural groups, as emphasised in the use of the term 'genocide', but crucially also the individuals within those groups. Post-conflict healing holds that societies require rebuilding from the level of the individual upward, in concert with nationwide pursuits.

Reconstruction from the level of the individual is a complicated undertaking, because individuals' needs are both highly varied and difficult to assess without evaluating the specific case of every person in the post-conflict society. As Mahmood Mamdani argues, however, overcoming individuals' feelings of trauma, resentment and victimhood after conflict is vital because these perceptions have long-lasting effects, producing subsequent feelings of victimhood in future generations that plant the seeds of further violence. Mamdani argues that, in the Rwandan case, a Hutu self-view of victimhood, particularly in the twentieth century, provided an emotional and psychological foundation for Hutu violence against Tutsi, as Hutu attempted to overcome their victim status and gain a greater sense of empowerment.[22] The inter-generational effects of trauma remind us of the need to facilitate healing not only to help

---

[21] D. Tutu, *No Future without Forgiveness*, New York: Doubleday, 1999, chs. 6, 7, 10 and 11.
[22] M. Mamdani, *When Victims Become Killers: Colonialism, Nativism, and the Genocide in Rwanda*, Princeton, NJ: Princeton University Press, 2001, chs. 4, 5 and 7.

individuals rebuild their lives but also to protect entire societies from descending into further conflict. Healing therefore is integral to achieving positive peace and ultimately reconciliation.

Healing concerns crucial questions of individual identity. Processes of healing comprise important internal and external elements, as healing entails what Malvern Lumsden describes as 'rebuilding a coherent sense of self and sense of community'.[23] Post-conflict healing relates to individuals' regaining a sense of inner wholeness; that is, healing of their own identity, as captured in the phrase 'to find oneself again'. Re-establishing individuals' sense of inner coherence also often requires rebuilding a sense of how they as individuals relate to their communities, from which they gain much of their sense of self-worth and the meaning of their lives. Lisa Schirch argues that it is often necessary to 'rehumanize' survivors and perpetrators after violence.[24] These individuals have forfeited much of their personal sense of humanity through either perpetrating, or being the victims of, mass crimes. Perpetrators often dehumanise their victims in order to justify their violent actions and, in turn, may suffer forms of dehumanisation themselves by committing crimes, when they forfeit feelings of common humanity and empathy towards their victims. Thus, healing requires rehumanising survivors and perpetrators to overcome the negative identities that they assumed during conflict.

FORGIVENESS

Similar to questions regarding healing, considerations of forgiveness represent a recent development in the study and practice of transitional justice. Forgiveness is an even more controversial and more rarely discussed issue in this context because it is so readily connected with religious perspectives to which many people do not subscribe. Some critics argue that any discussion of forgiveness will inevitably require forfeiting retributive or deterrent justice; that is, perpetrators will not receive the punishment they deserve or that may be necessary to discourage future criminality. Some critics also argue that forgiveness will entail the enforced forgetting of crimes and an unjust demand for survivors to

---

[23] M. Lumsden, 'Breaking the Cycle of Violence', *Journal of Peace Research*, 34, 4, November 1997, p.381.

[24] L. Schirch, 'Ritual Reconciliation: Transforming Identity/Reframing Conflict', in M. Abu-Nimer (ed.), *Reconciliation, Justice, and Coexistence: Theory and Practice*, Lanham, Md.: Lexington Books, 2001, p.152.

'move on' from their pain and loss.[25] For all of these reasons, it is often considered too emotionally costly or coercive to advocate forgiveness after mass violence.

Most political thought on post-conflict forgiveness has occurred within the past decade. However, Hannah Arendt explored the appropriateness of forgiveness in the aftermath of the Second World War and provided an important analysis of the relevance of this term after atrocity mass conflict. Arendt argues that 'forgiveness is the exact opposite of vengeance, which acts in the form of re-acting against an original trespassing, whereby far from putting an end to the consequences of the first misdeed, everybody remains bound to the process'.[26] Direct retribution, Arendt argues, fuels the cycle of violence. Therefore, forgiveness, which entails forgoing feelings of resentment and a desire for personal, direct retribution, is necessary to start afresh and to allow people to deal with memories of the past in a more constructive manner. 'Forgiveness does not imply forgetting ... "giving up", "turning the other cheek" or "letting the other off the hook"', argues Wendy Lambourne, but rather should be seen as a 'complex act of consciousness' that overcomes injury in order to restore lost relationships.[27] Forgiveness therefore requires active, sometimes public, acknowledgement of crimes committed, and leaves open the possibility that victims will seek redress from perpetrators and perhaps insist on punishing them.

On this basis, forgiveness does not inherently oppose all forms of punishment, provided it does not involve personal, direct retribution, or ongoing calls for retribution even after perpetrators have been punished. Because forgiveness suggests some form of renewed relationship between perpetrator and victim, it is often confused with reconciliation. The two concepts, however, are distinct. While forgiveness may, in practice, lead to parties' resolving their differences to the extent that a renewed form of relationship is possible, nothing in the concept of forgiveness requires parties to reconcile. A victim may justifiably forgive his or her transgressor

[25] See, for example, these two main criticisms of notions of forgiveness after the Rwandan genocide by genocide survivor Jean Baptiste Kayigamba in 'Without Justice, No Reconciliation: A Survivor's Experience', in P. Clark and Z.D. Kaufman (eds.), *After Genocide: Transitional Justice, Post-Conflict Reconstruction and Reconciliation in Rwanda and Beyond*, London: Hurst & Co. Publishers, 2009, pp.33–42.

[26] H. Arendt, *The Human Condition*, Chicago, Ill.: University of Chicago Press, 1958, p.241.

[27] W. Lambourne, 'The Pursuit of Justice and Reconciliation: Responding to Genocide in Cambodia and Rwanda', *Columbia International Affairs Online*, June 1999, www.ciaonet.org/isa/law01, p.4.

and still refuse to engage with him or her again, perhaps for fear of repeat offences. Forgiveness requires only that a victim forgo feelings of resentment and a desire for direct revenge against the perpetrator.

RECONCILIATION

Finally, where truth and justice have traditionally been the more common objectives of post-conflict institutions, reconciliation has recently become a focal theme. More regular considerations of reconciliation in transitional-justice debates, however, have rarely cultivated a clear understanding of what reconciliation is and how it may be achieved. It is important therefore to define what 'reconciliation' means. In the broadest possible sense, reconciliation involves the rebuilding of fractured individual and communal relationships after conflict, with a view towards encouraging meaningful interaction and cooperation between former antagonists. Reconciliation entails much more than peaceful coexistence, which requires only that parties no longer act violently towards one another. Non-violence may mean that the parties concerned simply avoid each other, seeking separation rather than mended relationships. Reconciliation, however, requires the reshaping of parties' relationships, to lay the foundation for future engagement between them. John Paul Lederach contends that a 'relationship-centric' interpretation of reconciliation holds that responses to conflict must penetrate to the level of individual relationships.[28] 'To enter reconciliation processes', Lederach argues, 'is to enter the domain of the internal world, the inner understandings, fears and hopes, perceptions and interpretations of the relationship itself.'[29] This internal dimension greatly affects reconciliation at the communal or national level, because these structures necessarily comprise individuals who have experienced violence. In this sense, reconciliation, when defined in terms of rebuilding individual relations, lays the foundation for rebuilding wider social relations after conflict.

Reconciliation is both a process and an endpoint, requiring individuals and groups to interact and cooperate in often difficult circumstances, to discover solutions to their problems and thus to build stronger future

---

[28] J. Lederach, 'Five Qualities of Practice in Support of Reconciliation Processes', in R. Helmick and R. Petersen (eds.), *Forgiveness and Reconciliation: Religion, Public Policy, and Conflict Transformation*, Philadelphia, Pa.: Templeton Foundation Press, 2001, p.185.

[29] *Ibid.*, p.185.

relationships. Reconciliation is both backward- and forward-looking, seeking to address the causes of past conflict in order to produce a more positive dynamic in the future. Any process of reconciliation must honestly and directly address the root causes of conflict, and the overwhelming feelings of grievance and anger that may have compounded over generations and led to violence, if the parties concerned are to overcome serious divisions in the future.

In defining reconciliation, it is also necessary to differentiate it from two terms with which is it often confused: peace and healing. First, reconciliation differs from peace or any of its related processes such as peacekeeping or peacebuilding. Peace, as discussed above, should be viewed as a prerequisite of reconciliation. If violence continues, it is nearly impossible for individuals and groups to consider rebuilding their relationships. The broader, systemic, society-wide peacebuilding aims of ending violence and safeguarding against future conflict therefore pave the way for reconciliation's deeper, inter-personal, relationship-focused processes.

Second, reconciliation differs from healing, which refers to the ability of individuals and groups to overcome trauma, experienced during or after conflict. Authors such as Johan Galtung often conflate reconciliation and healing: for Galtung, reconciliation entails 'the process of healing the traumas of both victims and perpetrators after violence, providing a closure of the bad relation'.[30] Reconciliation, however, with its focus on rebuilding broken relationships, constitutes much more than overcoming trauma, although this – like peacebuilding – is often an important prerequisite of reconciliation. Many individuals and groups may not feel that they have suffered extreme trauma after conflict. Nonetheless, their relationships may be severely damaged, for a host of reasons other than trauma, and they may therefore seek some form of reconciliation. In other cases, traumatised individuals may need to overcome feelings of anguish, loss or hatred towards others before they can feel ready to reconcile with them.

CONCLUSION

This chapter has traced the theoretical contours of the six key transitional justice themes with which the sources analysed in this book

---

[30] J. Galtung, 'After Violence, Reconstruction, Reconciliation, and Resolution: Coping with Visible and Invisible Effects of War and Violence', in Abu-Nimer, *Reconciliation, Justice and Coexistence*, p.3.

associate gacaca. Because many sources provide varied or confused interpretations of each term or conflate these terms with one another, this
chapter has provided a clearer understanding of what each term entails
and, where conflation is likely, how each objective differs from closely
related terms. As later chapters highlight, sources on gacaca interpret
each of these themes in more detailed ways than they are discussed here.
Interpreting my sources' views on and practice of gacaca, the later analysis highlights how gacaca connects these six profound aims (and two
of the three pragmatic objectives discussed later) in particular ways, creating a galaxy of inter-related objectives, reflecting its holistic approach
to post-conflict reconstruction. One overall focus in this book is how, in
terms of different sources' interpretations of gacaca, but more importantly the population's practice of gacaca, these themes manifest, and the
problematic or successful practical outcomes that result from gacaca's
simultaneous pursuit of different types of aims.

CHAPTER 2

MOULDING TRADITION: THE HISTORY, LAW AND HYBRIDITY OF GACACA

INTRODUCTION

This chapter clarifies the genesis and modalities of gacaca and situates it within the broader realm of transitional justice. Much confusion currently surrounds how best to define the history and function of gacaca and how to locate it relative to other transitional justice processes around the world. Questions regarding gacaca abound: is it fundamentally a legal institution, a social institution with certain quasi-legal functions or something entirely different? What is it designed to achieve and how should we judge its effectiveness as a response to the needs of the Rwandan population after the genocide? In later chapters, I argue that most critiques, especially those from non-Rwandan legal commentators, mischaracterise what gacaca is and what it is designed to achieve. Therefore, it is not surprising that most commentators provide unconvincing accounts of the effectiveness of gacaca as a post-conflict remedy. In particular, many legal critics mistakenly characterise gacaca as a form of mob justice, in which the rights of individuals are sacrificed for the sake of the cheap and rapid prosecution of genocide suspects, or simply as a means of centralised state control. Many of the Rwandan government's characterisations of gacaca are also problematic, especially its attempt to portray gacaca as an indigenous mechanism with which the population identifies and in which it readily wishes to participate. Later chapters will show that legal critics are misguided in dismissing gacaca as an illegitimate system for punishing genocide perpetrators, while the Rwandan government (and some commentators) wrongly romanticise gacaca as a form of time-honoured justice automatically acceptable to all Rwandans.

Gacaca is more complex and multifaceted than most sources have so far suggested. This chapter shows that gacaca displays what I term 'internal hybridity', referring to its wide range of historical influences and types of objectives and processes. Hybridity is an increasingly common theme in the study and practice of transitional justice and post-conflict reconstruction and usually refers to systems of, rather than single, institutions. In recent years, a growing trend has emerged in institutional responses to complex conflict and post-conflict situations that advocates 'legal pluralism' or hybrid structures in which 'two or more legal systems coexist in the same social field'.[1] Today, legal pluralism in transitional-justice terms usually involves some type of international criminal tribunal and a locally directed truth commission, as in the cases of Sierra Leone and Timor-Leste, although discussions of community-based practices are also becoming more common in this regard. The primary purpose of such hybridity of institutions is to facilitate holism. A holistic approach to transitional justice contends that multiple political, social and legal institutions, operating concurrently in a system that maximises the capabilities of each one, can contribute more effectively than a single institution to the reconstruction of the entire society. Holistic approaches seek to respond to the various physical, psychological and psychosocial needs of individuals and groups during and after conflict.

While much attention has been paid to hybridity in terms of legal pluralism when responding to mass crimes, gacaca displays a form of internal hybridity that most commentators have overlooked, while also being embedded in the hybrid system along with the national courts and the ICTR. The concept of internal hybridity entails that gacaca embodies different types of objectives and processes that normally would require multiple institutions. This chapter underscores gacaca's internal hybridity and general dynamism. Better understanding gacaca's history and methods will allow us to more effectively critique its practical operation later in this book.

Linking the various strands of argument in this chapter is the contention that gacaca responds to various pragmatic and complex social needs in Rwandan society and therefore manifests a level of dynamism and complexity commensurate to that of the post-genocide situation. The hybridity of gacaca as a modern-traditional institution and of its aims and methods is necessary to facilitate the sorts of holistic responses that the post-genocide environment demands. This chapter also highlights that gacaca

[1] S.E. Merry, 'Legal Pluralism', *Law and Society Review*, 22, 1988, p.870.

is the product of protracted debates and complex political compromises involving different factions of a divided state and disagreements among international and domestic actors over the most appropriate responses to genocide crimes. Understanding how the Rwandan state came to select a transformed version of traditional gacaca helps explain many of the current contradictions and tensions within gacaca. This political analysis also underscores key fissures within the state that determine much of Rwanda's overall reconstruction process. Contrary to orthodox opinion on Rwanda, the government is not a united, homogeneous entity capable of consistently enacting coherent, centralised policy with limited elite or public consultation. The experience of gacaca highlights the tenuous nature of factions within the Rwandan state and the crucial political negotiations and concessions necessary to formulate major policy decisions, especially on questions of justice, reconciliation, reconstruction and development.

HISTORICAL DEVELOPMENT OF GACACA

This section traces the historical evolution of gacaca from a traditional mechanism of conflict resolution, through several phases of debate and reform within Rwanda, to its current manifestation as a hybrid response to genocide crimes. The following section then outlines the mechanics of gacaca, based on relevant legal documents, and the relationship between gacaca and the other two existing judicial systems charged with handling genocide cases: the Rwandan national courts and the ICTR. Together these sections counter a romanticised mythology about gacaca that over time has become increasingly common, particularly among non-Rwandans. In many journalistic and academic accounts of gacaca, the institution is referred to as a 'traditional' or 'village' practice, implying that gacaca, as a ritual and a set of ideas, is deeply entrenched in Rwandan society, particularly in rural communities, and automatically comprehensible to, and considered legitimate by, the population.[2] Some elements of the Rwandan government, especially in early discussions

[2] See, for example, A. Blomfield, 'Village Courts Will Try Thousands over Rwandan Genocide', *Daily Telegraph*, 5 October 2001, www.telegraph.co.uk/news/worldnews/africaandindianocean/rwanda/1358581/village-courts-will-try-thousands-over-Rwandan-genocide.html; R. Carroll, 'Rwandans Face Village Justice', *Guardian*, 5 July 2004, www.guardian.co.uk/international/story/0,3604,1253924,00.html; IRIN News, 'Rwanda: Plans to Reform Traditional Courts', 16 June 2004, www.irinnews.org/print.asp?ReportID=41693; H. Vespereni, 'Rwandans Back People's Courts', BBC News, 5 October 2001, news.bbc.co.uk/1/hi/world/africa/1581236.stm; N. Weisbord, 'Traditional Justice for a Genocide', *International Herald Tribune*, 26 September 2003, www.iht.com/articles/111291.html.

49

around gacaca, also describe it in this way.[3] Overall this chapter argues that, rather than seeing gacaca as a static, traditional system, we should view it as designed specifically to meet the needs of the post-genocide environment and as a dynamic practice that in the modern context comes in various forms, both state-run and outside of any official political or judicial structures.

Even before 1994, gacaca was a constantly evolving phenomenon; the genocide represented the most radical leap in this evolution. Gacaca was not an automatic choice as an institution to deal with genocide crimes, largely because its historical methods were not designed to deal with such complex cases. The eventual decision to adopt gacaca in this context was highly controversial. Rather than viewing post-genocide gacaca as *indigenous*, which connotes a native enterprise, occurring 'naturally' and inevitably accepted by the local population, we should view it as *endogenous*: initiated and synthesised within Rwandan society but – because of the complicated nature of that synthesis, and how markedly current gacaca differs from the original practice that partly inspired it – viewed by much of the population as a new, and perhaps confusing or even disagreeable, entity. As we will see later in this chapter, the complex historical evolution of gacaca, culminating in the current institution, is vital to explaining its more specific, hybrid methods and objectives.

In the months following the genocide in Rwanda, around 120,000 genocide suspects, mostly Hutu, were rounded up and transported to jails around the country built to hold only 45,000 inmates.[4] Most detainees were never formally charged with any crime and were forced to live in hellish conditions: underfed, drinking dirty water and crammed into tiny rooms where they were often made to sleep in latticework formations for lack of space.[5] During the genocide, the Rwandan judicial system – which manifested signs of debilitation before 1994 – was nearly destroyed completely, as the infrastructure of the national courts was decimated and many judges and lawyers were

[3] See, for example, C. Murigande, 'Report on Urugwiro Talks from May 1998 to March 1999', *Report on the National Summit of Unity and Reconciliation*, Kigali: National Unity and Reconciliation Committee (NURC), 18–20 October 2000, pp.31–4. Even by 2006, however, the NURC was still describing post-genocide gacaca as the revival of a 'sleeping but not dead model of justice' upon which 'people in their sectors continued relying' (NURC, *Training Manual on Conflict Management*, Kigali: NURC, February 2006, p.43).
[4] International Centre for Prison Studies (King's College), 'Prison Brief for Rwanda', London: ICPS, 2002, www.kcl.ac.uk/depsta/rel/icps/worldbrief/africa_records.php?code=39.
[5] Author's fieldnotes, Butare Central Prison, 4 February 2003.

killed or fled the country.[6] With the existing judicial system incapable
of dealing with massive numbers of suspects, the government sought
new mechanisms to hear genocide cases. As then Vice President and
now President Paul Kagame said in 1998, 'Presently, the maintenance
of 120,000 prisoners costs US$20 million per year, for which we receive
assistance from the international community. This cannot continue
in the long-term: we have to find other solutions.'[7] In response to the
social, political, economic and legal problems created by the overcrowded prisons, the Rwandan government in 2001 instituted gacaca
to try lower-level genocide suspects, most of whom had been imprisoned for more than a decade. In March 2005, gacaca entered its most
crucial phase, as it expanded nationwide and in some communities
began judging and sentencing the first wave of genocide suspects,
some of whom, as a result of their conviction at gacaca, have now been
sentenced to new prison terms. Gacaca continues to judge and sentence genocide suspects imprisoned since 1994 and has in recent years
identified many new suspects who were not rounded up during the initial incarceration process but now face justice at gacaca.[8]

---

[6] AI, 'Rwanda: Gacaca – A Question of Justice', AI Doc. AFR 47/007/2002, December 2002,
pp.12–13.

[7] P. Kagame, quoted in S. Vandeginste, 'A Truth and Reconciliation Approach to the Genocide
and Crimes against Humanity in Rwanda', Antwerp: Centre for the Study of the Great Lakes
Region of Africa, May 1998, p.45.

[8] There is considerable debate about exactly how many new genocide suspects gacaca has identified. The Rwandan government estimates that up to 1 million genocide suspects have been
prosecuted, after gacaca has unearthed hundreds of thousands of new cases since 2002 (author's
government interviews, Domitilla Mukantaganzwa, Executive Secretary, National Service of
Gacaca Jurisdictions, Kigali, 24 April 2009). There is little evidence so far to suggest that so
many new cases – approximately an increase of 800 per cent to the initial number of genocide
suspects – have been identified. Interviews at gacaca provincial offices and at the community
level suggest that the numbers are likely to be considerably lower than the government claims.
National Service of Gacaca Jurisdictions (NSGJ) officials in the northern and southern provinces reported approximately 300 per cent and 400 per cent increases respectively in the number of genocide suspects identified by gacaca. At the community level, Alphonse and Cypriet,
two detainees who had confessed to committing crimes during the genocide and whom I interviewed on several occasions in 2003, and again in 2006, 2008 and 2009, claimed that, in their
local jurisdictions, gacaca had led to roughly a 100 per cent increase in the number of genocide
suspects identified: in Alphonse's community, around fifty individuals had confessed to genocide crimes while in prison after the 1994 round-up of suspects, and gacaca had subsequently
identified sixty-five new suspects; in Cypriet's community, fifty-five new suspects had been identified, alongside the forty who had initially confessed (author's detainee follow-up interviews,
Alphonse, Nyamata, Kigali Ngali, 11 June 2006; Cypriet, Nyamata, Kigali Ngali, 11 June 2006).
Based on these findings, it is more likely that gacaca has dealt with around 1 million *cases* rather
than *suspects*, as many suspects are accused of committing multiple crimes and many crimes were
committed by groups.

Pre-genocide gacaca

Little has been written about how gacaca functioned before the Belgian colonial era. Historians record that at the turn of the twentieth century gacaca did not exist as a permanent judicial institution but was based instead on unwritten law and assembled only when conflicts arose within or between families, particularly in rural Rwanda.[9] Gacaca hearings, usually held outdoors either on a patch of grass or in the village courtyard, were overseen by male heads of households, and women were forbidden from taking part, unless as claimants or defendants. The traditional aim of gacaca, according to Abbé Smaragde Mbonyintege, was to 'sanction the violation of rules that [were] shared by the community, with the sole objective of reconciliation'.[10] Such an objective drew heavily from the traditional Rwandan cosmology that considered the family and the wider community as the most valuable human units. In this worldview, individuals gained their sense of worth primarily through their embeddedness in communities, from their connections first to family and then to their wider community. For this reason, punishments at gacaca were inadequate if they acted solely as punitive measures. Sentencing at gacaca was intended instead to re-establish social cohesion, incorporating restorative processes that allowed individuals found guilty to regain their standing in the community. Gacaca judges never imposed prison terms on those found guilty, although in some instances they did banish individuals from the community for a short period but always with the option for them to return eventually.[11]

Early in the twentieth century, gacaca was the main method of ensuring social order in communities across Rwanda, dealing principally with uncomplicated cases referring to land use, livestock, damage to property, marriage or inheritance. The methods employed in hearing these cases were relatively straightforward. Gacaca brought conflicting

[9] F. Reyntjens, 'Le *Gacaca* ou la justice du gazon au Rwanda', *Politique Africaine*, December 1990, p.32.

[10] A.S. Mbonyintege, 'Gacaca ishobora ite kongera kuba izira y'umwiyinge bw'abanyarwanda', *Urumuri rwa Kristu*, 15 August 1995, p.15 (translation by C. Ntampaka and S. Vandeginste), quoted in S. Vandeginste, 'Justice, Reconciliation and Reparation after Genocide and Crimes against Humanity: The Proposed Establishment of Popular Gacaca Tribunals in Rwanda', paper delivered to All-Africa Conference on African Principles of Conflict Resolution and Reconciliation, Addis Ababa, 8–12 November 1999, p.15.

[11] A. Karekezi, 'Juridictions gacaca: lutte contre l'impunité et promotion de la réconciliation nationale', in E. Ntaganda (ed.), *Les Juridictions gacaca et les processus de réconciliation nationale*, Cahiers de Centre de Gestion des Conflits (no. 3), Butare: Université Nationale du Rwanda, May 2001, p.32.

parties before community elders to hear grievances, to allow defendants to respond to any charges and finally to pass judgments based on the evidence heard. In an ideal gacaca hearing, defendants would first – after prompting from the judges – confess their crimes, express remorse and ask for forgiveness from those whom they had injured. Gacaca judges would then demand that confessors provide restitution to their victims, and the process would culminate in the sharing of beer, wine or food – usually provided by the guilty party – to symbolise the reconciliation of the parties involved.[12]

With time, gacaca became more institutionalised and stratified, particularly as colonial powers gained greater control over the national judicial system. An important political method employed by the Belgian colonial regime in Rwanda was to appoint local (and because of the Belgians' perception, based on social-Darwinist ideology, of the Tutsi as a superior race to the Hutu), usually Tutsi, administrators to maintain order on the colonialists' behalf. In the case of gacaca, these local Tutsi administrators appointed the elders in charge of hearings. Gacaca continued to function according to local, unwritten law but, whereas hearings had previously occurred in communities only as they were required and were carried out in front of judges who were usually elders of the families involved, politically appointed judges soon began holding gacaca sessions once a week in each sector of the country.[13] All male inhabitants of the community – not only those involved directly in specific cases – were encouraged to participate.[14]

In 1943 – in an early form of hybrid system for dealing with common crimes – the Belgian administration in Rwanda officially recognised gacaca as a legitimate judicial mechanism functioning alongside the national court system, though this concurrence was never enshrined in law.[15] The colonial regime encouraged citizens to weigh the relative strengths and weaknesses of the two systems (e.g., the speed and locality of gacaca versus the greater juridical sophistication of the official courts) and to choose accordingly where they wished to have their cases heard. Filip Reyntjens argues that gacaca and the national courts each developed separate 'clientele'[16] who engaged in a type of 'forum

[12] Vandeginste, 'Justice, Reconciliation and Reparation', p.15.
[13] Karekezi, 'Juridictions gacaca', p.32.
[14] Reyntjens, 'Le Gacaca', p.33.
[15] C. Ntampaka, 'Le Gacaca: une juridiction pénale populaire', Agence Intergouvernementale de la Francophonie, www.droit.francophonie.org/acct/rjf/actu/13Ntampa.htm.
[16] Reyntjens, 'Le Gacaca', p.37.

shopping':[17] rural claimants, who were typically farmers with cases concerning land rights, payment of debts, inheritance or personal disputes, tended to seek hearings at gacaca; urban dwellers with more complex cases, for example involving work contracts, often took their disputes to the official courts. In his analysis of gacaca in a largely agricultural region of Butare province in 1986 and 1987, Reyntjens calculates that over an eight-month period nearly 93 per cent of the approximately 1,200 judicial cases heard took place at gacaca rather than in the formal courts.[18]

The next major phase in the evolution of gacaca saw it develop from an essentially judicial structure to one fulfilling a wider administrative role after Rwanda gained independence from Belgium. Historian Charles Ntampaka argues that this change ensued as it became custom for defendants who were dissatisfied with the result of their hearings at gacaca, for example at the level of their cell (the smallest administrative unit within Rwandan local government, which usually comprises ten or more extended families or on average 830 citizens[19]) to appeal the judges' decision to the next superior administrative official such as the mayor or prefect of the sector (comprising around six cells or 5,000 citizens[20]) or even to judges in the official courts. These administrators effectively became temporary gacaca judges, fulfilling the role typically afforded heads of families and village elders. In the hands of these administrators, gacaca became a much more active enterprise. Whereas in the past gacaca hearings were assembled only at the behest of parties in conflict, post-independence administrators often called parties to gacaca without any request being made by members of the community.[21] According to Ntampaka, gacaca was 'no longer a family-based forum of reflection for the renewal of social harmony but it became instead a forum in which locally elected judges from the official courts could collect evidence, particularly in civil matters, and hand down judgements based on the testimonies they heard'.[22]

[17] *Ibid.*, p.40.
[18] *Ibid.*, p.38.
[19] Vandeginste, 'Justice, Reconciliation and Reparation', p.18.
[20] *Ibid.*, p.18.
[21] C. Ntampaka, 'Le Gacaca devenu une justice aux mains des victimes', *Umubano*, March 1999, www.umubano.be/02_fr/magazine/s_gacaca.htm.
[22] Ntampaka, 'Le *Gacaca*', p.8 (author's translation).

Post-genocide debates over transitional justice

The post-genocide period marks the most radical evolution of gacaca, during which its internal hybridity became a central feature. Although gacaca was not officially sanctioned to hear the majority of genocide-related cases until 2001, it was debated officially as a potential mechanism soon after the end of the genocide. As early as 1995, the Rwandan government and even the UN questioned whether gacaca might be appropriate for prosecuting certain genocide crimes. At an international conference in Kigali in October 1995, the government considered both a general amnesty and gacaca as possible methods for dealing with genocide suspects. Amnesty was rejected on the grounds that it would inflame many genocide survivors' perceived desire for vengeance. The government dismissed gacaca on the grounds that it violated existing Rwandan law regarding the need to formally prosecute serious crimes, particularly murder.[23] During this same period, many commentators, including José Kabago, observed an increase in the use of gacaca in rural areas, most likely as a response to the breakdown of the more official court system.[24] These gacaca courts rarely handled the major crimes connected to the genocide but rather focused on the more common infractions with which gacaca was traditionally associated.

In 1996 and 1997, the notion of gacaca as a potential response to mass violations of human rights was sidelined in official discussions. Instead, the government, with major assistance from international NGOs such as the Belgian organisation Avocats Sans Frontières (ASF) and the Danish Centre for Human Rights (DCHR), began a major overhaul of the national courts. The dire state of the post-genocide judicial system forced the government and international donors to embark on a nationwide campaign of training new judges and lawyers. The national court system also suffered from a lengthy history of corruption and repression, as before the genocide the courts were highly politicised and invariably a tool of an authoritarian executive. These factors necessitated the post-genocide vetting and training of judicial personnel.

In an attempt to further speed the hearing and prosecution of genocide cases in the national courts, the government passed the Organic Law of August 1996, which – as explored in greater detail in the following

---

[23] Republic of Rwanda, 'Minutes of the Symposium on Gacaca', Hotel Umubano, Kigali, 6–7 March 2000, p.13.
[24] J. Kagabo, 'Minutes of the Symposium on Gacaca', Hotel Umubano, Kigali, 6–7 March 2000, p.51.

section – divided genocide suspects into four categories depending on the severity of their crimes and established a plea-bargaining scheme that offered decreased sentences in exchange for suspects' confessions.[25] The Chief Prosecutor of the Supreme Court launched genocide investigations across the country, establishing judicial panels comprising lay magistrates who received four months' legal training, while several hundred judicial police inspectors compiled dossiers on the genocide prison population.[26]

The national courts were initially slow in hearing the cases of genocide suspects. By 2000 the courts had heard only 2,500 cases, less than 3 per cent of the genocide backlog. Of those cases, around 500 accused were acquitted and 400 received the death penalty. Plea-bargaining in these cases was extremely rare, with fewer than 20 per cent of defendants pleading guilty. It was clear that, at this rate, the vast majority of genocide cases would never be heard, necessitating the search for alternative mechanisms to process the immense backlog.[27]

Discussions turned to the possibility of employing a South Africa-style truth commission. As Jeremy Sarkin points out, there is a precedent of employing such an institution in Rwanda. After the signing of the Arusha Accords in 1993, a truth commission was established in Rwanda to investigate human-rights abuses committed between 1990 and 1993. Its work was severely undermined by ongoing violence in Rwanda in late 1993, but it was still able to produce a final report that detailed crimes against humanity committed during the civil-war period.[28] In 1997, the government considered, then rejected, the idea of using a truth commission to address genocide crimes, on the grounds that it would not adequately punish génocidaires.[29]

The year 1998 marked the re-emergence in public discourse of the potential use of gacaca for hearing and prosecuting genocide cases.

---

[25] Republic of Rwanda, 'Loi organique no. 8196 du 30/8/96 sur l'organisation des poursuites des infractions constitutives du crime de genocide ou de crimes contre l'humanité, commises à partir de 1er octobre 1990', *Official Gazette of the Republic of Rwanda*, 1 September 1996, Articles 2–9 (from here on, referred to as the 'Organic Law').

[26] UN Office of the High Commissioner for Human Rights, 'The Administration of Justice in Post-Genocide Rwanda', UN Doc. HRFOR/Justice/June 1996/E, June 1996.

[27] AI, 'Rwanda: The Troubled Course of Justice', AI Index AFR 47/10/00, April 2000, pp.2–3.

[28] J. Sarkin, 'The Necessity and Challenges of Establishing a Truth and Reconciliation Commission in Rwanda', *Human Rights Quarterly*, 21, 3, 1999, pp.777–8.

[29] For analyses of these debates regarding a truth commission in Rwanda, see Sarkin, 'Necessity and Challenges'; and M. Drumbl, 'Sclerosis: Retributive Justice and the Rwandan Genocide', *Punishment and Society*, 2, 3, 2000, p.296.

Between May 1998 and March 1999, President Pasteur Bizimungu held 'reflection meetings' each Saturday at Urugwiro Village in Kigali.[30] The purpose of these meetings was to gather political, social, legal and religious authorities to discuss the most pressing issues concerning national reconstruction.[31] Questions of justice and reconciliation featured heavily in the talks, and, in June 1998, the possibility of revitalising gacaca was again raised, primarily by a group of provincial prefects, most notably Protais Musoni, then-Prefect of Kibungo and now Minister of Local Government, Good Governance, Community Development and Social Affairs. Fatuma Ndangiza, Executive Secretary of the NURC, describes Musoni as the 'father of gacaca' and the individual chiefly responsible for convincing the government to reform gacaca to deal with genocide cases.[32]

On 17 October 1998, Bizimungu established a commission to investigate the possibility of restructuring gacaca into a system appropriate for handling genocide cases.[33] Musoni describes the debates at Urugwiro during this period as protracted and often heated, a fact not readily expressed by many state sources who tend to characterise the government's decision to transform the traditional practice of gacaca as rapid and almost inevitable.[34] The official report on the Urugwiro discussions gives a flavour of these disagreements, highlighting major dissension over justice issues and the possible use of gacaca in particular.[35] Interviews with key participants in the meetings draw out this theme even more clearly. Musoni recounts:

> The debates about whether and how we could use gacaca after the genocide were long and difficult. We were all in a room for a very long time – the President, government ministers, community leaders. The commission reporting to the President was made up of three prefects and various lawyers from the government, including several senior people in the Ministry of Justice. There were serious conflicts among us about what gacaca was supposed to be. The issue of the population's involvement in

---

[30] For a detailed synthesis of these meetings, see Republic of Rwanda, 'Report on the Reflection Meetings Held in the Office of the President of the Republic from May 1998 to March 1999', Kigali: Office of the President of the Republic, August 1999.

[31] For an overview of these meetings, see Murigande, 'Report on Urugwiro Talks', pp.22–34.

[32] Author's government interviews, Fatuma Ndangiza, Executive Secretary, NURC, Kigali, 10 June 2006.

[33] Republic of Rwanda, 'Report on the Reflection Meetings', p.9.

[34] Author's government interviews, Protais Musoni, Rwandan Minister of Local Government, Good Governance, Community Development and Social Affairs, Kigali, 13 June 2006.

[35] Republic of Rwanda, 'Report on the Reflection Meetings', pp.55–86.

gacaca was especially difficult. The lawyers kept saying, 'How can we let the people judge their own cases so soon after the genocide?' The prefects were pushing the participation angle. We believed the emphasis of gacaca should be like it was practised on the hills, where we came from: it should emphasise truth and reconciliation. Gacaca should be more than judgements. Punishment was important but it had to give us truth and reconciliation ... I personally wanted less emphasis on judgement in gacaca and a freer rein for the truth to come out. We should take gacaca slowly and help overcome the reluctance of the truth-tellers in the community.

...

At Urugwiro, we were highly conscious of the concerns of the international community. What would the rest of the world think of gacaca? We'd heard many of their concerns when gacaca was first mentioned during conferences after the genocide. We knew their fears of trusting the masses at gacaca would be very great ... Eventually, we found something that everyone in the room could agree to: a gacaca that kept the lawyers happy and gave the rest of us most of what we wanted.[36]

President Kagame, who was Vice President at the time of the Urugwiro discussions, confirmed Musoni's recollections:

Those talks were very difficult. I for one wasn't convinced that gacaca was the best approach. I still don't think gacaca gives us all we need and it has major limitations. But it gives us most things and certainly more than most other processes ... When we were talking [at Urugwiro] about how to achieve justice and reconciliation, I wanted something stronger than gacaca. The survivors were calling for strong justice. After all, they had been through genocide. Was gacaca going to be enough for them? ... Eventually I was persuaded that gacaca would help us deal with the massive numbers of genocide suspects who were in prison.[37]

Tharcisse Karugarama, currently Rwandan Minister of Justice, who participated in the Urugwiro talks in his capacity as Prosecutor General of the Appeals Court of Ruhengeri, also echoed Musoni, especially regarding the difficulties of convincing government lawyers of gacaca's virtues:

The main stumbling block in the discussions was the acceptability of the [gacaca] process to the legal fraternity. You know, lawyers are arrogant people and unfortunately I belong to that clan. In training, they

[36] Author's government interviews, Protais Musoni.
[37] Author's government interviews, Paul Kagame, President of the Republic of Rwanda, Kigali, 13 June 2006.

refer to each other as 'learned brother' and 'learned counsel' – they think that justice is their exclusive right. They think their exclusive right is the law without realising that justice is the domain of all the people. Law and justice are separate entities. Sometimes law delivers justice but not always. People don't know how to put on robes and wigs but that doesn't mean they don't know what justice is.

. . .

Around August 1997, I wrote something on gacaca, arguing that we could move around the country with mobile teams, screening genocide suspects. The document leaked and I went on the radio and television for three hours, fielding questions from journalists about how we could provide justice for genocide cases. I was saying that the entire justice system will collapse if we don't get away from classical trials. I wasn't envisaging gacaca as it's happening today – my proposal wouldn't have been as good as gacaca is now, but I was talking about similar principles, about how to involve the population and lay judges more.

. . .

Soon after, I received so much condemnation that I nearly went into exile. I was accused of simplifying the genocide, making it sound less horrific than it really was [to the extent that] you could just give justice to the population and not to professionals. Most survivors when they saw me in the street wouldn't even greet me. People were muttering that I was going to promote impunity. Members of the government accused me of seeking cheap popularity. Making matters worse was the fact that the prisoners and their relatives were in favour of my proposals, so the backlash was bad. Lawyers described me as stupid. The Chief Justice even called me a donkey and there were cartoons of me in the newspapers. You couldn't talk about gacaca or anything like it in 1997 ... Gacaca certainly did not come easily. Almost everyone inside the government opposed gacaca early on. Really they were misunderstanding the differences between justice and law. But Musoni and I and others were able to convince them that gacaca had many benefits.[38]

These interviews with Rwandan elites highlight major divisions among policy-makers on key questions of post-genocide justice and reconciliation. My interviews with Kagame, Musoni, Karugarama and other government officials indicate that four main divisions were apparent during the Urugwiro talks: between lawyers and non-lawyers; between urban and rural elites; between the RPF military and political hierarchy; and between members of the RPF who had fought or been present in Uganda

[38] Author's government interviews, Tharcisse Karugarama, Rwandan Minister of Justice, Kigali, 3 September 2008 (interview conducted jointly with Nicola Palmer).

or Rwanda during the civil war and the genocide and diasporic figures who had returned to Rwanda after the genocide. As Kagame describes above, the lawyers, urban elites and RPF (especially military) leaders who had lived through the conflict first-hand generally favoured 'stronger' forms of justice for genocide suspects than they perceived in the proposed use of gacaca. These groups opposed gacaca for slightly different reasons. Lawyers favoured more conventional judicial responses to genocide crimes that reflected their own legal training. Urban elites favoured similar legal measures because they would centralise accountability processes in Kigali, while lawyers and urban elites converged in their depictions of gacaca as a primitive, rural practice appropriate only for low-level community infractions, and their distrust of the population's capacity to address serious crimes themselves so soon after the genocide.[39] RPF leaders, particularly in the military, with first-hand experience of the genocide advocated strict justice for the crimes they had witnessed directly and invoked survivors' demands in the community for such measures.

On the other side, non-lawyers, rural elites, some RPF political officials and returned diasporic figures argued that conventional court processes for genocide crimes would prove inadequate in the face of hundreds of thousands of suspects still in prison and would fail to address crucial social issues of healing and reconciliation in the countryside. Some RPF political leaders advocated the use of gacaca by invoking principles of 'popular justice' from their days in Uganda supporting Yoweri Museveni's National Resistance Movement (NRM) and Uganda's history of using local councils (LCs) to address crimes in the community. Designed initially as fora for communal decision-making on day-to-day community issues, the LCs evolved into the primary local-level political and judicial institution throughout Uganda. The LCs, as they became known after Museveni's election victory in 1996, grew out of resistance councils (RCs) established by his forces during the Ugandan bush war to maintain law and order in rebel-held regions and to gather intelligence and mobilise recruitment in areas held by Milton Obote's army. Soon after the NRM's rise to power, Museveni proclaimed that 'popular justice' could help overcome the rampant corruption of political and judicial structures inherited from Amin and Obote and reinvigorate Ugandan community life.[40] In 1987, the Resistance Councils and Committees Statute

---

[39] See also, Republic of Rwanda, 'Report on the Reflection Meetings', p.60.
[40] Y. Museveni, *Sowing the Mustard Seed: The Struggle for Freedom and Democracy in Uganda*, London: Macmillan, 1997, p.30.

afforded the RCs the role of hearing low-level civil cases, as a means to overcoming the congestion of the magistrates courts and to making justice more accessible – physically and culturally – to local populations.[41] At Urugwiro, several RPF political leaders argued that gacaca could similarly aid Rwanda's attempts to decongest the national courts of their genocide caseload while also pursuing healing and reconciliation at the community level.[42]

Meanwhile, diasporic elites, particularly Tutsi who had returned from Europe and the USA, argued that the state needed to consider international opinion of Rwanda's post-genocide policies because foreign aid and diplomatic support were essential to the reconstruction process.[43] While Musoni's comments above emphasise international concerns over the use of gacaca to handle genocide cases, a government official who had been at the Urugwiro meetings and spoke to me on the grounds of anonymity highlighted another area of international disquiet:

> There was major pressure on the government because of the public executions of *génocidaires* like the ones in the Amahoro [Stadium]. There was anger from survivors because of the lack of justice and anger from the international community because of how we were [initially] going about justice, so it was very difficult. The world was sympathetic to us

[41] B. Baker, 'Popular Justice and Policing from Bush War to Democracy: Uganda, 1981–2004', *International Journal of the Sociology of Law*, 32, 4, 2004, p.336.

[42] Republic of Rwanda, 'Report on the Reflection Meetings', p.60. A cyclical genealogy of ideas has manifested recently, as the Ugandan government has considered the post-genocide version of gacaca as a model for its own considerations of community-based processes to deal with crimes committed by the Lord's Resistance Army in northern Uganda. In 2006, a Ugandan parliamentary committee was established to consider whether local (particularly Acholi) rituals could be codified and nationalised, similar to Rwanda's reform and formalisation of the gacaca courts. 'We are considering whether something like gacaca in Rwanda provides a model for us here in Uganda', a government official said. 'There are pros and cons to the use of traditional practices and we have to weigh up what the best approach is. But certainly we believe traditional methods can teach us a lot about dealing with the current situation' (author's interview, Ugandan Government Official, Kampala, 3 March 2006). The language of 'gacaca' has also gained significant currency in Ugandan public discussions. In an article in the Ugandan state-owned *New Vision* newspaper, one commentator characterised the 'free and fair' elections in Uganda in 1989, which he described as exhibiting little executive interference, as a 'gacaca (community) exercise devoid of vertical civic ... discourse' (A. Bisika, 'Otunnu Is Not Obama because Uganda Is Not USA', *The New Vision*, 2 September 2009).

[43] On this theme, see also B. Oomen, 'Donor-Driven Justice and its Discontents: The Case of Rwanda', *Development and Change*, 36, 5, 2005, pp.887–910. In 2002, Richard Sezibera, the Rwandan ambassador to the USA, said, 'We have modified the [traditional gacaca] process to meet international standards as much as possible and placed the gacaca courts under the control of our supreme court' (R. Sezibera, 'The Only Way to Bring Justice to Rwanda', *Washington Post*, 7 April 2002).

after the genocide because of what we'd been through but some people [at Urugwiro] were saying we needed to take a softer line. We had to act calmly and reasonably. We couldn't afford to lose international support because that would mean losing aid and being isolated again.[44]

This official stated that the key element that eventually convinced Kagame and others of the virtues of gacaca was concern over international perceptions of Rwanda's approach to post-genocide accountability.[45] The timing of the Urugwiro talks was especially important in this sense, commencing in May 1998, several weeks after a number of widely reported public executions of convicted *génocidaires* in stadia around Rwanda during the official genocide commemorations in April.[46] The parties at Urugwiro decided eventually that international apprehension over public executions of *génocidaires* outweighed any disquiet over reviving gacaca. The latter concerns could be addressed by instilling sufficient safeguards for due process as gacaca was reformed to handle genocide cases.

These descriptions of the Urugwiro meetings highlight the major divisions within the Rwandan government and the manifold concerns that were raised during debates over appropriate justice and reconciliation measures. In the section below, discussing the modalities of gacaca, it is clear that much of gacaca's hybridity, especially its combination of legal and non-legal objectives and methods, results from the crucial political compromises that led to gacaca's inception. Different parties within the government had varying experiences of the genocide, ranging from having fought the genocidal government directly to having lived thousands of miles away in 1994, and having been exposed variously to international opinion on Rwanda. These divergent experiences crucially shaped policy-makers' views on how best to address genocide crimes. Understanding gacaca's genesis is vital to understanding its complex features and, as we shall see, the continuing divisions in government circles over how to conduct gacaca across the country. A key theme in this book is that those government divisions – particularly between lawyers and non-lawyers and between RPF leaders who experienced the genocide first-hand and members of the returned diaspora – continue to shape key areas of state policy, principally regarding how to address the legacies of the genocide.

[44] Author's government interviews, anonymous Rwandan official, Kigali, 14 June 2006.
[45] *Ibid.*
[46] See, for example, BBC, 'From Butchery to Executions in Rwanda', 27 April 1998, www.news.bbc.co.uk/1/hi/programmes/from_our_own_correspondent/84120.stm.

In February 1999, after the UN Office of the High Commissioner for Human Rights assisted the post-Urugwiro study of gacaca, the UN Special Rapporteur stated, 'gacaca is not competent to hear crimes against humanity, but it could be utilized for purposes of testifying in connection with reconciliation.'[47] Ignoring the UN's advice, Bizimungu's commission produced a draft proposal in June 1999, detailing how gacaca jurisdictions might be divided among the various levels of local administration – cell, sector, district, province – with each level hearing and prosecuting cases according to the categories of crime outlined in the Organic Law.[48] Soon after, the Commission distributed the draft proposal in government and NGO circles and organised a sensitisation conference in Gitarama, which gathered mayors and other community leaders from around the country to explain the concept of gacaca to them and to canvass opinion of the proposed structure.[49] Following the conference, the newly established NURC was charged with conducting a detailed grass-roots analysis of the perceptions of the national population concerning justice and reconciliation broadly and specifically the gacaca proposal.[50] The result of these debates and analyses was the enactment of the Gacaca Law in January 2001.[51]

Gacaca begins

At the outset, the government stated that gacaca was designed to expedite justice for genocide crimes, while pursuing more subtle social goals such as reconciliation by encouraging direct community participation in genocide prosecutions. Gacaca was not intended to replace the national courts in the hearing of genocide cases but rather to relieve the immense pressure on the national system by addressing the vast numbers of low-level suspects, while leaving more senior accused

[47] UN Office of the High Commissioner for Human Rights, 'Report on the Situation of Human Rights in Rwanda', UN Doc. E/CN.4/1999/33, 8 February 1999, p.12. A member of the Office of the High Commissioner for Human Rights team responsible for the 1999 report later published a longer critique of the proposed gacaca process. See L. Werchick, 'Prospects for Justice in Rwanda's Citizen Tribunals', *Human Rights Brief*, 8, 3, 2001, pp.15–18.
[48] Vandeginste, 'Justice, Reconciliation and Reparation', pp.17–20.
[49] Ligue Rwandaise pour la Promotion et la Defense des Droits de l'Homme, 'Juridictions gacaca au Rwanda: résultats de la recherché sur les attitudes et opinions de la population rwandaise', Kigali: LIPRODHOR, August 2000, p.14.
[50] NURC, 'Nationwide Grassroots Consultations Report: Unity and Reconciliation Initiatives in Rwanda', Kigali: NURC, January 2001.
[51] Republic of Rwanda, 'Organic Law 40/2000 of 26/01/2001 Setting Up Gacaca Jurisdictions and Organising Prosecutions for Offences Constituting the Crime of Genocide or Crimes against Humanity Committed between 1 October 1993 and 31 December 1994', *Official Gazette of the*

to the national courts and the ICTR.[52] Soon after passing the Gacaca Law, the government, with the assistance of the DCHR, ran a nation-wide education campaign explaining the new law to the population.[53] Once the government believed that the population was sufficiently sensitised, it ran a 'pre-gacaca' programme of displaying genocide suspects before their home communities in what was billed as a dress rehearsal for a more fully fledged gacaca to be activated countrywide in 2002. Several local and international NGOs were permitted to

Republic of Rwanda, October 2000, Article 13 (from hereon, referred to as the 'Gacaca Law'). The Gacaca Law has been modified five times, as explored in greater detail below. The five documents that comprise these modifications are: Republic of Rwanda, 'Loi Organique No. 33/2001 du 22/6/2001 modifiant et completant Loi Organique No. 40/2000 du 26 Janvier 2001 portant creation des "juridictions gacaca" et organisation des poursuite des infractions constitutives du crime de genocide ou de crimes contre l'humanité, commises entre le 1 octobre 1990 et 31 decembre 1994', *Official Gazette of the Republic of Rwanda*, 22 June 2001 (from hereon, referred to as the 'Gacaca Law [Modified 2001]'); Republic of Rwanda, 'Organic Law No. 16/2004 of 19/6/2004 Establishing the Organisation, Competence and Functioning of Gacaca Courts Charged with Prosecuting and Trying the Perpetrators of the Crime of Genocide and other Crimes against Humanity, Committed between 1 October 1990 and 31 December 1994', *Official Gazette of the Republic of Rwanda*, 19 June 2004 (from hereon, referred to as the 'Gacaca Law [Modified 2004]'); Republic of Rwanda, 'Organic Law No. 28/2006 of 27/06/2006 Modifying and Complementing Organic Law No. 16/2004 of 19/06/2004 Establishing the Organisation, Competence and Functioning of Gacaca Courts Charged with Prosecuting and Trying the Perpetrators of the Crime of Genocide and Other Crimes against Humanity, Committed between October 1, 1990 and December 31, 1994', *Official Gazette of the Republic of Rwanda*, 27 June 2006 (from hereon, referred to as the 'Gacaca Law [Modified 2006]'); Republic of Rwanda, 'Organic Law No. 10/2007 of 01/03/2007 Modifying and Complementing Organic Law No. 16/2004 of 19/6/2004 Establishing the Organisation, Competence and Functioning of Gacaca Courts Charged with Prosecuting and Trying the Perpetrators of the Crime of Genocide and Other Crimes against Humanity, Committed between October 1, 1990 and December 31, 1994, as Modified and Complemented to Date', *Official Gazette of the Republic of Rwanda*, 3 January 2007 (from hereon, referred to as 'Gacaca Law [Modified 2007]'); and Republic of Rwanda, 'Organic Law No. 13/2008 of 19/05/2008 Modifying and Complementing Organic Law No. 16/2004 of 19/6/2004 Establishing the Organisation, Competence and Functioning of Gacaca Courts Charged with Prosecuting and Trying the Perpetrators of the Crime of Genocide and Other Crimes against Humanity, Committed between October 1, 1990 and December 31, 1994, as Modified and Complemented to Date', *Official Gazette of the Republic of Rwanda*, 19 May 2008 (from hereon, referred to as 'Gacaca Law [Modified 2008]'). Gacaca Law (Modified 2004) and Gacaca Law (Modified 2008) constitute a more significant rewriting of parts of the original Gacaca Law than do the other modified laws. The 2001, 2006 and 2007 revised document are concerned primarily with minor changes to the wording of several sections of the Gacaca Law, while the 2004 and 2008 versions comprise several important reforms of the gacaca process, outlined later in this chapter.

52 See, for example, Murigande, 'Report on Urugwiro Talks', pp.30–3.

53 F. Kerrigan, 'Some Issues of Truth, Justice and Reconciliation in Genocide Trials before Gacaca Tribunals in Rwanda', Copenhagen: DCHR, April 2002.

observe the hearings and to provide analyses for further government consideration.[54]

These pre-gacaca hearings ran similarly to the traditional method of gacaca discussed above, with the exception that government-selected 'procureurs' and their assistants, rather than family heads or communally elected judges, conducted hearings. The procureurs heard evidence from witnesses and survivors in detainees' communities and after considering the testimony, along with the evidence already contained in suspects' files, they decided whether or not there was sufficient evidence to warrant the reimprisonment of the detainees. During pre-gacaca, it was stressed that those suspects who were released on the grounds of insufficient evidence could be required to appear again before gacaca when it became fully operational, if subsequent evidence came to light.

An important development during the pre-gacaca process, as noted by observers from PRI, was the introduction of 'groupes de choc' or 'confession teams'.[55] These groups consisted of religious detainees who had confessed to crimes because of their faith and who attempted to convince other detainees and those present at gacaca hearings to do likewise. Confession teams were formed and subsequently encouraged in their activities during prison visits by evangelical church organisations such as Prison Fellowship Rwanda (PFR), who were particularly active in prisons in Kigali Ville and Ruhengeri provinces.[56] According to PRI, the confession teams 'give recalcitrant detainees who are presented, but not released, an "injection", a pep talk to confess ... [T]he government seems to accept this [unofficial] innovation, which is remarkable, given the often-difficult relationship between the relative secular state and the various religious denominations'.[57] As we will see in later chapters, from 2003 onwards groups opposing the confession teams emerged in the form of syndicates of suspects and members of the broader community who

---

[54] See for example, AI, 'Gacaca: A Question of Justice', pp.22–6; Penal Reform International (PRI), 'Interim Report on Research on Gacaca Jurisdictions and its Preparations (July–December 2001)', Kigali: PRI, January 2002, pp.16–25.

[55] Ibid., p.22. For a more detailed discussion of the influence of confession teams on the running of gacaca, see T. Morgan, 'Healing Genocide', Christianity Today, 31 March 2004, www.christianitytoday.com/ct/2004/004/ 4.76.html.

[56] PRI, 'Report on the Gacaca [Report V]', Kigali: PRI, September 2003, p.10. Catholic leaders have also printed articles in popular publications, exhorting detainees to confess to their crimes and the population to forgive those who confess. (See, for example, Evêques Catholiques du Rwanda, 'Juridictions gacaca: pour une justice qui reconcilie', Dialogue, 230, September–October 2002, pp.3–13.)

[57] PRI, 'Interim Report', p.22.

colluded to hide evidence from gacaca. The formation of groups such as the confession teams and the syndicates of suspects has greatly affected gacaca's ability to gather and weigh evidence.

Parallel to the government's initiation of gacaca, unofficial versions of the institution were also beginning to emerge around Rwanda. As subsequent chapters highlight, key features of these parallel forms of gacaca influence the Rwandan population's interpretations of the post-genocide institution's hybrid aims and methods. In particular, observers reported after the genocide that not only did gacaca continue to operate in its more traditional form in communities across the country, especially to deal with land issues, but two unofficial forms of gacaca examining genocide crimes had evolved.

First, a form of non-state gacaca emerged in a prison in Nyamata district of Kigali Ngali province in May 1998 and began in other prisons around the country between 1998 and 2001, at a time when the government was still debating the appropriateness of gacaca for dealing with genocide crimes.[58] In this 'prison gacaca', detainees divided themselves into groups according to geographical areas (and sometimes gender) and elected panels of *urumuri* (Kinyarwanda for 'the light') to act effectively as gacaca judges.[59] In these sessions, detainees confessed their crimes to the urumuri and those gathered at the assemblies. The urumuri recorded the confessions, asked for additional evidence from those assembled and stored the records of these sessions for use at official gacaca hearings outside of the prisons.[60] Carina Tertsakian argues that the government has 'been behind [prison gacaca] from the very beginning',[61] although as discussed later in this book, some former prisoners in Kigali Ngali claim that detainees initiated the process in 1998 and the government only began encouraging prison gacaca hearings after the beginning of official gacaca in 2002.

Second, an unofficial form of gacaca developed in many religious communities. 'Gacaca nkiristu' or 'Christian gacaca' has occurred mainly in rural Catholic communities in the provinces of Butare, Kibungo, Cyangugu, Kigali Ngali and Ruhengeri.[62] Christian gacaca employs

---

[58] Karekezi, 'Juridictions gacaca', p.34.
[59] C. Tertsakian, *Le Château: The Lives of Prisoners in Rwanda*, London: Arves Books, 2008, pp. 169, 34.
[60] PRI, 'PRI Research on Gacaca Report IV: The Guilty Plea Procedure, Cornerstone of the Rwandan Justice System', Kigali: PRI, 2003, p.12.
[61] Tertsakian, *Le Château*, p.365.
[62] Karekezi, 'Juridictions gacaca', p.34.

priests or other church officials in the role of gacaca judges. Parishioners are encouraged to confess their sins to the congregation – sometimes concerning genocide crimes and sometimes minor infractions affecting other church members – and to ask for forgiveness both from those whom they have injured and from the community as a whole. Alice Karekezi reports that embedded in Christian gacaca is the notion that, once an individual has confessed to certain sins, it is the 'divine obligation' of those personally injured and of the general congregation to forgive the confessor.[63] The assumption underlying this duty to forgive is that, because God has forgiven his children of the sins they have confessed to him, believers are obliged to forgive those who have transgressed them in daily life.

On 4 October 2001 – with a view to beginning a pilot phase of gacaca in selected locations around the country – the first round of elections for gacaca judges or *inyangamugayo* (Kinyarwanda for 'wise or respected elder') occurred in every cell in Rwanda.[64] In preparation for the elections, the community leaders of 'ten-house' groups, known as *nyumbakumi*, were charged with the responsibility of encouraging every adult in these households to vote for gacaca judges and to draw up lists of outstanding members of these households to be proposed as potential judges.[65] While some questions arose regarding the level of control surrounding the elections, most observers considered the ballot a great success, citing the massive turnout of voters around the country and how peacefully the elections were conducted.[66] Many commentators remarked on the importance of the discussions that surrounded the pre-selection of candidates. Potential gacaca judges were elected for their standing in the community, their dedication to the well-being of their neighbours and for their love of truth and justice. The discussion of these criteria resulted in the denunciation of many candidates for their participation in the genocide. Many observers therefore characterised the elections as instigating an important dialogue on issues such as truth, justice and reconciliation.[67] Some commentators went further and described – with some hyperbole – the election as a 'wedding party', a form of mass celebration across the country and proof that a dynamic sense of community

---

[63] *Ibid.*, p.34.

[64] S. Gasibirege, 'L'Élection des juges *inyangamugayo*: rupture ou continuité?' in E. Ntaganda (ed.), *De la paix à la justice: les enjeux de la réconciliation nationale*, Cahiers de Centre de Gestion des Conflits (no. 6), Butare: Université Nationale du Rwanda, November 2002, pp.93–127.

[65] PRI, 'Report IV', p.30.

[66] *Ibid.*, p.29.

[67] Gasibirege, 'L'Élection des juges *inyangamugayo*', p.98.

was alive in Rwanda.[68] The result of the vote was the election of more than 250,000 gacaca judges in cells across the nation.

In April 2002, these judges underwent six days of training, two days per week over three weeks, under the guidance of instructors drawn from a wide range of educated elites, including experienced judges and lawyers.[69] Training of gacaca judges focused on general legal principles, the basic tenets of the Organic and Gacaca Laws, and the specific procedures of gacaca, including management of gacaca hearings, gathering and analysis of evidence, categorisation of genocide suspects according to the severity of their crimes, sentencing those found guilty, methods of conflict resolution and identifying and assisting people suffering trauma.[70]

On 18 June 2002, the government officially inaugurated the gacaca jurisdictions, and seventy-three cells in twelve selected sectors, one per province, began a pilot phase of gacaca. The objective of these initial hearings was to introduce the methods of gacaca to the population and to identify problems and weaknesses in the system that could be overcome before gacaca became fully operational in all cells. During the pilot phase, these hearings did not involve passing judgments on genocide suspects but only the construction of lists of vital information that would assist in judgments in later phases of gacaca. The next section discusses the nature of these lists in greater detail.

In the first few months of the pilot phase, various local and international NGOs, including African Rights, AI and PRI, monitored gacaca and provided assessments to the government. These organisations cited various weaknesses in the gacaca system, including the inadequacy of training for judges, logistical difficulties such as assembling the required quorum of community members at gacaca hearings and transporting detainees to these hearings, and problems created by a lack of legal counsel and adequate judicial guidance.[71]

Gacaca extended nationwide and modified
Few changes were made to the running of gacaca between the end of the initial pilot phase of seventy-three cells and the introduction of a

[68] *Ibid.*, p.98 (author's translation).
[69] African Rights, 'Gacaca Justice: A Shared Responsibility', Kigali: African Rights, January 2003, p.4.
[70] AI, 'Gacaca: A Question of Justice', p.26.
[71] See, for example, African Rights, 'Gacaca Justice', pp.32–40; AI, 'Gacaca: A Question of Justice', p.27; PRI, 'PRI Research Team on Gacaca (Report III: April–June 2002)', Kigali: PRI, July 2002, pp.6–14.

further 623 cell jurisdictions on 25 November 2002.[72] The government intended to introduce gacaca in approximately another 10,000 cells in March 2003. This was delayed, however, by the slowness of the jurisdictions where gacaca was already operating and the spate of major political and social events, particularly the provisional release of approximately 23,000 detainees from prisons around Rwanda, the establishment of ingando for genocide suspects in January 2003 and the preparations for the first post-genocide presidential and parliamentary elections in the middle of 2003.[73]

In June 2004, the government responded to several perceived problems with the running of gacaca jurisdictions by enacting a modified version of the Gacaca Law, which coincided with the expansion of gacaca from 751 to more than 11,000 cell- and sector-level jurisdictions around the country.[74] The main purpose of the amended Gacaca Law was to streamline and strengthen the running of gacaca in key areas. Among other changes, the 2004 version of the Gacaca Law decreased the number of levels of gacaca jurisdictions and the number of judges required to run gacaca hearings, established fixed sentences for individuals found guilty of harming or harassing gacaca witnesses or interfering with judges' investigations of genocide-related crimes, and allowed victims of sexual crimes to give evidence *in camera* to a single judge of their choosing or, if they do not trust any of the judges concerned, to give evidence directly to the public prosecutor.[75] The main reasons given for these modifications to the number of judges and levels of jurisdictions were the government's desire to make the best use of the talents of the best qualified judges and thus to speed up the gacaca process by decreasing the number of unqualified judges and ensuring that the best judges were assigned the more difficult cases at a smaller number of jurisdictions. Codifying a system for sentencing those found guilty of intimidating witnesses or judges was a response to reported cases of detainees returning from ingando who injured or killed gacaca witnesses or

---

[72] IRIN News, 'Special Report on Hopes for Reconciliation under Gacaca Court System', 4 December 2002, www.irinnews.org/report.asp?ReportID=31241&SelectRegion=Great_Lakes&SelectCountry=RWANDA.

[73] Republic of Rwanda, 'La Situation actuelle des juridictions gacaca', Kigali: Supreme Court of Rwanda, 6th Chamber (Gacaca Commission), 25 June 2003, pp.1–2.

[74] IRIN News, 'Traditional Courts Inaugurated', 24 June 2004, www.irinnews.info/report.asp?Report ID=41860&SelectRegion=Great_Lakes&SelectCountry=RWANDA.

[75] Gacaca Law (Modified 2004), Articles 33–8, 13, 30, 38.

interfered with judges' running of gacaca investigations and hearings.[76] Providing greater privacy for victims of sexual crimes when they gave evidence constituted a response to reports of the widespread reluctance of such victims, particularly women who suffered rape or sexual torture during the genocide, to come forward at gacaca to discuss the crimes committed against them.[77] These changes paved the way for the beginning of the judgment phase of gacaca in some communities in March 2005. As detailed below, further significant rewriting of the Gacaca Law occurred in 2006 and 2008, with the objectives of again decreasing the caseload in the national courts and hastening the entire gacaca process to deal with its original caseload as well as the new cases arriving from the national courts.

The discussion above of the various historical developments of gacaca – from a traditional practice for hearing low-level criminal cases to the modern version intended to deal with genocide and crimes against humanity – underscores that gacaca is an organic, dynamic system that has undergone myriad changes in the past century and that a wide range of state and non-state actors has influenced its evolution. Gacaca is not a static, traditional institution, as some sources have contended, but rather a hybrid of traditional and modern elements. Many features of gacaca – in its various incarnations, before and after colonisation, in prisons and religious communities, in preparatory phases leading to its current form and in its handling of genocide crimes – have remained consistent, for example the conducting of hearings outdoors in communal spaces, the high value placed on public participation and the linkage of gacaca and notions of social cohesion and reconciliation. Meanwhile, important features of gacaca have changed over time, with the most radical phase of evolution occurring as it has been restructured to deal with genocide cases and as it has been continually revised to respond to difficulties encountered in jurisdictions around the country. The current manifestation of gacaca reverts to the traditional practice of employing judges

---

[76] IRIN News, 'Rwanda: Genocide Survivor Group Denounces Killings, Harassment', 16 December 2003, www.irinnews.org/report.asp?ReportID=38445&SelectRegion=Great_Lakes &SelectCountry=RWANDA.

[77] Ligue Rwandaise pour la Promotion et la Defense des Droits de l'Homme, 'Situation des droits de la personne au Rwanda en 2002: rapport annuel de la LIPRODHOR', Kigali: LIPRODHOR, June 2003, p.64. For a more detailed discussion of the reasons behind, and nature of, the changes to the Gacaca Law regarding sexual crimes, see HRW, 'Struggling to Survive: Barriers to Justice for Rape Victims in Rwanda', New York: HRW, September 2004, www.hrw.org/reports/2004/ rwanda0904/index.htm.

chosen by the communities in which hearings take place. As we have seen, during different periods in the twentieth century colonial and local-government officials played a greater role in the selection of gacaca judges, but in this regard modern gacaca displays an important similarity to gacaca as it existed in the pre-colonial era (although, as will be discussed in later chapters, the state still plays a vital role in the day-to-day operation of gacaca). Modern gacaca, however, diverges from the traditional system by relying on written law, involving women both as judges and members of the General Assembly, displaying a more systematic organisation between the administrative divisions of local government, and imposing prison sentences on those found guilty. Such developments counter the argument that gacaca in the post-genocide context is little more than a return to a well-established, widely understood indigenous form of conflict resolution that the Rwandan population will automatically accept.

As an endogenous rather than indigenous response to crimes, gacaca remoulds tradition to suit current circumstances. Gacaca was not an automatic choice as the primary transitional or reconstructive institution after the genocide, and the Rwandan government considered various other options before settling on gacaca. Furthermore, after gacaca was selected as a model for the main post-genocide justice institution, it did not inherently possess the concepts and methods necessary to address genocide crimes and therefore required major reform. As highlighted by the analysis above of government debates over gacaca, the Gacaca Law eventually adopted was the result of a political compromise between different factions, with a crucial division between lawyers and non-lawyers in the government, particularly over the issue of popular participation in gacaca, and between influential diasporic and non-diasporic political figures. Once gacaca was underway, senior state officials expressed dissatisfaction with many aspects of gacaca and called for the sorts of reforms represented in the 2004, 2006 and 2008 changes to the Gacaca Law. Kagame said in 2006, 'I still don't think gacaca gives us all we need and it has major limitations. But it gives us most things and certainly more than most other processes ... Today the genocide caseload is still massive, so with gacaca we may have to think of new ways to address this.'[78] As later chapters will show, the regular changes to gacaca's operation have greatly complicated popular participation in the process. For now, however, such changes point to the dynamism and evolution of gacaca.

[78] Author's government interviews, Paul Kagame.

Even during its so-called 'traditional' phase, gacaca as an institution and a set of ideas developed according to the needs of the population and the influences of outside forces such as local and colonial political elites. Similar ranges of local and external influences have shaped the evolution of gacaca since 1994. The single greatest catalyst of this evolution, however, has been the government's and the population's need to respond holistically to the massive social, cultural, legal and economic challenges resulting from the genocide.

MODALITIES OF GACACA

Having seen how gacaca has developed historically, it is now necessary to examine briefly how the modernised version of gacaca functions. Understanding the modalities of gacaca will be important for the exploration of its hybrid objectives and methods in later chapters. Two legal documents establish the modalities of gacaca, the Organic Law of 1996 and the Gacaca Law of 2001, with the latter modified five times, minimally in June 2001, June 2006 and March 2007, and more substantially in June 2004 and June 2008. The Organic Law is organised to prosecute 'the crime of genocide or crimes against humanity' or 'offences . . . committed in connection with the events surrounding genocide and crimes against humanity'.[79] The Organic Law defines 'genocide' and 'crimes against humanity' in accordance with three international conventions, to which Rwanda is a signatory: the 1948 UN Convention on the Prevention and Punishment of the Crime of Genocide, the 1949 Geneva Convention on the Protection of Civilian Persons in Time of War, and the 1968 Convention on the Non-Applicability of Statutory Limitations to War Crimes and Crimes against Humanity.[80] The Organic Law, and subsequently the Gacaca Law of 2001, divides genocide suspects into four categories of crimes committed between 1 October 1990 and 31 December 1994. When the Gacaca Law was modified in 2004, a key change was the merging of the old Categories 2 and 3 to form a synthesised Category 2, thus reducing the overall number of categories to three, which by the 2008 version of the Gacaca Law were organised as follows:[81]

---

[79] Organic Law, Article 1.
[80] Ibid., Article 1.
[81] In the original categorisation of crimes detailed in the Organic Law and the Gacaca Law of 2001, Category 2 comprised 'persons whose criminal acts or whose acts of criminal participation place them among perpetrators, conspirators or accomplices of intentional homicide or of serious assault against the person causing death', while Category 3 comprised 'persons

Category 1
  (a) any person who committed or was an accomplice in the commis-
      sion of an offence that puts him or her in the category of planners
      or organisers of the genocide or crimes against humanity;
  (b) any person who was at a national leadership level and that of the
      prefecture level: public administration, political parties, army,
      gendarmerie, religious denominations or in a militia group, and
      committed crimes of genocide or crimes against humanity or
      encouraged others to participate in such crimes, together with his
      or her accomplice;
  (c) any person who committed or was an accomplice in the com-
      mission of an offence that puts him or her among the category of
      people who incited, supervised and ringleaders of the genocide or
      crimes against humanity;
  (d) any person who was at the leadership level at the sub-prefecture
      and commune: public administration, political parties, army,
      gendarmerie, communal police, religious denominations or in a
      militia, who committed any crimes of genocide or other crimes
      against humanity or encouraged others to commit similar offences,
      together with his or her accomplice;
  (e) any person who committed the offence of rape or sexual torture,
      together with his or her accomplice.

Category 2
  (a) a notorious murderer who distinguished himself or herself in his
      or her location or wherever he or she passed due to the zeal and
      cruelty employed, together with his or her accomplice;
  (b) any person who tortured another even though such torture did not
      result in death, together with his or her accomplice;
  (c) any person who committed a dehumanising act on a dead body,
      together with his or her accomplice;
  (d) any person who committed or is an accomplice in the commis-
      sion of an offence that puts him or her on the list of people who
      killed or attacked others resulting in death, together with his or
      her accomplice;
  (e) any person who injured or attacked another with the intention to
      kill but such intention was not fulfilled, together with his or her
      accomplice;

whose criminal acts or whose acts of criminal participation make them guilty of other serious
assaults against the person' (Organic Law, Article 2; Gacaca Law, Article 51). In Gacaca Law
(Modified 2004), these two categories are merged to create a new Category 2, while the old
Category 4, which deals with individuals charged with property-related crimes, is now rendered
as Category 3 (Gacaca Law [Modified 2004], Article 51).

(f) any person who committed or aided another to commit an offence against another without intention to kill, together with his or her accomplice.

Category 3
A person who only committed an offence related to property. However, when the offender and the victim come to a settlement by themselves, settle the matter before the authorities or before the witnesses before commencement of this law, the offender shall not be prosecuted.[82]

Until 2008, gacaca had jurisdiction over suspects in Categories 2 and 3, while Category 1 cases were referred to the national court system and the ICTR. The 2008 modifications to the Gacaca Law shifted a range of Category 1 cases to gacaca, including those of suspected orchestrators of the genocide at the sub-prefecture and commune levels and suspected perpetrators of rape or sexual torture. The outstanding Category 1 cases concerning national or prefecture-level planners of the genocide remain solely the jurisdiction of the national courts and the ICTR.[83] Although no explicit principles exist for the distribution of suspects between the ICTR and the national courts, an unofficial division assumes that the ICTR will hear the cases of suspects considered to be among the most important planners and perpetrators of the genocide.[84] As discussed in later chapters, the divisions among the three tiers of post-genocide justice have narrowed in recent years, with increased evidence shared among them and moves to transfer cases of genocide suspects from the ICTR to the national courts.

For those suspects over whom gacaca has jurisdiction, the Gacaca Law divides the hearing of their cases, according to category, between the approximately 11,000 jurisdictions at two administrative levels. Each of these levels carries out a different task in the gacaca process. The cell is charged with the investigation of crimes committed within the cell during the specified period and with the production of four

---

[82] Gacaca Law (Modified 2008), Article 9.
[83] *Ibid.*, Articles 5–7.
[84] The ad-hoc division of jurisdiction between the ICTR and the national courts has on occasion created major tensions when the two bodies have sought jurisdiction over the same genocide suspects. See, for example, P. Gourevitch, 'Justice in Exile', *New York Times*, 24 June 1996, A15; and F. Mutagwera, 'Détentions et poursuites judiciaires au Rwanda', in J.-F. Dupaquier (ed.), *La Justice internationale face au drame rwandais*, Paris: Karthala, 1996, pp.17–36.

lists: first, of all those who lived in the cell before 1 October 1990; second, of all those who were killed in the cell during the specified period; third, of the damage to individuals or property inflicted during this time; finally, of suspects and their category of alleged crimes. The cell hears cases only of suspects in Category 3. Cases of suspects in Categories 1 and 2 are heard at the sector level. The sector also functions as the jurisdiction for the appeal of all cases heard in gacaca and the point from which certain Category 1 cases are forwarded to the national courts.[85]

A crucial issue for the effective running of gacaca is the election of judges. Gacaca is unique among post-conflict judicial structures around the world in its mass involvement of the population in the delivery of justice. Gacaca judges must be Rwandan nationals over the age of twenty-one years, without any previous criminal convictions or having ever been considered a genocide suspect (except in relation to property crimes), and an honest, trustworthy person, 'free from the spirit of sectarianism' but 'characterised by a spirit of speech sharing'.[86] Judges cannot at any time have been an elected official, government or NGO employee, trained judge or lawyer, or a member of the police, armed services or clergy. The stated motivation for this exclusion is to ensure that gacaca is a popular process, run by citizens at the local level and free from actual or perceived political or legal interference.

Both levels of gacaca – cell and sector – consist of a general assembly, a bench of judges, a president and a coordinating committee. At the cell level, the general assembly constitutes every resident of the cell over the age of eighteen years. In October 2001, general assemblies across the country elected nineteen judges to form cell-level benches of inyanga-mugayo while also nominating five representatives to form the general assembly at the sector level. The revised Gacaca Law in 2004 reduced the number of judges at both levels of jurisdiction to nine, with five deputies also nominated who could substitute for any of the nine judges if they were absent.[87] In July 2004, the gacaca judges who were elected in 2001

---

[85] Gacaca Law (Modified 2008), Articles 5–7.
[86] Ibid., Article 14. The phrase 'speech sharing' appears to entail that judges should be capable of encouraging the community to participate in gacaca hearings and of facilitating peaceful, productive discussions in the general assembly.
[87] Ibid., Articles 13 and 23.

decided among themselves which individuals would stay on as either judges or deputies, thus reducing the number of judges nationwide from approximately 250,000 to around 170,000.[88] Surveys into the make-up of benches of gacaca judges across Rwanda show that most judges are middle-aged, professional, educated members of the community, with women constituting around 35 per cent of all inyangamugayo at the cell level, and judges with higher education usually nominated to the sector level of gacaca.[89]

Gacaca judges are empowered to carry out various tasks, including summoning witnesses to testify at hearings, issuing search warrants and imposing punishments on those found guilty. Judges usually sit once a week before a required quorum of 100 members of the General Assembly. In Phase 1 of a gacaca jurisdiction, which ideally should comprise six weekly meetings (but invariably takes much longer), the Assembly gathers to determine a schedule of hearings and to begin compiling the four lists mentioned above. In Phase 2, which comprises the seventh meeting, the General Assembly gathers to produce a detailed dossier of evidence on each individual accused of a crime and listed during the sixth meeting of Phase 1. The accused then have the opportunity to respond to the evidence brought against them during Phase 3 of gacaca, after which in Phase 4 the judges weigh all of the evidence they have heard and pass judgment on defendants.[90] The president chairs all meetings and is responsible for leading an orderly, directed discussion that encourages truthful testimony and creates a space for victims and survivors to describe their personal pain and loss.

A key role of the president in this scenario is to maintain order within the Assembly, especially as the discussion can become emotionally charged and testimonies may diverge. The Ministry of the Interior is tasked with guaranteeing the security of judges, suspects and the community at large during gacaca hearings, usually by providing one or two armed security guards for all sessions.[91] The president must also

---

[88] IRIN News, 'Plans to Reform Traditional Courts'; IRIN News, 'Traditional Courts Inaugurated'.

[89] PRI, 'Interim Report', p.32; African Rights, 'Gacaca Justice', p.6.

[90] In very few gacaca jurisdictions do the three phases occur as quickly as originally planned. For example, by June 2003, only sixteen of the seventy-three pilot gacaca jurisdictions inaugurated in June 2002 had completed both Phases 1 and 2 of the gacaca process and none had yet begun Phase 3 (Republic of Rwanda, 'Situation actuelle des juridictions gacaca', pp.1–2.)

[91] Republic of Rwanda, 'Les Parténaires du processus gacaca', Official Rwandan Government website, www.inkiko-gacaca.gov.rw/fr/partenaires.html.

encourage those who may be reluctant to speak – especially women and the young – to testify. In particularly emotional or complex cases where witnesses may be unwilling to testify in front of a large gathering, judges (or in cases involving sexual violence, a single judge) may convene *in camera* with a witness to hear evidence. As discussed in greater detail below, lawyers are forbidden from assisting either suspects or witnesses at any stage of a hearing as their involvement is seen as a potential threat to the open, non-adversarial approach of gacaca. Gacaca's insistence on delivering justice without lawyers constitutes one of the primary reasons legal critics and human-rights groups have been so hostile towards the institution.

After hearing evidence against a suspect, judges may retire *in camera* to consider the individual's guilt, before which judges are expected to withdraw themselves from any cases involving friends or family members to the second degree of relation. The president will attempt to reach a consensus among the judges before deciding on the person's guilt. However, in cases where consensus is impossible, a majority decision by the nine judges will suffice. The bench must then announce its decision concerning a suspect's guilt to the general assembly, either at the same meeting or the next, at which point those convicted of crimes are entitled to appeal the bench's decision, first to the gacaca jurisdiction that initially heard their case or, if they remain dissatisfied with this judgment, to the sector level of gacaca and upward.[92]

The Gacaca Law dictates that punishment should be meted out in various ways. Individuals who refuse to testify at gacaca or are found to have provided false testimony are subject to a prison term of three to six months.[93] A centrepiece of the gacaca judicial structure is a predetermined matrix of sentences that incorporates a system of confession and plea-bargaining that is foreign to the European judicial system but finds a place in some jurisdictions in the USA (see Table 2.1). According to this matrix, suspects can decrease their sentences by at least half if they confess their crimes. Another important feature of the gacaca sentencing mechanism is the combination of prison terms and community service.

The sentencing structure, as established by the Gacaca Law, operates as shown in Table 2.1.[94]

---

[92] Gacaca Law (Modified 2008), Articles 7, 23 and 24.
[93] Gacaca Law (Modified 2004), Article 29.
[94] Gacaca Law (Modified 2004), Articles 72–81; Gacaca Law (Modified 2008), Articles 17–22.

TABLE 2.1 Gacaca sentencing scheme

Judgment category	Guilty with no confession	Guilty with confession during trial	Guilty with confession before trial	Minors (14- to 18years-old) when offence committed [95]
1	Life imprisonment with special provisions	25–30 year prison term; possibility of commuting half to community service	20–4 year prison term; possibility of commuting half to community service	10–20 year prison term if guilty without confession; 8–9 year prison term following confession during trial or 6.5–7.5 year prison term following confession before trial
2 (a–e) (judged at sector level; appeals to sector level)	10–15 year prison term	6.5–7.5 year prison term; possibility of commuting half to community service and having one-third suspended	6–7 year prison term; possibility of commuting half to community service and having one-third suspended	10–15 year prison term if guilty without confession; otherwise, half of adult sentence; possibility of commuting half to community service and having one-third suspended, except when no confession is made
2 (f) (judged at sector level; appeals to sector level)	5–7 year prison term; possibility of commuting half to community service	3–5 year prison term; possibility of commuting half to community service and having one-third suspended	1–3 year prison term; possibility of commuting half to community service and having one-third suspended	Half of adult sentence; possibility of commuting half to community service
3 (judged at cell level; appeals to sector level)	Reparations for damage caused or equivalent community service			

[95] Minors who were less than fourteen years old at the time of the offence cannot be prosecuted at gacaca but instead are placed in special solidarity camps (*ibid.*, Article 20).

Most community service is carried out in *travaux d'intérêts généraux* (TIG) camps, which are administered by Rwanda Correctional Services and involve convicted perpetrators in community work programmes such as road-building, clearing ground, making bricks and rebuilding houses for genocide survivors.

Finally, an indication of the breadth of its objectives, gacaca draws together a wide range of government departments. The NSGJ, which previously constituted a specialised chamber of the Supreme Court until the modified Gacaca Law of 2004 rendered it an independent government entity, is the primary institution charged with administering the gacaca process. The National Human Rights Commission and several international NGOs are actively engaged in the monitoring of gacaca and proposing reforms. Meanwhile, the Ministry of Justice is in charge of running education campaigns to sensitise and mobilise the population to participate in gacaca.[96] In particular, the ingando – administered jointly by the Ministry of Justice and the NURC – are a key component of the process to educate the population, especially suspects, about the aims and methods of gacaca.[97] Finally, the Ministry of Health, with the assistance of the NURC, has trained a small number of trauma counsellors to deal with people's psychological difficulties as a result of their participation in gacaca.[98]

At the time of writing, the Rwandan government was considering maintaining the gacaca system beyond the completion of the genocide caseload in order to deal with the mounting number of day-to-day crimes in the community. The government considers gacaca to have been such a success in decreasing the burden on the national courts in handling genocide crimes that it could fulfil a similar purpose regarding everyday crimes.[99] Projected national budgets indicate a substantial increase in funding to the gacaca jurisdictions well after the expected completion

---

[96] Republic of Rwanda, 'Les Parténaires du processus gacaca'.

[97] In November 2003, the Ministry of Justice, the NURC and the Gacaca Commission also ran short solidarity camps for 800 gacaca judges from selected communities around Rwanda. These camps were designed to encourage judges to share their experiences from different gacaca jurisdictions and to discuss possible reforms of gacaca. IRIN News, 'Gacaca Judges Undergo "Solidarity Training"', 24 November 2003, www.irinnews.info/report.asp?ReportID=38065& SelectRegion=Great_Lakes&SelectCountry=RWANDA.

[98] IRIN News, 'Trauma Counsellors Trained', 16 January 2004, www.irinnews.org/report.asp?ReportID=38977&SelectRegion=Great_Lakes&SelectCountry=RWANDA.

[99] Author's government interviews, Tharcisse Karugarama.

of the genocide caseload in 2010, suggesting gacaca will continue to play a major role in the national criminal-justice framework.[100]

This future version of gacaca may replace a current community-level institution known as 'mediation committees' or *abunzi*, which the government instituted in 2003 to resolve disputes unrelated to genocide crimes. The abunzi comprise twelve community members considered to be of high integrity, of whom the conflictual parties may choose three to mediate their particular dispute. According to the Kigali-based Institut de Recherche et de Dialogue pour la Paix:

> The abunzi emphasise the role of the family as a critical 'first step' in the resolution of domestic disputes; conflicts over divorce and inheritance, for example, have to go through abunzi before they can be transferred to a formal court. The mediators will first try to reconcile both parties, before devising a settlement based upon local laws and customs. Any party who is dissatisfied with the settlement may then refer the matter to the courts.[101]

In this regard, the abunzi resemble strongly the colonial and post-independence versions of gacaca, as permanent, state-sanctioned structures designed to deal with everyday conflicts in the community. Gacaca's eventual replacement of the abunzi will represent a cyclical evolution of gacaca, as it reverts to this historical status, with the exception that it will, like the genocide version, be enshrined in national law. It is likely that the population's experience of gacaca in handling genocide crimes will greatly affect popular interpretations of, and participation in, the future version of gacaca. The analysis of gacaca's efficacy in later chapters will therefore be important for interpreting its probable success as a long-term judicial mechanism. Having described the history of gacaca's evolution through the twentieth century and after the genocide and the nature of its current philosophy and modalities – especially its endogenous construction of hybrid aims and methods – I turn now to the question of how we should best interpret gacaca's aims, with an eye towards offering an appropriate critical analysis of gacaca later in this book.

---

[100] Republic of Rwanda, 'Annex II.6: State Expenditure by Budget Agency – 2009–2012', Kigali: Ministry of Finance, July 2009.

[101] Institut de Recherche et de Dialogue pour la Paix (IRDP), A *Time for Peace: Canvassing the Views of Rwanda's People in the Search for Lasting Peace*, Kigali: IRDP, August 2008.

CHAPTER 3

INTERPRETING GACACA: THE RATIONALE FOR ANALYSING A DYNAMIC SOCIO-LEGAL INSTITUTION

INTRODUCTION

As I argued in Chapter 2, gacaca is an intricate, multifaceted social practice that draws on a wide range of legal, political and cultural influences over several generations to produce the hybrid system that is now designed to deal with genocide cases. Given gacaca's complex evolution during the twentieth century and the marked reform of the institution after the genocide, it is not surprising that great confusion and contestation over the objectives of the practice manifest both in the critical literature and in the daily running of gacaca. My purpose in this and subsequent chapters is to ask three questions: exactly what is gacaca designed to achieve, how should we analyse its effectiveness as a response to the needs of the Rwandan population after the genocide, and in practical terms how well has gacaca performed?

This chapter briefly discusses the current controversy among many observers concerning gacaca as an institution dealing with genocide and related crimes and the confusion among many participants regarding gacaca's objectives. In order to lay a foundation for the interpretation of gacaca's objectives and the analysis of its practical function in the following chapters – which is designed in part to overcome this confusion regarding the purposes of the institution and to show that much of the controversy over gacaca is based on a misinterpretation of these objectives – this chapter outlines the rationale that underpins the interpretation of gacaca's aims and methods throughout this book. Various social, political and legal commentators have criticised gacaca on a number of grounds, particularly regarding perceived violations of individual rights, but what is lacking in the critical literature is a clear notion of how to judge gacaca's effectiveness. This chapter describes the basis on which I critique gacaca in the remainder of this book. The final section of this chapter outlines the dominant discourse on gacaca, particularly from non-Rwandan legal scholars and human-rights observers, which holds that gacaca is an institution designed essentially to punish those guilty of genocide in order to eradicate the culture of impunity and thus to safeguard against future crimes; that is, to provide for *deterrent justice*. One of the main reasons for offering a more grounded and nuanced interpretation of gacaca's objectives in this book is to highlight the shortcomings of the prevailing discourse on gacaca.

The following chapters interpret gacaca on the basis of the legal documents governing the institution,[1] public pronouncements by and interviews with Rwandan government officials, commentators' perspectives on gacaca (including observations of gacaca hearings by ASF[2] and other researchers), my first-hand observations of gacaca hearings and interviews with genocide suspects, survivors, gacaca judges and the general population. I argue that gacaca is designed to pursue a combination of *pragmatic* and *profound* aims. There is little controversy among most observers of gacaca over what I interpret in Chapter 6 as gacaca's three main pragmatic objectives – *processing the immense backlog of genocide cases, improving living conditions in the jails* and *helping to foster economic development* – though it is not always clear how these objectives may be pursued through gacaca and whether they in turn contribute to the fulfilment of gacaca's profound objectives. Few commentators would question that these pragmatic aims play an important role in the design and running of gacaca. However, I argue that these commentators have not always adequately described why and how gacaca pursues these objectives and therefore it is necessary to interpret these aims more closely than has been done so far.

Chapters 7–10 outline and interpret the profound objectives of gacaca which, relative to the dominant discourse, constitute a new, more

[1] In this book, I analyse eight documents that partially express the government's design of, and intentions for, gacaca: the seven key legal documents governing gacaca, as outlined in the previous chapter (the Organic Law of 1996, the original Gacaca Law of January 2001, and the five modified versions of the Gacaca Law), and Republic of Rwanda, 'Manuel explicatif sur la loi organique portant création des juridictions gacaca', Kigali: Supreme Court of Rwanda, 6th Chamber (Gacaca Commission), 2001. This final document is the manual used to aid judges in their carrying-out of gacaca duties (from now on, referred to as the 'Gacaca Manual').

[2] ASF, 'Les "Juridictions gacaca" au jour le jour', ASF, 19 June 2002–27 July 2003, www.asf.be/FR/Frameset.htm (from now on, referred to as 'ASF Gacaca Reports').

wide-ranging interpretation of its aims. Chapter 11 argues that there are two main reasons why the prevailing orthodoxy is flawed and why a new analysis of gacaca's aims is required, one related to the methodology employed by most observers in their interpretations of gacaca and another concerning problems with the specific objectives that these critics associate with gacaca. In particular, most commentators have ignored the essential ethos of gacaca and many of its external social and cultural influences. Most commentators have consequently misinterpreted the main methods and objectives of gacaca, leading them to criticise it for failing to achieve outcomes for which it was never intended.

In reply to the dominant discourse on gacaca, I argue that six key objectives emerge in its design and daily operation: *truth, peace, justice* (not only retributive or deterrent, but also restorative), *healing, forgiveness* and *reconciliation*. I examine in detail how each of these objectives is defined and manifests practically according to various official, popular and critical sources and how the pursuit of each objective displays a distinctive ethos of *popular ownership, participation and public engagement* which drives gacaca as a whole and which most observers disregard in their analyses of gacaca. My interpretation of gacaca's objectives then lays the foundation for the analysis of gacaca's practical efficacy.

CONTROVERSY AND CONFUSION OVER GACACA

The introduction of gacaca to deal with genocide crimes has worried many observers, especially international lawyers and human-rights monitors concerned principally with due process for genocide suspects. Gacaca's most controversial feature is the mass involvement of the population in hearing and prosecuting complex genocide cases. Lawyers are barred from all hearings because the makers of gacaca argue that in order to create an environment in which the community feels comfortable to discuss the fractious issues of genocide crimes and ethnic discord, it is necessary to avoid the adversarial nature of more conventional courts, where victims rarely have the chance to talk openly of the pain they have suffered or to engage meaningfully with perpetrators. Excluding lawyers from gacaca is also meant to maximise the community's sense of ownership over the process and consequently its personal and interpersonal effects.[3] Many international

---

[3] See, for example, P. Kagame, 'Kagame Speaks on Eve of the Launch of Gacaca Trials', excerpt of radio interview the BBC, reprinted on official government website, Republic of Rwanda, 5 October 2001, www.rwanda1.com/government/president/interviews/2001/gacaca.html.

observers, however, are concerned about the potential for intimidation of witnesses and unfair trials for, or direct reprisals against, genocide suspects at gacaca.[4] In a community that is so traumatised and riven with ethnic tensions, these critics fear that gacaca may spark a return to the violence of the past.

Alongside these international concerns, the modernisation of gacaca has also caused great confusion and disagreement among many Rwandans. Particularly in the early stages of gacaca, many participants equated the post-genocide institution with its traditional precursor. More importantly, many genocide survivors believed that those found guilty of genocide crimes would receive the sorts of relatively lenient punishments that had been handed down to perpetrators at traditional gacaca hearings or even an amnesty.[5]

Meanwhile, the Gacaca Law is itself a complex synthesis of Western law and historical Rwandan practices, incorporating a plea-bargaining system that has some parallels in Western legal contexts and methods of communal dialogue and deliberation drawn from traditional gacaca; a hybrid resulting from the array of international and local actors who were instrumental in reforming gacaca after the genocide. This complex genesis makes gacaca difficult to categorise. Furthermore, as gacaca relies heavily on popular involvement at all levels of the institution, from the election of judges through to the sentencing of genocide criminals on the basis of communal discussions and provision of evidence, the population has often shaped gacaca according to the needs of particular communities. As later chapters will show, this has meant that gacaca, especially in towns and villages far from Kigali, has often diverged from the original intentions of the makers of the institution.

A concrete example from my observation of a gacaca hearing in Ruhengenge district of Kigali Ville province on 6 April 2003 will help illustrate the sorts of contestations over the aims of gacaca that often emerge during hearings and their crucial practical impact.[6] Conflicts between participants in gacaca constitute an important reason for more finely interpreting its objectives. Before the start of this gacaca hearing,

---

[4] See, for example, African Rights, 'Gacaca Justice', pp.38–46; and AI, 'Gacaca: A Question of Justice', pp.35–40.
[5] See, for example, survivor interviews, Grégoire, Butare, Kibingo, 14 May 2003; Nathan, Kigali Ngali, Nyamata, 19 May 2003; Tharcisse, Gisenyi, Gisenyi Ville, 23 May 2003.
[6] Author's gacaca observations, Kigali Ville, Ruhengenge, 6 April 2003.

the president of the judges' bench ordered a group of women to drag two large blue tarpaulins, containing the recently exhumed remains of genocide victims in the community, beneath the thatched shelter where the hearing would take place. The week before, two detainees from Kigali Central Prison had confessed in front of this gacaca to the murder of several children during the genocide and to dumping their bodies in a mass grave on the edge of the cell. On hearing this confession, the president ordered the exhumation of the site that the detainees had described and the storage of the remains discovered there.

The two tarpaulins were opened at the gacaca hearing of 6 April to display a pile of rotten clothes in one and a heap of cracked and decayed bones, evidently those of children, in the other. On seeing the remains, the general assembly showed signs of great distress. Women and children began crying. Several men shouted angrily at the president for allowing such traumatising evidence to be displayed at an already-fraught gacaca hearing, where the general assembly was constructing a list of people who had died in the cell during the genocide. This gacaca hearing occurred in an especially emotional environment in early April, at the start of a month-long national remembrance of the victims of the genocide and the day before 7 April, which marks the official anniversary of the start of the genocide in 1994. Why, several members of the general assembly asked, was the president of the gacaca displaying these remains when many in the community were already experiencing such high levels of trauma?

In my interviews in this community over several weeks before this hearing, I discovered that many in the general assembly had developed a view of gacaca as an important means of discovering the truth of what happened to their loved ones in 1994. This discovery had in turn aided many survivors' ability to deal with emotions of anger and loss by providing the necessary facts about the death of their friends and family, thus allowing them to understand precisely what had happened and to speak more clearly and assuredly about their experiences. For these survivors, the distress of the exhumation appeared to undo much of the good associated with the hearing of gacaca testimonies to this point.[7] The president replied that the exhumation of the children's remains served a dual purpose: on the one hand, it verified the testimony of the two detainees at the previous gacaca regarding the location of the mass grave and, with later forensic analysis, it would

[7] *Ibid.*

help verify how many children were buried there and how they had been killed. The exhumation was also a way of publicly shaming the detainees who committed these crimes. A third purpose related to the exhumation, which the president did not mention, was that relatives of those whose remains were discovered could now bury their loved ones in an appropriate manner.[8]

This situation underscores that different interpretations of the purposes and aims of gacaca can become confused and produce discord within the communities involved. For many participants in the general assembly at Ruhengenge, the objective of gacaca was to establish the degree of truth necessary to aid survivors' healing. They argued that the judges should have excluded any investigations that re-traumatised survivors. The president, however, argued that an important aim of gacaca was also to *verify* the truth of testimonies heard at gacaca – to reach the clearest possible understanding of what occurred during the genocide, even if this increased levels of trauma for participants – and, in turn, to deliver some form of justice to the perpetrators, for example through public shaming. Though the president did not argue this specifically, it was also possible that causing short-term trauma by ordering the exhumation was justified because those who had lost friends and relatives during the genocide could now experience more profound and long-lasting healing, for example by burying their loved ones appropriately. This example shows that different participants can interpret gacaca's *raison d'être* in myriad ways: in this particular instance, as a forum for the broad search for the truth, a realm of truth-recovery within the limits of healing, a means for pursuing some form of retributive or deterrent justice, or as a facilitator of long-term healing.

As the following chapters will show, situations such as the one just described are unavoidable given the degree of current misunderstanding and confusion regarding gacaca's objectives. Such disagreements also highlight the crucial personal, emotional dimensions of gacaca. Given the immense impact of the genocide on individuals and communities and of people's direct involvement in gacaca hearings, participants invest enormous and manifold hopes in gacaca. Many participants in gacaca, as well as the political leaders and commentators who help

---

[8] This third interpretation of the events surrounding the exhumation at Ruhengenge was suggested to me by Martin Ngoga, Rwandan Deputy Prosecutor General, during a panel session at the conference, 'The Rwandan Genocide and Transitional Justice: Commemorating the 10th Anniversary of the Genocide', St Antony's College, University of Oxford, 15 May 2004.

shape the system, articulate a wide and often inchoate array of interpretations. This confusion poses difficulties both for judges and members of the general assembly who participate directly in gacaca and for observers and commentators who monitor how effectively gacaca operates. Major disagreements nevertheless emphasise the importance of individual and communal agency in gacaca and the vital role of the general population in running and shaping the institution, often with highly unpredictable results.

POPULAR ETHOS OF GACACA

Different individuals and groups in Rwanda interpret gacaca as an institution in various ways. Different groups also define in divergent ways the various terms with which gacaca is purportedly linked, such as the nine pragmatic and profound aims mentioned above. The nature of these interpretations, both of the objectives themselves as concepts and of their connections to the gacaca process, often reflects what particular individuals and groups believe they may gain from gacaca rather than any reasoned articulation of the community-wide role that gacaca plays. Therefore, it is necessary to critically examine the interpretations of all interested parties, whether from an official, popular or critical standpoint, and to assume that none of these groups possesses an inherently more valuable understanding of what gacaca should achieve. My point in investigating the nine objectives mentioned earlier is that the association of these aims with gacaca draws from the Rwandan social, cultural and political sphere and not from a distantly related theoretical or philosophical realm that I seek to impose on any analysis of gacaca.

Gacaca is a dynamic enterprise that draws on a wide range of legal, political, cultural and religious sources. Therefore, one secondary aim of later chapters is to investigate the influences that other social forces have had on gacaca – often differing between geographical regions but underpinned by a particular Rwandan worldview – and that affect the population's expectations of the institution. Failing to recognise the influences that other social phenomena exert on gacaca, as most writers in this field have so far, leads to a limited understanding of the values that gacaca embodies and in turn to an unsatisfactory conceptual framework with which to critically assess gacaca. Any attempt to critique gacaca must address the issue of how the people engaged in this process interpret the practice and from which social and cultural sources – apart from the legal documents and pronouncements by government leaders that initially shape the institution – they draw these interpretations.

The often unexpected ways in which the Rwandan public perceives gacaca will therefore have a significant bearing on how the institution functions. Basing my argument on the assumption of possible differences between official and popular views of gacaca raises an important methodological question: when interpreting the objectives of gacaca, how should we balance an analysis of the government's intentions with the practical manifestation of the institution in the community? Will the most compelling aims of gacaca emanate from the government's perspective of gacaca, as expressed in the legal texts establishing the institution and public pronouncements by political leaders, or from the views and practices of the general population engaged in gacaca? If disagreement occurs between official and popular understandings of gacaca, should one interpretation trump the other? In general, the assumption underpinning the analysis in subsequent chapters is that neither the government's nor the population's views carry any special weight in the critical interpretation of gacaca. My approach is to treat official and popular interpretations of gacaca as equal sources of analysis, examining the two side by side – often aided by the analysis of other commentators – with the understanding that on occasion the government's expression of gacaca and its aims will prove more responsive to the needs of the post-genocide society and more coherent than the population's own expressions of gacaca, and vice versa. Furthermore, neither the Rwandan population nor the Rwandan state is monolithic and therefore it will be necessary to interrogate the crucial disagreements within these categories of actors in order to fully comprehend immanent understandings of gacaca.

It is important to justify the contention that the population's views on gacaca should warrant a central status when interpreting gacaca's objectives and judging its effectiveness. It may appear that such an approach gives undue consideration to what many observers may view as merely participants' misunderstandings or deliberate contraventions of the laws governing gacaca – in essence, a 'warping' of the original intentions of the makers of gacaca that should carry no moral or practical weight in our understanding of gacaca. There are, however, very good reasons for closely analysing the ways in which everyday Rwandans' interpretations of gacaca, as represented in their verbal discussions of the institution and in their practices and interactions during gacaca hearings, contribute to the function of the institution. The fundamental reason why interpreting popular perceptions of, and participation in, gacaca is important for understanding gacaca as a whole is because the driving ethos of gacaca is one of popular ownership and participation. The Rwandan government emphasises the importance of popular agency, and most Rwandans, at least in their verbal expressions, also view themselves and not the state as the driving force behind gacaca.[9] As argued in more detail later, the government and population often overstate the extent to which everyday Rwandans are free to participate in gacaca. Nonetheless, the spirit of gacaca emphasises that the community should play a central role in all aspects of the process and that the objectives of gacaca should not be pursued through the agency of national or local elites but through communal engagement in a public setting.

The government stresses that gacaca judges must allow the general assembly, with minimal interference from judges or other community leaders, to openly discuss cases and wider (often emotional, non-legal) issues stemming from the genocide. Fatuma Ndangiza, Executive Secretary of the NURC, describes gacaca as 'a form of justice originating from and serving Rwandan culture' and a demonstration of 'Rwandans' ability to manage their [own] conflicts'.[10] As the Gacaca Manual, which the government produced with the assistance of ASF in order to guide judges in their daily running of gacaca, exhorts: 'Don't

[9] Various government and academic surveys reported near the beginning of the gacaca process that there was much enthusiasm among the Rwandan population for participating in gacaca. For example, Stella Babalola reports that 87 per cent of interviewees claimed that they wanted to participate in hearings. (S. Babalola, 'Perceptions about the Gacaca Law in Rwanda: Evidence from a Multi-Method Study', in Ntaganda, Les Juridictions Gacaca, p.114.) Babalola and Simon Gasibirege report that 89.4 per cent of interviewees believe that it is the responsibility of every Rwandan to testify at gacaca (S. Gasibirege and S. Babalola, 'Perceptions about the Gacaca Law in Rwanda: Evidence from a Multi-Method Study', Special Publication [No. 19], Baltimore, Md.: Johns Hopkins University School of Public Health, Center for Communication Programs, April 2001, p.11.). Meanwhile, according to an NURC survey, 91 per cent of the population believes that prosecution witnesses will want to participate in gacaca in order to expose genocide and related crimes NURC, 'Opinion Survey on Participation in Gacaca and National Reconciliation', Kigali: NURC, January 2003, Annexe 4, p.13). However, my own observations of gacaca hearings and those of other observers indicate that one of gacaca's biggest problems has been low turnouts in many communities. (Examples are described in author's gacaca observations, Ruhengeri, Buhoma, 4 May 2003; Butare, Save, 15 May 2003.) I explore the issue of why many gacaca jurisdictions have struggled to encourage their members to attend hearings in my critical analysis of gacaca in later chapters.
[10] F. Ndangiza, 'Transitional Justice and Reconciliation', paper delivered to the Conference on Policy Research, Ottawa, 21 November 2002, p.7.

forget that the population is the main actor in the Gacaca Jurisdictions and that you represent the population.'[11] Judges are on hand primarily to encourage what Hannington Tayebwa, former Head of Judicial Services at the Ministry of Justice, calls 'facilitated problem-solving', which holds that the general assembly should engage in a largely open discussion at gacaca hearings, in which judges act as mediators to help the community achieve certain legal and social objectives.[12] Gacaca judges function essentially as democratically-elected officials, pursuing the good of the populace by allowing the general assembly to control much of the running of gacaca, except in instances when judges believe that communal discussions may lead to damaging levels of discord or violence.[13]

Much of the Rwandan public shares the government's understanding of the importance of popular participation in gacaca. In my interviews, many Rwandans discuss at length the importance of public dialogue during gacaca hearings and the need for all members of the community to openly discuss their experiences and concerns. As Boniface, a genocide survivor in Kacyiru district of Kigali Ville, said,

> At gacaca the truth frees us from the weight we have carried around since the genocide. Gacaca is important because it allows us to be together and to hear the truth and to learn to live together again ... I will go to gacaca and ask the prisoners who come from the jail to speak the truth about what they did ... There are many lies at gacaca. But the community will refute them and the judges will get to the truth and make a record of the prisoners' crimes. Then I will feel as if all these things have finished and life will start again.[14]

A gacaca judge in Buhoma district of Ruhengeri province stated similarly, 'Gacaca is important because it brings everyone together, to talk together. When we come together, we find unity ... Sometimes there is even too much talking and I have to slow the people down.'[15] Many Rwandans view gacaca as a forum in which all members of the

---

[11] Gacaca Manual, p.10 (author's translation).

[12] Author's government interviews, Hannington Tayebwa, Head of Judicial Services, Ministry of Justice, Kigali, 30 January 2003.

[13] Guidelines governing respectful discourse and the role of gacaca judges in maintaining order during gacaca hearings are found in the Gacaca Manual, pp.26–7.

[14] Author's survivor interviews, Boniface, Kigali Ville, Kacyiru, 22 May 2003 (author's translation).

[15] Author's inyangamugayo interviews, Alice, Ruhengeri, Buhoma, 4 May 2003 (author's translation).

community, suspects, survivors and the general population, can debate and discuss legal and non-legal issues resulting from the genocide.

Gacaca's popular ethos necessitates an analysis of popular perspectives if we are to rigorously interpret its aims. This is a difficult undertaking because the volatile nature of gacaca makes it a moving target. It is impossible to propose a single, paradigmatic interpretation of gacaca and its aims because gacaca is shaped largely by the needs, beliefs and methods of local communities. These local factors vary greatly between, and within, different communities, and over time, leading inevitably to ambiguous, changeable and frequently contested understandings of gacaca. This dynamism should make us wary of interpreting the aims of gacaca too rigidly. Nevertheless, to neglect the ramifications of popular ownership of gacaca is to neglect the important public spirit of the institution and thus to fail to judge it on its own terms. As I argue in the following chapters, many non-Rwandan commentators' interpretations of gacaca and its objectives are flawed in critical respects, principally their neglect of the popular nature of the institution. It is therefore necessary to offer a more grounded interpretation than exists currently, however limited that interpretation may be as a result of the dynamic nature of gacaca.

DOMINANT DISCOURSE ON GACACA

How have most commentators interpreted gacaca? Is there a single, overriding view that drives most critiques of the institution in the existing literature? As mentioned in the Introduction, the study of gacaca is a rapidly growing field and already many detailed and varied accounts have emerged. A small number of Rwandan academics and observers have discussed the importance of gacaca for pursuing various objectives, including reconciliation.[16] The views of these authors are not incorporated into what I describe as the dominant discourse on gacaca because, in terms of the existing literature on this subject, their work currently

---

[16] See, for example, Karekezi, 'Juridictions gacaca', pp.9–96; S. Gasibirege, 'Recherche qualitative sur les attitudes des Rwandais vis-à-vis des juridictions-gacaca', in Ntaganda, Les Juridictions gacaca, pp.121–71; S. Gasibirege, 'Résultats définitifs de l'enquête quantitative sur les attitudes des Rwandais vis-à-vis des juridictions-gacaca', in Ntaganda, De la paix à la Justice, pp.38–92; Gasibirege, 'L'Élection des juges inyangamugayo'; Gasibirege and Babalola, 'Perceptions about the Gacaca Law in Rwanda'; Ntampaka, 'Le gacaca: une juridiction pénale populaire'; C. Ntampaka, 'Le Gacaca Rwandais: une justice répressive participative', Dossiers de la Revue de Droit Pénal et de Criminologie, 2001, pp.211–25.

constitutes a minority (albeit crucial) view. The analysis here does, however, draw on Rwandan authors' interpretations to critique the dominant discourse on gacaca. Over time, it is likely that the local literature on gacaca will grow and some local authors may respond more directly to the critiques of gacaca by non-Rwandan legal commentators.

The majority of published critiques comes from non-Rwandan observers and draws on a form of human-rights analysis that views justice as the primary virtue by which gacaca should be evaluated. That most non-Rwandan observers of gacaca come from a legal background means they tend to interpret gacaca strictly as a judicial remedy to the legacies of the genocide. Discerning the success of gacaca in terms of social outcomes other than deterrent justice, such as reconciliation, is thus sidelined, rendering these virtues as secondary considerations to these forms of justice, if in fact they are considered at all.

While most commentators – especially those from human-rights groups such as AI and HRW, whose arguments are explored in detail below – consider justice and the protection of human rights as the primary lens through which to interpret and analyse gacaca, they define justice in a very particular fashion. The form of justice that most commentators employ when analysing gacaca is *formal* in method and *deterrent* in outcome. Regarding the formal nature of this version of justice, the dominant discourse on gacaca draws on a long-standing tradition in Western philosophy that holds that justice should be a neutrally determined, universal virtue and free from all value-laden claims made by specific individuals or groups.[17] The only way to achieve this neutrally-determined justice, according to this view, is to follow predetermined principles and procedures. In the context of gacaca, formal justice requires that the modalities of the institution adhere to commonly accepted precepts of due process, such as those requiring defendants to have access to legal counsel of their choosing and for cases to be heard by a neutral, disinterested judiciary.

According to the current orthodoxy, the most important outcome of the gacaca process is the punishment of genocide perpetrators, which will help eradicate the culture of impunity that many non-Rwandan commentators believe prevailed in Rwanda before and during the genocide. In this view, justice will be achieved and gacaca will be deemed

---

[17] The paradigmatic example of this view comes from John Rawls in his model of distributive justice, as presented in J. Rawls, *A Theory of Justice*, Oxford: Clarendon Press, 1972.

successful only when genocide perpetrators have been found guilty and sentenced according to the severity of their crimes. Any failure to mete out punishment to those found guilty of genocide crimes, and to do so according to commonly accepted principles of due process, will render gacaca an unjust and illegitimate institution.

Several examples of human-rights critiques of gacaca illustrate the most common arguments against gacaca. All three critiques assume that gacaca is an institution aimed primarily at formal, deterrent justice. On this basis, they conclude that gacaca is an unjust and illegitimate attempt to deal with the legacies of the genocide.

In a report published in December 2002, AI argues,

> the legislation establishing the Gacaca Jurisdictions fails to guarantee minimum fair trial standards that are guaranteed in international treaties ratified by the Rwandese government ... [G]acaca trials need to conform to international standards of fairness so that the government's efforts to end impunity ... are effective. If justice is not seen to be done, public confidence in the judiciary will not be restored and the government will have lost an opportunity to show its determination to respect human rights.[18]

Elsewhere, AI argues that it is

> principally concerned with the extrajudicial nature of the gacaca tribunals. The gacaca legislation does not incorporate international standards of fair trial. Defendants appearing before the tribunals are not afforded applicable judicial guarantees so as to ensure that the proceedings are fair, even though some could face maximum sentences of life imprisonment.[19]

Five years later, AI repeated similar criticisms of gacaca, namely that it 'fails to meet international standards for fair trial and lacks independence, impartiality and transparency'.[20] HRW echoed this view in 2009, equating gacaca with the US government's military commissions in Guantanamo Bay: 'Human Rights Watch knows of no criminal justice system other than Rwanda's highly discredited gacaca courts in which

---

[18] AI, 'Gacaca: A Question of Justice', p.2.

[19] AI, 'Rwanda: Gacaca – Gambling with Justice', press release, AI Index AFR 47/003/2002, 19 June 2002, p.1. For a detailed exploration of AI's approach to gacaca and how, for example it differs from PRI's, see A. Meyerstein, 'Between Law and Culture: Rwanda's Gacaca and Postcolonial Legacy', *Law and Social Inquiry*, 32, 2, spring 2007, pp.467–508.

[20] AI, 'Rwanda: Fear for Safety/Legal Concern: François-Xavier Byuma (m)\n\n', AI Index AFR 47/007/2007, 9 May 2007, p.1.

hearsay is admitted before a jury of non-lawyers, as would be the case with the revised military commissions.'[21]

In July 2002, HRW analysts Kenneth Roth and Alison Des Forges published an article critical of interpretations of gacaca expressed by writer Helena Cobban. According to Cobban, deterrent justice is not gacaca's only function and, for example, 'therapy' or the healing of wounds after the genocide for both genocide perpetrators and survivors are also among gacaca's aims.[22] In response, Roth and Des Forges argue,

> [I]t is precisely at a time of atrocities … that a policy of trial and punishment is essential. Justice reinforces social norms and deters some would-be perpetrators … [O]ne can only imagine the long line of perpetrators who would choose therapy instead of prison cells. Before we agree to counselling instead of punishment [through gacaca], we owe it to the victims of the Rwandan genocide – and to all future victims of genocide – to contemplate the [idea of therapy at gacaca] from their perspective.[23]

For now, it is not necessary to question the validity of Roth's and Des Forges' specific critique of Cobban's argument. What is important to note here instead is the primacy that groups such as AI and HRW afford

[21] HRW, 'US: Revival of Guantanamo Military Commissions a Blow to Justice', New York: HRW, 15 May 2009.

[22] H. Cobban, 'The Legacies of Collective Violence: The Rwandan Genocide and the Limits of Law', *Boston Review*, April/May 2002, www.bostonreview.net/BR27.2/cobban.html. Cobban – along with Kasaija Phillip Apuuli, Erin Daly, Mark Drumbl, Arthur Molenaar, the Norwegian Helsinki Committee for Human Rights (NHCH, L. Danielle Tully, Peter Uvin and Stef Vandeginste – offers one of the few critiques of gacaca by a non-Rwandan source that emphasises the role of gacaca in pursuing social outcomes other than retributive or deterrent justice. (See K.P. Apuuli, 'Procedural Due Process and the Prosecution of Genocide Suspects in Rwanda', *Journal of Genocide Research*, 11, 1, March 2009, pp.11–30; E. Daly, 'Between Punitive Justice and Reconstructive Justice: The Gacaca Courts in Rwanda', *New York University Journal of International Law and Politics*, 34, 2002, pp.355–96; Drumbl, 'Punishment, Postgenocide'; M. Drumbl, *Atrocity, Punishment, and International Law*, Cambridge: Cambridge University Press, 2007; A. Molenaar, 'Gacaca: Grassroots Justice after Genocide – The Key to Reconciliation in Rwanda?', Research Report 77/2005, Leiden: African Studies Centre, 2005; NHCHR, 'Prosecuting Genocide in Rwanda: The Gacaca System and the International Criminal Tribunal for Rwanda', Oslo: NHCHR, September 2002, pp.14–18; L.D. Tully, 'Human Rights Compliance and the Gacaca Jurisdictions in Rwanda', *Boston College International and Comparative Law Review*, 26, 2, 2003, pp.385–414; P. Uvin, 'The Gacaca Tribunals in Rwanda [Case Study]', in D. Bloomfield, T. Barnes and L. Huyse [eds.], *Reconciliation after Violent Conflict: A Handbook*, Stockholm: International Institute for Democracy and Electoral Assistance, 2003, pp.116–21; P. Uvin, 'The Introduction of a Modernized Gacaca for Judging Suspects of Participation in the Genocide and the Massacres of 1994 in Rwanda', discussion paper prepared for the Belgian Secretary of State for Development Cooperation, 2000; S. Vandeginste, 'Justice, Reconciliation and Reparation').

[23] Des Forges and Roth, 'Justice or Therapy?'

methods of 'trial and punishment' in the context of gacaca, with the aim of deterring potential criminals, and the implication that, according to this discourse, these methods must comply with international standards of judicial procedure. Nowhere in the literature do human-rights critics explicitly state that deterrent justice is the *only* objective of gacaca, although quotes such as the one above from Roth and Des Forges come close to making such a point. However, objectives that legal commentators imply do not relate to methods of punishment, and more specifically to ideas of deterrence, such as 'therapy', 'healing', 'rehabilitation' or 'reconciliation', are generally treated with scepticism, if in fact they are considered at all.[24] Therefore, we can conclude that the prevailing discourse considers deterrent justice to be the primary objective of gacaca.

The current academic literature on gacaca is now quite substantial, and most critiques – particularly from non-Rwandan authors – have mirrored the human-rights arguments cited above. For example, Allison Corey and Sandra Joireman argue that gacaca threatens security in Rwanda by failing to adequately punish *génocidaires* in two key respects.[25] First, they argue that gacaca fails to punish perpetrators in a formal sense, as embodied in principles of due process such

[24] For similar formal, deterrent-justice interpretations of gacaca that draw on little if any empirical evidence, see: African Rights, 'Gacaca Justice'; M.G. Bolocan, 'Rwandan Gacaca: An Experiment in Transitional Justice', *Journal of Dispute Resolution*, 2004, pp.355–400; W. Burke-White, 'A Community of Courts: Toward a System of International Criminal Law Enforcement', *Michigan Journal of International Law*, 24, 1, fall 2002, pp.54–61; J. Fierens, 'Gacaca Courts: Between Fantasy and Reality', *Journal of International Criminal Justice*, 3, 2005, pp.896–919; D. Haile, 'Rwanda's Experiment with People's Courts (Gacaca) and the Tragedy of Unexamined Humanitarianism', Institute of Development Policy and Management Discussion Paper, Antwerp: University of Antwerp, January 2008; K.J. Heller, 'What Happens to the Acquitted?', *Leiden Journal of International Law*, 21, 2008, pp.663–80; S. Ngesi and C. Villa-Vicencio, 'Rwanda: Balancing the Weight of History', in E. Doxtader and C. Villa-Vicencio (eds.), *Through Fire with Water: The Roots of Division and the Potential for Reconciliation in Africa*, Claremont: Institute for Justice and Reconciliation, 2003, pp.20–3; PRI, 'Research Team on Gacaca'. (It should be noted, however, that PRI appears to hold a somewhat inconsistent view of gacaca's objectives, in some key documents expressing an exclusively formal, deterrent interpretation of gacaca and in others highlighting the role of gacaca in facilitating other outcomes such as reconciliation, via means other than legal due process. For an example of PRI's exploration of gacaca's capacity for facilitating reconciliation, and via negotiation, see PRI, 'Gacaca Courts in Rwanda', Kigali: PRI, 2003; PRI, 'Report on the Gacaca [Report V]'; J. Sarkin, 'Gacaca Courts and Genocide', in C. Villa-Vicencio and T. Savage (eds.), *Rwanda and South Africa in Dialogue: Addressing the Legacies of Genocide and a Crime against Humanity*, Cape Town: Institute for Justice and Reconciliation, 2001, pp.54–91; Werchick, 'Prospects for Justice in Rwanda's Citizen Tribunals'.

[25] A. Corey and S. Joireman, 'Retributive Justice: The Gacaca Courts in Rwanda', *African Affairs*, 103, 2004, pp.73–89. See also S. Joireman, 'Justice for a Genocide?', *Global Review of Ethnopolitics*, 2, 2, January 2003, pp.65–6.

as participants' right to legal counsel and to have their cases heard by neutral, third parties, rather than by members of the community who themselves may be involved in the cases under consideration. Second, they argue that gacaca fails to uphold principles of judicial fairness by focusing only on crimes committed by *génocidaires* and neglecting crimes against Hutu committed by members of the Tutsi minority and the RPF. Corey and Joireman argue that this selectivity of cases to be heard at gacaca leads to a form of 'politicized justice', which intensifies 'a desire for vengeance among the Hutu majority ... thereby contributing to, rather than curtailing, the risk of ethnic violence in the long run'.[26] Many observers, including those from AI and HRW, have criticised gacaca on these same grounds of legal due process and judicial fairness and have often accused the Rwandan government of directly interfering in gacaca cases to ensure its desired judicial results.[27] Corey's and Joireman's argument, however, differs slightly from these critiques by claiming that politicised justice will lead to insecurity rather than simply a derogation of a moral duty to try all crimes equally or a failed attempt to eradicate the culture of impunity, which appear to be the human-rights organisations' main justifications for pursuing punishment through gacaca.

In the current literature on gacaca, there are several variations of these formal critiques as outlined above. However, the examples from these human-rights organisations and academics are representative of the dominant discourse on gacaca. Some critics emphasise either the formal or deterrent shortcomings of gacaca more than others, while some emphasise both of these aspects. Both components of this view of justice, however, predominate in the existing literature and constitute a largely coherent view among most commentators of what gacaca is and what it is designed to achieve (or more crucially, given the critical nature of most commentaries, what gacaca supposedly is not and what it supposedly fails to achieve). Later chapters will show that the dominant discourse on gacaca is severely flawed for two main reasons: first, because it mistakenly views gacaca exclusively as a legal institution, which can be analysed solely through the legal statutes that underpin it; and second, because it interprets formal, deterrent justice as the only

---

[26] *Ibid.*, pp. 86, 74.
[27] Des Forges and Roth, 'Justice or Therapy?', pp.1–2; AI, 'Gacaca: A Question of Justice', pp.2–11. HRW, 'Law and Reality: Progress in Judicial Reform in Rwanda', New York: HRW, July 2008, pp.19–22.

objective of gacaca, while neglecting more fundamental aims, such as reconciliation, and more negotiated processes during hearings. In short, the dominant discourse fails to account for the hybrid nature of gacaca and the hybrid methods and objectives it embodies. We therefore require a more grounded interpretation of gacaca and its objectives if we are to appropriately critique its practical operation and to fully comprehend its impact on the post-genocide society.

CHAPTER 4

THE GACACA JOURNEY: THE ROUGH ROAD TO JUSTICE AND RECONCILIATION

INTRODUCTION

As we saw in Chapter 2, present-day gacaca is the result of years of difficult argument in Rwandan society about the most appropriate social, legal and political responses to the backlog of genocide cases. Since gacaca was codified and operational, it has become embedded within, and heavily reliant upon the success of, a complex process involving the transfer of detainees from prison to their home communities, where eventually they face gacaca trials. It is necessary therefore to explore the personal, emotional responses of the population to the provisional release of genocide suspects, which affect popular interpretations and perceptions of gacaca. This chapter and the rest of the book refer to what I call the 'gacaca journey'. This journey comprises six phases: the imprisonment of genocide suspects; the release of selected suspects into eighteen ingando around Rwanda; suspects' three-month-long civic education in the camps; their release into their home communities; suspects' trials at gacaca; and finally, their sentencing and, in cases where they are found guilty of serious enough crimes, their return to prison and/ or participation in TIG. This is fundamentally the detainees' journey. However, it unavoidably affects the wider population, especially when detainees return to live among survivors in the same locations where they are accused of committing genocide crimes.

In this chapter, I provide a narrative of the entire gacaca journey, based on first-hand observations of key events during that period and interviews with participants. The journey is ongoing, as consecutive waves of detainees are released from prison to eventually face gacaca. The episodes in this chapter centre on interviews with three detainees whom I tracked through all stages of the gacaca journey and with their communities, recording changes over time in their views and interpretations of gacaca and its impact. My purpose here is to provide the narrative context within which gacaca operates and to lay the foundation for a more detailed analysis of gacaca in Chapters 5–11. This chapter begins with an overview of the first three phases of the gacaca journey. It then uses my interviews and field observations to describe the later stages.

THE JOURNEY BEGINS: FROM PRISON TO INGANDO

The conditions in Rwanda's prisons were until recently among the worst in the world. Before the start of gacaca, most of the tens of thousands of genocide suspects in prison were never charged formally with any crime and most lived in appalling conditions. Various NGOs called on the Rwandan government to drastically improve the situation in the genocide jails,[1] and the Red Cross assisted in building several extra detention facilities to help lessen the problem of overcrowding.[2] A national overhaul of the detention system in recent years culminated in the construction of Mpanga Prison near Nyanza in south-western Rwanda, with $7 million donated by the Dutch government to build the facility capable of holding 7,500 detainees.[3] In August 2009, the Rwandan government signed an agreement with the Special Court for Sierra Leone allowing the latter to send convicted perpetrators to Mpanga, which it started doing in October 2009.[4] The government also intends Mpanga to hold any high-level genocide suspects passed over from the ICTR, if the tribunal judges permit the transfer of cases to the national courts in the future.

Until the provisional release of genocide suspects, the massive over-population of Rwanda's jails caused anger and consternation among

---

[1] See, for example, AI, 'Gacaca: A Question of Justice', p.8.

[2] United Nations, 'Situation in Rwanda: International Assistance for a Solution to the Problems of Refugees, the Restoration of Total Peace, Reconstruction and Socio-Economic Development in Rwanda (Report of the Secretary-General)', UN Doc. A/51/353, 12 September 1996, p.8.

[3] International Justice Tribune, 'Mpanga, A Stronghold for the UN in Rwanda', 5 May 2009, www.rnw.nl/int-justice/article/mpanga-stronghold-un-rwanda.

[4] Reuters, 'Sierra Leone Court Sends Convicts to Rwandan Prison', 31 October 2009, www.reuters.com/article/latestCrisis/idUSLV126612.

all groups in society. Many survivors whom I interviewed argued that, while it was necessary to hold the suspects in prison until they could be tried, the population was suffering from detainees' inability to publicly tell the truth about their crimes.[5] Members of the general population complained that the government was unable to adequately provide food and clothing for detainees, a responsibility that fell to their families, who as well as supporting relatives in jail, suffered financially from detainees' inability to contribute to community livelihoods.[6]

By the end of 2002, the situation in the genocide prisons had become unsustainable. On 1 January 2003, a government communiqué broadcast over state-owned radio announced that an undisclosed number of genocide suspects would be provisionally released to hasten their appearance before gacaca.[7] According to detainees and survivors, the communiqué was followed by a radio announcer's commentary that created great confusion among many Rwandans. The commentary suggested that all genocide suspects would soon be liberated.[8] This led to mass celebrations in prisons across the country. 'We were dancing and singing and hugging one another', a detainee in Butare Central Prison said. 'People began packing their bags and waiting by the gates, thinking they would be going home soon.'[9] Many survivors interpreted the radio message in the same way and were fearful that so many suspects would be released. 'The radio said that all of the [genocide] prisoners were coming back', said one survivor in Kigali Ville. 'We were very scared. We didn't understand what was happening. No one explained to us why the prisoners were returning like this.'[10]

When it became clear that the 1 January communiqué had caused widespread fear and confusion, government officials travelled to every genocide prison and various towns and villages to explain the nature of the release of detainees. According to detainees at Butare Central Prison, officials told them that not all genocide suspects would be liberated at this stage but only the very young, elderly and sick detainees, followed

[5] Author's survivor interviews, Grégoire, Butare; Boniface, Kigali Ville; Jean-Michel, Kigali Ville, Kacyiru, 22 May 2003; Patience, Gisenyi, Gisenyi Ville, 23 May 2003.
[6] Author's general population interviews, George, Ruhengeri, Ruhengeri Ville, 4 May 2003; Robert, Butare, Kibingo, 14 May 2003; Henri, Kigali Ngali, Nyamata, 19 May 2003.
[7] For a translated summary of this communiqué, see Republic of Rwanda, 'Communiqué (Summary, Original in Kinyarwanda)', 7 January 2003, www.gov.rw/government/070103.html.
[8] Author's prison fieldnotes; author's survivor interviews, Jean-Michel, Kigali Ville; Julienne, Butare, Kibingo, 14 May 2003.
[9] Author's prison fieldnotes.
[10] Author's survivor interviews, Christiane, Kigali Ville, Kacyiru, 22 May 2003.

by selected prisoners who had already confessed to their crimes and therefore were considered ready to appear before gacaca. Not all suspects who had already confessed to their crimes, however, would be released. Furthermore, they would not be released directly into their home communities but first into ingando, where they would receive a civic education to prepare them for life in the outside world and ultimately for gacaca. The government emphasised that this was a provisional release and that anyone found to have made a false confession would return immediately to prison. Moreover, if suspects were eventually found guilty at gacaca, they faced the possibility of a return to jail, depending on the severity of their crimes.[11]

These government clarifications caused mixed responses both inside and beyond the jails. Some survivors were heartened to know that not all detainees would be released and that the suspects would have to pass through ingando before returning to their home communities. Many survivors worried, though, that because confession was a prerequisite for most detainees' liberation, suspects would confess falsely to benefit from this provision. Some detainees claimed that their fellow inmates acted in precisely this fashion. 'After the officials told us who would be released, everyone [in the jail] started confessing', one prisoner said. 'Everyone was writing confessions on pieces of paper and taking them to the warden's office. Those who didn't know how to write found a friend who could write for them.'[12] Some detainees claimed that some fellow inmates faked sickness to secure an early release.[13] Some prisoners also complained that most detainees released on health grounds or because they were elderly did not have to pass through ingando but instead returned directly to their home communities.[14]

The issue of confession is central to the gacaca journey: to embark on the journey, suspects must first admit to their crimes. This entails a conscious decision by detainees to participate in the process. Consequently, there is little doubt that many detainees confess to crimes significantly less severe than those they actually committed during the genocide. Many detainees wager that the benefits of an early, provisional release and decreased sentences under gacaca's plea-bargaining scheme far outweigh the risk of being found guilty of crimes to which they have not yet confessed. In many cases, however, the community confronts suspects with the true nature of their crimes when they come face to

[11] Author's prison fieldnotes.
[12] Ibid.   [13] Ibid.   [14] Ibid.

face at gacaca, at which point detainees convicted of crimes more severe than those they originally admitted will receive harsher penalties than suspects who confess fully at the earliest opportunity. Issues of truth-telling and many detainees' tendency to gamble on false confessions are explored in greater depth in Chapter 7.

Survivors were not the only group to react furiously to the announcement of the prisoner releases. The announcement also caused anger and resentment among detainees who were told that they would not be going home. In particular, detainees who claimed that they were innocent of genocide crimes argued that it was unjust that those who confessed to, and therefore were guilty of, crimes would be liberated, while the innocent remained in jail. Some detainees went on hunger strikes to protest the rejection of their applications for release.[15] At a prison workshop run by World Vision for detainees in Butare who remained in jail, a sixty-eight-year-old man joked, 'The warden told me I was slightly too young to be released. If only I could've borrowed a couple of years from someone else.'[16] Another man worried that, when the suspects who were released early reached their home communities, they would tell lies about those still in jail.[17]

The government released an undisclosed number of elderly and sick detainees directly into their home communities on 10 January 2003 (most of whom never appeared before gacaca) and on 28 January released approximately 20,000 detainees into eighteen ingando in the country's twelve prefectures.[18] After several waves of provisional releases, by October 2008 around 85,000 genocide suspects had returned to their home communities.[19] Following the first release in 2003, the mood of the detainees leaving Kigali Central Prison was celebratory but muted. 'This is an extraordinary day', one prisoner said, 'but we are not home yet. There are still the camps to come. But we have waited many years for this day and soon we will go home.'[20]

The ingando were officially inaugurated at a ceremony at Gashora in Kigali Ngali province on 31 January 2003. For the next three months, the first wave of detainees received a wide range of lessons and participated in group work programmes, often rebuilding survivors' homes destroyed during the genocide. I visited four ingando during this

[15] *Ibid.* [16] *Ibid.* [17] *Ibid.*
[18] Author's government interviews, Jean de Dieu Mucyo.
[19] International Centre for Prison Studies, 'Prison Brief for Rwanda', King's College London, www.kcl.ac.uk/depsta/law/research/icps/worldbrief/wpb_country.php?country=39.
[20] Author's general fieldnotes, prison release, Kigali Ville, 28 January 2003.

period, in Kigali Ville, Gashora, Butare and Ruhengeri. The Gashora camp was one of the largest in the country, holding around 2,100 suspects, while the Ruhengeri camp was one of the smallest, with 469 detainees.[21] The camps afforded suspects much more living space than the prisons; most camps had a football field where detainees were permitted to play matches at the end of each day. Detainees received more regular and higher quality meals in the camps and were often allowed to visit their communities, either to visit sick relatives or to meet survivors in preparation for gacaca. One source of frustration for many detainees and their families, however, was the fact that the government initially told them that suspects would spend two months in the camps before being released. When the two months passed, detainees were informed that – for reasons unexplained – they would have to stay in the camps for an indefinite period, which eventually amounted to one extra month.[22]

The civic education that detainees received in the ingando had little bearing on most survivors' fears and concerns regarding the release of the accused. Rose, a thirty-six-year-old survivor in Nyamata whose son, three nephews and two nieces were murdered during the genocide – she suspected by Hutu neighbours – said,

> Can we trust [the detainees] not to repeat what they did to us before? They might not have received enough lessons from the government [in the ingando] … For most of survivors, the release [is] a mockery. Haven't we suffered enough already?[23]

The government's main aim in establishing the camps was to teach lessons to the detainees before they returned to their communities. Sara Bawaya, a trained psychologist and one of two NURC coordinators of the Gashora ingando (who later became the Director of Civic Education at the NURC), explained the government's purposes in establishing the camps:

> If you look around you here, you will see that these are good people in this camp. I can't really work out why they participated in genocide … Now they do everything we tell them to. We need to teach them now because, with a bad government, they will repeat the genocide. It's like

---

[21] Author's solidarity camp fieldnotes, Gashora, 18 April 2003; Ruhengeri, 3 May 2003.

[22] Author's solidarity camp interviews, Gashora (no. 1), 18 April 2003; Gashora (no. 3), 18 April 2003; Butare (no. 1), 28 April 2003.

[23] Author's survivor interviews, Rose, Kigali Ngali, Nyamata, 19 May 2003 (author's translation).

when a baby is born and reaches 7 years. By then … it's too late to teach it anything else. But what we hope these people will learn is, 'if I do wrong, a good government will get me.' That way, they won't repeat the genocide … And if we educate them, then they will educate their children, and this will become an education for future generations … The government is the most important agent in making people good or bad.[24]

Little systematic research has so far been conducted into the use of ingando in Rwanda. Like gacaca, ingando represents the Rwandan government's invocation of a return to 'tradition' in resolving past conflicts and inculcating civic values in Rwandan society. As highlighted by Bawaya's comment that '[t]he government is the most important agent in making people good or bad', ingando – which Ndangiza calls 'reconciliation camps' – is founded on the notion that the state must educate the populace in how to live harmoniously and prosperously.[25] Patrick Mazimpaka, former Rwandan presidential envoy to the Great Lakes, describes the basis of ingando as the Kinyarwanda concept '*ubu-rere buruta ubuvuke*: people are not born with values; values can only be internalized through practice and education. And we have to have specific education for reconciliation and democratization.'[26]

Such views draw strongly on RPF ideology, replete with Marxist overtones derived from the NRM experience in Uganda, where leaders, including Yoweri Museveni, had been immersed in Marxism during their student years at the University of Dar es Salaam and later in Frente de Libertação de Moçambique (FRELIMO) training camps in Mozambique.[27] Ingando draws on NRM concepts of 'political education' as embodied in Ugandan institutions such as *chaka-mchaka*, a form of indoctrination camp used during the Ugandan bush war for military cadres and as mobile schools for the broader population, which focused on the history of flawed politics in Uganda and the NRM's self-identified role as political rectifier.[28] The RPF used ingando for political and military education in its formative years in Uganda and during

---

[24] Author's solidarity camp fieldnotes, Gashora, 18 April 2003.
[25] Author's government interviews, Ndangiza, 10 June 2006.
[26] P. Mazimpaka, 'Reconciliation and Democratization Processes after the Genocide', in *Reconciliation and Democratization: Experiences and Lessons Learned in Reconciliation and Democratization from Germany, South Africa, Namibia and Rwanda*, Kigali: NURC, October 2003, p.22.
[27] O.O. Amaza, *Museveni's Long March: From FRELIMO to the National Resistance Movement*, London: Pluto Press, 1996.
[28] See, for example, M. Katumanga, 'Folk Poetry as a Weapon of Struggle: An Analysis of the Chaka Mchaka Resistance Songs of the National Resistance Movement/Army of Uganda', in

the 1990–3 civil war in Rwanda. In the post-genocide context, ingando has been employed since 1999 in the reintegration of ex-FAR (Forces Armées Rwandaises) and ex-interahamwe combatants from the eastern DRC and since 2003 for confessed genocide perpetrators as part of their provisional release before facing gacaca. Frank Rusagara, Director of Military History at the Rwandan Defence Forces, describes ingando historically as

> a military encampment or assembly area … where the troops received their final briefing while readying for a military expedition … In such gatherings, the individuals were reminded to subject their interests to the national ideal and give Rwanda their all … That was the idea behind the institution of Ingando as a vehicle for reintegration of captured ex-FAR and militia into the RPF/A.[29]

In recent years, a wide range of social and cultural groups have undergone civic education in ingando, including schoolteachers, university lecturers, students, business- and tradespeople and civil servants.[30] My purpose here is not to provide an in-depth analysis of ingando but rather a brief overview of the institution in so far as the Rwandan government has employed it to support the gacaca process.

In each of the four ingando I visited, officials refused to show me the teaching materials they used in their lessons. However, from lesson notes gathered from detainees during my interviews, I was able to identify the main themes of the camp pedagogy.[31] Each camp employed different teachers, who taught a slightly different curriculum, although several topics were consistent across the four camps.

K. Njogu and H. Maupeu (eds.), *Songs and Politics in Eastern Africa*, Dar es Salaam: Mkuki na Nyota Publishers, 2007, pp.129–55.

[29] F. Rusagara, *Resilience of a Nation: A History of the Military in Rwanda*, Kigali: Fountain Publishers Rwanda, 2009, p.193.

[30] Author's government interviews, Sara Bawaya, Director of Civic Education, NURC, Kigali, 24 August 2008.

[31] In 2006, the NURC published the official, standardised ingando curriculum, drawing on the lessons that had been taught to date in different camps around the country. The curriculum comprises forty-four topics, including 'Peace, Reconciliation and Good Governance', 'Social Consciousness and Social Revolution', 'The Ethnic Issue in Rwanda and the African Great Lakes Region', 'Genocide and its Concept', 'Prevention, Resolution and Management of Conflicts in Human Society', 'Gacaca Jurisdictions and Communal Work (TIG)', 'The Role of Religious Confessions in Healing and Development', 'Trauma and its Treatment' and 'Government's Program in the 7-Year Period, 2003–2010, and Vision 2020' (Republic of Rwanda, 'Imfashanyigisho Y'Ingando N'Andi Mahugurwa', Kigali: NURC, October 2006).

An early theme that lessons in all camps covered was what officials called 'overcoming bad governance', which referred to the need for all Rwandans to resist the divisive or genocidal policies of past colonial or national political regimes and to embrace the supposedly more inclusive, harmonious policies of the Kagame government.[32] Detainees were taught that Belgian colonists divided Rwandans into three ethnic groups and distributed identity cards, laying the foundation for genocide. Such views echo arguments made during Bizimungu's meetings at Urugwiro in 1999: 'Before the Europeans' arrival, Rwandans were understanding each other, [and] the Country was characterized by unity.'[33] Sylvestre, a farmer and a detainee in the Ruhengeri ingando, said, 'This is the first time I have heard about the history of Rwanda and what our bad leaders did to us. Now I know where all our problems came from – they came from the bad leaders.'[34]

Detainees were then taught how they could become what Ruth, a suspect in the Kigali Ville ingando, recorded in her notes as 'agents of change'.[35] As agents of change, detainees were told that they should return to their communities and spread the government's message that there was no place in Rwandan society for the ethnic divisions of the past and that 'we are all Rwandans now.'[36] To build a peaceful and stable country, Rwandans should draw on their underlying unity and traditional Rwandan educational and conflict resolution processes such as ingando and gacaca to resolve problems in the future. Detainees were instructed on the detailed modalities of gacaca, particularly its plea-bargaining system and how they would benefit from early confessions to their crimes. They were taught that gacaca would allow the community to 'talk about its problems together' and to achieve justice and reconciliation.[37] All Rwandans were needed to participate in gacaca, to resolve past conflicts and to regain a sense of national unity that first the colonists and later the genocidal regime had destroyed. 'Gacaca lets us solve our own problems', Sylvestre, the detainee in Ruhengeri, recorded in his lesson notes. 'Outsiders cannot help us, only ourselves.'[38] Most detainees described the

---

[32] Solidarity camp lesson notes, Ruth, Kigali Ville, 12 April 2003 (author's translation); Alphonse, Gashora, 18 April 2003 (author's translation).

[33] Republic of Rwanda, 'Report on the Reflection Meetings', p.11.

[34] Author's solidarity camp interviews, Ruhengeri (no. 4), 3 May 2003 (author's translation).

[35] Solidarity camp lesson notes, Ruth (author's translation).

[36] Ibid. (author's translation).

[37] Solidarity camp lesson notes, Sylvestre, Ruhengeri, 3 May 2003 (author's translation).

[38] Ibid. (author's translation).

ingando lessons as useful and believed that they would help them reintegrate more quickly and smoothly into their home communities.

THE FATEFUL ROAD: RETURN OF THE FIRST GENOCIDE SUSPECTS TO THEIR HOME COMMUNITIES

Just as the international community largely ignored the genocide in 1994, it was also almost entirely absent on the most momentous day in Rwanda since the genocide. Only two foreign media agencies, BBC Radio and the Canadian television network CTV, were on hand on 5 May 2003, when more than 20,000 confessed genocide perpetrators were provisionally released into their home communities, after spending nearly a decade in prison.[39] I expected to fight my way through hordes of journalists to talk to the detainees before they boarded buses, returning to the same communities where they committed their crimes. Instead, I walked unimpeded into the Kinyinya ingando on the outskirts of Kigali. After some hasty negotiations, I persuaded camp officials to let me ride on a run-down, white Mercedes-Benz bus carrying seventy detainees to an undisclosed drop-off point somewhere south, near the Burundi border.

First, though, I went looking for Laurent, a short, grey-moustached forty-two-year-old Hutu detainee, whom I met when I first visited the Kinyinya camp three weeks earlier. When I first interviewed Laurent, unlike most suspects he refused to describe the crimes to which he had confessed.[40] A camp official later told me that Laurent had confessed to murdering three men and a woman in 1994.[41] I wanted to know how he was feeling now as he prepared to return to his community.

I found Laurent sheltering from the blazing afternoon sun beneath a blue tarpaulin, a tattered bag of clothes by his side and his left knee heavily bandaged. 'I'm sick and I have to walk home today', he said. 'I'm sad because I have no family left. What am I going back to? I'm going back to nothing.' All of Laurent's family, themselves Hutu, were killed during the genocide. All around, detainees were hugging one another and exchanging addresses. 'When I see these people outside of the camp',

---

[39] The full narrative of the detainees' journey from the Kigali Ville solidarity camp to Gashora is recorded in author's general fieldnotes, solidarity camp release, 5 May 2003.

[40] Author's solidarity camp interviews, Kigali Ville (no. 13), 12 April 2003.

[41] Author's solidarity camp fieldnotes, Kigali Ville, 12 April 2003.

Laurent said, 'they will be like my brothers and sisters.' Laurent picked up his bags and began limping towards the camp gates. I asked him why he was not riding on the bus with the rest of us. 'My name isn't on the list of people to ride in the bus', he said. 'I'm sick and my leg is bad but [the camp officials] tell me I have to walk home.'[42]

I boarded the bus with the last of the detainees. The men onboard waved ecstatically to their friends as the bus pulled out of the camp. Once outside the gates, they began dancing and singing in celebration, stomping in unison and rocking the bus back and forth. The lone, fresh-faced security guard in a maroon uniform smiled and kept the beat by banging the butt of his rifle on the floor. Waving, cheering Hutu lined the streets to welcome the returning prisoners as if they were a liberation army. Shopkeepers and schoolchildren in khaki uniforms and bright blue dresses screamed and waved as the bus bounced along the rutted, dusty tracks out of Kigali.

One detainee, Karisa, sat silently near the front as the rest of the bus celebrated behind him. He told me that he had confessed to being an *infiltré*, one of the thousands of interahamwe who fled into the jungles of Zaire after the RPF victory in 1994 and had continued to attack Tutsi civilians in North and South Kivu. Hutu-dominated rebel groups currently operating in the eastern DRC such as the Forces Démocratiques de Libération du Rwanda (FDLR) comprise large numbers of suspected perpetrators of the 1994 genocide. Following the Sun City accords in December 2002 between the Congolese government and rebel groups fighting in the east, there have been several attempts to enact disarmament, demobilisation and reintegration (DDR) processes for ex-combatants in the DRC, often involving the return of Hutu militiamen to Rwanda. Since 2007, however, few repatriated combatants from the DRC have passed through gacaca or other justice processes often because they were too young in 1994 to be prosecuted for genocide crimes. Instead, most returned fighters have undergone periods of civic education in ingando before returning to civilian life or being reintegrated into the Rwandan army.[43] Long before any DDR process, Karisa was captured in 1996 and jailed as a genocide suspect. 'Today is an amazing day', he said. 'All I want to do is walk the streets of Kigali for one or two hours. I want to remember what it's like to walk those streets.' Karisa was from Bicumbi in central Rwanda but he said that he wanted to find his

---

[42] Author's general fieldnotes, solidarity camp release (author's translation).
[43] Author's observer interviews, Faith Malka, Research Fellow, Institute of Policy Analysis and Research, Kigali, 22 August 2008.

older brother who he had heard was living somewhere near Butare in the south-west. 'We have a new life now', he said. 'Everything is new. But what will happen to us now? None of us can know.'[44]

The detainees fell silent as the bus rolled further away from Kigali. For weeks, rumours had been circulating that Tutsi lynch mobs would be waiting when 300 trucks and buses of released prisoners like this one arrived in marketplaces all over Rwanda.[45] Some of these detainees would also be found guilty at gacaca and sentenced to further years in prison. The coming months would therefore be only a short, and in their eyes, cruel, taste of liberty.

Some of the detainees grew angry that the bus had not stopped in Kigali to drop off those who lived near the ingando. 'Where are we going?' one of them demanded of the driver, who ignored him. The detainee's name was Diomède and he was nineteen years old, meaning that he was only ten years old during the genocide. He told me that he had confessed to being in a group of three boys who killed another boy with a machete and hacked the Achilles tendons of an old man whom they left for the interahamwe to finish off.[46]

The road wound south following the Nyabarongo river which snakes through a fertile valley of thick, green vegetation, surrounded by hills of cocoa plants, sunflowers and banana palms. The bus driver stopped in Nyamata, the largest town in Kigali Ngali province, to buy a bottle of water. The detainees, furious that we still had not reached the drop-off point, swarmed forward, yelling violently at the driver as he climbed back into the cabin. Some of them tried to push past him and out of the door. The security guard leapt to his feet and brandished his rifle, herding the men back down the bus. The driver calmed them by explaining that the drop-off point was not far away. Some of the detainees slid windows open and bought a handful of cigarettes from the market sellers below. Down the aisle, from detainee to detainee, the cigarettes were passed silently, one drag at a time, with almost ritualistic reverence. 'We haven't had a cigarette the whole time we were in prison', Karisa said. 'Can you imagine?'[47]

It took forty-five minutes to travel the last 15 kilometres of corrugated road. No one spoke. We pulled into a small village and the bus stopped. Schoolchildren watched as the detainees picked up their bags

[44] Author's general fieldnotes, solidarity camp release (author's translation).
[45] Author's general fieldnotes, 1 February 2003, 12 April 2003, 22 April 2003.
[46] Author's general fieldnotes, solidarity camp release (author's translation).
[47] Ibid. (author's translation).

and stepped slowly into the village courtyard. Except for several officials who greeted the detainees as they walked off the bus, no adults were visible. The officials took the men to an open-sided room where one official began lecturing them. The suspects would remain in this village for the night, another official told me, then they would be sent home on foot tomorrow. The intention behind this approach seemed to be to release the detainees slowly and in small numbers back to their home communities to minimise the possibility of reprisals by survivors.

One by one, adult villagers emerged from the surrounding houses, to catch a glimpse of the prisoners. They stood at a distance and whispered to one another. The return of these detainees attracted no fanfare; that would come when they arrived in their home villages. The official's lecture ended and the gathering dispersed. I found Karisa, who told me, 'There are only a few survivors in this village, so we can sleep here tonight in peace.'[48] An official approached me and said that I should leave, explaining that no outsiders were permitted to follow the detainees home the next day.

The driver and I climbed into the empty bus which bounced and jolted its way through the fading evening light back to Kigali. When I got off, I scanned the dark circle of hills surrounding the city: out there on the hills, all over the country, the confessed *génocidaires* were going home. The return of the detainees caused fear and confusion in many communities.[49] Generally, the release occurred peacefully, although several reports emerged of violent attacks against some returning suspects.[50] In a high-profile case, detainees who returned to Gitarama province were found guilty of murdering survivors whom they believed would testify against them at gacaca.[51] These appeared, however, to be isolated incidents.

In May 2003, the government rearrested 787 provisionally released detainees and a further 5,770 detainees in June 2003. This caused much uncertainty, particularly among suspects' families. The government was slow to explain exactly why released detainees were being rearrested. Between the two periods of rearrests, the government announced that

[48] *Ibid.* (author's translation).
[49] Author's survivor interviews, Patrice, Ruhengeri, Ruhengeri Ville, 4 May 2003; Grégoire, Butare; Julienne, Butare; Rose, Kigali Ngali; Juliette, Kigali Ville, Kacyiru, 22 May 2003; Christiane, Kigali Ville.
[50] Author's government interviews, Alexis Rusagara, Deputy Coordinator of Solidarity Camps, NURC, Kigali, 13 May 2003.
[51] IRIN News, 'Genocide Survivor Group Denounces Killings'.

an investigation by the national survivors group Ibuka unearthed evidence showing that many released detainees had lied about the crimes they committed during the genocide. The government also claimed that some of the rearrested detainees had committed crimes in the ingando, such as selling drugs or committing rape while working on labour programmes in the community.[52] The rearrested detainees returned to prison, to begin the gacaca journey again, while the remaining detainees who had been released stayed in their home communities, awaiting summonses to testify at gacaca.

THE PERSONAL JOURNEY: THREE SUSPECTS RETURN HOME

This section provides three separate narratives of detainees whom I interviewed at all stages of the gacaca journey. The final section of this chapter highlights the most salient similarities and differences among their experiences, identifying some of the crucial personal, emotional issues that genocide suspects face during this process and their relevance for the entire gacaca process. A key feature of this aspect of the analysis is that it draws on interviews with the same individuals and their surrounding communities over six years, which allows for useful examination of shifts in attitudes and relations and of the direct impact of these changes on individuals and communities as gacaca has evolved. This approach is important, given gacaca's capacity to alter over time and produce different societal results in the same locations during different periods. Repeat visits also allowed the building of trust with interviewees, deepening the conversations and allowing greater insights into gacaca and its effects.

Laurent

Laurent was the genocide suspect in the Kigali Ville ingando with the injured leg mentioned in the previous section, who a camp official claimed had confessed to killing three men and a woman. Laurent had been married but his wife and children were killed during the genocide. He was a practising Catholic and had studied for one year at the National University of Rwanda in Butare. Before the genocide, Laurent was an accountant, working for traders in the main market of Kacyiru

---

[52] IRIN News, 'More Genocide Suspects Rearrested', 11 June 2003, www.irinnews.org/print.asp? ReportID=34679.

district of Kigali Ville province. I met him three times: in the ingando, on the day of his release and later, when he was living in Remera district of Kigali Ville. When I first met Laurent in the camp, he said that he was uncertain of the reception he would receive from his community when he returned. 'Now that I have left prison', he said, 'I'm going into a new world outside … I don't know how my neighbours will react.' He said that it would be difficult to achieve reconciliation between suspects and survivors and he feared that many of his fellow detainees had unrealistic views of what reconciliation would require. 'We need reconciliation without sentimentality', Laurent said.

> Reconciliation doesn't come from the sky. It comes bit by bit. It means living together, saying sorry, asking for forgiveness. It is much more than words – it is actions.[53]

When I met Laurent a second time, on the day of his release from the ingando, he again expressed uncertainty about the reception he would receive in his home community. He also described his sadness at leaving many of his fellow detainees who had become like his family.[54] Several weeks after his release, I met Laurent again, near his new home in Remera. He told me that, after his release, several friends took him into their house and cared for him; as a result, his leg healed quickly. His friends were now funding his way through a computer course, and he hoped to earn a living as a computer repairman. 'I want to learn new skills so that I can support myself', Laurent said. 'But these skills will be wasted after gacaca if I go back to prison.' He said that he had not yet returned to the community where he committed his crimes and he would not contact anyone in his old community until he saw them at gacaca. 'Gacaca is slow', he said, 'so I won't see these people for a very long time … I have waited ten years for justice and I can't wait much longer. I am an old man and I don't want to wait.'[55]

When asked whether he thought that the ingando lessons had been beneficial for life in the wider society, Laurent said,

> I still consult my notes, not often, but sometimes. It's important to remember what we learnt there. Some [detainees] will forget everything. They are the stubborn, insolent ones. They are unteachable. I'm not like them.

[53] Author's solidarity camp interviews, Kigali Ville (no. 13) (author's translation).
[54] Author's general fieldnotes, solidarity camp release.
[55] Author's detainee follow-up interviews, Laurent, Kigali Ville, Remera, 20 May 2003 (author's translation).

Laurent said that his future was very uncertain and that he often feared what would happen to him. In the immediate situation, he had no money and no work. 'There is no one to support me', he said. 'I can't rely on my friends for much longer.' At the end of the third interview, Laurent said, 'Sometimes I think life was better when I was in prison. I knew people there and they knew me'. Life outside of prison, he claimed, meant only loneliness and poverty.[56]

In 2006, I returned to look for Laurent in Remera. Several neighbours said they had not seen him for many months but there were rumours that he had left the community or died.[57] One neighbour said that Laurent had finished his computer course and therefore had probably found a job closer to town, but another neighbour said that was unlikely because 'everyone uses computers in town but they get them fixed in Remera'.[58] A gacaca judge in the local jurisdiction said that Laurent's case was still pending and the judges were concerned that he had fled the community. 'No one disappears for very long, though', he said. 'Where can you hide in Rwanda? I'm sure he'll be brought back soon.'[59]

By 2008, when I next returned to Remera, Laurent's neighbours were certain he would not be back, citing rumours that he had died in another district. One middle-aged woman said, 'Laurent was from another place. He had moved here after leaving jail and people knew him but he had very few friends and I'm quite sure he had no family.'[60] I failed to find the friends who had paid for Laurent's computer course. The generally blasé reactions from Laurent's neighbours suggested he had correctly predicted that he would not replicate in the outside world the closeness of relationships he had forged in prison.

Cypriet

Cypriet was a sixty-three-year-old farmer from Bugesera district in Kigali Ngali province whom I met five times: in the Gashora ingando in 2003 and several weeks later, following his provisional release into his home community, where I also visited him in 2006, 2008 and 2009. He was married, a practising Catholic and had attended primary school up to the fifth year. After the genocide, Cypriet fled to eastern Zaire as he feared

[56] *Ibid.* (author's translation).
[57] Author's general fieldnotes, 13 June 2006.
[58] Author's general population interviews, Kigali Ville, Remera, 13 June 2006.
[59] Author's inyangamugayo interviews, Kigali Ville, Remera, 13 June 2006.
[60] Author's general population interviews, Kigali Ville, Remera, 15 August 2008.

'bad things were going to happen to any Hutu left behind'.[61] Soon after he returned to Rwanda in 1997, he was arrested, charged with genocide crimes and sent to Rilima Prison.

Later, after being provisionally released into the Gashora ingando, Cypriet had become a close friend of another genocide suspect, Alphonse, whose experience is described below. In the camp, Cypriet told me that he had confessed to being part of a group that committed murder during the genocide but that he himself had not killed anyone. He claimed to feel remorse for what he had done, but he believed that people committed crimes during the genocide solely because 'they were told by bad authorities that they had to kill'. Cypriet said that he expected to receive a warm welcome from his community after his release and that he was confident that gacaca would 'help connect us [detainees] with our neighbours again'. He expected to receive a pardon at gacaca because he himself did not commit crimes during the genocide.[62]

When I met Cypriet (along with Alphonse) several weeks later in the central marketplace of a village 30 kilometres south-west of Nyamata, he was much less optimistic about the release process. He claimed to have actively avoided meeting survivors in his village because 'it is difficult to know the state of survivors' hearts'. He had also heard that many survivors reacted angrily to detainees when they returned from the camps. Cypriet did not know when he would be called before gacaca but he was not concerned about his trial because 'gacaca will not put the blame [for genocide crimes] on anyone, because it will be like the old gacaca.' Cypriet said that the future was highly uncertain, especially because his family was very poor and their crops were not producing enough to 'feed one more mouth', now that he had returned from prison.[63]

By 2006, when I next met Cypriet, it was clear that the years had taken an immense toll on him. His face was drawn, his body gaunt and hunched over. He had moved to a new home on the outskirts of the community, 50 metres off the main track and nestled among maize crops and banana palms. Cypriet pointed to several large gashes in the mud bricks of his house and said that two months earlier a group of genocide survivors had attacked his home with hoes and pangas. He had not yet raised the money to fix the house. 'The same thing happened when I first came

[61] Author's solidarity camp interviews, Gashora (no. 1).
[62] Ibid. (author's translation).
[63] Author's detainee follow-up interviews, Cypriet, Kigali Ngali, Nyamata, 18 May 2003 (author's translation).

back from Congo', he said. 'People here used axes and pangas to destroy my walls. I know who they are because they shouted things at my wife as she was walking to the farm. They said I was a *génocidaire* and should be in jail.'[64]

Cypriet's experience of gacaca had been much less positive than he anticipated during our 2003 discussions. By 2006, his case had been heard at gacaca and he was awaiting his sentence. 'I'm worried about gacaca', he said.

> Many survivors there gave false information about me. The community mentioned many more crimes than I actually committed ... At the start, the judges agreed with me that I was innocent but now they're consider- ing the new information from the survivors ... I've gone to gacaca every time there has been a hearing here. I haven't missed a single hearing. The judges do good work but not all of them are wise. They do what they can but they often believe people's lies.

Cypriet said he had resigned himself to being found guilty at gacaca and that he would probably be sentenced to community service. This wor- ried him greatly as he believed he was physically too weak to build roads or houses or tend communal gardens, as many other suspects convicted at gacaca had been forced to do. 'I may have to go to TIG', he said. 'I'm waiting on the judges' response. If I'm told to go, I'll go. I have no choice.' He said that at gacaca he had condemned others who had com- mitted murder during the genocide and therefore he expected leniency from the judges in exchange for his cooperation. 'I didn't commit any crimes [during the genocide]', he said, 'so I'm still hoping the truth will prevail. That is what I'm praying. But I think the judges will say I should be punished.'[65]

A sign of Cypriet's frailty, the next two times I visited his home – in 2008 and 2009 – he was bedridden with malaria and unable to speak to me. 'He has been like this since he came back [from prison]', his wife Agnès said. 'We have to ask young relatives and friends to help with the farming because he is too weak.'[66] The judges in Cypriet's gacaca juris- diction agreed with this assessment. Although they found him guilty of aiding the group murder of a forty-three-year-old Tutsi man during the

---

[64] Author's detainee follow-up interviews, Cypriet, Kigali Ngali, Bugesera, 11 June 2006 (author's translation).
[65] *Ibid.*
[66] Author's detainee follow-up interviews, Agnès, Kigali Ngali, Bugesera, 21 April 2009 (author's translation).

genocide, they determined that he was physically incapable of participating in community service. One of the gacaca judges told me:

> We were convinced that he had committed that one crime but not some
> of the others [that people were accusing him of]. This happens at gacaca –
> people say many things … We knew about the attacks on his house, how
> he had been threatened when he came back to the community. His wife
> also spoke about this at gacaca. We listened to everything. We decided
> he had already spent many years in jail and this should decrease his sen-
> tence. He was supposed to do TIG [as his punishment] but, as you have
> seen, he is very old and weak. You cannot ask an old man like that to do
> TIG.[67]

Alphonse

Alphonse was a thirty-six-year-old merchant from Bugesera district in
Kigali Ngali province whom I met six times: at the inauguration of the
ingando in Gashora (soon after he was released from the nearby Rilima
Prison), towards the end of his stay in the Gashora camp, several weeks
after his release into his home community and in his house in 2006,
2008 and 2009. He was not married, was a practising Catholic and had
attended secondary school up to the fourth year. At the inauguration of
ingando, Alphonse told me that he had confessed to murdering several
people during the genocide, which placed him in Category 2 of crimes.
Although he claimed that he had been forced to kill, his Catholic faith
convinced him that it was necessary to confess. He did not feel guilty
about what he had done, however, and he expected his community to
welcome him warmly. 'I did many good things in the community', he
said, 'and they will remember me and will be pleased to see me again.'[68]
Alphonse also said that he had been an urumuri during prison gacaca
hearings at Rilima in 1998 and he believed this would help him greatly
when navigating the official gacaca process in his community. He said
that detainees had started prison gacaca hearings themselves as they
needed to believe that 'some kind of justice was underway' but several
years later, when the official gacaca process started, government officials
became more involved, encouraging detainees to participate in prison
gacaca, especially as a means to gather more confessions from genocide
suspects.[69]

---

[67] Author's inyangamugayo interviews, Kigali Ngali, Bugesera, 21 April 2009.
[68] Author's general fieldnotes, solidarity camp inauguration, 31 January 2003 (author's translation).
[69] *Ibid.*

By the second time I met Alphonse, he had become a highly respected member of the ingando community, identified by camp officials as a leader who could encourage other detainees to participate during lessons. Alphonse said that he had encouraged many detainees who had already confessed to admit to other crimes which they had hidden from prison and camp officials. 'It is better for people to tell the truth now', he said. 'Gacaca is only worrying for those who have hidden the truth.' Alphonse claimed that he personally had no fear of gacaca. 'I'm innocent of all crimes', he said, 'and my neighbours know me. I'm sure they will pardon me.' He said that gacaca would be important for 'solving high and low problems' concerning national and personal issues, and that gacaca would encourage Hutu and Tutsi to live together again, 'as they did in the past'.[70]

When I met Alphonse for the third time, several weeks later in the marketplace south-west of Nyamata where I also interviewed Cypriet, he had been released from the Gashora camp and expressed similar optimism as before. Alphonse claimed to have met many survivors in Nyamata and his current community: 'I sought them out, we talked for a very long time and they bought me drinks', he said. The ingando lessons, he argued, had been important for teaching him how to cohabit with survivors and that 'if everyone respects the local leaders, then we will live together in peace.' Alphonse said that he felt calm about facing his community at gacaca. 'Gacaca has not yet started here', he said,

> but I am ready to testify … Gacaca will start after the [Constitutional] referendum … I will tell the truth and the victims will forgive me. There is no question about that. I expect only good things at gacaca, no more punishment, just cohabitation.[71]

Alphonse said that, since returning to his home community, he had helped local authorities locate the mass grave where his victims were buried. The officials were now busy investigating his crimes. Alphonse repeated that he had been forced to kill and therefore he would not be sent back to prison. 'My worry today is not gacaca', he said. 'I have already been punished for what I did. My only worry is that I want to start a business here but I'm still waiting for the capital. My family has to support me and they are very poor.' His father and one older brother, both Hutu,

---

[70] Author's solidarity camp interviews, Gashora (no. 12) (author's translation).
[71] Author's detainee follow-up interviews, Alphonse, Kigali Ngali, Bugesera, 18 May 2003 (author's translation).

were killed during the genocide – later, when we had developed greater rapport, Alphonse told me who he believed had killed them, as discussed below – meaning that, with Alphonse in prison, the family had lost their three primary breadwinners, plunging them into deep poverty. Like Cypriet, Alphonse's family had also incurred great expense by moving to a house on the outskirts of community, ensuring he would not have to live close to genocide survivors after returning from ingando.[72]

I interviewed several survivors who lived near Alphonse's new house. They admitted to feeling uneasy about his presence in the community. 'We knew the people he killed in 1994', said Chantal, a forty-six-year-old woman whose parents and two cousins had been murdered during the genocide. 'He has just come to live in that house. We don't know why he has moved here but it worries us, as he has done many bad things.'[73] Zephyr, a thirty-three-year-old man who fled to Tanzania during the genocide and returned to the community in 1999, said,

> I knew Alphonse before the genocide – I used to see him often in the marketplace where he worked. But you cannot describe what he did [in 1994]. It is as though it was a different man from the one I knew. I never knew him well but that was a different man, the one who did those things … Now he is back living here and I am not sure what to think about that.[74]

On a Sunday morning in June 2006, I found Alphonse at a Catholic church several kilometres from where I had met him three years earlier. Some children ran ahead into the church to alert him to my presence and he came out to greet me. Alphonse took me to a small adobe building nearby and after the church service five nuns joined us. He said we would soon talk about his experiences since I had last seen him, but first we had to eat. Two other nuns brought pots of rice, beans, okra and stringy pieces of beef and a large calabash of banana beer, which was passed around the table. After the meal, the nuns left Alphonse and me alone. Alphonse said we should visit his home and we walked for fifteen minutes down red dirt paths that wound through banana palms and bright, yellow-flowered acacia trees until we reached a deeply rutted track that sloped upward to his house.[75]

---

[72] *Ibid.* (author's translation).
[73] Author's survivor interviews, Chantal, Kigali Ngali, Bugesera, 18 May 2003.
[74] Author's survivor interviews, Zephyr, Kigali Ngali, Bugesera, 18 May 2003.
[75] Author's detainee follow-up interviews, Alphonse, Kigali Ngali, Bugesera, 11 June 2006.

After greeting Alphonse's mother, two brothers, his sister-in-law and several nieces and nephews, he and I went inside and sat on low stools in a back room. Alphonse said that his family was facing great hardship. Since we had last met, one of his younger brothers had died, further depleting the number of male workers in the family. 'That was in 2003', Alphonse said,

> and things started to get very hard. There were several marriages in the family and, as you know, marriages cost money. There were times when we didn't have enough to eat. I contacted friends who couldn't help us because they also lacked the means. In 2004, our farm began producing again and we had enough to eat, although the drought was bad and many crops died. We survived – the local authorities advised us how to survive … In 2005, I discovered a younger brother whom I hadn't seen in years and he advised me to start a business, like the one I used to run. But I didn't have the money to start this, so I'm still farming … I've had to look after the children of my brother who died because last year their mother died of AIDS and they have become my responsibility … Slowly, little by little, I'm solving my problems but it is very difficult.[76]

Alphonse explained again that his family had moved house in 2003 to get away from genocide survivors who were threatening him, including harassing him in the market and throwing rocks on his roof during the night. 'Many of my friends are survivors', he said,

> but at first even some of them were scared of me [when I came back from jail]. They wondered if the government was trustworthy when it said that the prisoners should come back to the community … Many people died here in 1994 and many people are still scared because of the returned prisoners. The survivors are worried and they don't believe that things can be peaceful again. Many of them live together now in new houses because the government has built these houses for survivors … Some survivors have been seeking revenge. Some of them have killed our families and we don't know why those perpetrators haven't been sent to jail … I know some of these survivors don't want Hutu on the hills … The government helps the survivors but not other ethnic groups.[77]

Alphonse stood and beckoned me to a window in an adjacent room. 'You see that house over there?' he said, pointing through the banana palms to another mud-brick home about 50 metres away. He explained that in the house lived an elderly lady named Muteteli, the mother of

---

[76] *Ibid.*   [77] *Ibid.*

two children whom he had killed during the genocide. He said that, in an attempt to get away from the survivors near the marketplace, it was preferable to live even this close to Muteteli because she was too old to threaten him. Alphonse said he rarely spoke to her, even though they tilled the same plot of maize crop. He took me outside and we walked for five minutes down a thin, sloping path with maize and banana plants high on both sides. When we reached Alphonse's farm, he explained, 'She starts working in the soil from that end and I start from this end. Because she is older than me, she works quite slowly. When we work, we say very little.' I asked him whether there was palpable tension between them. He replied, 'Yes, it's difficult between us. But what choice do we have? She's the head of her household and I'm the head of mine. It's our responsibility to work so we can feed our families ... We don't talk about the past because we have to feed our families.'[78]

Alphonse described crucial instances, however, when he and Muteteli had been forced to talk about the past. He explained that on three occasions, after they had worked together all week on their field, they had gone to gacaca on the Sunday morning and Muteteli had stood to testify against him regarding the murder of her children. 'It was hard', he said. 'Each time that she tried to speak, she couldn't. The judges would ask her to speak and she would cry.' At each of the three hearings, the judges told Alphonse to respond to Muteteli's testimony; each time he had said that she was speaking the truth. The morning after each gacaca, Alphonse and Muteteli returned to their land and continued working as they had previously.[79] Later that day, after I had spoken to Alphonse, I visited Muteteli to request an interview, but she said that she was not willing to speak to me.

Alphonse described the overall experience of gacaca in the community as difficult. He said that personally gacaca had been positive so far, owing largely to his good relationship with the gacaca judges in his community. For others, though, gacaca had not been so straightforward. 'Many people tell lies at gacaca, the suspects as well as the survivors', Alphonse said. 'I've always told the truth since coming back [from prison] and I've told others to tell the truth but not everyone does.' Nevertheless, the dossiers of evidence collected from detainees' confessions in prison and transferred to the gacaca judges, along with the judges' deliberations

[78] Ibid.   [79] Ibid.

with the general assembly during gacaca hearings, had unearthed most cases of false evidence. Alphonse said,

> Many suspects keep saying that they have no reason to confess. They say things like, 'I was sick during the genocide, I wasn't there.' But eventually the truth comes out because someone will refute them. A lot of new people have been identified [as genocide suspects]. Some of them were even in mass today. Some others have hidden in Kigali and the judges are trying to bring them back.[80]

From his conversations with the inyangamugayo, Alphonse believed that he would not face further punishment for his crimes, given the time he had already spent in jail; at worst, he would have to participate in community service. 'I'm hoping my punishment is already over', he said. 'All of those crimes were caused by the authorities. They were caused by the bad leaders who forced people to kill … It's true that some people killed by themselves without any force [from the authorities] but most people, like me, were forced to kill.' Alphonse said that the wait for his gacaca sentence was deeply unsettling but he remained positive about the future:

> Things will get better soon. The population will tell the truth and the judges will judge people according to the law … The government says that it wants reconciliation but first it must stop the survivors who want revenge. There are many survivors who want to attack those who have come back from prison. It's possible there will be new problems between different groups but I think things will start to improve soon.[81]

Alphonse said that one source of major tension at gacaca was the fact that Hutu were unable to seek justice for crimes committed against their loved ones during and after the genocide. It was at this point that Alphonse told me that the RPF had killed his father and brother a month after the genocide ended. 'Some friends found their bodies lying on the road, far from our old house', he said. 'RPF soldiers had come through the marketplace and were on all the roads … I've seen the same soldiers come back here, even this year. It's like they're mocking us.' Alphonse said that several of his nieces and nephews had raised the issue of his father's and brother's deaths during gacaca hearings but the judges and some members of the general assembly responded angrily that these were

---

[80] *Ibid.*   [81] *Ibid.*

irrelevant cases for gacaca because they did not concern genocide crimes against Tutsi.[82]

I returned to interview Alphonse in his home in September 2008, by which time he had been sentenced by gacaca. As he predicted, he received only six months of community service for the crimes he had confessed but, to his great surprise, he was found guilty of aiding an additional murder. 'Some survivors invented this story', he said.

> You remember I told you before that many survivors have been looking for revenge? They were angry that gacaca wouldn't send me back to prison and they gave false testimony that I had been with others when they killed a man down there in the valley. I thought the judges would just laugh at them. Those judges know me well and they know what I did [during the genocide]. But Ibuka put pressure on them and they decided that I was guilty and should go back to prison for three years ... Most of the judges have good experience but others have less and some of them also tell lies. I said I hadn't received good justice, so I appealed my case.[83]

Alphonse appealed to the sector-level gacaca and marshalled a group of survivors to testify on his behalf. He also appealed against the cell-level gacaca's original decision to sentence him to one year's community service for his confessed crimes, on grounds of his early confession and the time he had already spent in prison. After his appeal, the sector-level judges quashed the charges against him of aiding murder and reduced his sentence for the remaining crimes to six months' community service. 'The problem [at the cell level]', he said, 'was that people didn't know the law. Many people were looking for revenge and the authorities were pressuring them ... These people needed the law to guide them. At the appeals hearing, things were better because people knew the law.' Alphonse said there were two main barriers to discovering the truth at gacaca: members of Ibuka who pressured people in the community to give false testimony and coerced judges to accept this and people who had returned to the community after lengthy periods away – especially Tutsi who had fled the country during the genocide or Tutsi who had never lived in the community before – who Alphonse said gave false evidence at gacaca because they could not have known what happened during the genocide.[84]

---

[82] Ibid.

[83] Author's detainee follow-up interviews, Alphonse, Kigali Ngali, Bugesera, 9 September 2008 (author's translation).

[84] Ibid.

Overall, Alphonse said, people in the community were satisfied with gacaca, believing that it had handed down reasonable sentences, accounting for the lengthy periods that most suspects had already spent in jail. Nevertheless, he said that some individuals had been convicted and sentenced to very long prison terms, including a close friend of his who had been sentenced to thirty years in Muhanga Prison. Alphonse said that some families in the community had written to the Executive Secretary of the NSGJ regarding the harsh sentences being delivered by the local gacaca judges; they were still awaiting a reply. 'Gacaca has been good here', Alphonse said,

> because most of the detainees are now back with their families. Some have gone back to jail but most are here now and working on their farms again. But there are many people who don't like gacaca. They liked it at the beginning but they have lost faith in the judges ... I blame Ibuka. Things were fine at gacaca and we were talking like family until Ibuka became involved. Ibuka has been pushing gacaca not to release detainees, even if they are innocent. Ibuka members come to hearings and encourage lies. How would they know anything? Most of those people were hiding in the bushes [during the genocide]. They saw nothing ... There's always a change during [the genocide commemorations in] April. Ibuka stirs up trouble, going around saying that this person killed that many Tutsi and should beg the survivors for forgiveness. These problems sometimes last until July.[85]

Alphonse also believed that Ibuka would complicate gacaca's ability to prosecute Category 1 cases after the recent change in the Gacaca Law: 'The judges for the Category 1 cases have already been vetted by Ibuka, so it will be their process. In this sector, five of the judges are definitely chosen by Ibuka, so my conclusion is that gacaca can't work for those cases.'

While many families of genocide suspects were pleased that gacaca had enabled their loved ones to return home, Alphonse said, they still saw gacaca as a one-sided process that ignored crimes committed against Hutu during and after the genocide. 'When people heard that the Category 1 cases were coming to gacaca', Alphonse said, 'some Hutu women complained of rape during the genocide and the attacks on them but the judges just ignored them. At gacaca, Tutsi women can talk about rape but not Hutu women.'

[85] Ibid.

Alphonse described relations among returned detainees, survivors and their respective families as generally calm:

> We live and work together. There is a sense of unity here but it is still limited. People haven't really reconciled … I find dealing with survivors very easy because they know me. They visit me and I visit them. Sometimes people say negative things about me but not very often.[86]

I interviewed the same survivors in the community as I had in 2003. In the main, they echoed Alphonse's depiction of local relations. 'There is no open conflict here', said Zephyr, the survivor quoted above,

> but everything has changed. It isn't like before, when we worked closely together, when Hutu and Tutsi intermarried and Hutu children were considered Tutsi children. People are more careful … Many people think the perpetrators should have been punished more. They see them come back from TIG and they say, 'Is that the end of justice for them?'[87]

Chantal, also quoted above, said, 'There is no reconciliation here. There is no more violence but there isn't reconciliation. Even in church, Hutu sit on one side and Tutsi on the other … When we go to gacaca, the Hutu families sit there and the Tutsi families sit here.' Chantal echoed Zephyr's concerns regarding the punishments handed down to many convicted perpetrators. 'We all know the prisoners can't go back to jail. The jails are still full, and we need the prisoners here to work on the farms. But if you kill people, if you kill six or seven people, and you spend only six or seven months doing TIG, that isn't right. The inyangamugayo should have been stricter with the guilty ones.'[88]

Alphonse stated that the introduction of the abunzi system in his sector had proven useful for the resolution of day-to-day disputes, which would typically remain unresolved because people could not afford to take their cases to the national courts. 'The people I know who have used the abunzi have said the process was very effective', he said. 'One time I wrote a submission for the abunzi to use in a family dispute and the abunzi appreciated that.'

Alphonse's hopes for the future had not diminished, despite his family's economic and emotional hardship. He said that he hoped one day to marry, build a house and buy a motorcycle. He had helped create an association of thirty-five local farmers who started a microfinance

---

[86] *Ibid.*

[87] Author's survivor interviews, Zephyr, Kigali Ngali, Bugesera, 9 September 2008.

[88] Author's survivor interviews, Chantal, Kigali Ngali, Bugesera, 9 September 2008.

scheme and were 'getting a little money from this'. The association had
been disrupted, however, by preparations for the upcoming parliamentary elections, which entailed regular rallies that all adult members
of the community were required to attend. Alphonse said that, even
though he was angry at the RPF for killing his father and brother, he
had – for the sake of expediency – decided to become a member of the
RPF political wing. 'I've become a member like so many others who
were sensitised to join en masse', Alphonse said. 'The survivors who
carry out revenge killings here don't like the RPF. They say the government does nothing and they have to take care of things for themselves … In this sector, if you're not RPF, you're considered against the
state and you risk yourself, especially if you belong to the PSD [Social
Democratic Party].' Alphonse laughed again and pointed to the corner
of the room. 'The RPF even gave me that hat and told me to sensitise
others. The RPF stopped the genocide and they started gacaca but we
still have big problems here. But, as I said, if you don't vote RPF, you
risk yourself. People will only vote RPF by force. It's not real democracy
here.'[89]

When I returned to Alphonse's home in April 2009, he was away at
his farm and I sat on a wooden bench in the family courtyard waiting for
him. His sister-in-law sat on a low stool out the front of the house, sifting
beans in a large steel bowl. By the time Alphonse arrived, his sister-in-
law was cooking in a small wood-and-chicken-wire enclosure adjoining
the house and smoke was billowing into the courtyard. Alphonse took
me around the back of the house and showed me the cow that his family
had recently acquired. He said on average the cow produced four litres of
milk each day and, because the eight members of his household required
only two litres per day, neighbours were constantly coming by to ask for
a share. 'Many things have happened since the last time you were here',
Alphonse said. 'We have made a little money from the farmers' association and that is why we have the cow. Our farm has done well, so we
now produce more maize, corn and sweet potatoes than we need and
there is always a little to sell.' Alphonse said he had become the leader of
the farmers' microfinance cooperative, which now boasted seventy-eight
members. This, however, was not the biggest development in Alphonse's
life: 'I am engaged and will be married in August', he said, beaming.
'I'm building a new house near this one so that my wife and I will have

---

[89] Author's detainee follow-up interviews, Alphonse, 9 September 2008 (author's translation).

somewhere to live. Building a house costs a lot of money but this is what a husband must do. It means there is no money for starting a proper business, like a shop in the market, but a wife and a house come first and maybe there will be a business later.'[90]

Alphonse recalled our conversations about gacaca and abunzi the year before and said that the trends he had identified then had continued. For him personally, the gacaca journey had ended because he had completed his community service. On a broader scale, though, gacaca was creating problems in the community. Alphonse said that, generally, gacaca had dealt effectively with Category 2 crimes, sending few convicted perpetrators back to prison and using community service to improve local roads and build new communal stalls in the central market. However, significant difficulties had arisen during Category 1 and 3 cases. 'There are big problems with the Category 1 suspects', Alphonse said. 'They tell only lies and they never confess to what they did during the genocide. This leaves the rest of us to deal with the consequences. We all had to confess to what we did and now we hear these authorities at gacaca saying only, "It was the Tutsi who killed the President [Habyarimana]. We did nothing".' Alphonse said that during the genocide he had spent several weeks in Gitarama and he had seen some of the authorities from his sector telling the local people, 'You see those houses? Go and kill the Tutsi.'

Alphonse claimed that gacaca's handling of Category 3 cases regarding property crimes had proven highly divisive in the community. 'The judges have been asking many people to pay compensation for the property they stole in 1994. But then many survivors start asking for ten times as much property as they had then.' Alphonse picked up a stick from the ground and traced the calculations on his arm.

> Some people lost their house during the genocide and now they ask for 2 million francs. Two million! Or they claim they should receive five goats when everyone knows they only had one. The Christians here are more honest but most survivors just tell lies. They demand compensation for almost everything – cows, beans, windows, tables, everything. But people here are very poor. The prisoners come home and their families have nothing, so how can they give compensation?[91]

[90] Author's detainee follow-up interviews, Alphonse, Kigali Ngali, Bugesera, 21 April 2009 (author's translation).
[91] *Ibid.*

As in 2008, Alphonse said that gacaca was suffering from widespread false testimony. He believed he heard more truthful evidence when he was an urumuri during prison gacaca in Rilima in 1998 than in most official gacaca hearings in his community. He said that feelings of anger and revenge were also hampering gacaca, particularly in the climate of the current commemorations of the fifteenth anniversary of the genocide. 'I could see the change in people's attitudes when I started testifying at gacaca', Alphonse said. 'I could see the vengeance in the survivors' eyes and they started saying incredible things, inventing stories about me.' Many Hutu in the community believed that their own suffering during the genocide was being ignored at gacaca hearings and nationwide during the official memorial month. 'Everyone commemorates quietly here. They go to the meetings at the sector office. If they disagree with anything, they shut their mouth for fear of going to prison … The Hutu people here say, "I need commemoration for *my* family during the period of revenge [after the genocide]". People are asking when *their* commemoration will happen.'[92] Alphonse said that he continued to see military officers walking around the community who had committed crimes against Hutu in the months after the genocide. He said that some officers had moved into the homes of Hutu who had fled as refugees into neighbouring countries after the genocide or had fled from gacaca into Burundi and Tanzania.

Alphonse summarised the community's variable experience of gacaca as follows:

> Gacaca has done a good job of connecting many crimes to the people who committed them. In those cases it has helped people reconcile. For many people here, their relations are better. They live and work together and there are no disputes. But not everyone has had this. Gacaca has sometimes made things worse.

As in 2008, Alphonse said that the introduction of abunzi into the community had helped resolve everyday disputes. 'People no longer have to go to the higher courts', he said. 'The abunzi are good for reconciliation and they influence people to do positive things.' However, Alphonse said that many of the continuing antagonisms driven by people's experiences at gacaca penetrated too deeply into their

---

[92] *Ibid.* (interviewee's emphasis).

lives for the abunzi to have any lasting impact on relations in the community.[93]

INITIAL OBSERVATIONS FROM DETAINEE NARRATIVES

These narratives of Laurent, Cypriet and Alphonse provide important insights into the personal issues that suspects face along the gacaca journey and some of the wider questions facing detainees and their communities generally. I outline only brief observations from these narratives here, then draw on them in more detail in later chapters. At the outset, the narratives of the three returned detainees show that suspects come from a range of backgrounds, having varying levels of education and types of occupations. Many suspects themselves lost family members during the genocide and, after many years in prison, now consider their fellow inmates as close friends or, in some cases, as substitute family. Detainees often face economic hardship after they are released as they return to families impoverished by the loss of breadwinners who either died during the genocide or have been in prison for many years.

In the ingando, Laurent, Cypriet and Alphonse expressed different expectations of the reception they would experience upon returning to their home communities. Cypriet and Alphonse expected a warm welcome, while Laurent was uncertain of the future, due largely to the fact that so many of his friends and family were killed during the genocide. Their expectations of community reactions heavily influenced the level of involvement they had with their neighbours, and particularly with survivors, after their return. Alphonse claimed to have talked and drunk with many survivors, while Laurent said that he had spoken to very few survivors. All three detainees, however, did not return to live in their old homes, moving instead to houses on the outskirts of their communities, to avoid confronting survivors every day. In my observations of communities to which provisionally released suspects returned, the movement of suspects and their families out of the sight of the community was extremely common.[94] Over time, Laurent and Cypriet in particular experienced difficult relations with genocide survivors, some of whom in

---

[93] Ibid.
[94] Author's general fieldnotes, 14 May 2003, 18–20 May 2003.

turn expressed fear or disquiet at the return of genocide suspects to the community.

The three detainees' expectations of their community's reception shaped their initial views on the prospects for reconciliation. Cypriet and Alphonse expected warm welcomes and therefore believed that it would be easy for perpetrators and survivors to live together again. Alphonse argued that local leaders would encourage peaceful cohabitation. Laurent, however, appeared to have the initial views of detainees such as Cypriet and Alphonse in mind when he argued, 'We need reconciliation without sentimentality. Reconciliation doesn't come from the sky.' Laurent was uncertain of the reception he would gain in his community and was therefore cautious about wider prospects of achieving reconciliation. There is a crucial contradiction in Cypriet's and Alphonse's claims that cohabitation can be easily facilitated after the genocide, given that, immediately after their release from the camps, they moved their households away from survivors. One irony of these narratives is that Laurent, who of the three detainees expressed the most hard-headed, pragmatic view of what reconciliation requires, did not expect – and perhaps did not want – to experience reconciliation, preferring life in prison where he felt among friends and surrogate family. Over time, however, Cypriet and Alphonse came to similar conclusions as Laurent regarding the difficulties of reconciliation, particularly after they had experienced fraught contact with genocide survivors.

Laurent, Cypriet and Alphonse all initially avoided attending gacaca and awaited summonses to hearings. They each said that gacaca was slow to begin in their communities. Each of them was anxious to have his case heard quickly but was resigned to a lengthy wait. The three detainees expressed generally positive views of gacaca, before and after their release from ingando. However, they expected very different outcomes from gacaca. Both Cypriet and Alphonse argued that gacaca would exonerate them: Alphonse because he claimed to have been forced to commit murder during the genocide and Cypriet because he claimed that he was only in a group of killers and that he himself was innocent. Both Cypriet and Alphonse argued – in line with their lessons in ingando – that the authorities had forced people to kill. They went beyond the teaching in the camps, though, by implying that this manipulation by elites absolved perpetrators of responsibility for their crimes. In contrast to Cypriet and Alphonse, Laurent expected gacaca to find him guilty and to send him back to prison. Contrary to their expectations, Cypriet and Alphonse were both found guilty at gacaca and sentenced to community service, although only Alphonse served his sentence, while Cypriet was deemed too old to participate in community work programmes. Cypriet and Alphonse both described the problem of false testimony at gacaca, although Alphonse stressed the importance of gacaca's appeals process for eventually discovering the truth about genocide crimes.

Given how bleakly he viewed his personal circumstances in the wider society, Laurent suggested that it would be beneficial to return to jail, where he had left his friends and where he would receive food, clothing and shelter from the government. For reasons of poverty, Cypriet also viewed the future with uncertainty and a degree of trepidation. Of the three detainees, only Alphonse expressed any sustained optimism about life outside of prison. Alphonse's optimism stemmed largely from his hope that his business background would bring him financial prosperity, and from his belief that his community would exonerate him at gacaca and allow him to return to something resembling his life before the genocide. By 2009, Cypriet's perspective on the future had remained generally the same, while Alphonse remained optimistic, particularly given his impending marriage and his family's improved material circumstances. I explore many aspects of these detainees' experiences – especially Alphonse's views on the lack of justice for RPF crimes – in later chapters.

CONCLUSION

The purpose of this chapter is to pave the way for a closer interpretation of gacaca's objectives and a critical analysis of its success so far in the following chapters. Understanding the nature of detainees' journeys toward gacaca, starting in prison and travelling to their home communities, is important for comprehending some of their key experiences and personal developments as they face justice through gacaca. The ingando are especially important for understanding the ideas about Rwandan history, the genocide, gacaca, and justice and reconciliation generally that the government imparts to detainees and the wider community. As subsequent chapters will show, however, the government's mishandling of key stages of the gacaca journey – particularly its lack of explanation to the community of why and how detainees would be provisionally released and suspects' lack of preparation for often fractious returns home – created unnecessary confusion and tensions in many places, thus dulling gacaca's effectiveness. The narratives in this chapter highlight that people's personal, emotional experiences have a significant impact on their participation in nationwide processes of justice and reconciliation such as gacaca. Given the central role that genocide suspects play in these processes, the ways in which the gacaca journey affects them will also affect their communities and consequently the entire post-genocide reconstruction process.

CHAPTER 5

GACACA'S MODUS OPERANDI: ENGAGEMENT THROUGH POPULAR PARTICIPATION

INTRODUCTION

The purpose of this chapter is to explore different sources' interpretations of gacaca's methods, while the following chapters focus on gacaca's objectives and how effectively it has pursued them. The first part of this chapter examines the ways in which *popular participation* is viewed by many sources as the modus operandi – and a principal virtue – of gacaca; a view opposed by many proponents of the dominant discourse on gacaca for whom only a formal, rather than a popular participatory, approach to transitional institutions is appropriate. The theme of popular participation is vital to our understanding of gacaca, given the high percentage of the Rwandan adult population that has personally engaged in the process, including attending hearings and providing first-hand evidence. Among transitional justice processes internationally, gacaca is unique in its direct involvement of such large numbers of civilians, many of whom have personally experienced mass conflict. The second part of this chapter contends that a central component of gacaca's modus operandi of popular participation is the need to foster genuine *engagement* between parties previously in conflict in order to rebuild fractured personal and communal relationships. As we shall see in later chapters, engagement is central to understanding how gacaca attempts to fulfil multiple legal and non-legal objectives simultaneously.

This chapter follows a structure that continues in Chapters 6–10: it outlines the Rwandan government's, the population's and commentators' perspectives on the given theme – in this case, popular participation – followed by a critical analysis of those perspectives. The purpose of the sections exploring official, popular and observer views is to analyse gacaca from multiple angles in order to gain the deepest possible understanding of its function and different parties' expectations of it. The critique of these three groups' views involves two dimensions of analysis: an inward dimension that focuses on the concepts and themes within the different perspectives and particularly whether such views are internally consistent and convincing; and an empirical dimension, comparing these views with the practice of gacaca, interpreted according to my observations of hearings and community interactions and interviews with participants.

MODUS OPERANDI OF GACACA: POPULAR PARTICIPATION

The central role that gacaca affords the population in the daily running and shaping of the institution is one of its most striking and controversial features. Many critics of gacaca have questioned the wisdom of allowing a traumatised and still heavily ethnically divided population to drive the country's main transitional process through its electing judges, instigating cases, providing evidence, determining the guilt or innocence of suspects and engaging in open, wide-ranging dialogue during hearings. Most transitional justice institutions around the world, whether war-crimes tribunals, truth commissions or variations of these bodies, seek, consciously or otherwise, to limit the population's involvement. The rationale for this exclusion is a belief that people emerging from mass conflict will have personally inflicted or suffered extreme trauma or grief and therefore will be too driven by their own experiences, desires and prejudices to help reconstruct the nation.[1] Consequently, the argument goes, outside parties – whether elites within the conflict society itself who may not have been caught up so directly in the violence or foreign bodies such as the UN – should be commissioned to plan and manage transitional processes. External facilitators are assumed to be more impartial in their attempts to formulate fair and effective long-term remedies to conflict.

At gacaca, the general population plays a very different role than in most transitional institutions. As I argued in Chapter 3, the underlying

---

[1] Recall from Chapter 2 that some participants in the Urugwiro negotiations in 1998 and 1999 voiced similar concerns about the proposed use of gacaca to deal with genocide crimes.

philosophy of modern gacaca draws on the ethos of the traditional version by recognising the importance of the community's ownership over, and direct involvement in, the process. Broadly speaking, most participants in gacaca interpret popular participation as the means by which gacaca pursues other objectives such as truth, justice and reconciliation. Few non-Rwandan commentators, most of whom express a version of the dominant discourse on gacaca, explicitly discuss popular participation and, where they do, they are normally highly critical of it. As already suggested, these commentators' emphasis on gacaca as a set of legal statutes to be analysed rather than as a social practice to be observed and assessed does not require an in-depth consideration of popular participation. Where proponents of the dominant discourse on gacaca do consider this theme, it is generally to critique the level of public involvement in, and the removal of external actors such as lawyers from, gacaca. This chapter argues that such criticisms of popular participation in gacaca are misguided.

Government's perspectives on popular participation in gacaca

The government's interpretations of popular involvement in gacaca emphasise its importance for facilitating relatively immediate goals, while also conveying a wider ideology concerning the roots of conflict in Rwanda and the need for a stronger sense of national unity. The government's perspective of popular participation draws heavily on the traditional version of gacaca, in which it was an ad-hoc institution upon which the local community called whenever conflicts arose. Before the colonial period, the local population rather than community leaders instigated gacaca hearings and the community participated directly in resolving local problems. The government portrays gacaca as fulfilling a similar purpose in the post-genocide environment. Fatuma Ndangiza, the Executive Secretary of the NURC, describes gacaca as 'a form of justice originating from and serving Rwandan culture' and a demonstration of 'Rwandans' ability to manage their [own] conflicts'.[2] One primary way in which the government has encouraged popular participation in gacaca has been to emphasise the population's ownership over a practice with which, officials argue, Rwandans are deeply familiar. According to this view, gacaca has proven effective in resolving conflicts in the past because the entire community has been involved in hearings. Gacaca

---

[2] F. Ndangiza, 'Transitional Justice and Reconciliation', p.7.

can therefore only succeed if the entire Rwandan population takes responsibility for achieving the expressed aims of the process.

Part of the government's discourse concerning the need to draw on Rwandan history to solve current problems emphasises – as we saw in Chapter 4 in the official lessons in the ingando and detainees' attitudes along the gacaca journey – the need to regain a sense of 'national unity' that colonial regimes and past 'manipulative' governments destroyed. As this and subsequent chapters highlight, the argument concerning the need to regain a lost sense of unity is a key component of the government's (and many detainees') views on most of gacaca's objectives.[3] Ndangiza argues that gacaca aims 'not to administer the classical system of justice, but to re-establish harmony and to bring citizens who were manipulated to commit crimes by the state intelligentsia, back to the right path'.[4] Underlying this perspective is the idea that the Rwandan people embody certain virtues, such as unity and social harmony, that previous leaders undermined. By reactivating and revitalising gacaca, the government argues that it will help the population rediscover these virtues.

The government regularly identifies the forms of dialogue and consensual decision-making practised at gacaca as means towards fostering more unified interactions in daily life. The theme of popular participation also gives a crucial insight into how the government explains the causes of the genocide to the population and how these sources of division and conflict should be quelled. The government blames 'outsiders' for creating divisions in Rwandan society by 'turning [Rwandan] tradition ... on [its] head' and propagating what Patrick Mazimpaka, then-presidential envoy to the Great Lakes, calls 'anti-values' in Rwandan society that require 'counter-values'.[5] The government argues that these outsiders are either the colonial administrators who sought to divide the community and to favour particular groups for their own political gain, or past Hutu leaders who actively excluded Tutsi from positions of influence and incited violence against them. Aloisea Inyumba describes the former interpretation of 'outsiders' when she claims, 'divisions were sown among Rwandans little by little by white people just as if a farmer sows his

[3] I do not consider unity as a separate objective of gacaca in this book because, as I will show, the government essentially conflates unity, which I consider to be an unconvincing aim, with reconciliation, which I argue is a legitimate objective of gacaca.

[4] F. Ndangiza, 'Transitional Justice and Reconciliation', p.4.

[5] Mazimpaka, 'Reconciliation and Democratization Processes', pp. 19, 23.

seeds'.[6] The latter view finds expression in the introduction to the Gacaca Law, which states that a major purpose of gacaca is to reconstitute 'the Rwandan Society that had been destroyed by bad leaders who incited the population into exterminating part of the Society'.[7] Ndangiza colourfully describes all Rwandans as needing to 'build within themselves a renewed sense of Rwandan nationality, in lieu of the fake identities derived of late from deforming mirrors', in which she considers external forces to be the main deformers of Rwandan identity.[8] Therefore, in order to overcome the divisions created by outsiders, Rwandans (i.e. 'insiders') must look to their own history and culture for solutions.

The government also views communal involvement in gacaca as a remedy to the failures of another group of 'outsiders': leaders of international institutions such as the ICTR, which are run by the same foreign governments that are perceived to have abandoned Rwanda during the genocide. The government views the ICTR as an expensive, ineffective institution that has little relevance for the population because it is so geographically removed, based in Tanzania, and because little justice has been carried out there, with only forty-five cases of those suspected of orchestrating the genocide heard to date, leading to thirty-eight convictions.[9] President Kagame argues that the ICTR

> has performed very poorly and consumed huge amounts of resources for doing very little ... The world is ready to keep wasting resources for doing nothing. The tribunal was not established to deal with the problem we are talking about, of genocide in Rwanda. It's dealing with paying huge salaries to UN workers or other individuals.[10]

Gacaca, on the other hand, the government argues, provides for the needs of Rwandans, thereby generating a greater sense of popular legitimacy, which is reinforced by the community's direct involvement in gacaca.

---

[6] A. Inyumba, 'Report on the Consultative Meetings Held at Grassroots Level by the Unity and Reconciliation Commission Executive Secretary' in NURC, *Report on the National Summit of Unity and Reconciliation*, 2000, p.41.

[7] Gacaca Law (Modified 2004), Introduction, p.2.

[8] F. Ndangiza, 'The Activities of the National Unity and Reconciliation Commission after the 2000 National Summit on Unity and Reconciliation', *Report of the National Summit on Unity and Reconciliation*, 2002, p.26.

[9] ICTR, official website, www.ictr.org.

[10] P. Kagame, interview with V. Brittain, 'The Arusha Tribunal Costs Too Much for Very Few Results', *African Geopolitics*, 11, summer 2003, www.african-geopolitics.org/show.aspx?ArticleId=3537.

Regarding the modalities of gacaca, the government argues that the general assembly constitutes the main participant during hearings. According to former Minister of Justice and Institutional Relations, Jean de Dieu Mucyo, '[T]he success of Gacaca largely depends on an active and unconditional participation by the population.'[11] Judges are on hand only to encourage what, as already quoted, Hannington Tayebwa from the Ministry of Justice calls 'facilitated problem-solving.'[12] From this standpoint, the general assembly should conduct an open discussion at gacaca hearings, in which judges act as facilitators. The government claims that its officials need to be involved in gacaca, though it rarely outlines what this should entail. 'Handling the Gacaca tribunals should be the business of the grassroots populations alone', argues Aloysie Cyanzayire, former Deputy Chief Justice of the Supreme Court and President of the Gacaca Commission. '[But] leaders, officials and workers should also be involved, especially in areas where they lived at the time of the 1994 genocide and massacres.'[13]

The Gacaca Law stipulates that the leaders charged with overseeing gacaca must not include lawyers. The primary rationale behind the exclusion of lawyers from all direct involvement in gacaca, and of groups such as police officers and clergy from being judges, is a desire to maintain the open, participatory spirit of gacaca. Individuals with specific expertise such as lawyers, the official argument goes, may dominate gacaca hearings and intimidate less-qualified participants. These elites should therefore be excluded from leadership roles in gacaca. 'There has been a major problem with elites confusing people', Ndangiza said in 2008, assessing gacaca's performance in terms of discovering the truth about genocide crimes. 'Much truth has come out and participation generally speaking has been high but elites participating in the process have been a problem. There has been low participation by elites and when they have participated, we have seen little truth come from them . . . There is a danger that they sophisticate everything and people get confused about what is going on.'[14] Such sentiments echo the concerns about Rwanda's history

---

[11] J. Mucyo, 'Minutes of the Symposium on Gacaca', Hotel Umubano, Kigali, 6–7 March 2000, p.11.

[12] Author's government interviews, Tayebwa, 30 January 2003.

[13] A. Cyanzayire, 'The Gacaca Tribunals: Reconciliatory Justice', *Report of the National Unity and Reconciliation Summit*, 2002, p.44.

[14] Author's government interviews, Fatuma Ndangiza, Executive Secretary, NURC, Kigali, 7 August 2008 (interview conducted jointly with Nicola Palmer).

of elite control over the population, which has led to discord and violence, and the need to invoke the more positive values considered inherent in the general population.

The government argues that giving fundamental control over the daily running of gacaca to the population will reinforce the popular understanding of traditional gacaca and fulfil the community's subsequent expectations of ownership over the current process. In turn, the population's ownership over gacaca is justified, the government claims, because the local population knows better than anyone what crimes were committed during the genocide and who is responsible for them. As Inyumba argues, 'The truth ... will be revealed since the people who witnessed the crimes being committed will give evidence.'[15] Augustin Nkusi, former Chief Legal Adviser to the Gacaca Commission and current Spokesperson for the Office of the Prosecutor General, states,

> At gacaca, the truth ultimately comes from the population. We know that people will tell who is responsible because they saw what [the perpetrators] did. They stood there as it happened and they saw everything with their own eyes. There will be no confusion about who is responsible for these things.[16]

If truth comes primarily from the population, the government argues, then gacaca should be organised to maximise communal participation in the pursuit and articulation of the truth.

Population's perspectives on popular participation in gacaca

The government's sustained discourse about the community's participation in gacaca has significantly influenced popular interpretations of gacaca's modus operandi. The popular perspective, among suspects, survivors and the wider population, echoes the official view of this theme, though without much of its nationalistic ideology. In particular, many Rwandans focus on the importance of engaging in dialogue during gacaca hearings and on the need for all members of the community to publicly discuss their experiences and concerns. As Alice, a gacaca judge in Buhoma district of Ruhengeri province, claims,

> Gacaca is important because it brings everyone together, to talk together. When we come together, we find unity ... Sometimes there is even too

---

[15] A. Inyumba, 'Restoring Human Dignity and Reconciling the People of Rwanda', *Media Development Index*, 4, 2001, www.wacc.org.uk/modules.php?name=News&file=print&sid=714.

[16] Author's government interviews, Nkusi, 2 February 2003.

much talking and I have to slow the people down. The women especially talk too much because they are used to talking much more than the men.[17]

Many everyday Rwandans believe that greater 'unity' is likely to result from this dialogue at gacaca, though they tend to describe this on a local rather than national level. Many Rwandans argue that parties at gacaca will carry this dialogue and the peaceful methods of conflict resolution embodied in the hearings into their everyday lives, leading to a greater sense of cohesion in previously fragmented communities. Many survivors view gacaca in a similar way to one man in Kigali Ville who described gacaca as a place where 'we all sit and talk like family'.[18] Valence, a forty-four-year-old genocide survivor in Bugesera, said, 'We use gacaca today in the way we always used it – to gather people to solve problems. The problem is the genocide and everything that happened here, not just in 1994 but even in earlier years, when there were many killings ... We talk at gacaca because we have to rebuild the family that has been broken apart.'[19]

This view of rebuilding a sense of 'family' in the community echoes the official argument that one likely outcome of gacaca will be the rediscovery of a lost sense of Rwandan unity. Like the traditional practice of gacaca and drawing largely on a notion of individual personhood as inextricably linked to communal identities, this perspective holds that the local population – essentially the 'family' to which individual community members belong – owns and runs gacaca in order to solve problems that arise within the family. Gacaca is thus interpreted as the search for internal solutions to internal problems. Recalling Alphonse's comments during the gacaca journey in the previous chapter, one of his frustrations with perceived Ibuka interference during gacaca hearings was that beforehand 'we were talking like family' and Ibuka's involvement stymied the community's interactions.

Various government and academic surveys in the early years of gacaca indicated widespread enthusiasm within the Rwandan population for active participation in hearings.[20] An important feature of several gacaca hearings observed by ASF is the extent to which some communities have instituted ad-hoc procedures to punish local people who fail to attend

[17] Author's gacaca interviews, Alice, Ruhengeri (author's translation).
[18] Author's survivor interviews, Boniface, Kigali Ville (author's translation).
[19] Author's survivor interviews, Valence, Kigali Ngali, Bugesera, 10 September 2008.
[20] NURC, 'Opinion Survey on Participation in Gacaca', Annexe 4, p.13.

gacaca hearings. In one cell in Kigali Ville, gacaca judges maintained a list of habitual absentees. In a cell in Kigali Ngali, the general assembly discussed whether it should impose fines on those who arrived late to hearings or failed to attend altogether.[21] PRI reports that some communities have discussed sanctioning the owners of bars and other businesses that open while gacaca hearings are underway.[22] While underlining the extent to which many members of the community do not attend gacaca, thus necessitating these punitive measures in the first place, such actions also display many Rwandans' view that the entire community should attend, and participate in, gacaca. In turn, these practices constitute one example of how local communities shape gacaca in ways that depart from the legal statutes and guiding principles outlined in the Gacaca Law or Gacaca Manual, which make no mention of punishment for absentees.

Meanwhile, a large section of the population expresses a degree of scepticism or fear of the level of interaction between antagonistic parties that gacaca entails. Marie-Claire, a survivor in Kigali Ngali whose husband and five children were killed during the genocide, said that she was fearful of meeting those who killed her loved ones. Therefore, she said, 'I won't go to gacaca unless I am forced to go.'[23] Several other survivors whom I interviewed expressed a similar reluctance to attend or participate in gacaca, either because they did not believe that it would benefit them in any way or because they feared publicly facing perpetrators.[24] Some family members of detainees said they did not expect to participate in gacaca hearings. 'It is hard for farmers to work and also go to gacaca', said Raoul, whose two brothers and two sisters were accused of committing genocide crimes. 'We are very poor and gacaca takes many hours.'[25] Jerôme, a sixty-three-year-old man in Kigali Ville whose three accused brothers were not among the released detainees, said, 'I am too old for gacaca. There is too much talking there. We should send the women to gacaca ... They will come back and tell us what is said.'[26]

---

[21] ASF gacaca reports, Kigali Ville, Kicukiro, Kagarama, Nyanza, 31 May 2003; Kigali Ngali, Rulindo, Rusagara, Nyamugari, 29 November 2002.

[22] PRI, 'Research on the Gacaca (Report V)', p.29.

[23] Author's survivor interviews, Marie-Claire, Kigali Ngali.

[24] Author's survivor interviews, Nathan, Kigali Ngali; Juliette, Kigali Ville; Augustin, Gisenyi, Gisenyi Ville, 23 May 2003.

[25] Author's general population interviews, Raoul, Kigali Ville, Kacyiru, 22 May 2003 (author's translation).

[26] Author's general population interviews, Jerôme, Kigali Ville, Kacyiru, 22 May 2003 (author's translation).

In contrast, some sources describe popular involvement at gacaca that are even more forceful than the government's own enthusiastic discourse. Whereas the official perspective tends to trumpet the personal and communal advantages of people's participation in gacaca, many Rwandans describe their involvement as fulfilling a duty to the government. This perspective manifests in practices such as some communities' sanction of absentees from gacaca but, more directly, in some individuals' descriptions of gacaca 'as doing the government's work'.[27] Many detainees in particular describe gacaca as 'helping the government solve the problems of the country'.[28] Here they do not articulate the personal or communal advantages of gacaca but rather their service to the state. Firmin, a detainee in the ingando in Gashora, admitted that he had confessed to committing genocide crimes because this was a way of 'helping the government fix the country's problems'.[29] Sylvain, a detainee recently released from the ingando in Gisenyi but whose two sons were still in prison, said, 'The government says we must go to gacaca, so we will go.'[30] It is realistic to expect that many people who express this version of participation as a duty do so not out of a genuine sense of loyalty to the government but rather out of fear that they may be branded as 'divisive' if they are not seen to support, or to participate fully in, gacaca. It is likely that many detainees who discuss participation in gacaca as a duty also do so in order to curry favour with government officials either in jail or in ingando to help facilitate their early release.

Commentators' perspectives on popular participation in gacaca

The critical literature on gacaca displays a wide range of views concerning popular participation in gacaca, from a focus on its facilitation of immediate objectives concerning the personal lives of participants to that of broader aims in the national political realm. Key differences emerge between the views of Rwandan and non-Rwandan commentators. While both camps generally agree that popular participation is the primary method by which gacaca operates, they disagree on its merits. Most Rwandan commentators express similar views to the government and the general population regarding the importance of the community's sense of ownership over gacaca. Non-Rwandan observers, on the

---

[27] Author's solidarity camp interviews, Kigali Ville (no. 4) (author's translation).

[28] Author's solidarity camp interviews, Ruhengeri (no. 7), 3 May 2003 (author's translation).

[29] Author's solidarity camp interviews, Gashora (no. 9), 18 April 2003 (author's translation).

[30] Author's general population interviews, Sylvain, Gisenyi, Gisenyi Ville, 23 May 2003 (author's translation).

other hand, are mostly critical of popular participation in gacaca and perceive in the community's central involvement a threat to legal due process and the protection of individual rights, especially for genocide suspects. Some non-Rwandan commentators also argue that the state plays a central role in the daily function of gacaca and therefore discussion of popular participation in the process is overstated.

First, Rwandan commentators express either a moderate or a far-ranging interpretation of popular participation in gacaca. In more moderate terms, Gasibirege argues that gacaca is above all a 'space for communication' where the population discusses their mutual concerns after the genocide.[31] Alice Karekezi, Alphonse Nshimiyimana and Beth Mutamba argue, 'The ability of gacaca to accomplish its goals of bringing justice, revealing the truth about the genocide, and contributing to reconciliation absolutely necessitates the strong participation of members of the local communities.'[32] Solomon Nsabiyera from World Vision argues that gacaca is important for 'overcoming the conspiracy of silence' that he believes prevails in Rwanda, as a result of survivors' reluctance to discuss traumatic experiences and because of continued animosity between Hutu and Tutsi.[33]

In the wider-ranging interpretation, some Rwandan commentators argue that mass involvement in gacaca increases the scope for popular decision-making within the community. They argue that public deliberations within gacaca influence the broader political realm by empowering previously disenfranchised citizens. Karekezi argues that gacaca encourages democratisation, empowering the population to engage with national issues in ways considered impossible before gacaca. The popular elections of gacaca judges in particular, she argues, 'represent an important moment for a population that was starting to think beyond the personal sphere', raising the question, 'could the general concern for the social reconstruction of Rwanda transcend people's particular interests?'[34] Gasibirege argues that, during the election of gacaca judges, the community came together in an unprecedented way and expressed

[31] Gasibirege, 'L'Élection des juges Inyangumagayo', p.102.
[32] A. Karekezi, A. Nshimiyimana and B. Mutamba, 'Localizing Justice: Gacaca Courts in Post-Genocide Rwanda', in E. Stover and H. Weinstein (eds.), My Neighbor, My Enemy: Justice and Community in the Aftermath of Mass Atrocity, Cambridge: Cambridge University Press, 2004, p.78.
[33] Author's observer interviews, Solomon Nsabiyera, Coordinator, Healing, Peace and Reconciliation Program, World Vision Rwanda, Kigali, 3 February 2003.
[34] Karekezi, 'Juridictions Gacaca', p. 89.

a belief in important virtues such as truth and justice as they chose judges who best embodied those values. The discussion of such virtues, Gasibirege argues, will have long-lasting effects on people's interactions in daily life and in the broader social and political realms.[35]

Karekezi argues that gacaca is especially likely to empower women who have otherwise been excluded from the most important social, cultural and political spheres at both the local and national levels.[36] In the past, women were excluded from being judges or providing testimony at gacaca. In the modernised institution, however, women play a key role both as leaders – constituting between 35 and 40 per cent of judges[37] – and general participants. From my observation of gacaca hearings between 2003 and 2010, women overall drive most discussions in the general assembly, expressing their views more forthrightly than men who often have to be cajoled into speaking.[38] Alice, the gacaca judge in Ruhengeri province quoted above, echoed this view when she said, 'Gacaca is important because it brings everyone together … The women especially talk too much because they are used to talking much more than the men.'[39] For Rwandan commentators such as Karekezi and Gasibirege, this increased popular involvement is not only important for the pursuit of particular aims within the confines of gacaca but also for greater popular participation in public life more broadly.

While some observers express great enthusiasm for mass participation in gacaca, many commentators – especially non-Rwandan proponents of the dominant discourse on gacaca – are sceptical of it. Many human-rights lawyers express doubts over the ability of a traumatised, divided population to make the sorts of careful, impartial decisions necessary for gacaca to fulfil its objectives. How, these critics ask, can genocide suspects and survivors – each group with its own set of needs and prejudices – be expected to pursue broader aims of accountability and social reconstruction?

---

[35] Gasibirege, 'L'Élection des juges inyangumagayo', p.107.

[36] Karekezi, 'Juridictions gacaca', p.78. Aloisea Inyumba, Executive Secretary of the NURC, echoes Karekezi, saying, 'The heart of … gacaca will be women' (A. Inyumba, quoted in J. Ciabattari, 'Rwanda Gambles on Renewal, Not Revenge', *Women's E-News*, 9 October 2000, www.womensenews.org/article.cfm/dyn/aid/301/context).

[37] Author's observer interviews, Klaas de Jonge, Research Coordinator, PRI, Kigali, 29 January 2003; Author's Government Interviews, Ndangiza, 10 June 2006.

[38] Author's summary from gacaca fieldnotes.

[39] Author's inyagamugayo interviews, Alice, Ruhengeri, Buhoma, May 2003 (author's translation).

First, many human-rights observers argue that, by involving the population so extensively, gacaca fails to guarantee legal due process for genocide suspects. In granting the community such a vital role in hearing and deciding genocide cases, they argue, gacaca cannot provide judicial mechanisms that are sufficiently transparent and impartial. AI argues, 'Since community members both provide the information regarding genocide offences and judge the suspected perpetrators, anything outside of their active and honest participation nullifies the fairness of gacaca tribunals.'[40] Such honest participation, most human-rights monitors state, is unlikely given the level of distrust and trauma prevalent in the community. If individuals lack confidence in those with whom they interact at gacaca, or if they are too traumatised or afraid, they are unlikely to cooperate in the institution or to pass fair judgments. Many critics argue that gacaca will simply become a form of mob justice.[41] Gacaca judges, whose role is to mediate hearings, some commentators argue, are also usually the family or neighbours of the suspects and survivors who participate in the general assembly. Therefore, they are likely to have vested interests in the outcomes of hearings. The danger of handing down partial judgments is exacerbated by the absence of legal counsel at gacaca. Critics argue, for example, that gacaca affords no protection to an innocent suspect who is accused unfairly by a general assembly and a panel of judges determined to see him or her punished.

Over time, non-Rwandan commentators on gacaca have voiced a second major criticism of the emphasis on popular participation in gacaca. Human-rights groups such as AI and HRW have argued that, rather than seeing the population as the central actor in gacaca, we should recognise the crucial role played by the Rwandan government. These critics often argue that the state interferes unjustifiably in many gacaca hearings, particularly to pressure judges to convict certain suspects.[42] This critique signifies a shift from the argument above regarding a lack of judicial safeguards, seeing the state rather than the population as the key reason that individual rights and due process may be violated through gacaca. Such concerns were central to HRW's amicus curiae to the ICTR in

---

[40] AI, 'Gacaca: A Question of Justice', p.3.

[41] See, for example, *ibid.*, pp.30–40; J. Prendergast and D. Smock, 'Postgenocidal Reconstruction: Building Peace in Rwanda and Burundi', United States Institute of Peace Special Report, United States Institute of Peace, September 1999, pp.18–19; African Rights, 'Gacaca Justice', pp.32–48.

[42] AI, 'Gacaca: A Question of Justice', pp.30–40. See also this critique from the HRW authors, A. Des Forges and T. Longman, 'Legal Responses to the Genocide in Rwanda', in Stover and Weinstein, *My Neighbor, My Enemy*, p.62.

2008, arguing against the possible transfer of suspects from Arusha to the Rwandan courts on the grounds that the individuals would not receive a fair trial in Rwanda, as highlighted by state interference in genocide trials in the national courts and gacaca.[43]

Non-Rwandan scholars such as Bert Ingelaere and Lars Waldorf have also argued that gacaca constitutes a 'state-driven, state-owned and top-down process'[44] and that, in Rwanda's experience, 'local justice is political justice'.[45] Waldorf criticises the degree of state coercion necessary to compel citizens to participate in gacaca and highlights what he describes as 'everyday forms of peasant resistance to state authority represented by many Rwandans' refusal to attend gacaca and therefore low turnouts in many jurisdictions.'[46] Ingelaere contends that, in the communities where he has observed gacaca,

> local authorities generally do not play an overtly active role in the ... proceedings but they are always present, together with some security forces, and they have received instructions from higher authorities that they need to monitor the Gacaca's activities closely and write reports. Some strictly judicial tasks such as information gathering have been assigned to the local authorities, with the population and judges only playing a secondary role.[47]

For these commentators, discussions of popular participation must reflect the practice of state control over the entire gacaca process.

Critique of sources' perspectives on popular participation in gacaca

The purpose of this section is to critically assess the official, popular and critical perspectives on popular participation in gacaca. This section

---

[43] ICTR, 'The Prosecutor vs. Fulgence Kayishema: Brief of Human Rights Watch as *Amicus Curiae* in Opposition to Rule 11 *bis* Transfer', Case No. ICTR-2001–67-I, 3 January 2008. HRW expands on the arguments presented in the Kayishema brief in its 2008 report on justice in Rwanda. See, HRW, 'Law and Reality: Progress in Judicial Reform in Rwanda', New York: HRW, 25 July 2008. For a response to these two documents, see P. Clark and N. Palmer, 'The International Community Fails Rwanda Again', Oxford Transitional Justice Research Working Paper Series, 5 May 2009, www.csls.ox.ac.uk/documents/ClarkandPalmer_Rwanda_Final.pdf.

[44] B. Ingelaere, 'The Gacaca Courts in Rwanda', in L. Huyse and M. Salter (eds.), *Traditional Justice and Reconciliation after Violent Conflict: Learning from African Experiences*, Stockholm: IDEA, 2008, p.54.

[45] L. Waldorf, 'Mass Justice for Mass Atrocity: Rethinking Local Justice as Transitional Justice', *Temple Law Review*, 79, spring 2006, p.3.

[46] *Ibid.*, p.19.

[47] Ingelaere, 'The Gacaca Courts in Rwanda', p.49.

analyses the perspectives of these three groups of actors in terms of the norms and ideas central to their interpretations, as well as how effectively they reflect the practical reality of gacaca's operation. Based on this normative and empirical analysis, this section proposes views that often differ substantially from the official, popular and critical perspectives.

First, there are several problems with the government's view of the role of popular participation in gacaca. One major problem with the official interpretation is its overstatement of the degree to which the community controls, and may freely participate in, gacaca. Popular participation in gacaca is not, as Mucyo argues above, unconditional. The government rarely discusses the extensive involvement of state actors in gacaca, which undermines the notion of gacaca as an entirely popular enterprise, driven by local agents. The government participates in numerous facets of the daily running of gacaca, including providing judges with dossiers detailing suspects' crimes and confessions, and sometimes intervening when hearings are perceived to diverge from the statutes and norms of the Gacaca Law and Gacaca Manual. During several gacaca hearings I attended, government officials intervened to correct certain judges' statements and to halt disruptive behaviour in the general assembly.[48] Officials sometimes passed notes to gacaca judges or moved among the general assembly, speaking quietly to participants who had been unruly during hearings.[49]

The greater problem with the government's view, however, concerns its expected outcomes of popular participation in gacaca. The government's discourse concerning a lost sense of national unity that must be regained through gacaca is highly unconvincing. An overview of Rwandan history makes it difficult to accept that the apparently lost sense of unity ever existed and that external actors such as colonial administrators are exclusively responsible for creating divisions in Rwandan society. Seeing the Rwandan population as the embodiment of key virtues that destructive elites have undermined and that now require rediscovery in the post-genocide environment is also implausible, given Rwanda's violent history and in particular the population's mass participation in the genocide. Even before the colonial era, although divisions between Hutu and

---

[48] Author's gacaca observations, Kigali Ville, Ruhengenge, Rugenge; Kigali Ville, Kacyiru, 11 May 2003; Butare, Save; Kigali Ngali, Nyamata, 19 May 2003. See also, ASF gacaca reports, Kigali Ngali, Ngenda, Kindama, Gikundamvura, 20 September 2002; Kigali Ville, Kanombe, Kanombe, Kamashashi, 28 May 2003.

[49] Author's gacaca obervations, Kigali Ville, Nyamirambo, 23 August 2008; Northern Province, Musanze, 22 April 2009.

146

Tutsi are not recorded as leading to violence, significant socio-economic divisions existed, creating widespread resentment and animosity, which sowed the seeds of armed conflict.

The notion of a pre-existing national unity is also inconsistent with other areas of official policy, especially the government's emphasis on the need to establish ingando for provisionally released detainees and other groups such as civil servants. The main purpose of the camps is to teach civic virtues to a population that the government perceives as lacking important social values. If these virtues already exist in the community, there seems little need to teach them. As we will see in later chapters, this theme highlights a tension at the heart of the government's vision of gacaca, between emphasising popular ownership and participation on the one hand and, on the other, the importance of the state in educating the populace or, as Sara Bawaya of the NURC was quoted in the last chapter, 'making people good or bad'. The government's entanglement of themes of popular ownership and state education often produces problems for the function of ingando and gacaca and the pursuit of various social objectives after the genocide.

Because the population echoes much of the official perspective of the community's participation in gacaca, many of the same criticisms just made can be directed towards the population's views, particularly where unity – the harmony of the 'family' – is assumed to be a latent feature of Rwandan society which gacaca will help rediscover. Two further components of the population's interpretation of popular participation in gacaca need to be countered. The view that the population should participate in gacaca because it has a duty to assist the government in achieving certain objectives is highly concerning. This view suggests that many people will simply go through the motions at gacaca. The objectives with which the population identifies gacaca, when they can justifiably and feasibly be pursued, should be pursued because the population views them as important for rebuilding personal relationships and Rwandan society as a whole, not because doing so will win favour with the state. The language of 'work' that surrounds some popular perceptions of participation in gacaca echoes many citizens' and political leaders' descriptions of their participation in the genocide or, as noted in the Introduction, in forced labour programmes that successive regimes used to subjugate certain groups in society.[50] The sense of divisive subservience

---

[50] For a detailed discussion of *génocidaires'* descriptions of committing murder and other crimes during the genocide as 'work', see Des Forges, *Leave None to Tell the Story*, p.209.

that this language entails is anathema to the spirit of public ownership over gacaca and to the ways in which gacaca should help undermine genocidal ideology.

Second, the population's generally enthusiastic statements regarding participation at gacaca have not always reflected popular practice across the country, namely that such involvement has fluctuated greatly.[51] From my observation of sixty-seven gacaca hearings in eleven communities between 2003 and 2010, there is a consistent trend in the population's involvement, both in terms of attendance levels and active dialogue. In these jurisdictions, attendance was high at three critical junctures in the gacaca process: first, when gacaca was getting underway and the population was compiling the initial lists of community information; second, at the beginning of the trial phase, which in most of these locations occurred in 2006 and 2007; and, finally, towards the end of gacaca, particularly as Category 1 suspects were being prosecuted at the sector level. These junctures marked moments of innovation and widespread community interest in gacaca: as it was commencing investigations and community evidence-gathering after many years of judicial inactivity regarding genocide crimes; when gacaca became a prosecutorial reality and the first suspects were brought from prison to testify during trials; and when high-profile suspects, including local mayors and prefects, were prosecuted in broad daylight. During these three phases of gacaca, attendance at hearings in the observed jurisdictions was consistently high (invariably above the legally required quorum of 100 adult participants and sometimes as high as several hundred), with only three hearings cancelled because a quorum in the general assembly had not been reached.[52] Furthermore, participants were actively involved during hearings, with large numbers of participants giving first-hand evidence and lengthy deliberations between judges and the general assembly.[53]

Between these three periods, however, the population in the observed jurisdictions participated much less during hearings, both in terms of the number of attendees and the quality of the communal discussions. Following the initial information phase, many people complained that gacaca hearings were long and tedious, often involving deliberations over the same evidence and focusing on minor details of past events,

---

[51] ASF has also recorded these varying levels of participation. See, for example, ASF, 'Monitoring of the Gacaca Courts, Judgement Phase, Analytical Report, March–September 2005', Brussels: ASF, 2005, pp.10–14.

[52] Author's summary from gacaca fieldnotes, 2003.

[53] *Ibid.*

particularly property that survivors claimed they had lost during the genocide and for which they claimed compensation. 'I have stopped going to gacaca because the people talk for hours and hours and we make no progress', said Faustin, a thirty-three-year-old farmer in Gisenyi. 'Some of the survivors say they had this many sacks of flour or this many millet plants until their neighbours stole them, then others will say these people are lying, and things get very tense. This kind of talk can go for hours.'[54] Other common explanations for non-attendance at gacaca during the information phase included that individuals were losing substantial time from work, with gacaca hearings taking up to a full day and sometimes held twice a week in certain locations; and many gacaca participants were perceived as lying and therefore the community was losing faith in the process.[55]

After the initial months of the trial phase of gacaca, participation also decreased in many communities for various reasons. Géraldine, a fifty-six-year-old farmer in Ruhengeri, echoed a common concern about gacaca-induced trauma: 'It is too difficult to constantly go to gacaca. You hear many terrible things there, over and over again those things that happened in the past. I have suffered nightmares because of what I hear at gacaca and the things it puts back in my mind.'[56] Throughout the trial phase numerous other interviewees cited emotional and psychological difficulties from the genocide testimony delivered at gacaca as the primary reason they stayed away from hearings.[57] Other respondents explained non-attendance, variously, on the basis of perceived corruption of gacaca judges, lack of faith in the testimony given by members of the general assembly, and the large number of returnees to the community from elsewhere in the region or overseas, who they said had little knowledge of local events during the genocide but nevertheless gave regular testimony at gacaca.[58] In the previous chapter, Alphonse

---

[54] Author's general population interviews, Faustin, Gisenyi, Nyabihu, 14 June 2006.
[55] Author's general population interviews, Thérèse, Ruhengeri, Ruhengeri Ville, 4 May 2003; Henri, Kigali Ngali, Nyamata, 19 May 2003. Author's survivor interviews, Romain, Butare, Kibingo, 14 May 2003; Jean-Michel, Kigali Ville, Kacyiru, 22 May 2003.
[56] Author's general population interviews, Géraldine, Ruhengeri, Burera, 15 June 2006.
[57] For example, author's general population interviews, Jules, Gisenyi, Nyabihu, 14 June 2006; Anitha, Gisenyi, Nyabihu, 14 June 2006; Apolline, Ruhengeri, Burera, 15 June 2006. Author's survivor interviews, Chemsa, Kigali Ngali, Bugesera, 10 September 2008; Liliane, Kigali Ngali, Bugesera, 10 September 2008; Blaise, Kigali Ngali, Bugesera, 21 April 2009; Gédéon, Kigali Ngali, Bugesera, 21 April 2009.
[58] Author's general population interviews, Keza, Ruhengeri, Burera, 15 June 2006; Deo, Ruhengeri, Burera, 15 June 2006; Solange, Kigali Ngali, Bugesera, 10 September 2008; Philbert, Kigali Ngali, Bugesera, 21 April 2009.

described all of these factors as major impediments to participation in his gacaca jurisdiction.

Finally, during seven years of gacaca observations, the general social and political atmosphere surrounding gacaca has crucially influenced the population's sense of well-being and affected popular involvement during hearings. Soon after the initial interest in gacaca during the pilot phase in 2002 and the extension of gacaca across the country in 2003 and 2005, interviewees consistently stated that the general atmosphere of tense uncertainty made them reluctant to attend gacaca. In the first eight months of 2003 alone, Rwandans faced a flurry of major national events that unsettled the populace: the first of several releases of genocide suspects from prison into the ingando and then into the community; the expansion of gacaca from 750 to nearly 9,000 jurisdictions; the government's banning of the MDR, the largest Hutu opposition party; a referendum on a new constitution; the first parliamentary and presidential elections since the genocide; Rwanda's increased involvement in conflict in the DRC; and an escalation of tensions with its neighbour and previous ally Uganda that many feared would lead to all-out war.

Conducting interviews in Ruhengeri, Gisenyi, Kigali Ville, Kigali Ngali and Butare provinces during this period, I heard a constant refrain of anxiety and confusion. In a village outside Ruhengeri, in the fertile volcanic hills near the border with Uganda, I met Gahiji, a fifty-five-year-old Tutsi farmer. He pointed to deep scars on his left cheek and said that during the genocide he had been attacked with a machete. Moments before the attack, he watched as his wife and two young sons were hacked to death only metres from where he stood. 'We heard on the radio in January that the *génocidaires* were coming back', he said. 'At first, we were very scared. Since then, the government has told us nothing.' He paused to take a long drink from a calabash. 'Now they talk of an election. We have to walk to the municipal office to register [to vote] and we lose a day's work on the farm. We just want to work and live in peace but that's impossible with all of these things going on.' Gahiji said that life had improved a little since the genocide: he had remarried, and his millet and maize crops had done well. 'But we live every day with the memories of what happened', he said. 'Sometimes it seems too much to keep going. But God gives us strength, and somehow we keep on living.'[59]

In 2003 and 2006, numerous interviewees living in communities near the Ugandan or Congolese borders cited insecurity and violence

---

[59] Author's survivor interviews, Gahiji, Ruhengeri, Buhoma, 4 May 2003.

in neighbouring countries as a key reason why they were reluctant to participate in gacaca.[60] Several hearings I attended in Ruhengeri and Gisenyi provinces in particular were called off because a quorum of participants could not be reached.[61] Théogène, a forty-two-year-old farmer in Gisenyi whom I interviewed after the gacaca hearing in his jurisdiction was cancelled in May 2003, said,

> There has been fighting again across the border and many Tutsi have been killed. People are on the move and taking all of their possessions with them. People here have loved ones [in North Kivu] and the fighting there worries them. They don't farm or go to the market or to church – they stay in their houses ... They don't go to gacaca because there they see the Hutu and everyone is agitated because of what is happening [across the border].[62]

Such statements highlight many Rwandans' continued sense of vulnerability – especially among those living in the northern and western provinces – and the impact of this on their willingness to participate in public gatherings such as gacaca, which inevitably raise further emotive and often destabilising or traumatising issues.

This evidence from eleven communities over a seven-year period highlights that gacaca is a highly fluid, dynamic process that relies heavily on the population's confidence and active involvement. At times, confidence and a desire to participate have been substantial in these communities, while at others they have decreased markedly. Whether people decide to attend gacaca hearings and participate depends greatly on the nature of the testimony and interactions during hearings and also on the prevailing social and political atmosphere. Even though many respondents stated that they were enthusiastic about participating in gacaca and believed popular ownership of the process was crucial, the observed reality of gacaca highlights that the population's participation in gacaca has varied substantially over time.

Finally, commentators' views on popular participation in gacaca pose various problems. The views of some Rwandan and non-Rwandan commentators are unconvincing for different reasons. Some Rwandan commentators overstate, in similar fashion to the government and

---

[60] Author's general population interviews, Stephen, Ruhengeri, Buhoma; Paul, Ruhengeri, Buhoma; Jules, Gisenyi, Nyabihu; Anitha, Gisenyi, Nyabihu; Keza, Ruhengeri, Burera; Deo, Ruhengeri, Burera.

[61] Author's gacaca observations, Ruhengeri, Buhoma, 5 May 2003; Ruhengeri, Buhoma, 6 May 2003; Gisenyi, Nyabihu, 23 May 2003; Gisenyi, Nyabihu, 14 June 2006.

[62] Author's general population interviews, Théogène, Gisenyi, Nyabihu, 23 May 2003.

population, the extent to which the community is able to direct, and participate in, gacaca. Many Rwandan commentators' views of popular participation at gacaca suggest that dialogue in the general assembly will be entirely free and open, with state officials and other external parties wielding little influence over hearings. These commentators are undoubtedly justified in underlining the importance of the face-to-face dialogue between suspects and survivors, which may not occur without gacaca. However, the community's dialogue is not as open and undirected as these sources suggest. As argued above, state officials play a significant role in ensuring security and adherence to the statutes and norms of the Gacaca Law and Gacaca Manual and may interfere for extraneous reasons. As Alphonse's statements in the previous chapter highlight, external bodies such as Ibuka also play an important role in many gacaca jurisdictions, a point echoed by several other participants in gacaca whom I interviewed.[63] The level of popular participation that occurs at gacaca is significant, and unusual among post-conflict institutions, but it is still much more moderate than some government officials, segments of the population and Rwandan commentators suggest.

Furthermore, it is highly questionable that popular participation in gacaca will lead to greater democratic engagement and general political decentralisation in Rwanda, at least to the extent that Karekezi and Gasibirege contend. The attempt to connect democratic trends in the running of gacaca with broader political participation relies heavily, first, on the population feeling sufficiently empowered to engage in the wider political realm and, second, on the government increasing the capacity of the population to participate in public life. It is not obvious that either of these conditions will soon be fulfilled. The public's sense of empowerment after gacaca depends heavily on its experiences at gacaca, the degree of trust generated there, and whether individuals feel that gacaca addresses their needs and concerns. It also seems highly unlikely that the government will seek any time soon to develop the political capabilities of the Hutu majority, especially in light of its moves in 2003 to dissolve the MDR, the largest – and generally considered moderate – Hutu opposition party, which amounts to denying Hutu any significant, official voice in the Rwandan parliament.[64] To

---

[63] Author's accused interviews, Alexandre, Gisenyi, Nyabihu, 14 June 2006; Benjamin, Gisenyi, Nyabihu, 14 June 2006; Sada, Kigali Ngali, Bugesera, 21 April 2009.

[64] See HRW, 'Preparing for Elections'.

encourage greater democratic engagement among the majority of the population at the local level, while denying the political participation of the majority at the national level, would be highly contradictory.

Gacaca unquestionably affords the population a rare opportunity to debate issues concerning national reconstruction and to participate in rebuilding processes. It must be recognised that gacaca has empowered many groups in society who have often been marginalised in national life, especially women and youth, who have played central roles as gacaca judges and as participants in the general assembly. Francine, a sector-level gacaca judge in Musanze district, said,

> Gacaca has allowed many women to speak publicly for the first time. They have spoken the truth clearly and talked openly about their personal experiences. I have seen this happen in my community. Gacaca has allowed women to gain courage, especially those who have husbands in jail. These women provide for their families, they are trodden down, but gacaca gives them strength. This proves that women are capable of doing anything as well as men, so gacaca has been important for showing their strengths ... Normally, in Rwanda women are apologetic but now [at gacaca] they are watching their men say sorry for their crimes, sometimes even apologising directly to women, and women have found this empowering.
>
> ... It is true that talking about rape at gacaca has been very difficult for women. It is hard for women to tell the truth if they have been raped. I expect many challenges when these new [Category 1] rape cases come to gacaca, but it will be easier this time because we will be behind closed doors and some women have already given testimony at gacaca, so they are less afraid.[65]

A recognition of gacaca's potential for empowerment partly explains the government's recent policy of establishing microfinance cooperatives for many gacaca judges, using the organisational skills they have developed during gacaca and providing some form of recompense for their unpaid labour as judges over many years.[66] It appears too that many gacaca judges will become abunzi or continue as inyangamugayo if the government follows through on its planned extension of gacaca to deal with everyday crimes after the genocide caseload is complete, suggesting

---

[65] Author's inyangamugayo interviews, Francine, Northern Province, Musanze, 29 August 2008 (interview conducted jointly with Nicola Palmer).

[66] Author's government interviews, Denis Bikesha, Director of Training, Mobilisation and Sensitisation, National Service of Gacaca Jurisdictions, Kigali, 14 August 2008.

judges will continue to play a vital role in Rwandan society. Francine said that inyangamugayo are likely to fulfil such a function:

> After gacaca, if problems arise in the community, people can still go to the inyangamugayo to resolve problems without resorting to state institutions. If there are problems between survivors and the general population, we can bring families together to resolve problems. We will always be intermediaries after gacaca and we will continue to train the people in the importance of gacaca and its values, because gacaca is important for resolving problems ... The inyangamugayo are not tired but courageous and ready to continue working in their communities.[67]

Nevertheless, because of government restrictions on political participation and empowerment at the national level, it is highly questionable whether popular participation within the confines of gacaca will lead to the community's greater involvement in democratic enterprises outside of gacaca and thus substantially alter the national political landscape.

The views of popular participation in gacaca expressed by most non-Rwandan commentators, who in the main are critical of this method or believe that it is overstated, pose a different set of problems. Responding to the criticisms of these authors, most of whom subscribe to the dominant discourse on gacaca, takes us to the heart of how the ethos and modus operandi of gacaca differ from those of more conventional transitional institutions. There are three main problems with non-Rwandan commentators' critique of popular participation in gacaca, two related to the critique itself and the other to the alternative modus operandi that these critics propose (often implicitly) in place of popular involvement.

First, the criticism that gacaca will weaken judicial safeguards as a result of greater communal participation is highly flawed. The key problems with this complaint are that it ignores the various safeguards that are in place in gacaca to protect suspects from potential miscarriages of justice and how gacaca has operated in practice.[68] Gacaca cannot protect against all miscarriages of justice but it is unjustified to argue that

---

[67] Author's inyangamugayo interviews, Francine, Northern Province.

[68] Maya Sosnov, for example, argues that for gacaca to be considered a legitimate form of justice 'the government should focus on establishing an appellate process within gacaca and within the criminal court system that enables people who do not feel they received a fair hearing to challenge their conviction' – ignoring the fact that such an appeals system already exists in gacaca and within the Rwandan national court structure (M. Sosnov, 'The Adjudication of Genocide: Gacaca and the Road to Reconciliation in Rwanda', *Denver Journal of International Law and Policy*, 125, 2007–2008, p.150).

gacaca in no way protects individual rights. That judges are required to pass judgments and sentences on the basis of a consensus (or, when failing to achieve consensus, on a majority) of nine judges, rather than on the opinion of a single judge, constructs an important layer of protection for the accused. Judges must discuss cases in camera, where they are less influenced by the views of the community, before reaching a decision and communicating it to the general assembly. This forces judges to debate cases in private, often at great length, thus adding a crucial element of slow, critical consideration. My research indicates that, nationwide, approximately 25 per cent of gacaca cases have resulted in acquittals.[69] The high acquittal rate may not be particularly surprising given that, reflecting the society as a whole, the majority of popularly elected gacaca judges are Hutu and may be inclined to judge their fellow Hutu sympathetically when they have been accused of genocide crimes. This situation is far from the brand of mob justice predicted by many human-rights observers of gacaca.

Furthermore, if individuals found guilty at gacaca believe they have not received a fair hearing, they may appeal the decision first to the jurisdiction where they were initially tried and, if still dissatisfied, to the next higher jurisdiction. As Alphonse's experience described in the previous chapter highlights, many suspects successfully appeal their gacaca cases. Twenty-nine of the eighty-two genocide suspects I interviewed around Rwanda after the commencement of the gacaca trial phase in 2005 said they had appealed their convictions or sentences. Twenty-four of these suspects, all of whom were subsequently either exonerated or had their sentences decreased, stated that they were satisfied with the decisions handed down at the appeals level.[70] Measures such as gacaca's appeals process are particularly important for protecting innocent suspects, who may feel that they cannot receive a fair trial in their home communities. Human-rights critics who equate popular participation in gacaca with lynch law ignore these protective features that are central to the gacaca process.

The Gacaca Law and Gacaca Manual also afford judges significant powers to control the content and tenor of evidence given at gacaca, in order to maintain decorum and security during hearings. Judges may

[69] Author's government interviews, Karugarama; Rugege, 2008; Bikesha; Epimaque Nteziryayo, Provincial Coordinator, National Service of Gacaca Jurisdictions, Northern Province, 28 August 2008.
[70] Author's gacaca fieldnotes, 2006–9.

stop individual testimony, banish antagonistic participants or halt entire hearings if they believe that certain testimony damages the overall pursuits of gacaca, or if there is a threat of violence towards judges or members of the general assembly.[71] One such intervention by a judge occurred at a gacaca hearing I attended in Kacyiru district of Kigali Ville. On a patch of grass beside a football field, a detainee wearing a bright red T-shirt, who had been released from an ingando less than a week before, arrived halfway through the hearing. A woman sitting in the general assembly spotted him and accused him of having burnt the roof of a house belonging to an old woman in the community, whose murder was being discussed. After the woman described the alleged act of arson, the accused man stood at the back of the gathering and began shouting first at the woman who was giving evidence, then at the president of the judges' panel for allowing this testimony to continue. The president told him to stop talking and to let the woman speak. The accused man refused and kept shouting. Some friends of the man also began shouting at the president to stop the woman from talking. A group of other women in the gathering told the man to sit and wait for his turn to speak, which he did momentarily, but he soon leapt to his feet again. The president could do little as the man screamed at the assembly, 'I know many things that I will never tell. Everyone here today should be on that list of killers.' Eventually, after the president left the bench at the front of the gathering to speak directly to the released detainee, the latter sat down and allowed the hearing to continue.[72]

Examples such as this one highlight the tense atmosphere at many gacaca hearings and the judges' important mediation role, neither of which the government readily recognises. The government's descriptions of a near-absolute degree of popular participation in gacaca exacerbate commentators' concerns over the potential for miscarriages of justice. The government may be its own worst enemy in defending gacaca against the criticisms of human-rights observers concerning due process. The more moderate account of popular participation in gacaca that I propose here recognises the mediation role played by gacaca judges and, to a lesser extent, government officials, and therefore significant safeguards for suspects, especially protecting the innocent from miscarriages of justice, and for all participants, in terms of protection from physical and verbal attack during gacaca hearings. I assess gacaca's performance

---

[71] Gacaca Law (Modified 2004), Article 30.
[72] Author's gacaca observations, Kigali Ville, Kacyiru, 11 May 2003.

in terms of delivering justice for genocide crimes in greater detail in Chapter 8.

Second, non-Rwandan commentators overstate the extent to which government officials interfere in gacaca hearings and jeopardise notions of popular participation. At the outset, this critique is inconsistent with the argument – often made by the same commentators, including AI and HRW – that gacaca is likely to result in mob justice, in which the state and other actors are powerless to intervene. In substantive terms, few of the non-Rwandan critics who make this point support the case with evidence from observed gacaca hearings.[73] Ingelaere argues broadly that 'local authorities do not play an overtly active role' during hearings but they have been instructed to write reports for higher authorities. However, he does not elaborate on concrete instances where such reports have been written and the impact of this on the running of gacaca. Waldorf meanwhile cites examples of state coercion only in high-profile cases such as those involving Major General Laurent Munyakazi, a high-ranking Hutu military official, and Father Guy Theunis, a Belgian priest. While my own observations, as highlighted above, indicate that state officials do from time to time intervene directly in hearings, this is a generally uncommon occurrence and usually confined to communities close to Kigali, where there is invariably a greater state presence. On three occasions that I have witnessed, government officials have intervened during hearings and been told by judges to desist from speaking on the grounds that the community should be free to debate the genocide evidence at hand. On all occasions, the officials followed the judges' orders.[74] Such instances of judges standing their ground represent important moments of local agency that remain under-recognised in most non-Rwandan critiques of gacaca.

[73] Authors who make this point such as Maya Goldstein Bolocan base their arguments only on (often misleading) interpretations of the Gacaca Law. For example, Bolocan argues, 'The position of the defendant may be further compromised by the fact that the Gacaca courts may, whenever necessary, be assisted by legal experts appointed by the National Service [of Gacaca Jurisdictions] whom, by virtue of their legal qualifications, may exercise considerable influence over the Gacaca judges ... [D]efendants do not have access to their case file prior to the hearings, and will not be able to present witnesses in their defense nor to cross-examine witnesses' (Bolocan, 'Rwandan Gacaca', pp.388–9). However, Bolocan cites no empirical evidence for the broad statement that the NSGJ 'may exercise considerable influence over the Gacaca judges'. Her statements regarding defendants' inability to access case files and present defence witnesses are both legally flawed – as the Gacaca Law contains no such prohibitions – and contrary to the practice of gacaca, in which defendants regularly mount their defence using such means.

[74] Author's gacaca observations, Kigali Ville, Butamwa, 21 May 2003; Kigali Ville, Remera, 13 June 2006; Kigali Ville, Mwendo, 16 August 2008.

There is evidence, including from my own observations, that state officials in some locations actively encourage – or even coerce – the population to participate in gacaca hearings. However, there is little evidence
to suggest that this is a widespread phenomenon – the large number of
hearings that have been cancelled due to low turnouts suggests quite the
opposite – nor that it would undermine the importance of popular participation in gacaca.[75] Waldorf's argument regarding coercion is problematic: he argues first that low turnouts at hearings represent 'peasant
resistance' to state compellance of participation in gacaca and then later
that '[l]ow participation rates have forced the state to employ coercion'.[76]
He attributes the slowness of the initial information phase of gacaca
to low participation during hearings.[77] However, I observed substantial
participation during the information phase, with some of the highest
turnouts at any point in the gacaca process, given that the population
during that period viewed gacaca as novel and a source of relief after the
long absence of any accountability process for genocide crimes. From my
observations, I concur with Waldorf that the information phase was very
slow and this diminished the population's enthusiasm for participation
in gacaca, at least until the beginning of trials. The primary cause of this
slowness, though, I contend, was not a lack of participation but rather
the overly forensic nature of the early information-gathering, especially arduous and highly contested discussions in the general assembly
regarding property that people had lost during the genocide.

There is a further problem with some observers' arguments concerning
government coercion of popular participation, namely that they centre
around how spontaneously the population chooses to attend hearings
rather than how actively it provides and debates testimony once hearings
are underway. It is unclear why a state that requires citizens to participate
in a legal process to which they could directly provide evidence should
be seen as engaging in unjustifiable coercion. In such cases, there appears
to be little difference between the actions of the Rwandan government
and the legal requirement in many countries for citizens with relevant

---

[75] Max Rettig, for example, states erroneously, 'The Rwandan government obliges every citizen to
attend gacaca. As of April 2007, citizens must carry a booklet in which local authorities mark
attendance' (M. Rettig, 'Gacaca: Truth, Justice, and Reconciliation in Postconflict Rwanda',
African Studies Review, 51, 3, December 2008, p.37). Local officials may have enacted such a
policy in Sovu, the community in Southern Province, where Rettig conducted his gacaca fieldwork, but it is certainly not a national policy, and attendance books were never employed in the
communities across the different regions where I conducted my fieldwork.

[76] Waldorf, 'Mass Justice for Mass Atrocity', p.20.

[77] *Ibid.*, p.19.

evidence or who have been summoned to jury service to actively participate in trials.

Non-Rwandan commentators' critique in this regard also presupposes
that the Rwandan state is capable of penetrating deeply into the 11,000
jurisdictions where gacaca operates in order to fundamentally control
the gacaca process as a whole. As Timothy Longman, Scott Straus and
Lee Ann Fujii highlight in their analyses of the causes of the genocide
and the motivations of those who committed murder, even a highly
centralised bureaucracy such as Rwanda's has limited reach into communal life. These authors counter a common view of the genocide as
solely the result of government command from the centre to the periph-
ery, highlighting that state orders were often rejected, there was regular
dissension between elites and the general population at the community
level, and in some places more localised motivations, such as fear and
greed, better explain people's decision to kill.[78] Similarly, gacaca manifests some cases of government interference, but these should not be
generalised to characterise the process as a whole, or to undermine the
importance of popular agency in gacaca. In analysing the operation of
gacaca, Longman (who initially expressed some concerns about the possibility of state control over gacaca[79]) argues, 'Several factors help to protect the independence of the gacaca courts ... [T]he sheer number of
judges on each panel helps to make influencing them more difficult ...
Related to this, the sheer number of courts will make it difficult for any
individual or group to influence the entire process.'[80]

A recent case highlights the Rwandan government's limited knowledge
of many developments in gacaca jurisdictions far from Kigali. In 2006, the
Rwandan and UK governments signed a memorandum of understanding
to facilitate the extradition of four genocide suspects from the UK to
Rwanda. Defence lawyers for the accused succeeded in appealing to the
UK High Court against their extradition.[81] During the High Court case,

---

[78] T. Longman, 'Genocide and Socio-Political Change: Massacres in Two Rwandan Villages',
ISSUE: A Journal of Opinion, 23, 2, 1995, pp.18–21; S. Straus, *The Order of Genocide: Race,
Power, and War in Rwanda*, Ithaca, NY: Cornell University Press, 2006, especially chs. 3 and 5;
L.A. Fujii, *Killing Neighbors: Webs of Violence in Rwanda*, Ithaca, NY: Cornell University Press,
2009, especially chs. 3 and 5.

[79] Des Forges and Longman, 'Legal Responses to the Genocide in Rwanda', p.62.

[80] T. Longman, 'Justice at the Grassroots? Gacaca Trials in Rwanda', in N. Roht-Arriaza and
J. Mariezcurrena (eds.), *Transitional Justice in the Twenty-First Century: Beyond Truth versus
Justice*, Cambridge: Cambridge University Press, 2006, p.215.

[81] *Brown and Others v. Government of Rwanda and Another*, [2009] All ER (D) 98 (Apr), Queen's
Bench Division, Divisional High Court, London, 8 April 2009.

family members of two of the accused, Emmanuel Nteziryayo and Celestin Ugirashebuja, who were living in Rwanda alerted the defence team that their loved ones had already been tried *in absentia* by gacaca jurisdictions in Southern Province.[82] At the time, it was contrary to Rwandan criminal law for individuals pending extradition from foreign states to be prosecuted through gacaca. Kigali-based officials in the National Public Prosecution Authority and the NSGJ were unaware of the attempt by sector-level gacaca judges to prosecute Nteziryayo and Ugirashebuja.[83] This example highlights that even in the cases of high-profile genocide suspects, central government authorities are often uninformed of developments in far-flung gacaca jurisdictions. Given the potential legal complications for the Rwandan government precipitated by Nteziryayo's and Ugirashebuja's domestic prosecution before their extradition from the UK was resolved, the Kigali authorities would certainly have had a keen interest – and the legal basis – to intervene to halt these gacaca trials. However, they were unaware of these events in the countryside and therefore made no attempts to intervene. This example underscores why we should be highly sceptical of analyses characterising gacaca as simply another means of Rwandan state control over the entire country. Such accounts greatly overestimate the ability of the government to monitor and influence directly a court system as diffuse as gacaca. As I will show in later chapters, evidence from communities around Rwanda also highlights that the population moulds the objectives and methods of gacaca in ways that often diverge substantially from government intentions, underscoring the importance of popular agency in gacaca.

The third major problem with non-Rwandan observers' criticisms of popular participation in gacaca is their proposed alternative modus operandi. As argued in Chapter 3, the dominant discourse criticises gacaca for failing to provide for formal justice. This critique provides an implicit, alternative view of how gacaca should operate. The formal approach to gacaca would apply what human-rights critics consider a form of legal due process, such as the one assumed to operate in institutions such as the ICTR, but which they perceive as currently lacking in gacaca. Judges would limit interactions in the general assembly to discussions of facts considered critical to determining the guilt or innocence of suspects. Members of the general assembly would be

---

[82] Author's email correspondence, UK Government officials, London, 26 February 2010.
[83] Author's government interviews, Martin Ngoga, Prosecutor General, Kigali, 12 April 2010; Domitilla Mukantaganzawa, Executive Secretary, National Service of Gacaca Jurisdictions, Kigali, 21 April 2010.

encouraged to respond only to questions from judges and not to debate
with one another during hearings. Lawyers in turn would be present to
advise survivors and suspects on how best to construct their respective arguments and to intervene in hearings if they believe that judges
are contravening the Gacaca Law.[84] The claim concerning the need
for lawyers at gacaca is the only part of this formal alternative that
the dominant discourse on gacaca outlines explicitly and consistently.
The other components of this alternative approach just outlined are
nevertheless consistent with the sorts of procedural criticisms that
proponents of the dominant discourse direct at gacaca. Therefore, if
the orchestrators of gacaca were to reform the institution in line with
such criticisms, then gacaca would need to incorporate all of the formal elements just expressed.

The formal alternative to gacaca is inadequate for both political and
practical reasons. At the political level, the main problem with the formal approach to gacaca is that it defies the spirit of gacaca discernible
from the government's and population's views. The population expects
to participate in largely open, undirected hearings, in front of judges they
have elected, and to debate and discuss both legal and non-legal issues.
The population expects that gacaca will function very differently from a
conventional courtroom. The formal approach implied by human-rights
critics would prove alienating, distancing the population from the work-
ings of a judicial system in which it would be entitled to participate only
when called as witnesses and only in response to questions from judges
and lawyers. Such strictures would greatly limit interactions between
participants in gacaca.

Embodied in the various Rwandan sources' interpretations of popular
participation in gacaca is a *discursive* understanding of the way gacaca is
expected to operate. According to the discursive view, participants in
gacaca should feel free to discuss issues that are crucial to their personal

[84] As Meyerstein points out, not all organisations that highlight due-process concerns with gacaca
advocate wide-ranging reform of the process: 'Both AI and PRI note deficiencies in due process
in gacaca, but seek different remedies for these problems. Accordingly, what emerges from PRI's
reports are not complaints about judges' ignorance of international criminal or humanitarian
law, but rather recommendations that judges be better trained in the Organic Law's procedures themselves, as well as be better compensated for their work. Similarly, the lack of defense
counsel per se is not registered by Rwandan participants or the PRI researchers themselves
as problematic. PRI notes the need for a more adequate defense of the accused, but, unlike
AI, nowhere do they recommend changing the structure of the gacaca to include individual
defense counsel as a necessary means of improving the fairness of proceedings' (Meyerstein,
'Between Law and Culture', p.484).

and communal experiences during and after the genocide. Whatever 'truth' may be discovered in gacaca will be reached through communal dialogue, not through the views of elites imparted to the population. Such dialogue may be messy, may take a long time and may in the end produce rather inconclusive results; there can be no doubting the risks inherent in the discursive approach embodied in gacaca. However, much of the population views the action of communal dialogue as inherently valuable. It contends that gacaca draws together people who may have, for reasons of protracted conflict, found it difficult to discuss matters of individual and mutual importance in the past. In this view, gacaca encourages participants to discuss crucial issues in an open environment where the community as a whole may benefit from hearing, and contributing to, such dialogue.

Because the formal alternative seeks to minimise communal involvement by giving an increased role to judges and lawyers, it directly opposes most Rwandans' self-definitions and their dialogical interpretation of gacaca. Viewing the negotiated approach as a potential cause of further acrimony and violence, the formal version of gacaca advocates an alternative that would lack popular legitimacy. Critics who advocate a more formal approach to questions of justice generally, and who specifically criticise gacaca for failing to meet formal requirements, would undermine the popular participatory spirit of gacaca and therefore seek to impose on gacaca a set of guidelines that the population is unlikely to consider appropriate. Because the Gacaca Law and Gacaca Manual enshrine the centrality of the population's acceptance of, and involvement in, gacaca, as argued in Chapter 3, the question of ensuring gacaca's popular legitimacy is of the utmost importance.

Apart from the political problems already outlined, two main practical problems with the formal alternative display its undesirability and unfeasibility. First, the proposal made by human-rights critics that lawyers be included in the gacaca process fails for both pragmatic and normative reasons. On a pragmatic level, Rwanda lacks the number of lawyers necessary to ensure that hundreds of thousands of genocide suspects have equal representation at gacaca. Most of the country's lawyers died during the genocide, a small number have since been trained and even fewer international lawyers are on hand to assist. This practical constraint is in turn ethically significant. To allow some individuals to benefit from the assistance of lawyers, while others, operating within the same hearing and who may be arguing against those acting on expert legal advice, are unable to gain access to lawyers for financial or other reasons, is to introduce an unacceptable form of inequality of assistance into the gacaca process. It is preferable therefore to remove lawyers completely from gacaca, thus ensuring that no participants in gacaca gain an advantage over others by having access to legal assistance that is not available to all participants.

In practice, lawyers continue to play an important unofficial role in gacaca, especially as many participants consult lawyers between gacaca hearings regarding how best to frame their evidence when their turn comes to testify. One lawyer in Musanze district said,

> I haven't dealt directly with genocide cases but I sometimes advise on gacaca cases, particularly for individuals who have been convicted. They often come to me asking what they should do ... I advise them as best I can, knowing the Gacaca Law and also how gacaca works. I go to gacaca, not as a lawyer but just as a normal member of the community, so I know how gacaca functions. I can't advise people during hearings but there is nothing stopping me advising them if they come to my office.[85]

Nevertheless, to allow lawyers to operate within hearings, particularly to speak on participants' behalf, would have the deleterious effects outlined above.

Second, the strictly formal approach to gacaca severely limits the range of issues that the community can discuss and debate during hearings. This narrower discourse is not only problematic because it fails to meet most Rwandans' expectations of how gacaca should operate, and therefore lacks popular legitimacy, but at a pragmatic level it means that the community cannot pursue certain objectives (particularly those that may not necessarily relate directly to formal justice). The formal approach would limit gacaca hearings to discussions of legal facts, to the exclusion of many emotionally motivated expressions which, as we have seen, much of the population considers valuable functions of gacaca.

The shrinking of the dialogical space inherent in the formal approach to gacaca would stymie gacaca's pursuit of both legal and non-legal ends. Regarding legal objectives, communal dialogue in an open forum, where issues can be debated and discussed, is important for gacaca judges to make reasoned decisions about genocide cases.

---

[85] Author's general population interviews, anonymous lawyer, Northern Province, Musanze, 28 August 2008 (interview conducted jointly with Nicola Palmer).

Survivors in particular can ask questions directly of those who committed crimes, which rarely occurs in more conventional legal settings, and the accused are permitted to respond. Judges may also hear evidence in an open, communal setting that they would not necessarily glean if they were limited to hearing testimony only from witnesses whom they had called. This more fluid exchange of views, in which judges act as mediators, can provide crucial information for determining the guilt or innocence of genocide suspects. The human-rights interpretation, which holds that significant communal involvement in a dialogically based legal setting automatically leads to unfair or biased decision-making, therefore neglects several important ways in which the discursive approach to discovering legal 'facts' may not only be safeguarded against miscarriages of justice, as gacaca is designed to do, but may even in some instances be more legally beneficial than more conventional methods of criminal justice.

Concerning non-legal ends, the formal model of gacaca would bar participants from expressing views and emotions that do not necessarily concern judicial cases but are nonetheless considered important for other reasons. As I have already shown, many survivors view this greater sense of freedom of expression during gacaca hearings, relative to those in conventional courtrooms, as important for fulfilling their emotional and psychological needs after the genocide. Furthermore, the presence of lawyers, as the formal approach to gacaca requires, would undermine the content and tone of open, largely undirected, communal discourse that is otherwise possible during gacaca hearings. The presence of lawyers would significantly alter the dynamic between members of the general assembly, increasing the use of technical legal language and modes of argumentation, and alter power dynamics as fully trained lawyers operate in a space where (often minimally trained) judges are supposed to be the primary facilitators of gacaca. In such a situation, the population would feel more inhibited and intimidated than in a forum where they are among their neighbours, giving evidence before judges whom they have elected. In advocating the inclusion of lawyers in the gacaca process, critics of the institution risk undermining the popular ethos of gacaca and the modes of dialogue that ensue at gacaca.

Thus, to summarise, all of the Rwandan sources investigated here – official, popular and critical – view popular participation in gacaca not only as the modus operandi of gacaca but more importantly as a valuable systemic expression of a Rwandan worldview of human identity as

communally embedded and 'truth', both legal and non-legal, as a negotiated outcome reached via communal discussion in public settings. In the
main, these sources overstate the extent to which the population can
engage in a completely open, undirected communal dialogue at gacaca.
State officials and gacaca judges in fact play a vital role in mediating the
dialogical space at gacaca, often in order to maintain a sense of order
and security and to ensure that gacaca pursues the objectives for which
it is designed. However, this elite involvement in gacaca is still relatively
minimal.

In contrast, most non-Rwandan commentators, basing their views
on the formal interpretation of legal process, argue that the level of
popular participation that they discern in gacaca inevitably entails a
form of mob justice. The formal perspective holds that any criminal-
justice system comprising significant communal, dialogical processes
inevitably constitutes a biased, unjust system that cannot safeguard
individual rights. The more moderate view of popular participation at
gacaca proposed here – with its emphasis on the community's participation in a largely open dialogical space, mediated by gacaca judges
and the state and constrained by the Gacaca Law – shows that human-
rights critics are wrong to criticise gacaca for failing to provide for
impartial decision-making and to safeguard individual rights. The
spirit of gacaca enshrines local actors as the most crucial participants.
This popular ethos must be maintained if the majority of Rwandans
are to view gacaca as a legitimate remedy to the legacies of the genocide. Mediators, however, still play a key role in helping the population
achieve its intended objectives through gacaca, increasing the population's trust in gacaca and thus bolstering gacaca's popular legitimacy.
The modus operandi of gacaca therefore entails largely unrestricted
popular participation within clearly defined boundaries designed to
protect individual rights and to direct communal discussions towards
fulfilling gacaca's aims. It is gacaca's hybridity – in this case, the combination of discursive methods and formal constraints – that most
sources overlook.

LINKING POPULAR PARTICIPATION TO GACACA'S PROFOUND OBJECTIVES: ENGAGEMENT – THE BRIDGE TO RECONCILIATION

A key outcome of the more intimate communal interactions that are
possible in gacaca relative to other post-conflict institutions, and a

theme that will prove crucial to our understanding of how gacaca is capable of simultaneously pursuing multiple post-genocide objectives, is the *engagement* that gacaca facilitates. A useful definition of engagement, which can be applied in the context of gacaca, comes from Norman Porter in his analysis of the potential for reconciliation in Northern Ireland. Porter emphasises the reconciliatory necessity of creating fora for public discourse and debate, in which a vital element is open and fair engagement between previously antagonistic parties. Speaking in terms applicable beyond the Northern Irish context, Porter argues that meaningful engagement entails 'practices involving honest, committed encounters with others, not least those with whom we disagree most'.[86] In these settings, individuals make themselves vulnerable to others and the most important result is that 'through [these practices] others are opened up to us and we to them, others are permitted to be heard in their terms and we in ours'.[87]

Engagement is a critical component of gacaca, given the degree to which the entire community is encouraged to participate and interact face to face at all levels of the institution. As I argue in later chapters, there can be no reconciliation (nor several of gacaca's other aims) without genuine engagement between parties previously in conflict. Engagement occurs via different means at gacaca: from the public discussions surrounding the election of judges through the various phases of the hearings themselves; the focus of the latter being the often non-legal and largely undirected dialogue in the general assembly in which judges act as mediators rather than direct participants. In particular, engagement entails antagonistic parties debating the root causes of their conflicts. It recognises that there will be deep-seated animosity between individuals and between groups after an event as destructive as genocide. One criticism of the ICTR expressed by some participants in gacaca is that, by undergoing trials hundreds of miles away in Arusha, high-level perpetrators avoid direct confrontation with the communities against whom they committed genocide crimes and therefore receive insufficient justice. Fidèle, a gacaca judge in Musanze district, said,

> In Arusha the big fish are there. The victims travel there but in gacaca everyone is already here: survivors, perpetrators, judges. They are all here in the community. That is the difference. If we want prisoners to

[86] N. Porter, *The Elusive Quest: Reconciliation in Northern Ireland*, Belfast: The Blackstaff Press, 2003, p.108.
[87] *Ibid.*, p.108.

come, they come, they tell the truth, they apologise and ask for forgiveness. We can see if they are touched, if they are sincere. But in Arusha it isn't possible for survivors to experience this. They can't tell whether the accused are sincere. Those in Arusha haven't asked for forgiveness. Those in Arusha have committed many crimes here, they should face us, the Rwandan family, but they avoid us by being there.[88]

Similar sentiments were expressed during a case in 2009 concerning the Rwandan genocide suspect, François Bazaramba, who had fled to Finland. Members of the Finnish court where Bazaramba was on trial travelled to his former village in southern Rwanda. A Finnish journalist travelling with the court interviewed a local inyangamugayo named Mamasani about the conducting of the trial overseas. The journalist reported, '[Mamasani] feels that the final truth in [the trial] could be reached only if Bazaramba and the witnesses in the case would come before the local people. "When he is not there, people can say anything they like." Mamasani feels that a Gacaca court would be the right place to deal with the Bazaramba case.'[89] In such interpretations, justice delivered through the ICTR or foreign courts is perceived as less rigorous for genocide suspects because it foregoes no direct engagement with the general population, save the small number of everyday Rwandans called as witnesses in ICTR cases.[90] Conversely, survivors such as Esther Mujawayo celebrate the fact that gacaca requires suspects to confront their communities directly. 'After 1994', Mujawayo writes, 'a deafening silence descended upon the whole population ... No one, absolutely no one could have imagined that one day the killers would speak ... With gacaca, the word [about the genocide] has spread.'[91]

As the following chapters highlight, implicit in gacaca is the view that reconciliation after the genocide will require difficult dialogue, a genuine confrontation with the sources of conflict, and parties' mutual

---

[88] Author's inyangamugayo interviews, Musanze District, Northern Province, Rwanda, 29 August 2008, notes on file with author (interview conducted jointly with Nicola Palmer).

[89] *Helsingin Sanomat*, 'Prosecutor in Genocide Case Takes Court on Tour of Rwanda Village', 17 September 2009, www.hs.fi/english/article/Prosecutor+in+genocide+case+takes+court+on+to ur+of+Rwanda+village/ 1135249393557.

[90] Elizabeth Neuffer recorded similar views from Rwandan survivors: 'having [ICTR] trials outside Rwanda deprives genocide survivors of something they need in order for reconciliation: the need to confront those whose orders left them mutilated or robbed ... of their families' (E. Neuffer, *The Key to My Neighbor's House: Seeking Justice in Bosnia and Rwanda*, London: Bloomsbury, 2000, p.377).

[91] E. Mujawayo and S. Belhaddad, *La Fleur de Stéphanie: Rwanda entre réconciliation et déni*, Paris: Flammarion, 2006, p.74 (author's translation).

dedication to rebuilding fractured relationships. Such a confrontation may on occasion prove detrimental to chances of reconciliation if it only produces further acrimony, and such experiences are legion in the life-span of gacaca. Engagement is not an inherently positive dynamic; when not managed effectively, it is equally capable of fomenting discord. For engagement to produce positive results, it requires the immense dedication of the parties involved, a genuine sense of trust between them and effective forms of mediation to ensure that this sense of trust is maintained. The forms of engagement that gacaca facilitates distinguish it from other transitional institutions such as war-crimes tribunals, which rarely allow open or meaningful interactions between victims and perpetrators and limit discourse to legal matters, to the exclusion of more emotional concerns.

One likely product of engagement at gacaca, which should be foreshadowed at this early stage, is the largely unpredictable outcomes. As I argued in Chapter 3, gacaca is a dynamic enterprise that involves an ever-evolving process of people's interactions and subsequent reshapings of the institution in order to meet newly realised needs and challenges. These interactions may not always be beneficial or even secure; instances of acrimony are unavoidable given the level of engagement that gacaca entails. There is an element of risk in allowing members of fractured communities to engage so closely with one another. Mediators must contain antagonisms at gacaca and direct the population's engagement towards reconciliatory ends.

Despite the undeniable unpredictability of gacaca and the risks involved, engagement is a central concept in gacaca because it acts as the main conduit through which gacaca, with its emphasis on popular participation, simultaneously pursues a range of pragmatic and profound objectives, including reconciliation. Engagement is therefore crucial to our understanding of how gacaca simultaneously pursues pragmatic and profound objectives that at the outset may seem unrelated or even mutually exclusive. As argued later, when mediated effectively, engagement can produce reconciliatory results between parties previously in conflict which institutions that fail to recognise the need for engagement rarely produce.

CHAPTER 6

GACACA'S PRAGMATIC OBJECTIVES

INTRODUCTION

Part of what makes gacaca such a complex social institution and difficult to interpret is the fact that various sources view it as a response to both pragmatic and more subtle socio-cultural needs in post-genocide Rwanda. Interpreting gacaca entails exploring areas as diverse as people's material well-being and their capacity to rebuild fractured relationships. The Rwandan government faces serious practical difficulties in rebuilding the nation, particularly processing the backlog of cases of genocide suspects and a lack of material resources, which hamper efforts to reduce poverty and to rebuild physical and social infrastructure after the genocide. This chapter focuses on the ways in which gacaca is designed partly as a remedy to some of the state's pragmatic, judicial and economic problems. While gacaca unquestionably has lofty aims concerning reconstructing lives and people's relationships, it is also driven by these sorts of practical dilemmas that confront most post-conflict societies. Chapters 7–10 focus on the contribution of gacaca to the fulfilment of profound objectives, which relate more to the social needs of discrete communities and Rwandan society as a whole. Alongside gacaca's hybrid modalities of creating a public, discursive space within legal boundaries, the remaining chapters highlight gacaca's hybrid objectives, which cover these pragmatic and profound concerns.

This chapter examines three pragmatic objectives to which the government and commentators (and to a lesser extent the population) have linked gacaca: processing the backlog of genocide cases and improving living conditions in the prisons (two objectives that this chapter explores together under the heading of 'problems concerning overcrowded prisons'); and fostering economic development. These objectives are relatively uncontroversial vis-à-vis the dominant discourse on gacaca described in Chapter 3 because, as this chapter will show, they concern ideas and practices of formal, deterrent justice, which constitutes the primary lens through which most observers view gacaca. Nevertheless, the interpretation of gacaca's three pragmatic objectives here differs in some key respects from most observers' understandings of these aims. As in the previous chapter, the analysis of gacaca's pragmatic objectives comprises first an outline of the government's, population's and commentators' views on the particular objective under consideration, followed by an internal and empirical critique of those sources' interpretations. This chapter contends – in opposition to several of these sources' interpretations of gacaca's pragmatic aims – that gacaca has generally proven more effective at processing the backlog of genocide cases and improving living conditions in the prisons than fostering economic development.

ALLEVIATING PROBLEMS CONCERNING OVERCROWDED PRISONS

The first pragmatic concern with which various sources associate gacaca is addressing a range of social, political and economic problems regarding the overpopulation of Rwanda's prisons. According to official, popular and critical sources, gacaca provides a remedy to two separate problems in this regard. First, some sources argue that gacaca will help process the immense backlog of genocide cases more quickly than the national court system or the ICTR. This is a practical and ethical objective, reflecting the need to prosecute detainees who have languished for years in inhumane jails without formal charges. This objective differs from the discussion of specific processes and forms of justice, which I consider in Chapter 8, by focusing only on the speedier *initiation* of genocide cases. The issues surrounding justice in Chapter 8 will focus on the *actual process* and the *outcomes* of gacaca trials.

Second, some sources argue that, by processing the backlog of genocide cases, gacaca will lead to the release of large numbers of detainees and thus will improve living conditions in Rwanda's prisons, including for suspects unrelated to the genocide. This too is a practical concern with a vital moral dimension, as the government must provide reasonable conditions for suspects whom it chooses to incarcerate. According to the sources analysed here, these two objectives are linked by a common process: the need to hasten the hearing of genocide cases through gacaca, which, some sources argue, will deal more efficiently with the backlog of cases and improve the living environment in the prisons by releasing the innocent or perpetrators of certain categories of crimes, thus decreasing the overall number of suspects in jail.

This section shows that the government primarily, and to a lesser extent the population, associates gacaca with expediting genocide cases and improving living conditions in the prisons. Commentators on gacaca remain largely silent on these issues, most likely because, in wanting to advocate due process for genocide suspects, they are wary of any claim that gacaca will provide hastier, and therefore (according to many sources) possibly unfair, trials. Nonetheless, some commentators do consider processing genocide cases more efficiently as an important objective of gacaca. After analysing the claims of the government, the population and observers of gacaca and assessing the empirical evidence from my observations of gacaca and its impact, this section argues that – with important caveats – gacaca has successfully decreased the backlog of cases and improved the living environment in the jails.

Government's perspectives on alleviating problems concerning overcrowded prisons

While the government rarely expresses its intentions regarding dealing with overcrowded prisons, for fear of alienating genocide survivors by raising too loudly the issue of potentially releasing suspects into the community, it undoubtedly believes that expediting genocide cases is one of gacaca's main objectives. At the National Summit of Unity and Reconciliation in Kigali in 2000, Aloisea Inyumba, then-Executive Secretary of the NURC, argued,

> People who lost their relatives wish that trials are speeded up so that perpetrators of crimes are punished. They fear to see the culture of impunity prolonged. There are people who say that their relatives are detained for 5 years while they are innocent … They wish that [the] Gacaca courts will be quickly operational and will be explained to them.[1]

---

[1] A. Inyumba, 'Report on the Consultative Meetings', p.43.

Implicit in the Gacaca Law is the idea that gacaca will rapidly hear suspects' cases. In the Law, the judicial process comprising a suspect's response to accusations in the general assembly, the assembly's public discussion of the suspect's evidence, and the judges' decision regarding the guilt or innocence of the suspect and the handing down of appropriate punishments for those found guilty is described as being fulfilled in two or three weekly hearings.[2] That the laws governing gacaca allow for the general assembly to consider the evidence concerning multiple cases during the same hearings – and the fact that such a multitude of gacaca jurisdictions function simultaneously in different communities – implies a faster judicial process than has previously been possible.[3] Though the government never states this explicitly, its primary aim in hastening genocide trials appears to be processing the backlog of genocide cases rather than improving living conditions in the prisons.

As explored in the section on gacaca's modalities in Chapter 2, the government has also reformed the Gacaca Law on several occasions, with one primary purpose being to further speed the hearing of genocide cases. Over time, sections of the government, including the President's Office, have grown frustrated with the slow pace of gacaca, believing that it consumes valuable resources and distracts from attempts to pursue national development. In 2006, President Kagame said,

> We have faced many difficulties in trying to speed up gacaca ... We need to stress that gacaca is not open-ended because, as a nation, we have other aims, such as developing our economy and building the country's skills base. Today the genocide caseload is still massive, so with gacaca we may have to think of new ways to address this ... Even an amnesty is possible, especially for low-level perpetrators. Anything is possible, even for more serious cases. What we have attempted here is justice on a massive scale but the costs have also been immense.[4]

Kagame's views echo his continuing ambivalence towards the gacaca process, as highlighted in Chapter 2, as well as the government's growing rhetoric in recent years that the country must move 'beyond' questions of addressing genocide crimes to pursue other national objectives such as economic growth and poverty alleviation.

---

[2] Gacaca Law (Modified 2004), Articles 64–9.
[3] *Ibid.*, Articles 64–9.
[4] Author's government interviews, Kagame, 2006.

Population's perspectives on alleviating problems concerning overcrowded prisons

The population rarely discusses the role of gacaca in dealing with problems concerning overcrowded jails. For many survivors, the issue of improving living conditions in the prisons is of little import, considering many detainees' horrendous crimes.[5] Many survivors are also too frightened to discuss gacaca's enabling the mass release of genocide suspects into the community.[6] Suspects themselves are often cautious about discussing their chances of being released, for fear of having their hopes dashed, or because they do not want to negatively influence prison officials' consideration of their cases by speaking too soon of their liberation.[7] The general population overall discusses these issues more openly, particularly the socio-economic impact at the community level of detainees returning from prison and the impact of the releases for their loved ones who remain in prison. Claver, a forty-seven-year-old brother of a recently returned detainee in Gisenyi, said, 'The prisoners coming home has made a big difference to our lives. We are very happy that they have come back. It brings us joy to reunite our family members who have been away for so long … People now have their loved ones back for farming, so they can produce more.'[8]

Both survivors and suspects discuss minimally gacaca's contribution to processing the backlog of genocide cases. Nathan, a genocide survivor in Nyamata district of Kigali Ngali, explained that one of the main reasons gacaca was necessary was that 'there is a great burden on the government to fix the overcrowded prisons. The most important thing about gacaca is that it will speed up the genocide trials and it will be better than Arusha.'[9] When asked why he confessed to committing crimes during the genocide, Thomas, a detainee in the Kigali Ville ingando, replied, 'When we confess, we adopt the policy of the country. We realise that the prisons are overcrowded and we need to help the government do the job of fixing that problem. The government needs help dealing with so many cases.'[10] For many detainees, however, a great advantage of

---

[5] See, for example, author's survivor interviews, Marie-Claire, Kigali Ngali, Nyamata, 19 May 2003; Boniface, Kigali Ville; Marianne, Kigali Ville; Tharcisse, Gisenyi.

[6] Summary of author's survivor interviews.

[7] Author's prison fieldnotes.

[8] Author's general population interviews, Claver, Gisenyi, Nyabihu, 14 June 2006.

[9] Author's survivor interviews, Nathan, Kigali Ngali (author's translation).

[10] Author's solidarity camp interviews, Kigali Ville (no. 4), 12 April 2003 (author's translation).

gacaca is not so much that it will 'help the government' but that it will help them by facilitating hastier trials.[11]

Commentators' perspectives on alleviating problems concerning overcrowded prisons

While much of the Rwandan population focuses on the pragmatic concerns motivating the decrease of the prison population, most commentators, especially non-Rwandan observers, emphasise – in a manner consistent with the dominant discourse on gacaca as an institution focused primarily on facilitating formal, deterrent justice – the *moral* importance of processing the enormous caseload of uncharged, untried genocide suspects. Many commentators who focus on the judicial component of decreasing the prison population are often the same commentators who previously highlighted the inadequacies of the national court system and argued that reforms were necessary to uphold the legal rights of genocide suspects.[12] These sources often tentatively advocate gacaca as a remedy to both the denial of prompt judicial hearings and the inhumane conditions in which detainees live. Erin Daly, for example, argues, '[t]he gacaca project has much to recommend it. It could very well help the obscene backlog of cases piling up in the conventional courts.'[13] Such commentators emphasise the human-rights violations committed by the Rwandan government in imprisoning so many suspects for so long in harsh conditions. A common argument by many human-rights organisations such as AI is that 'justice delayed is justice denied.'[14] Therefore, they argue that the Rwandan government should defend the human rights of genocide suspects by affording them speedier trials, though not at the cost of due process.

Critique of sources' perspectives on alleviating problems concerning overcrowded prisons through gacaca

How convincing are these arguments regarding gacaca's ability to expedite the genocide caseload and improve detainees' living conditions? This

---

[11] See, for example, author's solidarity camp interviews, Butare (no. 3), 29 April 2003; Butare (no. 15), 29 April 2003; Ruhengeri (no. 10), 3 May 2003; Ruhengeri (no. 11), 3 May 2003; Ruhengeri (no. 15), 3 May 2003.

[12] African Rights, 'Gacaca Justice', pp.1–3; AI, 'Troubled Course of Justice', pp.5–15, 33–40; HRW, 'Rwanda: Human Rights Developments', *World Report 2001*, HRW, December 2001, www.hrw.org/wr2k1/africa/rwanda.html.

[13] Daly, 'Between Punitive Justice and Reconstructive Justice', p.356.

[14] AI, 'Namibia: Caprivi Treason Trial – Justice Delayed Is Justice Denied!', AI Doc. AFR 42/002/2003, 4 August 2003.

section argues that gacaca has generally proven effective at addressing these problems, although with some important caveats. Regarding the first problem associated with overcrowding, that of dealing with the backlog of genocide cases, gacaca has overall fulfilled this objective by employing thousands of courts to simultaneously prosecute hundreds of thousands of cases. As discussed in Chapter 2, while the government grossly overstates the number of suspects prosecuted by gacaca, citing upwards of 1 million (probably because this matches its estimated number of victims killed during the genocide), gacaca has certainly succeeded in prosecuting hundreds of thousands of suspects. By mid-2010 it appears that gacaca will have completed the backlog of genocide cases, including the multitude of new suspects that the population has identified since gacaca began in 2002 and the tens of thousands of Category 1 cases transferred from the national courts to gacaca in 2008.

By clearing the backlog of genocide cases, gacaca has also overall improved living conditions in the prisons. Gacaca's ability to release detainees more rapidly has created more living space for detainees who remain. In October 2008, the International Centre for Prison Studies stated that 59,311 prisoners remained in Rwanda's jails, which had a capacity of 46,700, although this figure has not been updated since 2002 and does not account for the construction of new prisons around Rwanda.[15] These statistics indicate the significant decrease in the overall prison population, which stood at around 120,000 at the beginning of gacaca. The problem of overcrowded prisons in Rwanda has therefore generally been overcome. However, a key assumption of this claim – which none of the sources mentioned above discusses explicitly – is that gacaca has resulted in a sufficiently large number of detainees being found innocent, or guilty of low-level crimes, allowing them to return home. In practice, this assumption has not always held, as gacaca has found many genocide suspects guilty and reimprisoned them, including thousands of new suspects identified during gacaca who until recently had lived freely in the community. In some prisons, such as in Rilima, this has resulted in similar numbers of individuals being incarcerated after gacaca as before and thus many of the same problems of overcrowding as previously identified.[16]

Furthermore, improving living conditions in Rwanda's jails requires more than simply decreasing the number of detainees. From my field

---

[15] International Centre for Prison Studies, 'Prison Brief for Rwanda'.
[16] Author's prison fieldnotes, Rilima Prison, 21 April 2009.

observations, many of the buildings used to house detainees are so run-down that even a small number of suspects could not live there humane-ly.[17] Reducing the overall number of prisoners has freed up resources that the government can now deploy towards improving living conditions in the jails. There is little evidence, however, that the government has used newly available resources to improve conditions in the prisons rather than in other crucial areas of need elsewhere in Rwandan society, except in cases such as the new Mpanga Prison, built with recently acquired foreign aid. Gacaca therefore has, to some extent, improved living conditions in the nation's prisons but it has been less successful in this regard than in dealing with the backlog of genocide cases.

GACACA AND ECONOMIC DEVELOPMENT

The release into the community of tens of thousands of detainees, most of whom are young or middle-aged Hutu males, is commonly viewed as bolstering the nation's workforce, particularly in the agri-cultural sector. There is consequently a strong connection between reducing the number of detainees in Rwanda's jails and fostering eco-nomic development. As highlighted in this section, all three groups of sources analysed discuss gacaca's role in increasing the economic well-being of Rwandans.

The material needs of the population after the genocide are immense, as many people still suffer from a lack of food, adequate shelter, clothing and access to medical care. The extent to which anxiety over mater-ial well-being consumes the population is underscored in the findings of surveys conducted by Gasibirege and Babalola. Of 1,676 Rwandans asked to identify the country's major social problems after the genocide, 81.9 per cent cited poverty and economic hardship, while only 12.6 per cent cited the trial of genocide suspects and 4.4 per cent listed emotional problems resulting from the genocide.[18] The researchers emphasise that their findings are not intended to undermine the importance of the population's legal and psychosocial needs after the genocide but rather to highlight that everyday material deficiencies also require a remedy. '[M]ost of the problems of poverty', Gasibirege and Babalola argue, 'are perceived to be directly linked with the genocide and thereby expected to be resolved through the gacaca process. Concomitantly, with efforts

---

[17] Ibid.
[18] Gasibirege and Babalola, 'Perceptions about the Gacaca Law', p.7.

aimed at resolving the issue of the trial of genocide suspects, attention to poverty alleviation would minimize social unrest and help ensure a lasting peaceful environment in the country'.[19]

This section shows that official, popular and critical sources interpret gacaca as fostering economic development at three different levels: individual, community and national. As a result, these sources argue that gacaca will contribute to economic development in three distinct ways. First, some sources argue that gacaca will enable the release of large numbers of able-bodied prisoners into the community, thus bolstering the national workforce, especially in rural areas. Furthermore, many released detainees, if they are found guilty of relatively low-level genocide crimes at gacaca, can commute part of their sentences to group labour, which involves work programmes designed to benefit communities in a tangible, material sense. Second, some sources argue that releasing detainees will minimise, for both the government and detainees' loved ones, the maintenance costs associated with providing food, clothing and shelter for suspects in prison. Third, according to some sources, gacaca will improve the material well-being of many genocide survivors through compensation, either from the government or convicted perpetrators.

This section argues that, primarily, commentators on gacaca, and especially Rwandan observers, associate gacaca with economic development. To a lesser extent, the government also argues that economic development is an important objective of gacaca, while the population appears in the main to reject this claim. Analysing the views of the three groups of sources, this section argues that in most instances the link between gacaca and economic development is overstated and that too many factors beyond the remit of gacaca affect the population's material conditions.

Government's perspectives on economic development through gacaca

First, the government interprets gacaca as facilitating economic development at the individual, community and national levels and by all three of the methods mentioned above: bolstering the workforce, saving maintenance costs associated with the mass imprisonment of genocide suspects and providing compensation for survivors. The government argues that gacaca's hastening of the judicial process will produce economic benefits

---

[19] *Ibid.*, p.18.

at the national and community levels by returning farmers to their fields and thus increasing commodity production. Moreover, according to the official view, the release of detainees will reduce the financial burden on families who have often had to feed and clothe their loved ones during their incarceration because the government lacks the resources to care for the massive prison population. In 2000, then-Minister of Foreign Affairs and Cooperation, Charles Murigande, told the National Summit of Unity and Reconciliation, '[M]ore than 120,000 [genocide suspects] now detained must be fed [by the government] or receive food from their relatives, a situation that negatively affects [the] national economy.'[20] Gacaca, Murigande argued, would employ community service as a form of punishment for some convicted *génocidaires* and thus '[p]ass sentences that would help us to promote Rwanda's economy'.[21] In a 2009 report to the UN Human Rights Committee, Rwandan ambassador to the UN, Joseph Nsengimana, said that since 2005 gacaca's use of community service as a punishment had produced 14 billion Rwandan francs' worth of labour for the post-genocide reconstruction of the country.[22]

Regarding individual economic development, the Gacaca Law requires some convicted perpetrators to pay compensation to victims, which may improve survivors' material conditions. The component of the Gacaca Law governing compensation is largely ill defined, allowing both for victims to claim restitution directly from perpetrators and for the government to force perpetrators to pay funds into the national Compensation Fund for Victims of the Genocide and Crimes against Humanity.[23] The Fund, established initially as the Genocide Survivors' Fund (GSF) in 1999 and drawing in 5 per cent of the government's annual revenue, is designed to award damages to victims through various methods, including direct financial assistance, improved health care and educational scholarships.[24] The Compensation Fund, argues Mucyo, 'will be distributed proportionally among the victims on the basis of the harm they suffered, as established by the gacaca courts or common law

---

[20] Murigande, 'Report on Urugwiro Talks', p.30.

[21] *Ibid.*, p.31.

[22] Quoted in UN, 'Rwanda's History Stained by Massive Human Rights Violations, but Rule of Law System Painstakingly Constructed to Tackle Forces Seeking to Sow Division, Committee Told', UN Human Rights Committee, UN Doc. HR/CT/705, 19 March 2009.

[23] Gacaca Law (Modified 2004), Articles 94–96.

[24] USAID (Rwanda), 'Annual Report FY 2003', Kigali/New York: USAID, 10 May 2004, p.10; G. Gabiro, 'Rwanda Genocide: Paying for Reconciliation', Fondation Hirondelle, 19 December 2002, www.hirondelle.org/hirondelle.nsf/0/192d793b82d9b481c1256cb800591075?OpenDocument.

courts. In this way, each victim can receive at least some compensation, which is one pillar of reconciliation.'[25]

Population's perspectives on economic development through gacaca

In contrast, the population generally views little connection between gacaca and economic development, particularly at the individual or community levels. The popular perspective therefore questions not only the government's claimed connection between gacaca and economic growth but also the conclusion from Gasibirege and Babalola cited above that among the population 'most of the problems of poverty are perceived to be directly linked with the genocide and thereby expected to be resolved through the gacaca process.'[26] The first part of this statement is undoubtedly true: most Rwandans view poverty as a direct result of the genocide. My research suggests, however, that the population generally disagrees with the second part of the statement: that gacaca is expected to alleviate poverty.

At the outset, the population is sceptical that survivors will receive significant levels of compensation because of perpetrators' and the state's lack of resources that could be made available for this purpose. According to an NURC survey, 54 per cent of Rwandans expect that survivors will be dissatisfied with the level of reparations received directly from perpetrators or through the Compensation Fund.[27] The use of compensation as punishment draws on the traditional version of gacaca, which required offenders to replace property that had been damaged or stolen or to provide other goods of equal value. It is not surprising therefore that 86 per cent of the population believes that the families of genocide victims should receive compensation through gacaca, while 65 per cent believe that those found guilty of genocide crimes should directly compensate victims.[28] As Alphonse stated during the gacaca journey in Chapter 4, discussions around compensation during gacaca hearings had proven highly fractious; meanwhile, it appeared that few convicted perpetrators possessed the materials necessary to compensate their victims, although some survivors had benefited from the new houses provided by the government.

[25] J. Mucyo, 'Gacaca Courts and Genocide', in Villa-Vicencio and Savage, *Rwanda and South Africa in Dialogue*, p.52.
[26] Gasibirege and Babalola, 'Perceptions about the Gacaca Law', p.18.
[27] NURC, 'Opinion Survey on Participation in Gacaca', Annexe 4, p.29.
[28] Gasibirege and Babalola, 'Perceptions about the Gacaca Law', p.15.

A rare example from my interviews of a survivor explicitly linking gacaca with economic development, in this instance in a community and national sense, comes from Rose in Nyamata. Rose argued that gacaca's hastening of the judicial process and the mass return of genocide suspects to the community will mean that 'the money spent on prisoners will be put back into the community now', enabling the government to support poverty-alleviation schemes for which it previously lacked the resources because of its preoccupation with maintaining conditions in the jails.[29] The general population, principally families of detainees, makes a stronger connection between the release of prisoners and economic development. Bernard, a sixty-one-year-old man in Butare, whose three sons were imprisoned since 1994, two of whom had recently been released from the ingando, said,

> The years when my sons were in jail had a very big effect on our family. We are a poor family and my sons are needed on the farm. Other families have helped us since the genocide ... God has listened to us and things will get better now that my sons are home.[30]

For many Rwandans, though, current economic realities are so harsh that gacaca and other institutions are unlikely to improve their situation. 'Gacaca won't give me work', said Ruth, the detainee in the ingando at Kigali Ville quoted earlier, who was a high-school teacher before she claims to have been falsely accused of complicity in murder during the genocide.[31] Her husband died of malaria while she was in prison and her two daughters went missing, leaving her with few close relatives to provide for her in jail and after her release from the ingando. Because the accusations made against Ruth after the genocide would almost certainly bar her from finding work as a teacher again, she said, 'I will need much more assistance from the government if I'm going to survive. I don't know what I will do when I go home. There is no one there to help me now.'[32] As described in Chapter 4, many detainees – including Alphonse, Cypriet and Laurent, the three interviewed on the gacaca journey – report that they faced significant financial hardship after their release.

---

[29] Author's survivor interviews, Rose, Kigali Ngali (author's translation).

[30] Author's general population interviews, Etienne, Butare, Kibingo, 14 May 2003 (author's translation).

[31] Author's solidarity camp interviews, Kigali Ville (no. 12), 12 April 2003 (author's translation). Ruth, though denying complicity in committing murder, had confessed to theft during the genocide, hence her release from jail into the ingando.

[32] *Ibid.* (author's translation).

For some families of detainees, the release of their loved ones back into the community places a greater economic burden on them as they have to cover the living costs that the government partly covered in the prisons. Meanwhile, the general population views overcoming poverty as its biggest challenge after the genocide. Among survivors, the belief that gacaca *should* provide them with some form of compensation for the pain and loss they have suffered is widespread. However, few Rwandans genuinely believe that gacaca – and perhaps state programmes generally – will improve their material conditions.

Furthermore, participation in gacaca appears to have placed a significant financial burden on many Rwandans. As discussed in the previous chapter, the considerable time spent at gacaca that otherwise would be spent farming or engaging in other economic activity was a key reason that many people cited for their non-attendance at gacaca. Several inyangamugayo also claimed that gacaca placed significant financial pressure on them and their families because, despite not being paid by the government for their oversight of gacaca, they were required to direct hearings at least once a week and expended many hours gathering evidence and deliberating with their fellow judges.[33] In such cases, the population argues that gacaca has in fact undermined its economic well-being.

Commentators' perspectives on economic development through gacaca

The most extensive articulation of economic development as an aim of gacaca comes from commentators, who in the main focus on economic development at the community level. Similar to the government's view, the critical literature focuses on the economic impact of the returned workforce from the prisons and the use of community service as a punitive measure. The focus on community service as a mode of punishment is consistent with most commentators', particularly non-Rwandan observers', espousal of the dominant discourse on gacaca with its focus on deterrent justice. As Francesco Giotta, former Chief of Party of the Johns Hopkins University Rwanda Communications Project, told the Gacaca Symposium in 2000, 'One should not forget that the program of participatory justice does not only imply reduction of the sentence,

---

[33] Author's inyangamugayo interviews, Dunia, Kigali Ville, Remera, 13 June 2006; Francine, Northern District; Placide, Northern District, Musanze, 29 August 2008 (interview conducted jointly with Nicola Palmer).

but also deferral of imprisonment to public labour. This is tantamount to releasing [tens of thousands of] detainees in order to achieve over two billion hours of public labour.'[34] In this sense, the punishment of convicted perpetrators may contribute to the economic well-being of entire communities. A UK Department for International Development commissioned report by Oxford Policy Management in 2003 states similarly that gacaca would alleviate economic pressures at the community level:

> From an economic perspective, the continuation of large numbers of untried prisoners imposes considerable costs. There is a direct cost to the prison service. Prisoners' households also bear a considerable cost, both in terms of loss of labour power, but also in terms of the time that prisoners' wives spend travelling to and from the prisons to visit and feed their husbands. It is reasonable to assume that some prisoners will be found innocent and others will be freed on the basis that eight years is sufficient sentence for their crimes, thus reducing both prison and family costs. Gacaca should also return labour resources to the rural areas.[35]

PRI, which has reported on the use of community service since the outset of gacaca, argues that this approach to punishment may translate to individual economic development, particularly as convicted perpetrators learn new skills, such as brick-making and house construction, from their time in TIG camps. 'In an economic recession, and with difficult access to land', PRI argues, 'this can be a real asset for the *tigistes* who are for the most part farmers.'[36] Some Rwandan commentators also focus on gacaca's possible economic benefits for individuals. Karekezi argues, '[the release of prisoners] ... will relieve women and their families who come to care for their menfolk at the prisons. I see women visiting the prisons with their babies on their backs, and I tell myself, "These children who have grown up going to feed their fathers in prison, what kind of life do they lead?"'.[37] Karekezi states that keeping so many suspects in jail for so long places an immense emotional and financial burden on the general population. The overcrowding of prisons is therefore not only a problem

---

[34] F. Giotta, 'Minutes of the Symposium on Gacaca', Hotel Umubano, Kigali, 6–7 March 2000, p.45.

[35] Oxford Policy Management, 'The Impact of Increases in Public Expenditure on Poverty in Rwanda', Oxford: Oxford Policy Management, March 2003, p.106.

[36] PRI, 'Monitoring and Research Report No. IX on the Gacaca: Community Service (TIG) – Areas of Reflection', Kigali: PRI, March 2007, p.22.

[37] A. Karekezi, 'Minutes of the Symposium on Gacaca', Hotel Umubano, Kigali, 6–7 March 2000, p.34.

for detainees but also for their loved ones who carry the weight of their absence from homes and workplaces.

Critique of sources' perspectives on achieving economic development through gacaca

How successful then has gacaca been in fostering economic development at the three levels? Regarding the improvement of people's personal economic circumstances, we should not overemphasise the impact that punishment in the form of either compensation or forced labour has had on individuals, especially on survivors. Given the overriding poverty of the population, any level of compensation, whether it comes directly from convicted perpetrators or indirectly through the Compensation Fund, has been symbolic at best. As Waldorf has highlighted, the Compensation Fund has lain almost entirely dormant since the inception of gacaca, with little evidence that few if any survivors have benefited from it.[38] Furthermore, the key to improving individuals' post-genocide economic circumstances in the long term is not the modes of compensation available through gacaca (many of which constitute one-off forms of restitution) but rather systemic economic reforms sector that allow individuals to engage in effective income-generating processes. Other state- and community-initiated economic processes will be significantly more effective in this regard than gacaca.

It is also questionable the extent to which gacaca has aided the economic development of separate communities. Most of the arguments concerning gacaca's contribution to increased productivity at the community level rely on the same questionable assumption that underpins the arguments for solving the problems of overcrowded jails, namely that gacaca will hasten the judicial process, decrease the prison population and thus bolster the currently depleted workforce with released detainees. As we saw earlier, gacaca has not swelled communities' labour forces in this way in all parts of the country. As PRI also points out, some communities have benefited from the TIG process substantially more than others. Over time, the government has gradually increased the use of TIG camps, which gather convicted *génocidaires* in seven locations around Rwanda where they engage in group labour programmes, often far from their homes. This means that communities close to TIG

---

[38] Waldorf, 'Mass Justice for Mass Atrocity', pp.17–18.

camps tend to benefit directly from this community service, while those far away gain very little.[39]

Furthermore, some communities have experienced economic difficulties *because of* gacaca, as many people have spent at least one full day per week attending gacaca hearings; time that would otherwise have been used for work. As highlighted in the previous chapter, the economic burden upon rural participants in gacaca is one reason that some have stopped attending gacaca hearings. Gacaca's requirement of mass popular participation comes with a significant economic cost. Thus, we should conclude, overall gacaca has not significantly improved the economic situation at the community level.

At the national level, the huge expense of running gacaca across the country poses major problems for an already cash-strapped state. Again, the government has saved some resources, as gacaca has helped decrease the number of suspects in jail. The costs involved in maintaining gacaca in such a large number of communities, however, have cancelled out many gains made by decreasing the prison population. The government, among other expensive activities, has trained gacaca judges, transported detainees to and from prison when they testify at gacaca, and coordinated the centralised gathering of legal data from jurisdictions around the country. The government's initial budget estimate for the total running of gacaca was 6 billion Rwandan francs or approximately US$13 million,[40] the third highest funding for any priority government activity at the time.[41] By 2003, the government estimated that 35 billion francs or US$75 million was needed for gacaca to process the full backlog of genocide cases.[42] A review of Rwandan government budgets from 2002 to 2009 indicates that total government spending on the direct running of the gacaca jurisdictions amounts to approximately 22 billion francs or US$39 million, although this amount does not include gacaca-related expenditure by other government bodies such as the NURC, the Ministry of Justice and the Rwanda Correctional Services.[43] Gacaca is substantially cheaper to run than

[39] PRI, 'Community Service', pp.18–40.
[40] Fondation Hirondelle, 'Training of Gacaca Judges Starts 8 April 2002', 3 April 2002, www.hirondelle.org/hirondelle.nsf/0/192d793b82d9b481c1256cb800591075?OpenDocument.
[41] Oxford Policy Management, 'The Impact of Increases', p.105.
[42] C. Kayitana, quoted in S. Kanuma, 'Local Justice', *Developments*, 24, 2003, www.developments.org.uk/data/Issue24/local-justice.htm.
[43] Republic of Rwanda, 'Ministry of Finance and Economic Planning Budgets, 2002–2009', Ministry of Finance and Economic Planning, www.minecofin.gov.rw/en/inno-file_galleries.php.

more conventional justice institutions, especially when compared to the immense costs involved with the running of the ICTR, which to date has cost more than US$1 billion.[44] Several foreign governments, including Belgium, the Netherlands, Switzerland and the USA, have provided funds for gacaca, greatly decreasing the financial burden on the Rwandan government.[45] However, the costs associated with running gacaca are still immense, and even with this level of support, gacaca has significantly drained the nation's resources, affecting the government's abilities to facilitate national economic development.

Gacaca's ability to contribute significantly to individual, community and national economic development has been curtailed by the immense needs of the population, the government's lack of resources, and gacaca's variable impact on the size of the available workforce. Other institutions that focus solely on economic matters and possess a greater ability to restructure key facets of Rwanda's economy are likely to prove more effective in pursuing this outcome. Therefore, although gacaca may contribute in some minor senses to economic development at the three levels discussed, it has overall failed to fulfil this objective.

CONCLUSION

This chapter has discussed gacaca's pursuit of three pragmatic aims after the genocide – processing the backlog of genocide cases, improving living conditions in the prisons and fostering economic development – which some official, popular and critical sources argue should be viewed as objectives of gacaca. Gacaca has, to some extent, contributed to the first two objectives but displayed little potential for facilitating the third. As we will see in the following chapters, gacaca's hybrid objectives after the genocide – combining the pragmatic objectives explored here and a range of more profound objectives concerning social and cultural reconstruction – underscore the complexity and dynamism of the institution. However, the hybridity of gacaca's aims has also, in practice, often left it overstretched and incapable of fulfilling many of the population's expectations.

---

[44] Hirondelle News Agency, 'Cost of the ICTR to Reach $1 Billion by the End of 2007', 12 May 2006, www.allafrica.com/stories/200605120745.html.
[45] Author's government interviews, Kayitana.

CHAPTER 7

ACCUSER, LIBERATOR OR RECONCILER? TRUTH THROUGH GACACA

INTRODUCTION

The theme of truth, perhaps more than any other in this book, illuminates gacaca's hybridity, particularly its combination of formal and discursive methods and legal and non-legal objectives. The concept of truth within gacaca proves highly variable and contested, necessitating the dissection of the ideas implicit in sources' interpretations of this theme. Unearthing the tensions between different conceptions of truth, and the practical difficulties that these create, will show that a key debate regarding gacaca is how it should connect legal and non-legal aims and specifically conceptions of punishment and restoration of fractured social relations.

Official, popular and critical sources interpret truth through gacaca in various ways. These sources express a wider range of interpretations of truth than of any other potential objective of gacaca. These perspectives often clash and are themselves rarely articulated consistently or systematically. This chapter provides a more thorough interpretation of truth at gacaca, drawing partly on these sources but seeking to go beyond existing interpretations.

At the outset, we require a clearer conceptual framework in which to analyse truth through gacaca. Truth comes in many forms during gacaca hearings and participants pursue truth for myriad reasons. For example, at gacaca the overarching term 'truth' may refer equally to the testimony of a genocide survivor who describes his or her experiences during the genocide in order to help prove the guilt or innocence of a suspect, and the testimony of a survivor who describes personal experiences to gain official or communal acknowledgement of his or her feelings of anguish and loss. Sometimes individuals provide both of these forms of testimony in the same speech. It is not always easy to distinguish between 'legal truth' and 'truth' told for more personal, emotional reasons, or what I term here 'therapeutic truth', which is intended to facilitate healing. Delineating these purposes of truth is particularly difficult when all testimony from genocide survivors comprises deeply personal evidence that may, at least initially, appear to serve – and may, from the witness's perspective, be intended to serve – both a legal and therapeutic function.

Anthony Holiday identifies a similar tension in the pursuits of the TRC in South Africa between what he terms the truth about 'forensic' facts and 'psychological' facts. 'On the one hand', Holiday argues,

> there were the forensic facts of politico-legal history, concerning what had been done, by whom and to whom and the political purposes (if any) for which these crimes had been committed. There were, on the other hand, the psychological facts, pertaining to how people now felt about what had been done to them. The former set of facts served the interests of the TRC's truth-gathering task, while the latter set, once bared in public, would be grist to the mill of national reconciliation.[1]

In Holiday's interpretation, forensic facts equate roughly to what I call legal truth, in which evidence is delivered to prove the guilt or innocence of a suspect. Holiday's 'psychological facts', however, are different from my notion of 'therapeutic truth' in that they are intended more for wider, reconciliatory purposes than for personal, emotional ones. Holiday's psychological facts therefore comprise a third function of truth: what I call 'restorative truth', which concerns the expression or shaping of truth in order to rebuild relationships after conflict. Where therapeutic truth relates to the individual, restorative truth concerns the communal. These functions of truth often overlap at gacaca because, as argued in greater detail in the section on healing in Chapter 9, there is a symbiotic relationship between restoring individuals' sense of personal and emotional well-being after conflict and restoring relationships between individuals and between groups. At gacaca, a major tension lies in balancing the fulfilment of individual and communal needs regarding truth, given the likely clash between discovering truth for strictly

[1] A. Holiday, 'Forgiving and Forgetting: The Truth and Reconciliation Commission', in S. Nuttall and C. Coetzee (eds.), Negotiating the Past: The Making of Memory in South Africa, Oxford: Oxford University Press, 2000, p.54.

legal purposes, to aid participants in personally coming to terms with the past, or to rebuild fractured communal relationships. The need to comprehend the connections and tensions among legal, therapeutic and restorative truth at gacaca drives the analysis in this chapter.

Alongside these three functions of truth, this chapter delineates three *processes* of truth through gacaca that are discernible from my sources' views. First, gacaca incorporates a notion of *truth-telling*, as participants describe in an open forum their personal and collective experiences during and after the genocide. Truth-telling is a specific form of the popular participation in gacaca explored in Chapter 5. Where the earlier discussion focused on broad concepts and processes of popular participation, the exploration of truth-telling here is more specific. This analysis centres on the role of truth-telling as a facilitator of retributive, therapeutic or restorative ends. As argued in this chapter, truth-telling constitutes a *means* to retributive justice, healing and reconciliation. Therefore, where processes of truth-telling serve goals of retributive or restorative justice or healing, as they are discussed elsewhere in this book, it will not be necessary to completely reiterate the nature and effects of these processes here.

Second, gacaca involves elements of *truth-hearing*, or truth as the reception of truth-telling. Truth-hearing concerns the ways in which participants receive and respond to the content of others' discourse and the effects of these reactions; it is therefore closely linked to the concept of acknowledgement discussed in relation to healing in Chapter 9. Truth-telling and truth-hearing constitute halves of an overall process of dialogue at gacaca and key components of the broader pursuit of truth recovery.[2] Weighing legal evidence is an important example of truth-hearing, as witnesses attempt to prove the guilt or innocence of genocide suspects through their testimony, and judges and the general assembly debate the content of that testimony before passing judgments.

Third, gacaca incorporates a dimension of *truth-shaping*, or truth as a mediated outcome, which occurs when outside parties interpret and rearticulate the personal testimony of participants at gacaca in order to fulfil a function other than that originally intended by the participants. Where truth-hearing concerns participants' reception of truth-telling within the confines of gacaca, truth-shaping involves external actors and usually (though not always) concerns outcomes of truth-hearing outside

---

[2] For an excellent discussion of concepts and processes of truth-recovery, see, K. Simpson, *Truth Recovery in Northern Ireland: Critically Interpreting the Past*, Manchester: Manchester University Press, 2009.

of gacaca. For example, truth-shaping occurs when historians debate the significance of evidence heard at gacaca and then publish their findings in order to create a historical record of what occurred during the genocide.

Within each of these three processes – truth-telling, truth-hearing and truth-shaping – gacaca embodies the three functions of legal, therapeutic and restorative truth described above. In exploring the various ways in which official, popular and critical sources interpret truth at gacaca – and in offering my own analysis of this objective – this chapter employs the taxonomy of processes and functions of truth. This chapter argues that truth through gacaca manifests in various legal and non-legal forms and that participants often only arrive at what they consider to be the truth after protracted, communal negotiation. Exploring truth through gacaca further highlights the significant tension in the overall processes of gacaca, namely the fine balance required between popular ownership over gacaca and the need, in select instances, for gacaca judges to mediate communal discussions. Despite various tensions highlighted by the pursuit of truth, this chapter contends that gacaca has generally succeeded in facilitating truth-telling and truth-hearing and, to a lesser extent, truth-shaping. Gacaca constitutes a vital forum for Rwandans to describe and to better understand personal and collective narratives of the genocide, with a view to protecting against a reoccurrence of mass conflict.

Government's perspectives on truth through gacaca

The government interprets truth through gacaca primarily as truth-telling and truth-hearing, viewing both as essentially legal but also including therapeutic truth as a subordinate component. More recently, state officials have begun to discuss the importance of truth-shaping after gacaca, which involves teaching the population historical lessons based on the evidence of genocide crimes gathered from public testimony. The government's overall concern at gacaca is to encourage suspects and witnesses to tell the truth about crimes committed during the genocide and for the general assembly and gacaca judges to weigh fairly the evidence presented. Regarding truth-telling, the government emphasises that the population is best situated to tell the truth about crimes committed during the genocide. As quoted earlier, the Gacaca Manual exhorts judges not to 'forget that it is from the population that the truth will emerge'.[3]

---

[3] Gacaca Manual, p.10 (author's translation).

Much of the emphasis on the community's ownership over gacaca stems from an assumption that, because genocide crimes were often committed in full view of the community, as neighbours killed neighbours and even family members killed family members, then the population will know who committed these crimes and how they were perpetrated. The government argues that the population not only knows better than anyone else what happened during the genocide but gacaca allows more people to tell their truth than is possible in other judicial institutions.

As gacaca has developed, many state officials have tempered their optimism regarding the population's role in truth-telling. In particular, some officials have expressed growing concerns over widespread false testimony during gacaca hearings. 'We have faced major challenges with truth at gacaca', Oswald Rutinburana, Project Coordinator at the NURC, said in 2008.

> Many people are not willing to tell the truth and as a result there is a long process involved in sieving the information. People are not always straight. They go round and round, and the judges require smart tactics in finding out the truth. Eventually the truth is known but the process becomes very long.[4]

Fatuma Ndangiza, Executive Secretary of the NURC, echoed these views:

> Truth-telling has become our biggest challenge. In our original surveys, 90 per cent of people were favourable toward gacaca's objectives. They said they trusted the inyangamugayo but they had some concerns about whether they would hear the whole truth from the perpetrators ... Now many victims doubt that the truth will come out of gacaca. They hear

---

[4] Author's government interviews, Oswald Rutinburana, Programme Manager, NURC, Kigali, 1 August 2008 (interview conducted jointly with Nicola Palmer). The image of gacaca as a 'sieve' has increased steadily over time in government discussions. PRI reports that, upon visiting Ruyumba TIG camp in 2006, they heard *tigistes* singing a song called, 'The Sieve'. 'The *tigistes* symbolised the Gacaca courts and Community Service with a sieve', PRI says, 'wishing that every Rwandan would go before the Gacaca to be purified ... Thus, the role attributed to Community Service camps is ultimately quite similar to that of "re-education" in the solidarity camps, and the teachings offered there bear a resemblance [to those in the Community Service camps]' (PRI, 'PRI Monitoring and Research Report on Gacaca (Report IX): Community Service (TIG) – Areas of Reflection', Kigali: PRI, March 2007, p.52). Detainees in an ingando in Gisovu in 2003 characterised gacaca similarly as a 'filter' in a song recorded by PRI: 'This filter is a reconciling justice / Let us pass through this filter, the filter, the filter for Rwandans, / They are the gacaca courts' (PRI, 'Research Report on the Gacaca, Report VI: From Camp to Hill, the Reintegration of Released Prisoners', Kigali: PRI, May 2004, p.15).

many lies from the perpetrators and suddenly these new returnees [from the diaspora] are attending gacaca and talking about genocide events that they never saw with their own eyes.[5]

Regarding truth-hearing at gacaca, the government again emphasises the population's central role in recording and weighing evidence concerning genocide crimes. The Gacaca Law outlines various processes of legal truth-hearing, such as the general assembly's compilation of four key lists of evidence in the early phases of gacaca, naming and categorising suspects in terms of the severity of their crimes, and recording detainees' confessions and witnesses' testimony. The general assembly in turn debates the information gathered through such processes in order to determine the guilt or innocence of individual suspects.[6]

To a much lesser extent, official sources claim that truth-telling and truth-hearing at gacaca may comprise deeply personal forms of discourse that do not directly concern legal issues. For example, some state sources interpret the physical setting of gacaca as a forum in which survivors publicly describe what they experienced during and after the genocide. In this regard, survivors engage in therapeutic truth-telling in order to gain public recognition of their experiences. As the Gacaca Manual states, 'To help facilitate the emergence of the truth of what happened during the genocide and other massacres; to recognise the victims and the nature of the damages inflicted on them … these are the tasks of the Gacaca Jurisdictions.'[7] In this sense, truth-telling and truth-hearing are intended not solely to solve legal cases but also to help survivors regain some sense of belonging in the community as others listen to accounts of, and publicly recognise, their traumatic experiences. These truth processes may provide a sense of healing, as they help individuals regain a sense of personal worth by allowing them to tell their stories publicly to an empathetic audience.[8]

Finally, in recent years, the government has emphasised the importance of truth-shaping through gacaca, particularly the use of evidence gathered from hearings in teaching civic lessons to the population. 'We have gathered so much evidence over all these years', said Domitilla Mukantaganzwa, Executive Secretary of the NSGJ, in 2008. 'Now gacaca is contributing to changing people's minds about

---

[5] Author's government interviews, Ndangiza, 2008.
[6] Gacaca Law (Modified 2004), Articles 33–44.
[7] Gacaca Manual, p.12 (author's translation).
[8] The theme of 'healing as belonging' is explored in greater detail in Chapter 9.

the criminal-justice system. They have seen that gacaca has dealt with all levels of criminals. They have seen others accused, even by their own relatives, and they have learnt what good behaviour is, how they must live together in harmony'.[9] Such views echo earlier government statements regarding the need to educate the population through processes such as ingando and gacaca. For this reason, the government has built a Gacaca Documentation Centre in Kigali, which will house physical and digital archives of gacaca evidence. 'We will have a meticulous record of everything the population has discussed at gacaca', said Denis Bikesha, Director of Training, Mobilisation and Sensitisation at the NSGJ. 'People will come from all over to consult these records. They will understand the events that overwhelmed us in 1994 and they will know how to stop such things ever happening here again.'[10]

Population's perspectives on truth through gacaca
Echoing the official interpretation of truth through gacaca, the popular view focuses on the processes of truth-telling and truth-hearing, especially on legal functions of truth, but with greater emphasis than the government on non-legal functions. Truth-shaping finds almost no place in popular discussions of gacaca, except from some gacaca judges who believe that truth at gacaca will be important for teaching moral lessons to Rwandan citizens. The population identifies all three functions of truth-telling within gacaca: legal, therapeutic and restorative. In describing these three functions, the population argues that truth-telling is an important means towards three ends explored in depth in later chapters: retributive justice, healing and reconciliation. Because later chapters address in greater detail the relevance of truth-telling for the pursuit of these other objectives, this chapter highlights briefly the most salient popular interpretations for our immediate purposes.

First, the population argues that truth-telling serves an important legal function. Many survivors argue that they will participate readily in legal truth-telling, for example by giving eyewitness testimony concerning genocide crimes and by helping construct the four lists of evidence. Patrice, a sixty-two-year-old survivor in Ruhengeri, whose wife, two sons

---

[9] Author's government interviews, Domitilla Mukantaganzawa, Executive Secretary, National Service of Gacaca Jurisdictions, Kigali, 7 August 2008 (interview conducted jointly with Nicola Palmer).

[10] Author's government interviews, Denis Bikesha, Director of Training, Mobilisation and Sensitisation, National Service of Gacaca Jurisdictions, Kigali, 23 April 2009.

and one daughter were killed during the genocide, said, 'I hope that we [survivors] will be allowed to speak freely at gacaca. I have much to tell about what I saw during the genocide … I saw many crimes with my own eyes and I want to tell what I know at gacaca.'[11] Some survivors, however, are reluctant to give evidence at gacaca or wish simply to listen to others' testimony. Grégoire, a survivor in Butare, whose parents and all of his brothers and sisters were murdered during the genocide, claimed that he would engage in truth-hearing rather than truth-telling at gacaca:

> All of these prisoners have confessed to their crimes and I'm sure now that they are ready to tell us the truth, to say what they did. But I just want to look at them now. I don't want to say anything. I just want to look at them and watch what they do. I won't speak at gacaca. I will just listen.[12]

At the same time, many suspects argue that their truth-telling at gacaca, particularly as it incorporates public confession and apology, will lead to their exoneration if they believe that they are innocent of crimes or will allow them to benefit from gacaca's plea-bargaining system if they are guilty. Richard, a detainee in the ingando at Butare, who argued that he had been unjustly accused of complicity in murder during the genocide, said, 'The community will definitely accept what I say at gacaca. I will stand up and tell them everything I saw when these killings occurred and they will agree that I am telling the truth.'[13] As with several other objectives explored in this book, some detainees describe truth-telling at gacaca as simply fulfilling an obligation to the state. 'I will tell the truth when I stand at gacaca', said Firmin, a detainee in the ingando at Gashora, 'because the Parquet [public prosecutor] tells us to. This is our duty.'[14] More than half of the approximately 200 individuals interviewed in the broader community between 2003 and 2010, most of whom had relatives who were accused of genocide crimes, described the primary function of gacaca as the potential for truth-telling to exonerate their loved ones, whose innocence they maintained. All of these individuals said that they would testify or had already testified at gacaca in order to clear their loved ones' names.[15] 'Gacaca is a source of light that brings the truth', said Agathe, a forty-six-year-old widow in Nyamata, whose

---

[11] Author's survivor interviews, Patrice, Ruhengeri (author's translation).
[12] Author's survivor interviews, Grégoire, Butare (author's translation).
[13] Author's solidarity camp interviews, Butare (no. 15) (author's translation).
[14] Author's solidarity camp interviews, Gashora (no. 9) (author's translation).
[15] Author's fieldnotes, 2003–2009.

parents and three siblings were accused of genocide crimes and were still in prison. 'It will allow us to see who is guilty and who is innocent.'[16]

Second, many popular sources argue that truth-telling at gacaca serves an important therapeutic function. Both suspects and survivors argue that the opportunity to speak openly at gacaca about events and emotions concerning the genocide has contributed to their personal healing. Many guilty suspects claim to have gained a sense of release from feelings of shame and dislocation by confessing to, and apologising for, their crimes in front of their victims and the general assembly at gacaca. Many survivors, on the other hand, claim to have overcome feelings of loneliness by publicly describing the personal impact of genocide crimes and receiving communal acknowledgement of their pain. As Paul, a survivor whose father, two brothers and one sister were killed during the genocide, said after a gacaca hearing in Ruhengeri,

> Gacaca is important for us survivors because it helps us live and work in the community again ... All the survivors come together and talk about what has happened. We realise that we are in the same situation, that we have all had family who were killed. We understand each other and we realise that we are not alone.[17]

Third, much of the population argues that truth-telling at gacaca contributes to the restoration of relationships between individuals and to broader reconciliation. In particular, much of the population interprets gacaca as an important dialogical forum in which various individuals and groups discuss issues that the community might otherwise avoid. The most important feature of this space is its integrative nature. Following a gacaca hearing in Butamwa sector of Kigali Ville province, Michel, the president of the judges' panel, described the importance of truth-telling for reconciliation. 'Gacaca is important for reconciliation', he said, 'because what happens here is real justice where we are all together, criminals and the innocent, and people can talk to one another face to face.'[18]

The hope of many suspects and survivors – but, generally speaking, a desire expressed more readily by suspects whose main concern is their ability to reintegrate into their old communities – is that the capacity to

---

[16] Author's general population interviews, Agathe, Kigali Ngali, Nyamata, 19 May 2003 (author's translation).

[17] Author's gacaca interviews, Paul, Ruhengeri, Buhoma, 4 May 2003 (author's translation).

[18] Author's gacaca interviews, Michel, Kigali Ville, Butamwa, 21 May 2003 (author's translation).

speak openly at gacaca will lead to greater dialogue between participants after gacaca. Many detainees in the ingando, in particular, describe gacaca as a place where people will come together 'as a family as in the old days' and once again solve their own problems.[19] A more open form of truth-telling, on a broader range of issues, is possible within gacaca than in other post-conflict structures. The hope of many Rwandans is that this forum will allow them to engage with others – both with those who share their experiences and with those who may even have committed crimes against them – and thus achieve a greater sense of personal integration as a result of less prescribed or directed truth-telling. This view of open truth-telling largely reflects the influence of the traditional institution of gacaca, with its emphasis on local communities dealing with conflicts as they arise.

It must be noted, however, that while there is widespread enthusiasm among the population for engaging in truth-telling at gacaca, many Rwandans also express scepticism about the extent to which the discursive space created at gacaca will contribute to more meaningful engagement between genocide perpetrators and survivors outside of gacaca. Many Rwandans, especially genocide survivors, are wary of truth-telling at gacaca. Some survivors argue that the discursive forum at gacaca may simply become the scene of further acrimony and discord if debates between perpetrators, survivors and others in the general assembly grow heated. Juliette, a survivor in Kigali Ville, whose parents and two brothers were killed during the genocide, said, 'I dread going to gacaca. I don't want to see the people who killed my family. It scares me to think what will happen between us when we come face to face there.'[20] Chantal, the survivor in Alphonse's community quoted during the gacaca journey in Chapter 4, said, 'I go to gacaca but I go very reluctantly. At gacaca, you hear such terrible things, you cannot even imagine. Sometimes the judges come to my house during the week and ask me to come to gacaca because they know I have evidence to give.'[21] On numerous occasions during the gacaca hearings I observed, lengthy arguments broke out in the general assembly, and judges were often helpless to restore a sense of order. The example cited in Chapter 5 of the recently returned detainee who interrupted the gacaca hearing in Kacyiru, the same district of Kigali Ville where Juliette lived, illustrates this point.

---

[19] Author's solidarity camp interviews, Butare (no. 21) (author's translation).
[20] Author's survivor interviews, Juliette, Kigali Ville (author's translation).
[21] Author's survivor interviews, Chantal, Kigali Ngali.

While many survivors express concerns over the potential for acrimony during gacaca hearings, many also argue that to create a space in
which they can engage with perpetrators, whatever the nature of that
dialogue, is better than having no such space. When asked whether any
good could come out of gacaca, Juliette replied, 'Yes, because although
it scares me to see the prisoners, it will be good to hear them tell the
truth.'[22] Situations such as the one at the hearing in Kacyiru, however,
display the potential pitfalls of the open nature of truth-telling at gacaca.
As some segments of the population recognise, truth-telling at gacaca is
not inherently restorative. Much of the success of truth-telling depends
on the nature of truth-hearing; that is, the outcomes of dialogue and the
ways in which the community reacts to revelations at gacaca.

Regarding truth-hearing, popular interpretations generally differ from
the government's perspective by emphasising its non-legal functions.
As we will see concerning healing in Chapter 9, survivors in particular
often talk of the potential 'liberating' effects of gacaca, as truth-hearing
fulfils their desire to know what happened to their loved ones and thus
frees them from the burden of ignorance. Survivors argue that gacaca
will afford them a sense of 'finality', especially through the four lists of
information when the truth concerning people's personal experiences
is recorded, even in a legal form. Joseph, a survivor in Kigali Ville, said,
'[Eventually] the judges will get to the truth and make a record. Then I
will feel as if all these things have finished and life will start again.'[23]

Reflecting the importance of Christian doctrine for many Rwandans,
the population's perceptions of the liberating potential of truth-telling
and truth-hearing draw largely on the Christian perspective that 'the
truth shall set you free.'[24] In the biblical context, this idea refers to a new
believer's recognition of the truth of his or her sinfulness, and therefore
of his or her separation from God, and of the liberation from the state of
sin and subsequent entry into God's presence that are possible through
accepting the gift of salvation. Whether the nature of truth in the context of gacaca is the discovery of what occurred in the past (i.e. truth-
hearing) or the personal articulation of that truth (i.e. truth-telling),
both views recognise the potential for truth to liberate people from the
burdens of uncertainty and disconnection from the community that
result from personal injury or loss.

---

[22] Author's survivor interviews, Juliette, Kigali Ville (author's translation).
[23] Author's survivor interviews, Boniface, Kigali Ville (author's translation).
[24] *The Holy Bible (New International Version)*, John 8:32.

The Christian view of the liberating potential of truth-telling also largely explains the population's emphasis on confession as a key source of truth through gacaca. Confession signifies the perpetrator's voluntary recognition of the wrongfulness of his or her crimes. Public confession may aid survivors' catharsis through increasing their knowledge of exactly what happened in the past and opening the way for apology, reparation and even survivors' forgiveness of perpetrators. Thus, confession constitutes an important mode of truth-telling that may in turn help build trust, and restore relationships, between suspects and survivors. Many Rwandans' experiences of Christian gacaca have solidified these expressed connections among truth, liberation and restoration. Céleste, a widow in Butare, whose son and brother were still in prison, accused of perpetrating genocide crimes, said in reference to Christian gacaca,

> At gacaca, the judges will bring us to the truth, just as the gacaca with the priests shows us how we can find the truth. The priests taught us to talk together. They were very gentle with us, saying God loves peace and truth, so we also must love peace and truth.[25]

Survivors often live for years in ignorance of exactly what happened to their loved ones during the genocide. While many killings were carried out in full view of the community, many occurred clandestinely at night or far from victims' homes, and many survivors did not view crimes first-hand because they had fled their communities or were in hiding. Many survivors have never found the bodies of their loved ones. Survivors often describe never having dealt emotionally with the loss of relatives and friends because they could never fully realise nor articulate the precise nature of their loss. The uncertainty of the details of a person's death can hamper a survivor's ability to reconstruct that event in his or her mind and to shape it in such a way as to move beyond grief to a less stricken state of being. Stefan, a survivor in Ruhengeri whose parents and two children were killed during the genocide, said,

> I want to see how [the suspects'] eyes look after all these years … I want to know if they will tell the truth … The most important thing for me at gacaca is that I can find out who killed my family, their names, what their faces look like. I have wanted to know these things for many years. Can you imagine what it is like to never know these things?[26]

---

[25] Author's general population interviews, Céleste, Butare (author's translation).
[26] Author's survivor interviews, Stefan, Ruhengeri, Ruhengeri Ville, 5 May 2003 (author's translation).

Raoul, a farmer in Kigali Ville who described himself as 'a Hutu who didn't kill anyone', said that his father and two brothers were murdered during the genocide. 'I don't know who killed them', Raoul said, 'and I want to know. Maybe at gacaca I will finally find out who killed them. I'm angry because I don't already know these things.'[27] As the gacaca journey in Chapter 4 highlighted, some suspects suffer similarly from this uncertainty about the past, for example Alphonse's and his family's frustration that gacaca would not allow them to discover who killed his father and brother because these acts did not constitute genocide crimes. For much of the population, truth-hearing represents a vital means to healing, as people seek freedom from their ignorance of past events.

A telling example of personal trauma stemming from uncertainty over the fate of missing loved ones is found in the autobiography of British novelist, Martin Amis. Amis describes the torment he experienced from never knowing the precise details of the murder of his young cousin, Lucy Partington, by the serial killer, Frederick West. 'All his life', Amis says, '[West] had been a colossus of mendacity, the enemy and opposite of truth', and his final assault against truth was to commit suicide in prison before he could be tried for murder, taking with him to the grave the truth of the death of Partington and numerous others.[28] Amis says,

> I have before me a recent newspaper clipping which begins: 'The mother [of a missing girl, aged 22] said last night: "I cannot close my eyes for fear of what I might see."' Her words have a fundamental eloquence. It strikes you as counterintuitive at first, when you come across it in the literature: the fact that the families of those who have been murdered usually *do* want to know how the victims died. But the reason is transparent. They want to retard or narrow down the swarm of horrors that will present itself for contemplation. Afterwards, at least, when you close your eyes, you know what you are going to see.[29]

Implicit in the expressed importance of truth-hearing is a particular conception of human identity as largely constructed by the narratives of an individual's life. If important events of a person's life are unknown, then that individual may struggle to make sense of many of his or her experiences and may feel that he or she cannot overcome the pain of the past. The philosopher Alasdair MacIntyre argues that humans seek to arrange the various experiences and beliefs that constitute their life into

---

[27] Author's general population interviews, Raoul, Kigali Ville (author's translation).
[28] M. Amis, *Experience: A Memoir*, Toronto: Alfred A. Knopf Canada, 2000, p.196.
[29] *Ibid.*, p.197.

an 'ordered unity' that gives meaning to their life as a whole.[30] According to MacIntyre, all human lives involve the construction of narratives that contribute to this sense of ordered unity. Drawing partly on Aristotle's conception of human identity, MacIntyre argues that all human lives have a particular telos or a direction that defines the meaning of the events of a life, according to the role those events play in the pursuit of the telos. These events then take on a certain order, expressed in the form of a narrative, because they are arranged in relation to a particular direction for that life. A person therefore comes to understand the significance of a moment in life only by seeing how it fits into the rest of the narrative of his or her existence and, more importantly, how it leads to the fulfilment of his or her telos. As Roquentin, the protagonist of Jean-Paul Sartre's novel *La Nausée*, says, 'a man is always a teller of tales, he lives surrounded by his stories and the stories of others, he sees everything that happens to him through them; and he tries to live his own life as if he were telling a story.'[31] If genocide survivors do not know many of the key details of the events of their lives – in essence, if there are gaps in their personal stories – then they are likely to struggle to make sense of their experiences and may feel that life has lost much of its meaning. For this reason, many survivors state that gacaca plays a crucial role in helping them reconstruct the narratives of their lives by facilitating forms of truth-hearing that detail the events of the genocide.

It must be noted that some survivors express antipathy toward truth-hearing at gacaca and argue that they do not want to know all of the details of the past. Nathan, a Pentecostal pastor in Nyamata whose wife was killed in 1994, said, 'I am not always mentally stable when I think of what happened to my wife. I cannot identify her killers. I have heard news of who these people are but I am not sure and I think it is better not to know.'[32] Nathan explained that, for him personally, knowing who had killed his wife and how she died would not help him deal with the pain he had suffered and could even increase his trauma. However, he also recognised that gacaca 'sends different messages to different people' and that for many survivors in his congregation discovering the details of the deaths of their loved ones had provided a form of 'medicine'.[33]

---

[30] A. MacIntyre, *Three Rival Versions of Moral Enquiry: Encyclopedia, Genealogy and Tradition*, London: Duckworth, 1990, p.197.
[31] J.-P. Sartre, *Nausea*, trans. L. Alexander, New York: New Directions Publishing, 1964, p.56.
[32] Author's survivor interviews, Nathan, Kigali Ngali (author's translation).
[33] *Ibid.*

Apart from learning the facts about the past, some survivors argue that the community's acknowledgement of their experiences, through the community's truth-hearing, contributes to the reconstruction of personal narratives. As survivors debate and discuss various issues and themes regarding the genocide in the wider community, they may discern a greater meaning in the events to which these themes are attached. Paul, the survivor from Ruhengeri quoted earlier, said, 'We [survivors] realise that we are in the same situation, that we have all had family who were killed. We understand each other and we realise that we are not alone.'[34] Truth-hearing at gacaca thus has the potential to provide both the historical knowledge of events and the communal setting in which to most effectively and meaningfully interpret the past.

Finally, some gacaca judges, in contrast to the rest of the population, interpret truth-shaping as an important objective of gacaca. Judges rarely discuss truth-shaping explicitly in this context, although their behaviour during gacaca hearings often suggests that they consider gacaca to be an appropriate forum for this process. Truth-shaping involves community leaders' attempts to produce narratives of the genocide, based on evidence heard at gacaca, which they believe will bear meaning for the community as a whole. Gacaca judges often attempt to use evidence gleaned from hearings as a foundation for broader pedagogical pursuits, usually regarding notions of moral education. Faustin, a judge in a gacaca jurisdiction in Nyamata district of Kigali Ngali province, said, 'All gacaca judges must help the population learn lessons from the genocide. We are the moral teachers of the people.'[35] Some judges and community leaders use gacaca as a forum for their own political and social views, regardless of whether these views concern genocide-related matters. During one gacaca hearing I attended in Nyamata, the president of the judges' panel opened the hearing with a ten-minute speech about the community's obligation to vote at the upcoming national presidential and parliamentary elections. 'If you participate in gacaca', the president said, 'you must also vote in the elections. This is your duty as citizens of Rwanda.'[36] Sometimes other community leaders interfere in the running of gacaca. At a hearing in Kanombe district of Kigali Ville, an observer from ASF recorded that the start of the hearing was delayed by nearly an hour and a half when the president of the judges' panel allowed the vice-mayor of

---

[34] Author's gacaca interviews, Paul, Ruhengeri (author's translation).
[35] Author's gacaca interviews, Faustin, Kigali Ngali (author's translation).
[36] Author's gacaca observations, Kigali Ngali, Nyamata, 19 May 2003 (author's translation).

the district to give a lengthy speech about general patterns of health in the community and the upcoming election of local officials.[37]

Commentators' perspectives on truth through gacaca

Commentators on gacaca consider to varying degrees all three processes of truth, but with a particular emphasis on truth-shaping. Regarding truth-telling, most commentators recognise the potential virtues (and risks) of the dialogical space that gacaca creates. Gasibirege argues that gacaca represents a 'face-to-face confrontation with the truth' in which individuals also have to 'face up to their conscience' by discussing events they have witnessed at first hand.[38] This confrontation, Gasibirege argues, sometimes requires a painful dialogue at gacaca that nonetheless is necessary for Rwandans to comprehend the causes of their conflicts and to collectively formulate remedies to ethnic hatred.

Non-Rwandan commentators disagree substantially on the virtues of truth-telling through gacaca. Ingelaere and Waldorf, who have conducted extensive research into gacaca, are deeply sceptical of this part of the process on two primary grounds: first, that truth-telling through gacaca is primarily a 'top-down' process by which the state imposes legal and historical truths on the population and encourages punitiveness against Hutu; and second, that public testimony opposes a Rwandan cultural preference for silence and secrecy and thus violates embedded social norms.[39] Ingelaere believes these two elements are closely linked. He argues, quoting the anthropologist Danielle de Lame, 'A "cult of secrecy" and the "consensus of the subjects" are two intertwined aspects of Rwandan culture. They function as remnants of the traditional organization of society.[40] Waldorf, also quoting de Lame, argues, 'It is unrealistic to expect people to tell the truth about the genocide in gacaca given all the cultural and micro-political constraints (not to mention the threat of prison). There is a "pervasive" culture of secrecy in rural Rwanda.[41] Ingelaere and Waldorf argue that not only are there long-standing cultural barriers to truth-telling at gacaca, but the government has encouraged a discourse of accusations and denunciations through

---

[37] ASF gacaca reports, Kigali Ville, Kanombe.
[38] Gasibirege, 'Recherche qualitative', p.130 (author's translation).
[39] B. Ingelaere, '"Does the Truth Pass across the Fire without Burning?" Transitional Justice and its Discontents in Rwanda's Gacaca Courts', Institute of Development Policy and Management Discussion Paper, University of Antwerp, November 2007, p.35.
[40] Ibid., p.24.
[41] Waldorf, 'Mass Justice for Mass Atrocity', p.21.

gacaca to generate a punitive approach towards Hutu that undermines any form of open, discursive space.[42]

Alexandre Dauge-Roth implicitly opposes such depictions, especially the notion of a Rwandan tendency towards silence and secrecy, arguing that for the post-genocide population – and survivors in particular – silence represents the perpetuation of their trauma. '[N]umerous survivors bear witness to their suffering and its aftermath', Dauge-Roth says, 'seeing silence as an unacceptable option … [T]estimony is driven by a desire to voice the fact that survivors, rather than "having survived a trauma" are "still surviving".[43] Dauge-Roth also emphasises the importance for survivors' own post-genocide agency of bearing witness to the atrocities they have endured:

> In the context of genocide survival and its aftermath, to bear witness represents the possibility 'of' and a call 'for' a dialogic space where survivors seek to redefine the present meaning derived from their experience and its haunting resonance. In their attempt to re-envision and re-assert themselves through testimony, survivors move from a position of being subjected to political violence to a position that entails the promise of agency and the possibility of crafting the meaning of who they are.[44]

Mark Drumbl broadly supports Dauge-Roth's interpretation of the importance of the discursive space created by gacaca but he believes that today gacaca's 'discursive potential remains underexploited'.[45] Drumbl argues that gacaca has become increasingly 'adversarial' and 'judicialised', reflecting the Rwandan government's overly compliant response to international legal concerns over the openness and discursivity of the early phases of gacaca which has driven an increasing emphasis on gacaca's more legalistic and punitive aspects.[46]

Most commentators echo the government's interpretation of truth at gacaca as truth-hearing, with its emphasis on the importance of legal truth-hearing (in the form of the four lists constructed primarily from confession and witness testimony). A minority of commentators argues that truth-hearing involves the extra-legal acknowledgement of survivors' experiences in order to facilitate healing. Karekezi, for example,

---

[42] Ingelaere, '"Does the Truth Pass across the Fire without Burning?"', pp.24–5; Waldorf, 'Mass Justice for Mass Atrocity', pp.24–6.

[43] A. Dauge-Roth, 'Testimonial Encounter: Esther Mujawayo's Dialogic Art of Witnessing', *French Cultural Studies*, 20, 2009, pp.166–7.

[44] *Ibid.*, pp.167–8.

[45] Drumbl, *Atrocity, Punishment, and International Law*, p.96.

[46] *Ibid.*, pp.94–5.

argues that gacaca is a vital forum for 'the reconstruction of facts … [that leads to] catharsis'.[47]

The focus of most commentators, however, is on the process of truth-shaping in which leaders and observers distil supposedly broader truths from deliberations at gacaca hearings. These broader truths, according to many commentators, tend to take two forms – historical and moral – that are usually linked. The interpretation of truth-shaping as an historical enterprise comes mostly from academic commentators, many of whom are already engaged in, or hope some day to engage in, constructing detailed historical accounts of the genocide on the basis of evidence recorded at gacaca. Rwandan commentators for the most part have expressed greater concern than non-Rwandans for the need to engage in this kind of historical truth-shaping. Such an ethic motivated the publication of several lengthy accounts of the events of the genocide, based on months of interviews with survivors and the general population, for example the 1,200-page account published by African Rights, entitled *Rwanda: Death, Despair and Defiance*.[48] In 2003, African Rights embarked on a research project designed to gather testimonies from gacaca hearings across Rwanda in order to verify the historical details described in the original book.[49] Recording discursive material in this way is intended to produce lasting historical accounts that future generations may use for better comprehending the experiences of the genocide.

Some commentators also argue that truth-shaping should involve distilling moral lessons from the community's discourse at gacaca in order to inculcate civic virtues in the population. Gasibirege describes gacaca as a 'school of truth' in which judges embody virtues of truth, non-discrimination and justice, which the community in turn should learn and practise in daily life.[50] These values, he argues, will help eradicate the culture of impunity and help the population resolve future disputes. For some observers, truth-shaping through gacaca involves interrogating people's memories of past events in order to learn how to construct a better society. At the Symposium on Gacaca in Kigali in 2000, Karekezi described the importance of recording historical material from gacaca hearings in the following fashion: '[T]o make people speak during a trial like Gacaca is also to be able to reconstruct memory; to be able to have

---

[47] Karekezi, 'Juridictions gacaca', p.66 (author's translation).
[48] African Rights, *Death, Despair and Defiance*.
[49] Author's observer interviews, Pacifique Kabarisa, Head of Research, African Rights, Kigali, 31 January 2003.
[50] Gasibirege, 'L'Élection des juges inyangamugayo', p.107.

a memory that is acceptable for all Rwandans since they will all benefit from it.'[51] According to this perspective, where other objectives of gacaca contribute to social and political reconstruction after the genocide, truth-shaping at gacaca is a vital means towards moral reconstruction. Non-Rwandan commentators such as Ingelaere and Waldorf, however, argue that truth-shaping through gacaca amounts to a form of 'state-sanctioned truth' that imposes on the population a particular view of Rwandan identity and explanations of the genocide on the population.[52]

Finally, my research indicates that some judicial sources external to gacaca have been shaping truth gathered at gacaca towards legal ends in their own jurisdictions. In May 2003, Maria Warren, ICTR Chief of Information and Evidence, and Don Webster, ICTR Prosecuting Attorney, stated that the Tribunal was interested in using evidence from gacaca hearings in its own trials.[53] ICTR trial notes since then indicate that the Tribunal has actively pursued records of gacaca hearings to assist in its own cases.[54] In more recent years, ICTR defence counsel has begun paying close attention to evidence gathered by gacaca, particularly as the same witnesses sometimes provide divergent testimony in front of the ICTR and gacaca, allowing defence teams to question the reliability of their evidence in ICTR trials.[55] While the ICTR judges questioned the validity of the gacaca process when deciding in 2008 to block the transfer of suspects from the ICTR to the Rwandan national courts, both prosecution and defence teams at the ICTR have discovered significant legal use for the testimony delivered at gacaca.[56] This has led to regular investigative missions by ICTR staff to the NSGJ headquarters in Kigali and to various gacaca jurisdictions around Rwanda. One sector-level gacaca judge in Musanze district said,

> Many investigators from Arusha have come here looking for evidence. They bring translators and ask to see the records from our hearings,

---

[51] Karekezi, 'Minutes of the Symposium', p.33.

[52] Ingelaere, 'The Gacaca Courts in Rwanda', p.51.

[53] Author's ICTR interviews, Maria Warren, Chief of Information and Evidence, ICTR, Kigali, 15 May 2003; Don Webster, Senior Prosecuting Attorney, ICTR, Kigali, 15 May 2003.

[54] See, for example, ICTR, 'Minutes of Proceedings: Nyiramasuhuko, Case No. ICTR-98–42-T'.

[55] Author's email correspondence, Senior Defence Attorney, ICTR, Kigali, 22 October 2009.

[56] See, for example, ICTR, 'The Prosecutor vs. Ildephonse Hategekimana: Decision on Prosecutor's Request for the Referral of the Case of Ildephonse Hategekimana to Rwanda, Rule 11 *bis* of the Rules of Procedure and Evidence', Case No. ICTR-00–55B-R11 *bis*, 19 June 2008.

asking if this person or that one has given evidence to us. These visits have become so regular that, if we think certain evidence will be useful for the investigators, we record it in simpler language in our notebooks … The language that people speak here is not always easy for outsiders to understand. The people use many proverbs and tell many stories and outsiders often misinterpret this, so sometimes we change the language for them.[57]

This example underscores that, over time, gacaca has acquired new audiences, such as ICTR investigators, and their interest has altered the function of the process, in this case the ways in which the inyangamu-gayo record gacaca testimony. Such developments further highlight the dynamism of gacaca, as it morphs and evolves according to new actors and influences. This also shows the increasing tendency of the different levels of post-genocide justice institutions to intersect and interact, such that the ICTR sees practical benefit in gacaca's evidence-gathering and the operation of gacaca shifts in the wake of international involvement.

Overall landscape of perspectives on truth through gacaca

It is now worth drawing together the various processes and functions of truth through gacaca that the government, population and commentators describe to underline some of the connections and tensions inherent in these components of truth. Within the three processes of truth at gacaca – truth-telling, truth-hearing and truth-shaping – we may discern various functions of truth, as expressed in Table 7.1. These functions of truth embody very different aims within gacaca and consequently they often conflict with one another. This section then outlines the three processes of truth at gacaca and how these processes, and the functions of truth embodied within them, may conflict with, or reinforce, one another.

Before exploring the compatibilities and tensions between the processes and functions of truth described by the three groups of sources, two further identifiable functions of truth, which these sources do not mention explicitly, must feature in any analysis of truth through gacaca. First, some detainees' truth-telling, in the form of public confessions and apologies before the general assembly, constitutes a mode of punishment through shaming. In this function of truth-telling, the purpose is to publicly identify those guilty of committing crimes and to expose the nature

---

[57] Author's inyangamugayo interviews, Armand, Northern Province, Musanze, 2 September 2008.

of their crimes, in order to produce a sense of disgrace in the guilty individual and to express to the wider community that such criminal behaviour is morally unacceptable.[58] This viewpoint resonates deeply in small communities, where confessed criminals will live with an ever-tarnished reputation. Public exposure of individuals' crimes will decrease their standing in the community, painting them as untrustworthy or dishonourable characters.

As with many of the outcomes of gacaca examined here, truth-telling as shaming requires a careful balance by gacaca judges. They must make public examples of convicted perpetrators, to send a clear message to the community that such actions will not be tolerated and to publicly acknowledge the long-term effects of these actions on the victims, while at the same time facilitating the eventual reintegration of perpetrators into the community, so that they gain a renewed sense of belonging and contribute to the overall rebuilding of the fractured society. Judges must also ensure that individuals who are innocent of the crimes of which they are accused do not suffer the same indignity as the guilty, by forcefully proclaiming their innocence and rebuking any member of the general assembly who continues to accuse the innocent of the crimes of which they have already been acquitted.

Second, none of the sources explored here describes the role of external parties in counselling individuals who give evidence at gacaca. Outside actors, for example trauma counsellors appointed by the Ministry of Health, may help facilitate individuals' discourse towards more therapeutic ends. We may deduce therefore that a function of therapeutic truth-shaping is possible through gacaca, as counsellors advise individuals who have given traumatic evidence at gacaca on how best to deal emotionally and psychologically with the truths they have told.

Table 7.1 draws together the various processes and functions of truth through gacaca explored in this chapter.

Critique of sources' perspectives on truth through gacaca
It is now necessary to critique the official, popular and critical interpretations of truth through gacaca. Some elements of these interpretations prove more useful or convincing than others and it is therefore necessary to highlight these convincing elements and to reject or correct more problematic ones. The tensions between gacaca's concurrent pursuit

---

[58] For a longer discussion of this issue, see, for example, J. Braithwaite, *Crime, Shame and Reintegration*, Cambridge: Cambridge University Press, 1989.

TABLE 7.1 Processes and functions of truth through gacaca

Function process	Legal (truth as a means to retributive justice)	Therapeutic (truth as a means to healing)	Restorative (truth as a means to reconciliation)
Truth-telling (truth as action)	Punishment of criminals through public shaming as a result of their confessions and apologies during gacaca hearings.	Individuals' pursuit of healing through public disclosure of traumatic experiences stemming from the genocide, usually seeking empathy and public acknowledgement of their pain and loss.	Creation of a dialogical space (for truth-telling and truth-hearing) to encourage discussion, debate and engagement, with the eventual aim of restoring fractured individual and group relationships.
Truth-hearing (truth as immediate outcome)	Use of confession, eyewitness testimony and the public weighing of evidence in judging genocide cases.	(a) Survivors' discovery of historical facts concerning their personal experiences of the genocide, which contribute to healing (especially healing as liberation, as discussed in detail in Chapter 9) through their overcoming ignorance about the past. (b) Public acknowledgement of individuals' trauma, which contributes to their healing (especially healing as belonging).	Creation of a dialogical space (for truth-telling and truth-hearing) to encourage discussion, debate and engagement, with the eventual aim of restoring fractured individual and group relationships.

TABLE 7.1 (cont.)

Function process	Legal (truth as a means to retributive justice)	Therapeutic (truth as a means to healing)	Restorative (truth as a means to reconciliation)
Truth-shaping (truth as mediated outcome)	External parties' use of evidence gathered at gacaca for legal cases either in the national court system or the ICTR.	Post-gacaca, counsellors' (such as those provided by the Ministry of Health) assistance to individuals who have engaged in truth-telling and truth-hearing at gacaca in order to aid their long-term healing.	(a) Creation, from evidence heard at gacaca, of a historical record of the genocide for the purpose of encouraging further dialogue, engagement and reconciliation. (b) Distillation of lessons from gacaca hearings to inculcate civic virtues in the population and thus overcome negative values and beliefs that fuel conflict.

of legal and therapeutic truth and between its popular ethos and the need for external mediation are the main points upon which the various sources' interpretations of truth through gacaca coalesce. This section critiques these interpretations thematically, according to the processes of truth-telling, truth-hearing and especially truth-shaping, which I argue is the most problematic of the three processes described by the sources here.

First, the observed practice of gacaca over many years highlights more substantial problems with truth-telling at gacaca than many of the sources analysed here identify. As Cypriet and Alphonse discussed along the gacaca journey, many individuals tell lies during gacaca hearings, either to protect their loved ones from being found guilty or to fabricate accusations against others. In several communities, respondents discuss the creation of 'syndicates of liars', comprising returned genocide suspects who collude to hide evidence from gacaca. 'It is true that some prisoners formed these groups when they came back from jail', said Egide, a twenty-nine-year-old convicted perpetrator who had returned to Nyamata from Kigali Central Prison and was sentenced by gacaca to two years' community service for his genocide crimes. 'They promise each other not to tell what they know about the crimes committed here [during the genocide]. They also threaten and force survivors not to tell what they know.'[59] IRDP has also observed the problem of 'negative solidarity' among some suspects and their families, including 'some defendants who accept all the blame to protect other family members who might be implicated'.[60]

Some suspects have a major incentive to confess falsely to crimes in order to benefit from gacaca's plea-bargaining scheme. A case in Bugesera district of Kigali Ngali province amply illustrates this point. At a gacaca hearing by a small banana-frond-encircled lake in June 2006, a suspect came from a nearby prison to confess to his genocide crimes. Standing in front of around 200 people in the general assembly, he admitted to looting some property from a house on the edge of the community, near the main road leading to Nyamata. When the suspect finished speaking, the judges highlighted for the audience's benefit that he had admitted to committing Category 3 crimes involving property and that, if found guilty, he would need to give the same amount of goods or the financial equivalent to the victims of his crimes and perhaps perform some

[59] Author's general population interviews, Egide, Eastern Province, Nyamata, 21 April 2009.
[60] IRDP, *A Time for Peace*, p.107.

community service. The judges asked if anyone in the general assembly wished to respond to the suspect's confession. After a lengthy silence, an elderly lady stood at the back of the gathering and asked permission to speak. When this was granted, she launched into a searing tirade, saying, 'This man is lying and you judges are not doing your job because you should know that he is lying.' The judges were visibly shocked and asked the woman to explain herself. She said that she knew the suspect was lying because the house from which he claimed to have looted property was her house, and the judges should have known this because, six months earlier, they had convicted a different man for these same crimes.

The woman sat down and the judges conferred. After they had deliberated, they asked several questions of others sitting in the general assembly, then announced that the woman was correct that this case had already been completed at an earlier hearing. After asking several questions of the suspect, they stated that he had clearly provided a false confession. The suspect initially protested but soon admitted that this was true. It emerged that he was in fact innocent of all genocide crimes. After spending many years in prison, however, he had deemed it preferable to fabricate a confession to a low category of genocide crime, which would bring a minimal sentence, rather than spend further years in jail, with no immediate prospect of release. On this basis, the gacaca judges found the detainee guilty of perjury and sentenced him to two years in jail. In short, the suspect had gambled on gacaca's plea-bargaining system and lost.[61] Such cases confirm the fears expressed by genocide survivors in Chapter 4 that gacaca's use of plea-bargaining to extract confessions from suspects may lead to a spate of false confessions.

Evidence from gacaca hearings and interviews with participants also highlights that truth-telling is limited in two further key respects. As Alphonse indicated in Chapter 4, because gacaca often forbids the discussion of RPF crimes against Hutu, many Hutu see gacaca as a one-sided truth process.[62] Alphonse's relatives who tried to raise the issue of his father's and brother's alleged murder by RPF officers were stopped from doing so, causing them to lament the lack of truth about such crimes. Such

---

[61] Author's gacaca observations, Kigali Ngali, Bugesera, 12 June 2006.
[62] Author's gacaca observations, Ruhengeri, Cyeru, 6 May 2003; Gisenyi, Rubavu, 23 May 2003; Gisenyi, Rubavu, 14 June 2006.

examples highlight that, in the vast majority of gacaca jurisdictions, truth-telling is limited to the discussion of one important set of crimes, to the exclusion of another. However, it should also be noted that some gacaca jurisdictions do permit the open discussion of RPF crimes. During several gacaca hearings, I witnessed Hutu-dominated panels of inyangamugayo in western regions of Rwanda allow lengthy discussions of RPF atrocities.[63] However, none of these discussions resulted in investigations or prosecutions of such crimes, given there is no such provision in the Gacaca Law, which caused resentment in these communities. Nevertheless, that RPF crimes were publicly discussed in these locations again shows the limited reach of the state into gacaca jurisdictions far from Kigali and the scope for local communities to direct gacaca in ways that directly contest government policy. My interviews with central authorities in Kigali indicate that the wider public discussion of RPF crimes generated by gacaca is yet another reason government officials are split over the virtues of gacaca, echoing the divisions during the Urugwiro talks in 1999. Some key figures (principally President Kagame) oppose open discussions of RPF crimes, while others (including Protais Musoni and Tharcisse Karugarama) argue that the population should be free to debate all local issues stemming from the period covered by the Gacaca Law (1 October 1990 to 31 December 1994), although they stop short of stating that gacaca should be allowed to investigate or prosecute RPF crimes.[64] The limits of truth-telling through gacaca have caused substantial disagreement within the Rwandan state from the inception of gacaca to the present.

Gacaca has also experienced major problems regarding truth-telling about Category 1 crimes. The move of sexual violence cases from the national courts back to gacaca – after they were initially shifted from gacaca, due to victims' reluctance to provide public testimony of such crimes and problems of retraumatisation – has proven difficult because the population recalls its initial reluctance to discuss these issues at gacaca. Other popular sources criticise gacaca's handling of sexual violence cases for a different reason: following the change in the Gacaca Law, these cases at gacaca are now only heard *in camera*, whereas after nearly eight years of gacaca the population has become accustomed to open, participatory hearings. Some members of the general population argue that the whole community should be permitted to participate

[63] Author's gacaca observations, Ruhengeri, Cyeru, 6 May 2003; Gisenyi, Rubavu, 23 May 2003; Gisenyi, Rubavu, 14 June 2006.
[64] Author's government interviews, Kagame; Musoni; Tharcisse Karugarama, Minister of Justice, Kigali, 20 April 2010.

in these cases, especially as they may have relevant evidence and they wish to hear suspects confess publicly to their crimes.[65] Such a move is untenable, however, as it would simply recreate the original problems of retraumatisation and reluctance to provide testimony that characterised gacaca's handling of sexual violence cases before 2004. Meanwhile, Category 1 cases involving political leaders, such as mayors and prefects, have also proven problematic in terms of truth-telling, due to – as discussed in Chapter 5 – many elites' refusal to confess to their crimes in front of their communities. For all of these reasons, truth-telling at gacaca has encountered substantial impediments.

Second, unrecognised in numerous sources' descriptions of truth-telling through gacaca, is the extent to which, in the case of each of the three functions of truth-telling (legal, therapeutic and restorative), truth-telling alone is an insufficient means to the expressed outcomes. Whether truth-telling is interpreted as legal (public confession as shaming), therapeutic (healing through public disclosure) or restorative (engagement and dialogue in a communal forum), it is not so much the telling of the truth but rather the ways in which other parties respond to it, that is important. If, for example, survivors or the general assembly do not condemn the suspect who publicly confesses to his or her crimes, then truth-telling will fail to shame the suspect. Similarly, if the community does not display empathy towards the survivor who describes his or her traumatic personal experiences, then the individual will not receive the public acknowledgement necessary for healing. This requirement of truth-telling highlights the extent to which gacaca is crucially a communal enterprise that involves the general assembly in personal pursuits, such as individual healing.

Third, the importance of communal responses for the efficacy of truth at gacaca highlights problems in some sources' interpretations of truth-telling and truth-hearing. Together these processes of truth constitute the dynamic of communal dialogue at gacaca that some sources argue is vital for facilitating more meaningful engagement between parties with the eventual aim of restoring relationships. The need for the appropriate reception of individuals' truth-telling hints at the difficulties of communal dialogue at gacaca. Some detainees and Rwandan commentators suggest that participants in gacaca will engage relatively effortlessly in dialogue and that truth-telling and truth-hearing will lead quickly to

---

[65] Author's general population interviews, Prosper, Kigali Ville, Remera, 15 August 2008; Damien, Kigali Ville, Remera, 15 August 2008; Leala, Kigali Ngali, Bugesera, 21 April 2009.

reconciliation. Such views ignore the inevitable tensions created by public discourse at gacaca. As my observations of various gacaca hearings show, public discussions at gacaca are often acrimonious, as parties who have rarely, if ever, debated with one another on crucial issues assemble to seek solutions to the very real conflicts between them. These parties will not easily reach agreement on many of the issues discussed; the truths heard at gacaca will not provide the easy 'medicine' or 'mending of the social fabric' that some sources suggest (such statements are discussed in greater detail in Chapter 9). Instead, participants in gacaca will need to negotiate the truths told and heard at gacaca and will often require the mediation of judges and other community leaders to discover solutions to their problems. Nevertheless, as Timothy Longman argues, based on his fieldwork into gacaca, 'Even heated exchanges were sometimes quite positive, because they allowed hidden grievances and resentments to come to the surface, where the community could deal with them. Some of the gacaca sessions I attended included dramatic confrontations between witnesses and the people they accused, with people showing extraordinary courage and forthrightness in ways that could only be positive.'[66] Gacaca facilitates forms of engagement and confrontation that are necessary for parties to tackle their problems head-on but such interactions are highly unpredictable and often produce further divisions, necessitating sobriety regarding the impact of truth-telling and truth-hearing through gacaca.

Moreover, the dialogical space that gacaca creates must expand beyond gacaca into participants' daily lives, so that communal dialogue continues in the long term. Gacaca constitutes a vital starting point for these collective discussions. Contrary to Ingelaere's and Waldorf's arguments, my research indicates a high level of public deliberation and debate during many gacaca hearings and – as highlighted by the interviews with participants cited above – a strong desire among all groups in Rwandan society (often for different reasons) to engage in truth-telling and truth-hearing through gacaca. The desire for discursiveness resonates powerfully among many Rwandans, as also highlighted by Dauge-Roth and Longman.

There is a danger that depictions of secrecy and silence in Rwanda essentialise the entire society. The anthropological work of de Lame, which informs much of Ingelaere's and Waldorf's analyses, focuses on a

---

[66] T. Longman, 'An Assessment of Rwanda's Gacaca Courts', *Peace Review: A Journal of Social Justice*, 21, 3, 2009, pp.308–9.

single hill in Kibuye province in the 1980s and early 1990s, and de Lame herself is cautious about extrapolating from the 'hillside micro-culture' to the country as a whole.[67] Furthermore, Ingelaere and Waldorf employ de Lame's analysis selectively. While extending de Lame's characterisations regarding secrecy and silence in Kibuye to Rwanda generally, they continue to describe ethnicity as the primary cleavage in Rwandan society, even though de Lame finds from her Kibuye investigations that socio-economic cleavages were more important than ethnicity in structuring daily lives.[68] Certainly some Rwandans are reluctant to engage in truth-telling and truth-hearing through gacaca but this stems more from the immediate concerns discussed above, such as the time-consuming nature of gacaca hearings and the impact of regional insecurity, than from any innate Rwandan reluctance to engage in public discourse on divisive issues.

The open, constructive dialogical space is not an immutable feature of gacaca. One issue in this regard that has emerged over time is the growing legalism of trials in many communities. From my observations of gacaca jurisdictions, the tone of many hearings has become increasingly formal and people's interactions more stilted, indicating an over-familiarity or fatigue with the gacaca procedure or the legal complexity of many cases, particularly those in Category 1. Many participants have also started bringing copies of the Gacaca Law to hearings and referring to particular sections of it when they speak, which rarely happened in the early years of gacaca.[69]

An example of this legalism was a Category 1 trial in Nyamirambo district of Kigali Ville in August 2008. The hearing took place in a sector office with only sixteen men and four women present to give testimony in front of five inyangamugayo. One by one, as the participants were called to testify, they stood and gave slow, laborious evidence – almost in the form of dictation – which the secretary of the inyangamugayo recorded in her notebook. The president of the inyangamugayo continually asked the witnesses to slow down to allow the secretary to finish recording their testimony. Unlike gacaca hearings I had attended in Nyamirambo in previous years, there was almost no interaction between the judges and the general assembly or within the general asssembly.[70] The judges engaged

---

[67] D. de Lame, *A Hill among a Thousand: Transformation and Ruptures in Rural Rwanda*, Madison, Wisc.: University of Wisconsin Press, 2005, p.111.

[68] *Ibid.*, pp.62, 94–8.

[69] Author's gacaca observations, Kigali Ville, Nyamirambo, 23 August 2008; Northern Province, Musanze, 22 April 2009 (both hearings observed with Nicola Palmer).

[70] Author's gacaca observations, Kigali Ville, Nyamirambo, 21 May 2003; 22 May 2003; 13 June 2006.

in a vigorous cross-examination of several witnesses, who were testifying regarding a suspect – considered a 'notorious killer' in Category 1 – who was alleged to have used an AK-47 and grenades to kill Tutsi during the genocide. The suspect was absent from this trial. The judges asked one witness to clarify whether it was 'the RPF or the interahamwe' who were responsible for several shootings in the community on the days being described. The judges were particularly concerned about inconsistencies between the testimony given by one witness and the father of a boy who was shot and killed. At the end of the hearing, the secretary read back the testimony that the witnesses had delivered and altered parts of the record based on their clarifications. The witnesses then filed past the judges' bench to sign that they agreed with the secretary's record, and the gathering dispersed.[71] The key characteristics of this hearing were the singular focus on discovering the legal facts about the events under consideration, with almost no discussion of their personal, emotional impact on the individuals concerned, and little communal interaction among the participants.

It should be noted that not all Category 1 gacaca hearings display these characteristics. A Category 1 hearing in Musanze district – which began in a field beside the sector office but was moved indoors when rain began to fall – generated a turnout of more than 150 participants from the community and highly engaged discussions throughout.[72] A key difference in this case was that the trial involved several senior suspects, including officials from the local mayor's office, who were present throughout the hearing. This energised the general assembly, in contrast to the Nyamirambo hearing, where the suspect was absent.

Two days after the Nyamirambo trial a gacaca judge in Kacyiru district of Kigali Ville named Fantine, who was also a schoolteacher, explained, 'All inyangamugayo are under pressure to complete cases more quickly than before. The government wants to finish gacaca, so it is telling us to finish these cases fast. That is why many cases are now just about the facts – we hear testimony, we ask questions so that we know if someone is guilty or not.'[73] Over time, many government officials, including President Kagame, have stated a desire to hasten the gacaca process, to enable the country to begin addressing other important post-genocide object-ives, particularly economic development.[74] This has led to an enforced

---

[71] Author's gacaca observations, Kigali Ville, Nyamirambo, 23 August 2008.
[72] Author's gacaca observations, Northern Province, Musanze, 22 April 2009.
[73] Author's inyangamugayo interviews, Fantine, Kigali Ville, Kacyiru, 25 August 2008.
[74] Author's government interviews, Kagame, 2006.

speeding up of many trials, particularly close to Kigali where – as previously stated – state officials wield greater influence over the operation of gacaca. As a result, much of the truth-telling during hearings has become perfunctory, limiting the communal dialogue possible through gacaca.

Finally, the most problematic interpretations from the sources analysed here concern the process of truth-shaping. Problems in this regard centre on issues of agency and specifically on two questions: who should constitute the primary actors at gacaca and for whose benefit should they participate in gacaca? Again, these questions, although stemming from issues regarding truth, highlight major tensions within gacaca as an entire institution. Two particular problems with interpretations of truth-shaping highlight these broader issues of agency at gacaca: the problem of judges' and other leaders' sometimes heavy-handed interventions during gacaca hearings; and the problem of viewing 'truth' as easily definable once parties external to gacaca have distilled 'truths' from the discourse of direct participants.

First, attempts by judges and community leaders, such as clergy, to engage in truth-shaping during gacaca hearings often leads to unjustified interventions. As my own observations of several hearings show, these interventions are often gratuitous, irrelevant in the specific context of gacaca and highly disruptive to the aims of truth-telling and truth-hearing. Truth-shaping during hearings often deflects attention from survivors' discussions of their experiences and focuses instead on the broader lessons that gacaca judges and other community leaders wish to highlight. Leaders should show restraint and, in the main, allow the general assembly to direct discussions, except when these grow violent or verge into irrelevant areas.

Second, problems arise from some sources', particularly some Rwandan authors', interpretations of truth-shaping as the attempt by commentators or community leaders to teach civic virtues, to reinterpret the past and to reconstruct memory, usually on behalf of the population after it has engaged in gacaca. Some commentators assume that external elites will distil broader truths from the community's discourse at gacaca and that the community will readily accept the lessons that these leaders impart to them. At the outset, such a view ignores the extent to which the so-called 'truth' at gacaca is often contested and inevitably communally negotiated. The community reaches legal decisions and interpretations of emotional discourse only after lengthy debates at gacaca. The general assembly may question any statements from judges or other participants – as the elderly lady did in the perjury case described above – and may discuss them at length. Gacaca is vital for shaping people's understandings of the events of the genocide and its aftermath, particularly for survivors for whom public acknowledgement of their experiences is a vital component of their participation at gacaca. As we have already seen, there are many truths told and heard at gacaca and many functions of truth, and the community effectively understands the significance of these truths only via discursive means. Therefore, many participants in gacaca treat with immense scepticism attempts by elites to reinterpret these truths on their behalf. Umutoni, a thirty-seven-year-old survivor in Nyarugenge district of Kigali Ville whose parents and sister were killed during the genocide, said, 'Some of us are frustrated because these officials come to gacaca and talk so much. They listen to what the suspects say, then they tell us what they think it means. But we know what it all means because we have been coming to gacaca for all these years now.'[75]

External parties must respect the multiplicity, and the deeply personal nature, of the narratives that constitute the communal dialogue at gacaca. As Charles Meier argues, the production of historical narratives

> means listening to, testing, and ultimately making public [different parties'] respective subnarratives or partial stories. To resort to a musical analogy: written history must be contrapuntal, not harmonic. That is, it must allow the particular histories of [different] groups to be woven together linearly alongside each other so that the careful listener can follow them distinctly but simultaneously, hearing the whole together with the parts.[76]

In many instances it will be inappropriate to deploy personal narratives in an effort to teach lessons to the community as a whole. When too heavily detached from popular needs and concerns, truth-shaping at gacaca becomes simply another form of elite control or manipulation, using the population's emotional, private experiences of the genocide for official ends.

Moreover, reinterpreting the past or reconstructing memory are highly complex, controversial processes. Karekezi's argument that truth-shaping at gacaca will reconstruct 'a memory that is acceptable for all Rwandans' belies the impossibility of such a task. Inevitably, individuals and groups disagree about the nature and significance of the past.

---

[75] Author's survivor interviews, Umutoni, Kigali Ville, Nyarugenge, 24 August 2008.
[76] C. Meier, 'Doing History, Doing Justice: The Narrative of the Historian and of the Truth Commission', in Rotberg and Thompson, *Truth v. Justice*, pp.274–5.

History and memory are unavoidably contested; there can never be an 'official memory' to which all citizens subscribe.[77] Reconstructing people's memories of events will require substantial debate, within and outside of gacaca, as the infinite range of people's recollections of the genocide, and the various moral and ethical claims they attach to them, will undoubtedly clash, rendering it impossible to construct a universally accepted account of the past. As Nigerian novelist Wole Soyinka argues, 'collective memory ... is the very warp and weft of the tapestry of history that makes up society. Unravel and jettison a thread from that tapestry and society itself may become undone at the seams.'[78] People cleave strongly to their individual memories, because their identity is bounded by how they remember and interpret their experiences. Similarly, societies often struggle to re-evaluate their own understandings of history – their sense of collective memory – because so much of communal identity is tied up with recounting and interpreting the community's past.

These issues are central to the case of the government's Gacaca Documentation Centre, which is designed to create a historical record of the genocide and contribute to the deterrence of future crimes. Gacaca certainly provides one of the most extensive records of any mass atrocity in the world, gathering documents based on communal discussions in 11,000 jurisdictions around Rwanda. However, the content and quality of those records will vary greatly across the country, highlighting, among other things, the extent to which the genocide occurred more rapidly and viciously and caused greater trauma in some locations than in others. The gacaca record will show that genocide as a nationwide phenomenon was also an aggregation of thousands of micro-events that involved millions of individuals. A challenge for the government in constructing the Gacaca Documentation Centre will be to allow those vital national, community-level and personal dynamics to emerge, underscoring the variance of genocide events and their local impact across the country, rather than attempting to tell a singular, bounded, official narrative of the genocide and its meaning for the population.

In Rwanda the role of politicised ethnicity as a lens for different groups' interpretations of history has led to the creation of highly volatile, antagonistic group identities that are one of the root causes of violence. The politics

[77] For a broad discussion of this theme, see P. Clark and Z. Kaufman (eds.), *After Genocide: Transitional Justice, Post-Conflict Reconstruction and Reconciliation in Rwanda and Beyond*, New York: Columbia University Press; London: Hurst & Co., 2009, Part II.

[78] W. Soyinka, 'Memory, Truth and Healing', in I. Amadiume and A. An-Na'im (eds.), *The Politics of Memory: Truth, Healing and Social Justice*, London: Zed Books, 2000, p.21.

of attempting to counter or reconstruct memory in a country riven by ethnic conflict are extremely fraught. Nevertheless, the process of analysing
and interpreting the events and experiences described at gacaca is important, particularly given the limited national discussion that has ensued
since 1994 on the key issues of Rwandan ethnicity and the root causes of
the genocide. Academic commentators and other elites play a vital role in
distilling historical patterns and moral lessons from evidence gathered at
gacaca. They must recognise, however, the inevitable limitations of truth-
shaping at gacaca, which stem from the population's reluctance to allow
external parties to formulate lessons on their behalf and the inevitably
volatile, controversial nature of processes of historical reinterpretation and
memory reconstruction. Effective truth-shaping must be consultative and
must reflect a wide range of people's beliefs and memories.

CONCLUSION

This chapter has argued that gacaca facilitates three processes of truth –
truth-telling, truth-hearing and truth-shaping – each encompassing
three functions of truth: legal, therapeutic and restorative. Gacaca's
simultaneous pursuit of these processes and functions of truth has often
proven highly problematic, especially in trying to balance legal and non-
legal, and individual and communal, concerns after the genocide. As one
of the primary means to achieving retributive justice, healing and reconciliation, truth highlights many of the tensions inherent in the hybrid
pursuit of those ultimate objectives, especially tensions between retributive and restorative outcomes and between the fulfilment of personal and
collective needs. The processes by which the community discovers truth
at gacaca underscore tensions in the overall methods of gacaca, particularly between maintaining the central ethos of popular ownership over
gacaca and managing elite involvement in the institution, while empowering mediators to intervene when communal discourse undermines
gacaca's overall objectives. Nevertheless, evidence from a wide range of
communities indicates that gacaca provides a vital dialogical space in
which Rwandans tell and hear narratives about the events and effects
of the genocide. While challenges to truth-telling, truth-hearing and
particularly truth-shaping have emerged over time, gacaca has provided
a forum for collective discussions that have not occurred elsewhere in
Rwandan society. In doing so, gacaca has fulfilled a vital truth function
in pursuit of the sorts of ends explored in the following chapters, particularly justice, healing and reconciliation.

CHAPTER 8

LAW, ORDER AND RESTORATION: PEACE AND JUSTICE THROUGH GACACA

INTRODUCTION

This chapter explores two themes – peace and justice – that are often linked in the study of transitional societies and that some commentators argue are closely connected in the context of gacaca.[1] The analysis in this chapter draws heavily on the distinctions made in Chapter 1 between negative and positive peace and among retributive, deterrent and restorative justice. While some sources attempt to draw strict divisions between these types of peace and justice, they often represent interconnected concepts and practices. For example, this chapter highlights that restorative justice, which holds that the punishment of perpetrators must be shaped deliberately towards rebuilding fractured relations, does not oppose all notions of deterrent justice, but only those that hold – as some proponents of the dominant discourse on gacaca argue – that punishment alone is an adequate response to crimes such as genocide. Similarly, positive peace, with its emphasis on long-term maintenance of peace, requires first that communities achieve negative peace, in the form of non-violence. After displaying the connections between negative/positive peace and retributive/deterrent/restorative justice respectively, this chapter argues that gacaca has generally succeeded in facilitating peace and justice, although it has faced major obstacles to fulfilling these objectives.

---

[1] See, for example, N. Waddell and P. Clark (eds.), *Courting Conflict? Justice, Peace and the ICC in Africa*, London: Royal African Society, 2008.

GACACA AND PEACE

As we will see later in this chapter, many commentators argue that gacaca jeopardises the maintenance of peace and security in Rwanda. They contend that gacaca will not adequately punish those responsible for genocide crimes and will instead increase tensions in the community by allowing large numbers of suspects (and eventually large numbers of convicted perpetrators after they have completed their sentences) to live side by side with genocide survivors. Various official, popular and critical sources, however, argue that gacaca will contribute substantially to post-genocide peace. Many of these sources, especially suspects in the ingando, view gacaca as a means of securing their own 'peace of mind'. Because the role of gacaca in helping individuals find peace of mind refers ostensibly to the objective of healing, which is explored in Chapter 9, this chapter will focus on gacaca's role in facilitating *communal* peace.

This section explores these sources' interpretations, especially their relative emphases on negative or positive peace, regarding three separate issues: first, the interpretation of the nature of conflict to which gacaca is expected to provide peacebuilding responses; second, the practical ways in which gacaca facilitates peace and which actors engage in these activities; and finally, the expected outcomes of peacebuilding through gacaca. This section argues, based on a critical analysis of these sources and assessing empirical evidence, that gacaca has generally succeeded in promoting peace in Rwanda. Within the concept of positive peace, gacaca plays an important *educative* role by inculcating in the population ideas and methods of future cooperation and conflict resolution rather than in a strictly *deterrent* sense designed to eradicate the culture of impunity. Contrary to the views of some human-rights critics, this section argues that a degree of initial stability and security after the genocide may need to be forfeited for the sake of positive peace, provided instability resulting from gacaca does not lead to renewed violence. For the population to engage directly and honestly at gacaca, with the aim of achieving sustainable peace, it needs to – and, in many communities, has already – overcome initial feelings of instability to confront the root causes of the genocide in a genuine and constructive manner.

Government's perspectives on peace through gacaca

How do government sources interpret the role of gacaca in facilitating peace? An examination of public pronouncements by government officials shows first that a rather confused interpretation of the nature of conflict in Rwanda underpins the official perspective of peacebuilding through gacaca. On the one hand, as we saw concerning popular participation, some officials view gacaca as a form of 'facilitated problem-solving', aimed at providing a template for future conflict resolution.[2] Such a view anticipates continued conflict in Rwanda, whether the government interprets 'problems' as simply minor, day-to-day disputes or something more extreme; a distinction between low-level and major conflict that is rarely clear in official discussions. In this instance, the government believes that a significant level of conflict is natural and inevitable in society and that it is therefore necessary to find peaceful ways to handle it. On the other hand, as we saw earlier, the government's nationalistic rhetoric surrounding the need to regain a lost sense of unity implies that conflict is an aberration in a prevailing state of communal togetherness. The natural state of affairs, according to this view, is the peaceful coexistence of different groups in Rwanda, a coexistence that external forces have historically undermined but that the population can regain by drawing on traditional practices and values inherent in Rwandan culture.

The two views – one of gacaca as overcoming inevitable minor conflicts (in order to avoid major conflict in the future) and one of gacaca as restoring a natural sense of unity that was forfeited temporarily during the genocide – are not necessarily mutually exclusive. Although the government rarely discusses conflict in these terms, it is realistic to assume that even within the view of peaceful coexistence as a natural state of affairs, the government believes that low-level disputes are inevitable in communities around Rwanda. The key difference is one of emphasis, with the initial view underlining the need to cultivate new negotiation methods to avoid violence in the future and the latter invoking a sense of historical cohesion that Rwandans should rediscover in the present. Both perspectives sustain the idea that low-level conflict is unavoidable in any community, especially one recovering from mass violence. The government's rhetoric of national unity, however, emphasises one point that the view regarding ongoing problem-solving does not, namely that mass conflict in Rwanda is an aberration and that a broader sense of social unity is the natural state of affairs.

The government's interpretation of how gacaca facilitates peacebuilding follows from the view that low-level conflict in society is inevitable. One of the main ways in which the government attempts to teach the

---

[2] Author's government interviews, Tayebwa, 30 January 2003.

civic virtues of 'facilitated problem-solving' to the population is through the guidelines governing speech during gacaca hearings, as outlined in the Gacaca Manual. These guidelines include allowing more vulnerable members of the community (such as the elderly) to speak first and emphasising the need for all members of the community to tell the truth and to argue constructively without threatening violence.[3] These guidelines display the government's belief that conflict during gacaca hearings – and presumably in day-to-day life – is unavoidable, thus necessitating methods to ensure more peaceful, constructive interactions.

As enshrined in the Gacaca Law, gacaca's emphasis on consensual decision-making, as occurs among the inyangamugayo when deciding the guilt of suspects, underlines the importance of consultation and open deliberation rather than force when resolving conflicts.[4] Coupled with the common official argument that one broader aim of gacaca is to teach civic virtues to the population through ingando, gacaca and other mechanisms, these modes of 'problem-solving' offer a model for deliberation and conflict resolution outside of gacaca, with the long-term aim of building peace in Rwanda. Thus, the government views gacaca as providing for both negative and positive peace, allowing the population to deal with past and immediate problems and to cultivate virtues that will encourage peaceful problem-solving in the future. A similar perspective drives the government's current use of abunzi to deal with common infractions arising in the community and the potential use of gacaca beyond the completion of the genocide caseload to deal with these problems.

The outcome of peacebuilding at gacaca, according to government officials such as Augustin Nkusi, will be the 'stabilising' of Rwandan society and ensuring citizens' security by teaching them how to resolve their conflicts peacefully.[5] According to this view, peace resulting from gacaca is largely negative, defined as non-violence or maintaining the situation that prevails directly after the cessation of conflict. The government's interpretation, however, also incorporates a conception of positive peace by establishing forward-looking measures through gacaca to ensure that the population can deal calmly and collectively with conflicts in the future. A second component of positive peace in this interpretation is the government's emphasis on gacaca's role in helping to eradicate the

---

[3] Gacaca Manual, p.26.
[4] Gacaca Law (Modified 2004), Article 24.
[5] Author's government interviews, Nkusi, 2003 (author's translation).

culture of impunity by actively deterring future criminals. As the introduction to the Gacaca Law states, one of the government's key motivations for establishing gacaca is the 'necessity to eradicate forever the
culture of impunity in order to achieve justice and reconciliation in
Rwanda, and thus to adopt provisions enabling rapid prosecutions and
trials of perpetrators and accomplices of genocide, not only with the aim
of providing punishment, but also reconstituting the Rwandan Society
that had been destroyed by bad leaders'.[6] In this view, the punishment of
genocide perpetrators is not only a necessary response to past crimes –
that is, giving perpetrators what they *deserve* (i.e. retributive justice) – but
also a means of deterring similar crimes in the future (i.e. deterrent justice). Such prospective interpretations of peacebuilding through gacaca
cohere more readily with the government's view of conflict in Rwanda as
unavoidable rather than with its view of an innate national unity.

Population's perspectives on peace through gacaca
Overall, the population appears deeply divided over how to interpret the
role of gacaca in building peace. In the rare instances that the population discusses peace through gacaca, such descriptions usually come
from detainees in the ingando. Regarding the nature of conflict that
peacebuilding processes at gacaca should overcome, few Rwandans discuss the idea of conflict as an aberration. The population emphasises
instead the inevitability of ongoing conflict which gacaca will need to
address. Unsurprisingly, most Rwandans, and especially genocide survivors, describe conflict in terms of deep-rooted animosity, which causes
ongoing fear, anger and resentment. Nathan, the pastor and survivor in
Nyamata quoted earlier, said,

> Everyone is still fearful – the prisoners and the survivors. The biggest fear
> though is among those coming back from the prisons ... For those com-
> ing back, their fears are justified because the survivors are still angry. It
> depends how bad [the prisoners'] crimes were. But for the survivors, the
> genocide is still haunting ... There is a small chance of revenge attacks
> against the prisoners, but I think the government will constrain anyone
> who is looking for revenge.[7]

The narratives along the gacaca journey in Chapter 4 support these
assertions that many survivors are fearful and angry when suspects

[6] Gacaca Law (Modified 2004), p.2.
[7] Author's survivor interviews, Nathan, Kigali Ngali (author's translation).

return from prison and relations between survivors and suspects are often strained.

A minority of the population, however, expresses a view of conflict as an aberration in Rwandan society. As we have seen, many detainees in particular express a view of Rwandan community as a 'family' characterised by an inherent sense of peace and harmony. Echoing the government's rhetoric, they argue that, when conflict arises, people must simply rediscover the familial virtues embedded in Rwandan society.

Much of the population interprets gacaca's peacebuilding methods similarly to the government, although with greater emphasis on educative rather than deterrent methods of peacebuilding. Genocide suspects tend to emphasise gacaca's capacity for fostering negative peace, reflecting their overriding desire to avoid reprisals after they return to their communities. Pierre, a suspect at a gacaca hearing in Butamwa district of Kigali Ville, argued that gacaca could 'lessen the possibility of violence in the community', suggesting that without a face-to-face dialogue between suspects and survivors at gacaca, they would experience open conflict soon after detainees were released from the ingando.[8] Many detainees describe their primary motivation for confessing to genocide crimes as the need to 'live peacefully with others', which they believe will be impossible without participating in gacaca.[9] Without a show of remorse through a confession of their crimes, apology and request for forgiveness, these detainees argue, they will suffer violent reprisals when they return to the communities where they committed crimes. Nevertheless, my research indicates that only a small minority of confessed perpetrators expressed genuine remorse for their crimes, with most claiming either that they were merely 'present' when crimes were committed or they were coerced by political elites to commit these acts.[10]

Survivors, on the other hand, usually interpret gacaca as contributing to positive peace, displaying a greater concern for developing longer-term methods to resolve conflicts. Gacaca promotes peace, some survivors argue, by allowing them to debate important issues resulting from the genocide and to solve their own problems. Survivors assume that these

[8] Author's gacaca interviews, Pierre, Kigali Ville, Butamwa, 21 May 2003 (author's translation).
[9] Author's solidarity camp interviews, Kigali Ville (no. 5), 12 April 2003; Gashora (no. 10) (author's translation).
[10] See similar responses by perpetrators in J. Hatzfeld, *A Time for Machetes: The Rwandan Genocide – The Killers Speak*, London: Serpent's Tail, 2008, pp.148–55.

processes will be long term and will require difficult dialogue between the parties involved. 'Gacaca is the best way for survivors to find out the truth about the past and for us to learn about living in peace', said Christiane, a widow in Kigali Ville with three young children whose husband was killed during the genocide. 'I'm not sure if we can live together again after what has happened. But at gacaca we will learn how to talk together again, and maybe then we will be able to live together peacefully.'[11] Muvunyi, a thirty-seven-year-old survivor in Nyabihu district of Gisenyi, said, 'If the people can talk face to face at gacaca and learn how to be together again, then they will live peacefully in the future ... We lack peace in our hearts but gacaca allows us to bring out the anger.'[12]

Regarding gacaca's peace-related outcomes, the population expresses mixed views. While many Rwandans closely connect gacaca and peacebuilding, many also expect gacaca to exacerbate low-level conflicts between individuals and groups in the community, at least in the early stages of gacaca when detainees and survivors come face to face for the first time. The NURC survey into public views of gacaca shows that most Rwandans anticipate an initial increase in instability during gacaca hearings. According to this survey, 49 per cent of the general population and 74 per cent of survivors believe that testimony at gacaca will initially aggravate tensions between families.[13] Eighty-nine per cent of survivors and 49 per cent of detainees believe that they will feel personally insecure during hearings,[14] and 97 per cent of the overall population argue that security forces will find it difficult to maintain people's safety at gacaca.[15] Tharcisse, a father of five children and a widower in Gisenyi Ville whose wife was murdered during the genocide, said,

> It was wrong to release the prisoners from the camps ... Now that they're back in the community there may be more killings. Survivors might hunt down the killers. The killers might hunt down survivors. The government has told us nothing about what is going on ... It's impossible for us to live together again.[16]

---

[11] Author's survivor interviews, Christiane, Kigali Ville (author's translation).
[12] Author's survivor interviews, Muvunyi, Gisenyi, Nyabihu, 14 June 2006.
[13] NURC, 'Opinion Survey on Participation in Gacaca', Annexe 4, p.20.
[14] *Ibid.*, Annexe 4, p.23.
[15] *Ibid.*, Annexe 4, p.16.
[16] Author's survivor interviews, Tharcisse, Gisenyi (author's translation).

For genocide suspects, the fear of reprisals when they arrive back in their communities is widespread. Many suspects I interviewed – including those on the bus leaving the Kinyinya camp during the first wave of detainee releases in 2003 – described rumours they heard in the ingando of groups of survivors waiting to exact revenge on them as soon as they returned home. Révérien, a detainee in the ingando in Kigali Ville, said on the day of his release into his home community near Nyamata,

> I don't know who's waiting for me in the village. People talk about survivors waiting there for us, maybe wanting to hurt us. I hear stories of survivors waiting for us in the market. I don't know what to expect. It's very scary for us.[17]

Many suspects consequently fear coming face to face with survivors at gacaca. Whether this fear derives from some detainees' feelings of guilt, and thus a fear of having their crimes exposed at gacaca, or from a genuine belief that they may face verbal or physical attack, is unclear. Similarly, many survivors fear having to engage with suspects. Christiane, the survivor who said that gacaca was a place to 'learn about living in peace', also said,

> I got very scared when I first heard the radio message that the prisoners were going to be released ... I often see prisoners now in the streets and I get scared. I think to myself, 'Will they hurt me? Am I safe here? What will happen when I see them at gacaca?'[18]

Beyond these initial stages of confrontation at gacaca, much of the population believes that gacaca will contribute to positive peace, emphasising its role in facilitating long-term stability in Rwanda. Many popular sources claim that, while gacaca may initially increase tensions between participants, this initial phase of instability is necessary for fostering positive peace, by directing initial tensions towards a form of engagement at gacaca that allows the parties involved to live together in the future. The NURC survey shows that 84 per cent of the population believe that gacaca will help eradicate the culture of impunity and 92 per cent argue that gacaca will lay the foundation for sustainable peace and social harmony.[19] These statistics suggest that the population is willing to endure an initial increase in tension and acrimony at gacaca to achieve longer-term peace and stability, provided the initial confrontations are

[17] Author's solidarity camp interviews, Kigali Ville (no. 11), 5 May 2003 (author's translation).
[18] Author's survivor interviews, Christiane, Kigali Ville (author's translation).
[19] NURC, 'Opinion Survey on Participation in Gacaca', Annexe 4, p.1.

mediated to produce more positive outcomes. Jean-Baptiste, a survivor interviewed after a gacaca hearing in Nyamata, said that he had spoken twice at gacaca about his experiences during the genocide:

> I come to gacaca because I want to see the killers, even though seeing them will scare me ... At gacaca I told the people what I saw and this was very hard ... All my family were killed during the genocide – my father, my mother, two brothers and four sisters. I know who killed them. Those men are still in jail and haven't come to gacaca yet ... I'm scared about meeting them. But gacaca is good for survivors because we can ... tell people what happened to our families ... There will only be peace from now on.[20]

Emerithe, a survivor in Gisenyi, said,

> You know, gacaca is very difficult for survivors because we have to hear how our families were killed. People repeat these things over and over and it fills your mind for many days. But it is better to know these things than not to know. And it is better to talk about these things. The inyangamugayo help us to talk – sometimes they start talking first and others follow. Things have been more peaceful here since people started to talk about what happened in the past.[21]

Commentators' perspectives on peace through gacaca
Finally, the critical literature rarely considers explicitly the link between gacaca and peace. It is clear, though, that most commentators view conflict in Rwanda as largely unavoidable, given the extent to which ethnic and other divisions have shaped social and political life for decades. Therefore, most commentators assume that gacaca will not only need to deal with the profoundly felt legacies of past violence but also to facilitate processes designed to avoid violence and produce greater social harmony in the future. As Stef Vandeginste argues, gacaca faces seemingly insurmountable odds in terms of rebuilding a society riven by ethnic divisions, distrust between neighbours and between citizens and the state. 'The impact of genocide, war and failed political transition', he argues, 'has led to a context in which society itself has been the victim, i.e. where the social tissue which underpins the usual indigenous response has broken

---

[20] Author's gacaca interviews, Jean-Baptiste, Kigali Ngali, Nyamata, 19 May 2003 (author's translation).
[21] Author's survivor interviews, Emerithe, Gisenyi, Nyabihu, 14 June 2006.

down, and where the state has been an instrument of oppression rather than an instrument of protection of fundamental rights of its citizens.'[22]

For most commentators, the methods by which gacaca facilitates peace emphasise the need for long-term processes of overcoming conflict that duly recognise deeply rooted animosity in the community. The few commentators who discuss peace through gacaca focus on its ability to foster positive peace, usually defined in the educative rather than deterrent sense. Many Rwandan authors stress the need for a pedagogy of civic virtues to afford the population the means to peacefully resolve its problems. A rare instance of a commentator's discussing negative peace through gacaca comes from Karekezi, who echoes the government's view that gacaca must establish negative peace in terms of restoring stability and 'social equilibrium'.[23] Karekezi, however, also argues that this initial stage of peacebuilding is insufficient and that gacaca constitutes a forum for communal problem-solving that encourages more peaceful, long-term engagement; a view that interprets peace in the positive sense.[24] In this critical view, dialogue and communal problem-solving are gacaca's main means of shoring up negative peace. More importantly, these processes also provide for positive peace, particularly if gacaca imparts civic virtues of cooperation and communal discussion to the population, thus helping safeguard against future violence.

Like the population, the few commentators who address gacaca's contribution to peace argue that it is likely to increase discord between participants, particularly between suspects and survivors and especially in the early stages of the process. Xavier Gasimba argues that 'both the innocent and guilty fear gacaca' and that survivors and suspects have different but equally justified reasons to expect personal insecurity during hearings.[25] Where commentators divide is over their expectations of the results of initially difficult interactions at gacaca. Some non-Rwandan observers argue that such confrontations will jeorpardise peace, especially if participants are dissatisfied with the forms of punishment meted out at gacaca, which may cause resentment and the desire for vengeance. Corey and Joireman argue that gacaca will lead to short- and long-term insecurity in Rwanda: in the short term, because the security of witnesses and defendants cannot be guaranteed during

[22] Vandeginste, 'Justice, Reconciliation and Reparation', p.1.

[23] Karekezi, 'Juridictions gacaca', p.34.

[24] Ibid., p.55.

[25] X. Gasimba, 'Minutes of the Symposium on Gacaca', Hotel Umubano, Kigali, 6–7 March 2000, p.41.

and after acrimonious gacaca hearings; and in the long term, because gacaca fails to guarantee due process for genocide suspects, for example by denying them access to legal counsel, and because it deals only with crimes committed by Hutu *génocidaires* and not those by the RPF. Corey and Joireman argue that gacaca embodies a form of 'politicized justice' that will intensify 'a desire for vengeance among the Hutu majority ... thereby contributing to, rather than curtailing, the risk of ethnic violence in the long run'.[26]

On the other hand, some Rwandan observers, such as Gasibirege, argue that the engagement between parties that gacaca encourages is necessary for the population to learn to resolve difficult issues collectively. The election of gacaca judges, Gasibirege argues, encouraged the community to discuss the virtues that judges should embody, to discern the degree to which different candidates embodied these virtues, and thus to learn to deliberate openly and peacefully on issues vital to the well-being of the entire community. The election of gacaca judges, Gasibirege argues, was a 'key moment in the process of peace' and showed that, if community leaders could create a conducive atmosphere, then the population could learn future modes of conflict resolution through active, public engagement.[27]

Critique of sources' perspectives on peace through gacaca

It is necessary to critically analyse and, in several cases, to reject, the views of the government, population and commentators regarding the three issues concerning peace through gacaca: the nature of the conflict that gacaca's peacebuilding processes are expected to address; the nature of those processes and the actors involved; and the expected outcomes of peacebuilding through gacaca. An analysis of these issues shows that the government's interpretation of peace through gacaca is particularly problematic. First, regarding these sources' interpretations of the nature of the conflict to which gacaca responds, it is untenable to hold the view, expressed by some official and popular sources, of conflict as an aberration in Rwandan society. Given the history of Rwanda, especially periods of mass violence after 1959, but even during earlier periods of deep-seated socio-economic divisions between Hutu and Tutsi, it is impossible to accept the view that conflict in Rwanda is unusual. Conflict between

---

[26] Corey and Joireman, 'Retributive Justice', pp.86, 74.
[27] Gasibirege, 'L'Élection des juges inyangumagayo', p.94.

Hutu and Tutsi has become a tragic norm, especially as successive colonial and domestic regimes politicised ethnicity, after 1959, and sponsored campaigns of violence against particular groups. At a more mundane level, daily disputes are also unavoidable in any community as people's interests and perspectives inevitably conflict. This is especially the case in a country as densely populated and ethnically divided as Rwanda, where the capacity for disputes over natural resources and social and political power is immense. Therefore, an assumption underlying the structure and daily running of gacaca must be that disagreements and disputes will arise consistently wherever hearings take place and often during the hearings themselves. Gacaca must ensure that these forms of lower-level conflict do not escalate to violence. Furthermore, the history of violent conflict, usually ethnically motivated, serves as a warning to the orchestrators of gacaca that anger and resentment run deep in the community and that all peacebuilding processes must address the possibility that these sentiments may lead to violence in the future. As discussed in more detail below, my gacaca observations and participant interviews show that, while gacaca hearings create immediate tensions in some communities, they often, over time, foster new forms of dialogue and better relations, particularly when the judges effectively mediate the discussions during hearings. Without the conscious management of tensions within communities, however, gacaca often foments greater discord.

Regarding methods of peacebuilding, only commentators on gacaca are consistently convincing, justifiably emphasising the need, and capacity, for gacaca to incorporate long-term processes of positive peace. This argument follows from the assumption that low-level conflict is inevitable in any community and that in Rwanda violent conflict has recently been common. Simply avoiding violence – that is, achieving negative peace – for example as some suspects wish, hoping to avoid reprisals from survivors, is insufficient. As the history of Rwanda after 1959 shows, periods of apparently peaceful coexistence between Hutu and Tutsi have tended to give way to mass violence because, despite the supposedly harmonious circumstances, the root causes of conflict were not addressed. At gacaca, it is necessary therefore for participants to confront face to face the nature, and sources, of their conflicts and to openly and genuinely seek ways of overcoming them. Gacaca provides for this form of confrontation through the processes of engagement as described in Chapter 5, particularly with the emphasis on open, in-depth dialogue and debate on issues of communal importance.

There is no doubting the risk that the level of engagement required at gacaca entails, and suspects and survivors are justified in anticipating painful confrontations at gacaca. Leaders overseeing gacaca must be sensitive to the population's fears and concerns and to the possibility that gacaca will, at least initially, exacerbate some tensions. At the same time, Rwandan commentators such as Karekezi and Gasibirege (and non-Rwandans such as Longman) are right to argue that not all disputes at gacaca hamper the cause of peace. Engagement at gacaca requires difficult dialogue as participants cooperate in a genuine attempt to come to terms with the sources of their disputes. Gacaca judges and other leaders who shape the institution must strike a balance between allowing the open debate and discussion of contentious issues during gacaca hearings – which may result in immediate forms of discord – and intervening when such discord threatens to incite unmanageable conflict. The government's interpretation of gacaca's peacebuilding processes pays insufficient attention to the role of mediators such as gacaca judges in assisting the population to translate their engagement at gacaca into further engagement in their daily lives outside of gacaca. The government's perspective here is self-contradictory, given that it also emphasises the need for gacaca to embody a form of 'facilitated problem-solving', which implies a significant level of mediation. Because the government maintains an extreme argument regarding untrammelled popular participation in gacaca, as discussed earlier, it fails to account for the need for mediators to guide often acrimonious gacaca hearings towards more peaceful ends.

Disagreements during gacaca hearings are often healthy, provided they neither concern issues completely irrelevant to post-genocide reconstruction nor escalate into violence. Short-term, low-level conflict, in the form of the community's discussions of often-painful and contentious issues, is necessary for long-term peace, as the dialogue of gacaca hearings becomes a training ground for non-violent conflict resolution outside of gacaca. One example of this comes from the gacaca jurisdiction in Kacyiru district of Kigali Ville discussed in Chapter 5, where in 2003 a recently returned detainee disrupted a hearing, necessitating intervention by the president of the inyangamugayo. I returned to the same community in 2006 to observe two gacaca hearings and interview participants. By this time, the trial phase had commenced and a number of suspects had already been convicted and sentenced. I spoke to several members of the general assembly who had been present at the 2003 hearing. 'I remember the hearing you are referring to', said Donatien, a forty-four-year-old survivor who ran a small electronics stall in the nearby market.

> That was a very difficult time here because the prisoners were coming back. There were always disruptions during gacaca because people were shouting and arguing ... If you look at gacaca here now, you will see that things are different. The people are more focused. They speak more calmly. That is because life is more settled. The prisoners have all been back for several years and some of them have been doing TIG in another place and now some will go back to jail ... The survivors still live a difficult life because of their memories. You cannot forget the things you have gone through. But things are peaceful here now. There are no big problems.[28]

Chifura, a sixty-two-year-old woman whose son was awaiting trial for alleged murders committed during the genocide, said,

> It is a terrible thing to have to wait like this. My son has been back here for three years and still he doesn't know what will happen to him ... I go to gacaca most weeks and the people are calm. They know each other and they talk normally to each other. Mostly in this place, people are living peacefully, but if you have a loved one who has been accused, then it is not easy. You can't sleep well because you are always worried.[29]

My observations of gacaca hearings in this community confirmed Donatien's and Chifura's descriptions. Both hearings, which involved several suspects confessing publicly to their crimes and numerous members of the general assembly standing to provide evidence, were characterised by engaged participation and calm mediation by the judges. The atmosphere surrounding these hearings, as Donatien and Chifura described, was significantly less tense than in 2003 because people had become used to the returned detainees living in their midst and to the modalities of gacaca. Many people were still uncertain of the results that gacaca would produce, particularly the judgments and sentences that would be delivered, but there was little of the observed suspicion and acrimony from three years earlier.[30]

A lack of any form of disagreement or conflict during gacaca hearings, on the other hand, usually signifies a lack of meaningful engagement

---

[28] Author's survivor interviews, Donatien, Kigali Ville, Kacyiru, 13 June 2006.
[29] Author's gacaca interviews, Chifura, Kigali Ville, Kacyiru, 13 June 2006.
[30] Author's gacaca observations, Kigali Ville, Kacyiru, 13 June 2006; 20 June 2006.

between participants. The Category 1 gacaca hearing in Nyamirambo described in the previous chapter displayed an increased formalism and little of the communal engagement observed in the district in previous years. As we saw in Chapter 4, the detainees who experienced the gacaca journey often avoided confrontation with survivors by moving to the outskirts of their communities. In doing so, however, they forfeited any possibility of engaging with survivors and addressing their antagonisms. Because engagement is so crucial for restoration, gacaca judges require a deep sense of discernment: they must facilitate engagement in order to achieve the aims of gacaca, without interfering unnecessarily in the proceedings, but they must also intervene if the debates at gacaca become unproductive or violent.

Observers such as Corey and Joireman are rightly concerned that acrimony during gacaca hearings may have wider effects on relations in the community. Such possibilities, however, do not completely undermine the potential for gacaca to embody civic virtues of communal engagement, dialogue and debate that are important for building trust and long-term peace. Furthermore, the mediation of gacaca judges and the presence of government security personnel at all hearings safeguard against destructive altercations or violence. Corey and Joireman therefore mistakenly conclude that gacaca will *inevitably* lead to major, short-term insecurity.

While it is undoubtedly important for gacaca to facilitate long-term peacebuilding processes that aim primarily at positive peace, one component of some officials' and commentators' arguments for sustained processes is highly questionable: the importance of punishment of perpetrators at gacaca for deterring future criminals and thus ending impunity. It is not immediately obvious that punishment at gacaca will deter potential criminals and thus contribute to negative peace. There is little doubt that a culture of impunity before the genocide was a critical factor in enabling the genocide. However, it is not clear that punishing *génocidaires*, whether through gacaca, the national courts or the ICTR, will eradicate the culture of impunity. Various writers, sometimes focusing on other conflict societies, have questioned the assumed link between punishment and the deterrence of potential criminals.[31] Critics of the

---

[31] See, for example, J. Braithwaite, *Restorative Justice and Responsive Regulation*, Oxford: Oxford University Press, 2002, pp.102–28; D. Martin, 'Retribution Revisited: A Reconsideration of Feminist Criminal Law Reform Strategies', *Orgoode Hall Law Journal*, 36, 1, 1998, pp.162–4; M. Minow, *Between Vengeance and Forgiveness: Facing History after Genocide and Mass Violence*, Boston, Mass.: Beacon Press, 1998, pp.145–6.

deterrence view of punishment argue that the political and cultural leaders who orchestrate mass violence are likely to do so regardless of the judicial consequences of their actions.

Furthermore, the culture of impunity in Rwanda was only an enabler of the genocide, and it alone does not explain *why* so many people killed their friends, neighbours and family members. Other cultural and political factors, particularly fear during the civil-war period, ethnic hatred, material deprivation and incitement and intimidation by state officials, were more direct causes of the genocide.[32] If a post-conflict institution such as gacaca aims to build peace, then it must respond to the deep-rooted motivations of the population that led it to perpetrate mass violence. Deterrence through punishment may lead individuals to question the consequences of committing crimes but it cannot respond adequately to the complex political and psychosocial causes of crimes such as genocide. Even when confronted with the genuine possibility of punishment for their actions, perpetrators who are motivated by extreme fear or ethnic hatred may not be deterred from committing crimes. It is therefore more appropriate to focus – as some sections of the population and some commentators do – on how gacaca contributes to peacebuilding by providing long-term, sustainable responses to the root *causes* of mass conflict, rather than to the factors that allowed conflict. Punishment for perpetrators is still necessary to voice the community's outrage at crimes committed and perhaps to deter some offenders. Effective deterrent justice, however, requires deeper, concurrent peacebuilding processes if it is to genuinely contribute to long-term peace.

Regarding the likely outcomes of peacebuilding through gacaca, the population and commentators overall offer useful insights, while there are significant problems with the government's perspective. The population and commentators on gacaca justifiably emphasise the degree to which gacaca causes great concern among many survivors and suspects, particularly as they anticipate the face-to-face engagement and the discussions of often traumatic experiences that gacaca requires. Feelings of trepidation are inevitable before and during gacaca hearings because gacaca constitutes for many Rwandans the first time they have engaged so closely with other members of the community, especially those from different ethnic groups. However, most popular and critical sources analysed here are right to argue that initial periods of foreboding and arduous

---

[32] See, for example, Fujii, *Killing Neighbors*; Longman, 'Genocide and Socio-Political Change'; and Straus, *The Order of Genocide*.

forms of engagement during gacaca hearings are necessary if individuals and the community as a whole are to reap the rewards of engagement through gacaca.

The government is similarly justified in arguing that the mediated problem-solving of gacaca is critical to cultivating similar methods of peaceful conflict resolution for the future. Several suspects and survivors interviewed stated that gacaca had a discernible impact on modes of dialogue and conflict resolution in their general community, drawing on principles of mediation and negotiation. As Alphonse stated during the gacaca journey, in his community gacaca (dealing with genocide crimes) and the abunzi (handling daily infractions) operated symbiotically, each reinforcing their respective mediation and resolution processes. As we have seen, however, the government does not consistently emphasise the role of gacaca in preparing the population to deal with future conflicts. The government often argues instead that gacaca will simply allow the population to achieve negative peace by restoring a lost sense of national unity. Besides the mythical status of the 'lost' unity, the problem with such a view is that maintaining negative peace alone is insufficient for the creation of a functioning, sustainable society. Aiming only at non-violence, as the government argues that gacaca should, fails to foster more meaningful, future relationships between previously antagonistic individuals and groups. Because there is an absence of violence does not mean that the sources of violence have been eradicated and that they may not again take root in society. Thwarting the potential for future conflict and building a lasting peace entail actively facilitating the creation of stronger bonds between individuals and groups previously in conflict. Gacaca must restore trust and facilitate engagement, not only because these are good in and of themselves but because they contribute to long-term peace by giving people the resources to resolve their conflicts constructively and independently.

In this sense, peacebuilding at gacaca aims at much more than restoring some lost form of communal 'unity'; it aims to develop the capacity of the population to resolve inevitable conflicts. Achieving negative peace is a vital first step towards building trust and facilitating engagement; a society such as Rwanda must achieve a level of non-violence and stability before seeking to build stronger bonds between its citizens. However, achieving that stability appears to be the aim of processes preceding gacaca, which in turn is concerned more with building trust and facilitating engagement. The view expressed above by the survivor Jean-Baptiste is especially telling: he admitted that the prospect of facing genocide perpetrators at gacaca scared him immensely but nonetheless he believed that gacaca was 'good for survivors because we can speak the truth' and that the recognition that gacaca would allow parties to discuss their conflicts constructively convinced him that there would 'only be peace from now on'. Certainly not all suspects or survivors share this perspective. The government and gacaca judges must therefore help participants in gacaca overcome their initial fears and concerns in order to pursue gacaca's profound objectives.

In conclusion, gacaca has led to periods of increased instability, particularly in the early stages of hearings when suspects and survivors meet face to face for the first time and, to some extent, at the beginning of the trial phase when issues of guilt and innocence are at stake, following the lengthy information-gathering phase. That gacaca may create initial tensions, however, does not preclude it from facilitating negative peace, provided these tensions do not lead to violence. Gacaca has often consolidated a situation of non-violence, which is the requirement of negative peace, by providing an immediate form of mediated conflict resolution. Aided by gacaca's legal statutes that safeguard against violence in the general assembly and the presence of security personnel at all hearings, gacaca judges have helped many parties discuss their conflicts more usefully, despite the difficulties inherent in assembling antagonistic parties in such close confines.

Gacaca has also proven vital in the construction of positive peace. The same processes of mediated engagement that are important for negative peace in the short term are crucial for positive peace in the long term, particularly if the population learns key virtues of conflict resolution at gacaca that it can transfer into daily life, as some communities appear to have already experienced. Thus, gacaca constitutes a vital realm for *educative* positive peace. Certainly the prospects for positive peace will be heavily influenced by social and political developments outside of gacaca. However, gacaca currently constitutes a rare forum in which the engagement between previously antagonistic parties necessary for maintaining long-term peace can occur.

GACACA AND JUSTICE

In all official, popular and critical discussions, justice – along with truth – is the theme most readily identified as an objective of gacaca. This is not surprising given the immense backlog of genocide cases and the widespread moral conviction that perpetrators should be brought to account for their actions and receive the punishment they deserve. Nonetheless, the sources analysed here regularly disagree over exactly how justice should be pursued through gacaca. Among the most controversial issues captured in discussions of justice through gacaca is why justice is necessary after the genocide: is justice required simply to fulfil a moral obligation to deal with perpetrators (which, as we saw in Chapter 1, constitutes retributive justice), to deter future perpetrators from committing similar crimes (deterrent justice), or to facilitate wider aims, such as rebuilding broken relationships and renewing the social fabric (restorative justice)?

Broadly speaking, these sources' interpretations comprise views on the *processes* and *outcomes* of justice. Regarding processes, these sources interpret justice as pursued in two main ways: formally, according to pre-determined legal statutes, or through negotiation, in which the population determines discursively how justice will be dispensed and what form of justice genocide perpetrators will receive. In turn, these sources interpret the outcomes of justice in the three ways just mentioned: retributive, deterrent or restorative.

This section explores the views of the government, population and commentators concerning justice through gacaca, particularly as they regard distinctions and connections between formal and negotiated processes and among retributive, deterrent and restorative outcomes. This section analyses their views concerning the *form* of justice that they believe gacaca facilitates and the *means* by which gacaca will pursue it. Just as Chapter 5 argued that gacaca displays internal hybridity by combining formal with negotiated methods (with emphasis on the negotiated, and the formal acting simply as legal boundaries), this section shows that gacaca represents an ingenious hybrid of retributive, deterrent and restorative justice outcomes (where the ultimate aim is restorative). This synthesis enables gacaca to achieve legal outcomes, especially punishing genocide perpetrators, in ways that facilitate important non-legal results, such as restoring fractured individual and communal relationships.

In particular, this section highlights that gacaca embodies two elements for shaping punishment towards restorative ends: first, gacaca's modus operandi of popular participation contributes to restorative justice by encouraging dialogue and collaboration between parties as they give and weigh evidence related to criminal cases. These forms of engagement in many communities have helped rebuild trust and relationships between previously antagonistic parties. Second, gacaca's use of community service as a form of punishment for some *génocidaires* contributes to restoration by reintegrating perpetrators more rapidly into the community and involving them in communal work programmes. These programmes often entail perpetrators and survivors working side by side; a form of engagement that has further aided restoration in many parts of Rwanda.

Government's perspectives on justice through gacaca

How do the different sources define justice through gacaca? The official view emphasises the retributive and deterrent functions of punishing suspects found guilty of committing genocide, while maintaining that the punishment of perpetrators should be shaped towards more restorative ends. The government in the early years of gacaca expressed the restorative view more mutedly, probably for fear of alienating survivors who may view any diminution of punishment as unjust. The Gacaca Law emphasises the deterrent nature of punishment at gacaca by stating that gacaca is established in order to 'eradicate forever the culture of impunity' by adopting 'provisions enabling rapid prosecutions and trials of perpetrators and accomplices of genocide'.[33] Rapid trials are necessary, the government argues – highlighting the concerns of retributive justice for fulfilling a moral obligation to try suspects and to punish the guilty – to process the immense backlog of previously untried genocide cases and to improve on other judicial structures such as the Rwandan national courts and the ICTR. Underlining the importance of gacaca for restorative justice, however, the Gacaca Law goes on to state that gacaca is designed 'not only with the aim of providing punishment, but also reconstituting the Rwandan Society that had been destroyed by bad leaders'.[34]

Senior Rwandan judicial officials increasingly argue that gacaca is necessary for restorative justice after the genocide, although they highlight different nuances. The Prosecutor General, Martin Ngoga, emphasised the enormity of Rwanda's post-genocide challenges and the necessity for gacaca to deliver reconciliation. 'Justice here has been necessarily contextual', he said. 'Our country was nearly destroyed by the genocide, which some people forget … But justice has made huge contributions here. We don't ask anyone to sing our praises but, if you look at the results, gacaca has delivered justice that has helped reconcile our people.'[35] Professor Sam Rugege, Deputy Chief Justice of the Supreme

---

[33] Gacaca Law (Modified 2004), p.2.
[34] *Ibid.*, p.2.
[35] Author's government interviews, Martin Ngoga, Prosecutor General, Kigali, 5 September 2008 (interview conducted jointly with Nicola Palmer).

Court, cautioned against wishing reconciliation to happen too quickly but nevertheless stressed the importance of gacaca – and the law generally – in deterring future criminality and facilitating reconciliation. In 2006, Rugege said,

> Gacaca is our only chance of reconciliation … Reconciliation depends on Rwanda finishing the process of prosecuting genocide suspects … We have a difficult situation of balancing different concerns. There are of course problems with fast justice and fast reconciliation. Reconciliation is an unavoidably slow process. And justice must precede reconciliation. It's part of the process – in many ways, we have to get it out of the way so that reconciliation can become viable.
>
> … In terms of rebuilding this country after the genocide, the politics of the situation can be debated, including convincing the ordinary people of certain policies and approaches. But it's more effective to rebuild through the law than through politics and morality. Politics has much to do with it and it's important to sensitise the population. The NURC, for example, has a major role in the rebuilding. But law has an important role because it deters future perpetrators and it also encourages others to do right, to follow a better path and to live more harmoniously.[36]

Assessing gacaca's impact in 2008, Rugege emphasised the effect of gacaca on Rwanda's entire legal system and, as a consequence, on improving social relations and facilitating reconciliation:

> Gacaca has done a stunning job of handling genocide cases at the rate that it has … It has also had an impact on our entire legal system, which we reformed substantially in 2004 and have continued to reform ever since. We now use plea bargaining much more than before, and you can see the influence of gacaca in this regard. In the formal courts, confession now enables lesser sentences, even the possibility of halving sentences, and more perpetrators are confessing their crimes. This is the impact of gacaca … The abunzi have also helped greatly. The abunzi are like gacaca in that they promote good neighbourliness and reconciliation between warring parties, telling them, 'If you talk things through, you can settle it.' … Social development comes through laws. The law is a vehicle for change, which is why legal and judicial reform are so crucial in this context. Out of destruction can come good things. Gacaca is our centrepiece for dealing with genocide crimes but it has been more than

---

[36] Author's government interviews, Sam Rugege, Deputy Chief Justice, Supreme Court, Kigali, 8 June 2006.

just punishment. It has brought about reconciliation among those who were directly involved in the genocide.[37]

Meanwhile, Tharcisse Karugarama, the Minister of Justice, underscored gacaca's achievements but also warned against expecting the law to achieve too much in the post-genocide context. 'Look at what gacaca has accomplished', he said.

> We now have only 53,000 detainees in prison, including genocide and other cases. Where are the rest? They've been reintegrated into the community. Some have been acquitted, some have received light terms, most have done community service and have helped in rebuilding the country … Gacaca has delivered justice and you can see the benefits in the way people relate to each other on the hills … Justice isn't about laws. It's about fairness and restoring human dignity. I've been a prosecutor and a judge and I know you shouldn't confuse justice and legal dogma. Gacaca hasn't always been acceptable to the legal fraternity but that's just dogma. Gacaca has delivered a justice that restores people's dignity and gives them a way to live together.[38]

Concerning the specific means of restorative justice, the government describes only vaguely how gacaca helps facilitate restoration, which it sometimes defines opaquely as 'social cohesion'[39] or 'communal harmony'.[40] In the official view, it is clear how punishment will be achieved through negotiated and formal means but less clear how this will contribute to rebuilding relationships. The Gacaca Law emphasises that genocide suspects will be prosecuted via detailed processes of communal evidence-gathering and deliberation (i.e. by negotiation) and, if found guilty, punished according to the predetermined matrix of sentences outlined in Chapter 2 (i.e. by formal procedures). The government rarely describes, though, how these processes will help facilitate restoration. In the rare instances that official sources do discuss the shaping of punishment towards restoration, they argue that this will occur through dialogue and collaboration during gacaca hearings. These processes are partly designed, as Nkusi was quoted in the last chapter, to uncover legal evidence in order to prosecute genocide perpetrators but

---

[37] Author's government interviews, Sam Rugege, Deputy Chief Justice, Supreme Court, Kigali, 7 August 2008 (interview conducted jointly with Nicola Palmer).

[38] Author's government interviews, Tharcisse Karugarama, Minister of Justice, Kigali, 3 September 2008 (interview conducted jointly with Nicola Palmer).

[39] Gacaca Manual, p.8 (author's translation).

[40] Government interviews, Nkusi, 2003 (author's translation).

also to encourage the population to collaborate in such a way as to help them rebuild relationships after the genocide.[41] President Kagame also connected gacaca to restorative justice in this way: 'The justice that you see at gacaca supports reconciliation by involving the people in the process. It may not be the ideal way of doing things but it is what we have to work with.'[42] In this 2006 interview, Kagame conceded that gacaca was struggling under the weight of the enormous genocide caseload, including hundreds of thousands of newly identified cases, and therefore the government was considering other ways to expedite the judicial process:

> I have to stress that gacaca is not open-ended. It has to have an end. It won't just stop if we reach 2008 but, at the same time, it can't continue forever because we have other goals to pursue. Open-endedness would be negative for the whole country ... Even an amnesty is possible, especially for low-level perpetrators. You'll remember that we used an amnesty for some people in 2003. Anything is possible, even with some of the very serious cases. We'll give time to our various processes to deal with these cases but we're talking about justice on a massive scale and we have to look at other approaches.[43]

Recently, state officials have described the importance of community service in rebuilding fractured social relations, especially as convicted perpetrators perform communal works that directly benefit survivors. 'More reconciliation occurs when perpetrators return home from TIG after gacaca', said Ndangiza. 'Then they start rebuilding trust and the reconciliation process really starts. Some do TIG from home and they meet victims directly and this helps reconciliation.'[44]

Population's perspectives on justice through gacaca
As they do regarding various objectives, the population's interpretations of justice through gacaca largely mirror the government's views, emphasising the importance of retributive and deterrent, rather than restorative, justice. For survivors in particular, the overriding concern regarding justice is desert: to see genocide perpetrators punished for their egregious crimes. Survivors rarely discuss ways in which punishment may facilitate restoration. As Romain, a survivor in Butare, said, 'Punishment is absolutely necessary at gacaca. We must punish the bad people for what they

---

[41] *Ibid.*   [42] Author's government interviews, Kagame, 2006.
[43] *Ibid.*   [44] Author's government interviews, Ndangiza, 2008.

did. We can't simply let them go free after everything they did to us.[45] Meanwhile, suspects and their families are highly aware of the nature of the legal processes and the likely punishments that the guilty will face at gacaca. 'I know gacaca will punish me', said Vedaste, the detainee in the solidarity camp at Butare quoted earlier who had confessed to committing murder during the genocide,

> but it will also reconcile me to those around me because I have confessed, because I have told them the truth … I will probably have to return to prison because of my crimes and I will probably do some community work as punishment.[46]

Some suspects believe that they have already served their punishments during their many years in jail. Arubier, a detainee in the ingando in Kigali Ville, said, 'I was in prison long enough and now it is time for me to live in the community again. I have already paid my penalty.'[47] Of the three suspects interviewed along the gacaca journey, only Laurent believed there gacaca might convict and reimprison him, while Cypriet and Alphonse believed they would, at worst, have to perform community service.

Like the government, though, large segments of the population, including some survivors, argue that punishment at gacaca may also help achieve restorative ends. Michel, the president of the inyangamugayo in Butamwa district who earlier described gacaca as 'real justice where we are all together', argued that punishing criminals in the communal setting of gacaca was also 'important for reconciliation'.[48] Such a view encapsulates the sorts of processes at gacaca that some parts of the population believe will facilitate restorative justice. Like the government, the population describes the forms of dialogue and collaboration that are attached to the pursuit of retributive justice as also helping the population to 'learn to live side by side again'.[49] Thus, negotiated justice is expected to facilitate restorative justice, particularly for *individuals* previously in conflict who constitute the focus of most popular discussions of restorative justice through gacaca.

While many survivors described the importance of gacaca for restorative justice – especially in the early years of gacaca – many survivors

[45] Author's survivor interviews, Romain, Butare (author's translation).
[46] Author's solidarity camp interviews, Butare (no. 19) (author's translation).
[47] Author's solidarity camp interviews, Kigali Ville (no. 17), 12 April 2003 (author's translation).
[48] Author's gacaca interviews, Michel, Kigali Ville (author's translation).
[49] Author's survivor interviews, Boniface, Kigali Ville (author's translation).

increasingly criticise the lenient sentences handed down to many convicted *génocidaires*. Chantal and Zephyr, the survivors in Alphonse's
community quoted during the gacaca journey, echoed widespread views
among survivors when they criticised community service as insufficient
punishment, given the gravity of crimes committed during the genocide.
Chantal recognised that many detainees had already spent years in jail
and that there were understandable, pragmatic reasons for not returning
perpetrators to prison en masse. She argued, however, that the community service demanded of some perpetrators – 'you kill six or seven people
and you spend only six or seven months doing TIG' – was inadequate. In
contrast to many human-rights critics' claims that gacaca would lead to
mob justice and draconian punishments for genocide suspects, many survivors argue that convicted perpetrators have in the main benefited from
the government's need to rapidly empty the prisons and thus gacaca's
tendency towards lenient sentencing. It appears that some perpetrators
and their families share this view. As quoted in Chapter 4, Alphonse
said, 'Gacaca has been good here because most of the detainees are now
back with their families. Some have gone back to jail but most are here
now and working on their farms again.'

One specific participatory process at gacaca that the government rarely
discusses but the population argues is important for restorative justice is
confession, as represented in gacaca's plea-bargaining system. Some suspects such as Thomas quoted earlier and Alphonse during the gacaca
journey argue that confession is not only important for decreasing their
sentences, as public confession and apology are necessary for detainees
to benefit from plea bargaining, but will also aid their chances of reconciling with genocide survivors. When they confess to their crimes, some
detainees argue, they express their genuine contrition and a desire to
help rebuild relationships with their victims. Especially when confession
includes a public apology (and even a request for forgiveness) at gacaca
hearings, some detainees believe that confession will aid the restoration
of relationships with survivors and the broader community.

Not all suspects, however, view confession as contributing to restoration.
Some detainees argue that confession is simply important instrumentally
for decreasing their sentences. Antoine, a detainee in the ingando at
Gashora who had confessed to being in a group of murderers during the
genocide, though he denied directly taking part in any killings, said,

> Why did I confess? Some people from the government came to the prison
> and showed us a booklet ... [which] explained how we can reduce our

sentences if we confess to what we did during the genocide. If we don't confess, the booklet said, we might receive an endless sentence. So we should help gacaca by confessing.[50]

Such a view emphasises, as we will see in greater detail in discussions of reconciliation in Chapter 10, the influence of external parties, such as government officials, on detainees' confessions, and the extent to which notions of duty crucially affect many detainees' participation in gacaca. In my interviews, suspects interpret confession as important for restoration and for decreasing their sentences in roughly equal numbers. Some suspects in fact argue that confession will contribute to both of these ends, identifying personal and communal benefits.[51]

Commentators' perspectives on justice through gacaca

Commentators express a wide range of interpretations of justice through gacaca. Most commentators, and especially human-rights critics of gacaca, emphasise the need for retributive or deterrent, rather than restorative, justice. As we saw earlier regarding the dominant discourse on gacaca, groups such as AI and HRW emphasise gacaca's punitive role and concerns over the right of genocide suspects to a fair trial. These critics rarely describe explicitly what they believe the punishment of perpetrators will achieve. Consistent with their overriding concern for protecting human rights, however, they are likely to argue that punishment deters future human-rights violations and thus eradicates the culture of impunity that existed before and during the genocide.

On the rare occasions that non-Rwandan observers discuss restorative justice, it is usually to contrast this unfavourably with retributive or deterrent justice, as exemplified by Kenneth Roth's and Alison des Forges' critique of Helena Cobban cited in Chapter 3. British commentator Elizabeth Onyango from African Rights meanwhile argues that 'sometimes in gacaca, justice will have to be *diminished* so that people can pursue reconciliation.'[52] In this way, human-rights commentators seek to dissolve any possible link between retributive or deterrent justice and notions of restoration or reconciliation. Some critics argue that processes of retributive, deterrent and restorative justice manifest in gacaca – although most of these authors focus solely on the retributive

---

[50] Author's solidarity camp interviews, Gashora (no. 6) (author's translation).

[51] Author's solidarity camp interviews, Gashora (no. 10); Butare (no. 4), 29 April 2003.

[52] Author's observer interviews, Elizabeth Onyango, Advocate, African Rights, Kigali, 31 January 2003 (my emphasis added).

and deterrent – but that these forms of justice are mutually exclusive; that is, if gacaca is to pursue reconciliation through justice-related means, then it will sacrifice retributive or deterrent justice and thus violate certain individual rights.

There are several exceptions to these views among non-Rwandan commentators. Several scholars argue that gacaca has forfeited much of its restorative potential by overly focusing on retributive and deterrent justice. Mark Drumbl, for example, argues that gacaca could conceivably pursue both punishment and restoration – and in fact displayed signs of doing so in the early years of its operation – but over time has preferred state-driven 'punitiveness' over rebuilding fractured relations. 'These concerns do not vitiate gacaca for genocide's innovative relevance in the accountability process', Drumbl says, but rather suggest that gacaca's 'architects [should] reflect upon how instantiating some of its informal and communal aspects could boost its restorative and reconciliation potential.'[53] Bert Ingelaere is similarly concerned that gacaca is overly punitive, although – unlike Drumbl – he believes that gacaca has always had retributive justice at its core and that reconciliation was largely an afterthought.[54] Ingelaere argues,

> the substance of encounters [during hearings] is handled according to the purely prosecutorial logic which limits the discursive aspects normally connected with ritual doings or the dialogical and healing dimension of truth-telling processes. The ongoing Gacaca activities demonstrate only a limited potential to evolve towards trust between ethnic groups ... This results from the fact that the Gacaca courts function according to the logic of criminal trials and not as small truth and reconciliation commissions. In that way, the Gacaca process perpetuates the cleavages it is supposed to eradicate.[55]

Lars Waldorf meanwhile believes that by encouraging hundreds of thousands of new accusations against genocide suspects and the prosecution of high-profile critics of the RPF such as Munyakazi and Theunis, the government has 'politiciz[ed] gacaca' to such an extent that it constitutes 'the potential imposition of collective guilt on the Hutu majority'.[56]

As we saw in Chapter 5, most non-Rwandan commentators interpret the processes by which gacaca should pursue retributive or deterrent justice as

---

[53] Drumbl, *Atrocity, Punishment, and International Law*, p.99.
[54] Ingelaere, 'The Gacaca Courts in Rwanda', p.46.
[55] *Ibid.*, p.54.
[56] Waldorf, 'Mass Justice for Mass Atrocity', p.24.

necessarily formal. Because these commentators' overriding concern is for gacaca's capacity to protect individual rights, they argue that punishment at gacaca must be handed down according to predetermined legal statutes that safeguard those rights. These commentators argue that gacaca's legal statutes are the key to understanding how it delivers retributive or deterrent justice. In most cases, however, these commentators argue that the Gacaca Law does not sufficiently guarantee the protection of individual rights, particularly the right of genocide suspects to a fair, impartial trial. Therefore, while most commentators argue that retributive or deterrent justice is pursued formally through gacaca, they argue that gacaca fails to deliver *legitimate*, formal justice.

Harrell is one of the few non-Rwandan commentators to argue that formal processes at gacaca may contribute to restoration. He argues that the use of community service to punish some convicted perpetrators shows how gacaca may shape retributive or deterrent justice towards more restorative ends. As perpetrators participate in community labour programmes, Harrell argues, often working side by side with survivors, such interactions may – similarly to forms of communal collaboration during gacaca hearings – allow perpetrators and survivors to learn to work together and thus facilitate reconciliation. Harrell claims that it is not simply reintegration but rather the active participation of detainees in community labour programmes, and their engagement with the community, that contributes to restorative justice.[57]

PRI, which has conducted in-depth research into the function and likely outcomes of community service through gacaca since its inception, raises questions over the connections between community service and restoring relationships. PRI argues that community service through gacaca is in part designed to contribute to 'the social rehabilitation of detainees', which appears to entail a fundamentally restorative process.[58] PRI also argues, though, that many survivors will not perceive community service as a sufficient form of punishment for *génocidaires*, echoing my respondents' views above. On the question of gacaca's use of community service as punishment for genocide crimes, PRI quotes various survivors, one of whom states, 'It is inconceivable that a person who has killed should benefit from a reduced sentence. It is unthinkable to live with such a person and there is a risk that it may provoke another

---

[57] P. Harrell, *Rwanda's Gamble: Gacaca and a New Model of Transitional Justice*, New York: Writers Club Press, 2003, p.87.
[58] PRI, 'Interim Report', p.10.

genocide.'[59] Therefore, while PRI argues 'for reasons similar to Harrell's' that community service as a form of punishment displays some capacity to contribute to restoration, it also argues that many survivors' objections to this process pose serious difficulties for restorative pursuits.

Most Rwandan commentators argue that justice through gacaca should be interpreted as both retributive and restorative, consistent with many of their views concerning gacaca's pursuit of positive peace and reconciliation discussed elsewhere in this book. Jean-Claude Ngendandumwe, Coordinator of the Catholic Peace and Justice Commission, describes a common link between retributive and restorative justice espoused by Rwandan commentators:

> Justice at gacaca is very important for reconciliation ... Justice at gacaca is a form of state-controlled revenge, and this lessens the need for revenge by the community ... At gacaca everybody is watching and talking. The justice at gacaca is communal. It is not handed down by a judge. The way everyone takes part in doing justice at gacaca means that reconciliation is possible.[60]

Ngendandumwe argues that punishment through gacaca is necessary because it undermines a desire for revenge that he believes is prevalent in the community. Punishment alone, though, he argues, is not enough: as it is handed down in a communally determined fashion, the dialogue and collaboration that this entails is important for rebuilding fractured relationships.

Critique of sources' perspectives on justice through gacaca

How compelling are the official, popular and critical interpretations of justice through gacaca? This analytical section argues that some of these sources offer useful interpretations of the form of justice, whether retributive, deterrent or restorative or some combination of all three, which gacaca embodies and the means by which it pursues justice. In many cases, though, there are significant problems with these sources' views that must be countered. Crucially, the practice of justice through gacaca, as evidence has been gathered and trials have been conducted across the country, has varied greatly and rarely cohered with the perceptions and expectations of many of the sources analysed here.

---

[59] Unnamed survivor, quoted in *ibid.*, p.10.
[60] Author's observer interviews, Jean-Claude Ngendandumwe, Coordinator, Catholic Peace and Justice Commission, Kigali, 27 January 2003 (author's translation).

First, concerning the form of justice, some detainees and commentators such as Ngendandumwe argue convincingly that restorative justice is a key element of the gacaca process. The government and much of the population, particularly survivors, hint at the presence of restorative justice elements in gacaca, but they rarely discuss explicitly gacaca's attempts to shape the punishment of genocide perpetrators towards more reconciliatory ends. At gacaca, there is an undeniable moulding of punishment towards restoration, which the government should articulate more readily, especially to better prepare survivors for the personal and collective impact of reconciliatory processes at gacaca. A key element of traditional gacaca persists in the current context and provides a vital insight into how gacaca is designed fundamentally to pursue restorative justice: the need for punishment to incorporate processes that facilitate the reintegration of convicted perpetrators into their old communities. At gacaca, detainees reintegrate more rapidly as a result of plea-bargaining; in many cases, part or whole sentences for those found guilty will be commuted to community service. These elements of the justice process and its outcomes, as enshrined in the Gacaca Law, underscore the fundamentally restorative aims of gacaca, deploying punishment specifically to achieve reconciliatory ends. The hundreds of thousands of convicted genocide perpetrators who are now back in the community as a result of the gacaca process are testament to gacaca's importance as a restorative tool – a theme taken up in greater detail in Chapter 10.

While Drumbl, Ingelaere and Waldorf are right to question the extent to which gacaca's retributive elements have overridden the restorative, these concerns are overstated. While many gacaca trials have grown more formal and legalistic over time, in most communities this has been a relatively late development, occurring mainly in Category 1 cases. Before this, many gacaca hearings displayed the high degree of discursiveness discussed in the previous chapter, in which participants combined discussion of legal and non-legal truths in the same setting, pursuing a range of personal and communal objectives. Therefore, through most of its phases, gacaca has not functioned exclusively 'according to the logic of criminal trials' but rather has displayed a hybridity of retributive and restorative functions and has contributed substantially to rebuilding fractured bonds.

An important element of gacaca trials also responds to Waldorf's concerns regarding the imposition of collective guilt on the Hutu majority. Gacaca has consistently individualised guilt by requiring individual suspects to face justice in front of their communities. As discussed above, gacaca's high rate of acquittals also shows that the process has been successful at exonerating many accused individuals. Furthermore, the relatively lenient sentences handed down to many convicted perpetrators suggest that, rather than constituting an attempt by the government to criminalise Hutu, gacaca has generally erred on the side of softer, pragmatic justice for perpetrators, which has proven unsatisfactory for many genocide survivors. As we saw earlier, the government has taught many genocide suspects in ingando that previous elites who have manipulated the population are primarily responsible for the genocide. This fuels many suspects' lack of remorse for their crimes, which they instead tend to explain in terms of elite coercion or being caught up in the general mayhem of 1994. Such views suggest that many *génocidaires* do not feel guilty, casting doubt on Waldorf's assertion that gacaca has simply collectivised the guilt of Hutu.

Second, while I believe that gacaca has proven effective as a mode of restorative justice in many communities, the sources analysed here express problematic notions of gacaca's justice methods. Furthermore, they neglect several important features of restorative justice through gacaca that are identified here. Regarding the virtues of gacaca's participatory approach to justice, particularly the importance of confession and apology for rebuilding relationships, some sources overstate the ease with which such actions will facilitate restoration. Some detainees and commentators such as Harrell assume that the community, and especially survivors, will readily accept perpetrators' confessions to, and apologies for, their crimes and that these actions will quickly build trust between participants in gacaca. These sources then assume that this sense of trust will help rebuild bonds destroyed during the genocide. Such a view is too optimistic and fails to account for the deep, mutual distrust and resentment among many suspects, survivors and their families. As highlighted in Chapter 4, many survivors doubt whether suspects will tell the truth at gacaca and whether their confessions and apologies will be sincere. Particularly given the large reduction in sentences that some suspects can obtain through plea-bargaining, many survivors believe that suspects have only instrumental motives for confessing and apologising. Some suspects' statements regarding the personally instrumental benefits of confessing to their crimes, as well as practical experiences such as the perjury case in Bugesera discussed in Chapter 7, only increase survivors' scepticism.

Suspects, commentators and the minority of survivors who articulate this view, are undoubtedly right to argue that public confession and apology can help build trust in the community. However, they fail to account for inevitable difficulties in building trust, given the fear and suspicion that prevail in communities after the genocide. It will take many survivors a long time to trust perpetrators sufficiently to believe that they can engage actively in restorative practices and rebuild relationships with them. In many cases, gacaca simply provides an initial step in this process, allowing detainees to publicly confess their crimes in the hope that this will engender a sense of openness and trust with survivors. In turn, this sense of trust may lead to a degree of restoration long after the gacaca process is completed, when survivors see further proof of perpetrators' sincere desire to rebuild relationships.

My observations of gacaca hearings and interviews with participants also highlight that much trust in gacaca has been undermined by constant changes to the Gacaca Law. In particular, major reforms to gacaca – such as altering the categorisation of genocide crimes and the matrix of sentences, decreasing the number of administrative levels where hearings take place and the number of judges, and moving Category 1 (including sexual violence) cases from the national courts to gacaca – have caused great confusion in many communities. 'Sometimes we struggle to keep up with the law', said Yves, a gacaca judge in Kacyiru district of Kigali Ville in 2006. 'There are so many changes that affect us and sometimes we can't explain everything to the people because we don't understand it ourselves.'[61] While some changes to the Gacaca Law have helped streamline the process and responded to particular problems that have arisen, as discussed in Chapter 2, the constant alteration of fundamental aspects of gacaca has often undermined the population's comprehension of and confidence in the justice process and dulled its restorative potential.

Some sources' argument that community service as a form of punishment will help automatically facilitate restoration is also problematic. Although Harrell's claim that something more than the mere return of detainees to the community is necessary for restoration, he assumes, without sufficient substantiation, that community service will lead inevitably to this outcome. Many of the problems regarding community service as punishment echo survivors' suspicions of gacaca's plea-bargaining system as a whole, especially many survivors' view that community service is too lenient a form of punishment for many perpetrators.[62] If survivors do not believe that perpetrators have received a level of punishment

---

[61] Author's inyangamugayo interviews, Yves, Kigali Ville, Kacyiru, 13 June 2006.
[62] Much of PRI's recent analysis of community service for convicted *génocidaires* echoes this finding. See PRI, Report IX, pp.50–64.

commensurate to their crimes, then feelings of resentment and distrust will increase, destroying any chance of these parties rebuilding relationships. Viewing gacaca as delivering meagre justice to convicted perpetrators, many survivors question the government's dedication to those who suffered the genocide at first hand. 'The government doesn't really care about survivors', said Marceline, a thirty-five-year-old survivor in Ngenda district of Kigali Ngali province. 'They have forgotten us. The *génocidaires* are all back here now and we can do nothing about it. We have to live with those who killed our families, those who live freely here now and can get on with their lives as if nothing happened in the past.'[63]

Similarly, in western and northern Rwanda, many survivors question why large numbers of repatriates from the FDLR and other Congo-based Hutu rebel groups, many of whom are also suspected of committing genocide crimes in 1994, are allowed to return to their home communities without passing through gacaca or other justice institutions.[64] On the other hand, many returned prisoners and their families, while acknowledging that gacaca's sentencing scheme has been quite favourable, also believe that survivors have flourished disproportionately since the genocide because of the government's socio-economic favouritism. As Alphonse said during the gacaca journey in 2003, 'Many [survivors] live together now in new houses because the government has built these houses for survivors ... The government helps the survivors but not other ethnic groups.' As Alphonse also highlighted, many Hutu view gacaca as one-sided justice which provides no recourse for crimes committed by the RPF. All of these elements exacerbate the already tense atmosphere of mistrust and suspicion that pervades many communities and undermine gacaca's restorative objectives.

Employing community service to facilitate restorative justice also requires detainees to participate in projects that the broader community views as beneficial and not simply as means for the government to punish detainees without having to return them to already crowded prisons. Community service contributes most to restoration when detainees work side by side with survivors, deepening their sense of engagement that begins at gacaca. This engagement must be carefully mediated so that close interactions between perpetrators and survivors

---

[63] Author's survivor interviews, Marceline, Eastern Province, Ngenda, 21 April 2009.
[64] Author's survivor interviews, Elise, Gisenyi, Nyabihu, 14 June 2006; Carel, Gisenyi, Nyabihu, 14 June 2006; Fidel, Ruhengeri, Burera, 15 June 2006; Kayitesi, Ruhengeri, Burera, 15 June 2006.

do not undermine restorative processes and perhaps incite further violence. In many of my interviews, however, it is clear that community
service often takes place far from perpetrators' homes and involves little
direct contact between perpetrators and survivors. PRI and IRDP have
also identified this trend in their observations of the TIG process.[65]
When community service entails minimal interactions between perpetrators and survivors, and if few direct material benefits from labour
programmes accrue to survivors, this mode of punishment loses much
of its restorative value.

Third, the view expressed mainly by Rwandan commentators such
as Karekezi and Ngendandumwe that negotiated justice entails forms
of engagement at gacaca that are inherently restorative is problematic for reasons discussed elsewhere in this book. These commentators
rightly argue that negotiated justice is important for helping parties
come to terms with the causes of their conflicts, to find solutions to
these problems and, by collaborating in these ways, to rebuild relationships. However, the ways in which Karekezi and Ngendandumwe
interpret negotiated processes of justice overlook the extent to which
gacaca judges and other leaders heavily mediate this negotiation. More
importantly, they neglect the degree to which negotiated processes
require mediation to ensure that intense engagement does not further
inflame tensions but instead facilitates restoration. Further complicat-
ing matters, negotiation is not inherently restorative. As discussed earlier, the negotiation by many gacaca judges in recent years, for example,
has amounted to unduly hastening trials, in an attempt to complete
the genocide backlog as quickly as possible. This has often resulted in
truncated communal discussions during hearings and increased formalism, limiting meaningful engagement among participants and thus the
scope for rebuilding relations. When directed in ways that acknowledge
the very real barriers that individuals face when deciding to engage with
others, negotiation may help rebuild relationships between participants
in gacaca. Without mediation, however, negotiation may simply lead
to further acrimony and violence. These observations underscore once
again a key tension within gacaca as a whole, namely between the need
for oversight and mediation and the importance of communal ownership, confidence and engagement.

This section has argued that there are significant problems with different sources' views on restorative justice through gacaca. These sources

---

[65] PRI, Report IX, pp.20–40. IRDP, 'IRDP Bulletin No. 2', Kigali: IRDP, December 2007, p.31.

also neglect one further punitive process that, if mediated effectively, could contribute to restoration: compensation or restitution as punishment. Few sources analysed here recognise the restorative role of compensation or restitution through gacaca. In the case of property crimes, the Gacaca Law requires convicted perpetrators who have the necessary means to return looted goods.[66] Where the looted property is no longer available, perpetrators must provide 'repayment of the ransacked property or [carry] out ... work [to the value of] the property to be repaired'.[67] As mentioned in Chapter 5, the government has also established a Compensation Fund for survivors, which seeks to provide basic health and educational services as a form of restitution after the genocide. Neither the Gacaca Law nor public pronouncements by government officials, however, explicitly connect these compensation mechanisms with notions of restoration.

As we saw earlier regarding gacaca and economic development, many survivors express great confusion over exactly how they can access restitution from the Compensation Fund. Few survivors appear to have so far benefited from this scheme. Ndangiza conceded in 2008 that gacaca's reparations process had been largely ineffective, mainly, she argued, because there had been paltry international assistance to the Compensation Fund.[68] Nonetheless, given a more effective mechanism, compensation – particularly when it involves direct restitution from perpetrators to survivors – can contribute to restorative justice. Compensation as retribution can punish perpetrators in a public way and at a level commensurate to their crimes. In many instances, the Gacaca Law requires perpetrators to personally return looted goods to survivors or to participate in direct forms of community service, such as rebuilding victims' houses or replanting their gardens, which carry greater meaning than general labour programmes. By combining punishment of perpetrators with tangible material benefits for survivors – which are particularly important given the population's view, noted earlier, that overcoming poverty is its biggest challenge after the genocide – compensation as a form of punishment will win favour among many survivors. Compensation may therefore help generate trust and goodwill towards convicted perpetrators, which constitute a necessary foundation for restoration.

---

[66] Gacaca Law (Modified 2004), Article 95.
[67] Ibid., Article 95.   [68] Author's government interviews, Ndangiza, 2008.

CONCLUSION

Weighing the views of the sources analysed here and evidence from gacaca's practical operation, we can conclude that gacaca has generally succeeded in achieving retributive justice, as it has heard and weighed the evidence in hundreds of thousands of genocide cases and convicted and punished those found guilty. As expressed formally in the Gacaca Law, gacaca constitutes a detailed system for punishing genocide perpetrators that relies on few external institutions or processes to achieve retributive justice.

Pursuing deterrent and restorative justice through gacaca has proven more complicated. I have already discussed in the section on peace the limitations of punishment for successfully deterring future criminals, both in a general sense and specifically in the Rwandan context. It is questionable the extent to which potential perpetrators of mass crimes such as genocide will be deterred by the threat of punishment. Deterring future mass crimes, particularly when they are ethnically motivated, is likely to require confronting the deepest causes of ethnic antagonisms, rather than simply punishing those guilty of past crimes. Therefore, while punishment at gacaca contributes to the deterrence of future criminals, other, longer-term processes are necessary to achieve this end.

Restorative justice through gacaca also constitutes a complicated practical pursuit because it relies heavily on unpredictable negotiations between individuals and groups during and after gacaca, although in this regard gacaca has already proven more successful than in the pursuit of deterrent justice. Similar to gacaca's pursuit of positive peace, gacaca provides an important starting point for restorative justice, especially by returning so many convicted perpetrators to the community, initiating a process of restoration that must continue long after gacaca is completed. Wider social and political developments in turn heavily influence this ongoing process. Restoration requires maintaining trust between parties previously in conflict, a sense of trust that fluctuations within gacaca and negative external developments quickly undermine.

The need to carefully balance retributive, deterrent and restorative pursuits is also a difficult practical issue for restorative justice. Because many survivors believe that perpetrators have not received the degree of punishment they deserve, their sense of trust in gacaca and in those with whom they interact during hearings has decreased. Without this popular confidence, gacaca in some communities has struggled to achieve restorative justice.

The ways in which gacaca pursues justice after the genocide displays perhaps more than any other objective the unique nature of gacaca in the realm of transitional justice institutions. In particular, gacaca's hybrid combination of formal and negotiated processes that aim at retributive, deterrent, and ultimately restorative, ends highlights the holistic approach that gacaca takes to responding to the legacies of the genocide. Gacaca embodies the belief that to punish perpetrators in the aftermath of conflict is not enough if Rwandans are to rebuild individual relationships and to reconstruct the entire social fabric. Punishment is a necessary initial response but it must be shaped towards more constructive, reconciliatory goals. Gacaca's pursuit of retributive, deterrent and restorative justice shows how legal processes can contribute meaningfully to non-legal ends, for example as punishment, handed down in a negotiated fashion, and taking the form of community service or restitution, can help rebuild broken relationships.

Thus, gacaca gives substance to President Kagame's claim that '[w]e cannot talk of reconciliation without justice in the context of Rwanda.'[69] Most existing transitional justice institutions focus on either legal or non-legal responses to violence, seeking either to punish perpetrators or to reconstruct broken relationships while offering amnesties to perpetrators. Gacaca's pursuit of restorative justice entails responding to both legal and non-legal concerns after the genocide. Most commentators on gacaca have focused on only one aspect of gacaca's nature; human-rights critics, for example, focus only on gacaca's legal, retributive or deterrent responses. Such an emphasis misrepresents gacaca's hybridity, failing to acknowledge the ways in which gacaca punishes perpetrators (thus fulfilling a necessary moral obligation to respond adequately to crimes and the expectations of survivors), while delivering justice creatively to achieve wider, restorative outcomes.

[69] P. Kagame, 'Preventing Genocide: Threats and Responsibilities', paper delivered to the Stockholm International Forum, 26 January 2004, p.4.

CHAPTER 9

MENDING HEARTS AND MINDS: HEALING AND FORGIVENESS THROUGH GACACA

INTRODUCTION

This chapter explores two themes – healing and forgiveness – that are rarely considered in the context of transitional societies. This neglect probably stems from the centrality for healing and forgiveness of psychological, psychosocial and sometimes even spiritual issues – usually concerning individuals rather than societies as a whole – that most political and legal analysts consider irrelevant or at best secondary concerns after conflict. In the context of gacaca, however, official, popular and critical sources explicitly discuss healing and forgiveness, albeit in highly variable and often contradictory ways. The Rwandan population in particular links gacaca closely with healing and forgiveness, highlighting the need for rebuilding individual lives as well as the nation after the genocide. The population argues that gacaca should take a holistic approach, seeing individual and communal issues as related symbiotically.

Healing and forgiveness, more than any other themes explored in this book, underscore the importance of religious – particularly Christian – values and beliefs for popular interpretations of gacaca's objectives. The Rwandan population connects gacaca closely with notions of healing and forgiveness on the basis of Christian principles of mercy, grace, redemption and atonement. My findings concerning the importance of Christian theology for Rwandans' interpretations of gacaca echo Stephen Ellis's analysis of the importance of religious concepts of transformation for many Liberians recovering from their country's civil war. Ellis argues, 'Christian teaching is particularly attractive to any ex-fighter who wishes to make a radical break with his or her past, perhaps because of the Christian belief that the Holy Spirit is universal in nature and can enter anybody to provide instant transformation.'[1] This chapter argues that similar claims regarding the potential for redemption and atonement through a Christian faith inform much of the Rwandan population's pursuit of post-genocide healing and forgiveness.

This chapter contends that, given the inevitably long-term nature of pursuing healing and forgiveness, gacaca is limited in how feasibly it alone can pursue these objectives. Nevertheless, healing and forgiveness show more clearly than the other objectives considered in this book how the population moulds gacaca to meet its own needs, drawing heavily on local religious beliefs, in ways that extend far beyond the view of gacaca portrayed in its governing legal documents and pronouncements by state elites.

GACACA AND HEALING

This section focuses on healing in terms of addressing individuals' post-genocide trauma and therefore does not consider what may be termed 'communal healing' or 'communal rehabilitation', which refer to reconciliation or restoration of entire communities or societies. In analysing official, popular and critical interpretations of healing through gacaca, this section focuses on two questions: first, what *form* do these sources argue healing takes? This section identifies two main forms of healing through gacaca: the first, which I term 'healing as liberation', involves individuals' discovery of a sense of inner freedom from sources of psychological and emotional turmoil, such as survivors' ignorance about what happened to their loved ones during the genocide. The second form, which I call 'healing as belonging', relates to individuals' expressed desire to experience greater psychological and emotional wholeness through reconnecting with their community. In many sources' interpretations, there is significant overlap between healing as liberation and healing as belonging, and the two are often mutually reinforcing in the context of gacaca.

The second question addressed in this section is: what specific healing *processes* does gacaca embody? Gacaca incorporates various processes that contribute to healing as liberation and healing as belonging,

<hr>

[1] S. Ellis, *The Mask of Anarchy: The Destruction of Liberia and the Religious Dimension of an African Civil War*, London: Hurst & Co., 1999, p.268.

and on occasions to both simultaneously. Broadly, healing as liberation involves processes concerning the expression or reception of knowledge at gacaca and often comprises notions of personal redemption or atonement through truth. Some truth-related processes at gacaca constitute crucial means to healing. This section explores some of these processes, identified only briefly under healing as liberation, which were considered in greater depth in Chapter 7. Meanwhile, healing as belonging involves individuals receiving communal acknowledgement of their past experiences and often comprises notions of acceptance, memorial and their active engagement with the community. Healing as belonging therefore resembles key aspects of reconciliation or restoration, particularly their emphasis on the importance of engagement for rebuilding relationships fractured by violence. Where healing as belonging differs from reconciliation or restoration is by emphasising the personal, psychological or emotional effects of engagement at gacaca. Where reconciliation concerns rebuilding relationships, healing as belonging refers to restoring individuals' sense of inner wholeness. Both reconciliation and healing as belonging, however, depend heavily on positive forms of engagement.

Based on an analysis of official, popular and critical interpretations, this section argues that gacaca displays an undeniable capacity to facilitate healing as liberation and healing as belonging for both survivors and suspects. However, the sources analysed here generally overstate the extent to which gacaca alone can help individuals overcome post-genocide trauma and the speed with which they will experience healing. Gacaca should be viewed as the beginning of a protracted process of healing that will continue long after gacaca is over. Meanwhile, the pursuit of healing also depends crucially on developments in the wider social and political realms that affect the inner world of those recovering from the genocide.

Government's perspectives on healing through gacaca

In the early years of gacaca, the government generally paid minimal attention to issues of personal healing, undoubtedly reflecting its focus on nationwide issues, principally forms of justice. Recently, however, the government has increasingly discussed the problem of trauma in the community and the need for healing, although gacaca is often identified as a cause rather than healer of trauma. In 2008, Ndangiza, Executive Secretary of the NURC, said, 'Trauma healing is a very real issue for us now, especially for women. You have all these women who didn't disclose rape to their husbands and children, so how are they going to discuss rape at gacaca?'[2] The Ministry of Health is responsible for mental-health issues connected to gacaca, but the government rarely spells out exactly what the Ministry's role entails. At the National Summit on Unity and Reconciliation in October 2002, Cyanzayire, Deputy Chief Justice of the Supreme Court and President of the Gacaca Commission, made a rare, and vague, official reference on this point: 'The Ministry of Health, which has the responsibility to see to the trauma complications induced by genocide and massacres must step up actions in that regard, since those complications have been cropping up in Gacaca.'[3] Where government officials do discuss the role of healing, and where it relates to processes at gacaca, such statements usually come from officials in the NURC who engage more closely with the population through sensitisation programmes concerning gacaca's aims and methods. At the Symposium on Gacaca in 2000, Antoine Rutayisire, then a commissioner with the NURC, said,

> The social and psychological implications will be dealt with when one has finished with the legal aspects of gacaca ... [M]ost of the speakers [at this conference have] cited the legal angle ... Now the fundamental question is ... 'What are the social, cultural and psychosocial implications?'[4]

This statement identifies a source of discord within the government itself: some departments, particularly the Ministry of Justice, focus on legal (usually retributive) aspects of gacaca, while other departments, such as the NURC, are concerned primarily with the psychological and emotional outcomes of legal decisions. The personnel in these different parts of the government reflect many of the factional divides discussed in Chapter 2, with the Ministry of Justice incorporating many of the legal and RPF elites who initially opposed gacaca and the NURC comprising predominantly diasporic figures who did not live through the genocide and therefore tend to take a more psychosocial rather than punitive approach to gacaca. It is not obvious that, in managing gacaca, these different departments operate within the same philosophical and practical framework, nor that they are always coherently coordinated.

Rutinburana, Programme Coordinator for the NURC, argued that, while healing undoubtedly plays an important role in gacaca, its pursuit is likely to complicate that of other objectives. Rutinburana stated

---

[2] Author's government interviews, Ndangiza, 2008.
[3] Cyanzayire, 'The Gacaca Tribunals: Reconciliatory Justice', p.44.
[4] A. Rutayisire, 'Minutes of the Symposium', Hotel Umubano, Kigali, 6–7 March 2000, p.37.

that a key virtue of gacaca is that it can 'open then heal wounds', with a view towards facilitating both healing as liberation and healing as belonging.[5] In Rutinburana's interpretation, healing as liberation occurs when survivors discover important details about the past. 'Releasing people from ignorance' by providing knowledge of personal events during the genocide, Rutinburana argues, 'is an important healing process at gacaca'.[6] Ndangiza meanwhile discusses a version of healing of liberation for genocide suspects who unburden their consciences by confessing to their crimes. 'The churches have been very effective in the prisons at encouraging the detainees to confess', she said. 'Politicians are very limited in this area – they are not very good at teaching people's hearts. But the churches teach people that if they did bad in the past but now they confess, they can have reconciliation with God, with their neighbours, and now they can have heaven.'[7] Rutinburana also describes the importance of opening then healing wounds in terms of healing as belonging: 'Healing may come to those who share their experiences at gacaca', he argued. 'The survivors will find others who have had similar experiences and they will be able to talk about these things together.'[8] In this view, survivors' feeling that they are not alone in having suffered trauma and that others empathise with them – which they gain through engagement with others at gacaca – may help them deal with many of the psychological and emotional effects of the genocide.

Implicit in Rutinburana's comments regarding the need to first open wounds at gacaca is the recognition that healing will be painful, especially for survivors. Rutinburana argues that truth processes that aim at healing may result in the 're-traumatisation' of participants.[9] Similar to the tension between forms of truth and healing discussed in Chapter 3 in the context of the exhumation of mass graves in Ruhengenge district, the disclosure of the truth at gacaca, while sometimes contributing to healing, raises difficult personal and communal issues. It may be extremely painful at first for individuals to share their experiences publicly. Rutinburana argues, however, that remaining silent will only exacerbate people's feelings of pain and loss. Conversely, communal acknowledgement of experiences that survivors share publicly can increase their sense of belonging in the community. As Kayitana, former

---

[5] Author's government interviews, Rutinburana, 2003.
[6] *Ibid.*
[7] Author's government interviews, Ndangiza, 2006.
[8] *Ibid.*
[9] *Ibid.*

spokesperson of the Gacaca Commission, states, '[In the government] we believe a pill that is bitter is sometimes the one that heals.'[10]

Population's perspectives on healing through gacaca

Few Rwandans overall, and especially genocide survivors, openly discuss healing through gacaca, although the population still identifies healing as an objective of gacaca much more readily than the government. The population's general hesitancy in discussing healing reflects many Rwandans' reluctance to discuss their trauma, especially with researchers and other outsiders whom they may not trust immediately. There is nonetheless substantial evidence from my interviews and observations of gacaca hearings that the population generally views healing as an important aim of gacaca. In cases where they explicitly discuss healing, survivors and suspects tend to interpret it in reference to their own need to deal with the past. In my interviews, only one individual, Thomas, a detainee in the ingando at Kigali Ville, expressed concern for the healing of others. It was necessary to confess to his crimes, Thomas argued, because 'when we [detainees] are open with our victims about our actions in the past then we can help the survivors recover.'[11]

When survivors openly discuss healing through gacaca, they describe it primarily as healing as belonging. Many survivors argue that they have experienced, or expect to experience, healing through gacaca when the community acknowledges their suffering. They state that gacaca allows them to tell their stories in front of an empathetic audience and to hear similar stories from others. This storytelling contributes to their sense of reintegration into the community, overcoming their feelings of social dislocation since the genocide. Survivors, even when they live side by side with others who have suffered pain and loss, often feel a great sense of isolation and loneliness. Victims of mass conflict sometimes find it difficult to talk about their experiences, even if their listeners have endured similar tragedies. They often feel immense guilt that they have survived conflict while so many around them have died.[12] Simon, a survivor in Nyamata, found his wife dead in their house when he returned after the genocide, but he never found the bodies of his two children who he

---

[10] C. Kayitana, quoted in R. Walker, 'Rwanda Still Searching for Justice', BBC, 30 March 2004, www.news.bbc.co.uk/2/hi/africa/3557753.stm.

[11] Author's solidarity camp interviews, Kigali Ville (no. 4) (author's translation).

[12] See, for example, Z. Harel, B. Kahana and E. Kahana, 'The Effects of the Holocaust: Psychiatric, Behavioral, and Survivor Perspective', *Journal of Sociology and Social Welfare*, 11, 1984, pp.915–29.

presumed were also murdered. Simon said, 'I felt like I should have died too. It was only God who helped me keep my mind and heart intact.'[13] Traumatic experiences may also make it difficult for survivors to express their emotions for fear that prolonged discussion will trigger hurtful memories and thus increase trauma. This inability to discuss painful experiences exacerbates survivors' sense of isolation from those around them, creating a vicious cycle of silence and loneliness. Therefore, a key component of healing as belonging is the opening of empathetic dialogue to facilitate individuals' sense of reintegration into the wider community. In the post-genocide context, the concept of reintegration is most often associated with suspects who return to their home communities after years in jail. However, survivors also require reintegration into their communities in order to overcome the estrangement and anomie that result from violence-induced trauma.

Once a sense of commonality has been achieved, many survivors involve themselves more readily in the life of the community, so that greater participation in communal affairs augments their renewed sense of belonging. Some survivors describe gacaca as a forum in which they can begin to re-engage in communal life and previously estranged members of the community 'may learn to live together again'.[14] They therefore link forms of public engagement with the objective of healing. In language reminiscent of the government's view, but with greater emphasis on the personal dimension, many survivors interpret healing as 'rehabilitation' in which they underline their ability to regain a degree of standing in society and to function more fully in the wider community. As Paul, the survivor from Ruhengeri quoted in Chapter 7 whose father, two brothers and one sister were killed during the genocide, said, '[At gacaca], [w]e realise that we are in the same situation, that we have all had family who were killed. We understand each other and we realise that we are not alone.'[15] According to this view, healing as belonging enables future activity and restores survivors to their previous status as vital, productive members of society. Thus, this form of healing has a strong communal element, displaying the expressed need of many survivors to function in society as they did before the genocide.

Survivors also interpret healing in more internalised ways, focusing on their need to overcome personal emotional and psychological trauma,

[13] Author's survivor interviews, Simon, Kigali Ngali (author's translation).
[14] Author's survivor interviews, Boniface, Kigali Ville (author's translation).
[15] Author's gacaca interviews, Paul, Ruhengeri (author's translation).

sometimes in isolation but often through engagement with others at gacaca. Survivors refer here to types of healing as liberation. During my interviews, survivors commonly describe the need to regain a sense of 'peace of mind' or to be freed from mental anguish. Jean-Baptiste, the survivor in Nyamata quoted in the last chapter, said after a gacaca hearing,

> I have stood and spoken at gacaca two times now ... This was very difficult for me because it brought back many bad memories ... I didn't talk about [the murder of my entire family] for many years but talking to people now about what happened brings great peace to my mind.[16]

In 2003, a NURC survey of public opinion on gacaca recorded that 71 per cent of survivors identified regaining peace of mind as a key motivation for their participation during hearings.[17] One source of great pain and confusion for many survivors is uncertainty about what happened to their loved ones during the genocide. Survivors' desire to know the details of their loved ones' deaths – the identity of the killers, the methods and motives of the murderers, the location of victims' bodies – drives their participation in gacaca. While the knowledge of these facts may prove crucial for identifying and punishing those guilty of committing crimes, it is also vital for people's personal understanding of events and for their catharsis.

From survivors' descriptions, healing as belonging and healing as liberation often reinforce one another. Some state that they feel a greater sense of belonging to their community if they achieve a sufficient level of mental and emotional well-being that allows them to engage actively with others. In turn, a greater sense of reconnection with the community aids survivors' quest for peace of mind, or liberation from ignorance, as others provide the historical details that have painfully eluded them. Other members of the community may acknowledge survivors' suffering and in many cases share similar experiences. While healing as liberation and healing as belonging concern the well-being of individuals, these forms of healing at gacaca regularly involve the whole community.

A specific way in which gacaca helps facilitate survivors' healing as belonging is through providing a form of memorial for deceased loved ones. Remembering lost friends and relatives, typically through forms of communal mourning, often prove cathartic for the individuals involved and integrative for the parties who share in the remembrance.

---

[16] Author's gacaca interviews, Jean-Baptiste, Kigali Ngali (author's translation).
[17] NURC, 'Opinion Survey on Participation in Gacaca', Annexe 3, p.9.

My observations of gacaca hearings suggest that many survivors view gacaca as a place where they collectively remember those who have died. In Nyarufonzo district of Kigali Ville province, several women brought to a gacaca hearing framed photographs of loved ones who died during the genocide. They clutched these photographs tightly throughout the hearing and pointed to them when they stood and gave evidence. When the women sat down again, many of them cried and hugged each other. Elderly women moved from the fringes of the gathering to comfort those in distress. The women holding the photographs appeared to gain solace and strength from those who showed them concern, sitting up more confidently and soon participating again in the deliberations. The solidarity displayed by those around them affirmed them as members of the community and acknowledged their traumatic experiences. Bringing the photographs to gacaca also afforded a greater sense of humanity and dignity to the individuals whose deaths the general assembly was discussing. Though they were reluctant afterwards to discuss why they had brought the pictures, the women's aim seemed to be to give a face to the otherwise disembodied names that the judges recorded in their notebooks and to more meaningfully remember their deceased friends and family members. Thus, through their actions rather than their words, these women viewed gacaca as a memorial for their loved ones, a place where they could receive comfort from others in the community, and thus a possible source of healing as belonging.[18]

Memorialisation is particularly important for survivors who lament that they have never been able to bury their loved ones who died during the genocide. The bodies of many genocide victims were dumped into mass graves and pit latrines or thrown into rivers, making it impossible for survivors to recover their remains. Many survivors therefore feel that they have never properly mourned the deaths of their loved ones. Patience, a fifty-two-year-old widow whose husband died in 2002 but whose three children were murdered during the genocide, two allegedly by the same man, said,

> I never found my children's bodies. I cry every day and want to know where their bodies are. I want to bury my children's bones. Maybe at gacaca I will find where their bodies were thrown, and then I will stop crying ... One day I might be able to forgive the man who did these things but first I want to bury my children.[19]

---

[18] Author's gacaca observations, Kigali Ville, Butamwa, 21 May 2003.
[19] Author's survivor interviews, Patience, Gisenyi (author's translation).

Survivors such as Patience view gacaca as a place where they can discover the location of their loved ones' remains, which will help them overcome feelings of uncertainty over the events of the genocide. More importantly, once the remains of genocide victims are recovered, survivors may bury them and feel that they have afforded the deceased a fitting memorial. Liberation from uncertainty and forms of personal and public acknowledgement through burial and memorial are key processes of healing that some survivors connect closely with gacaca.

Not all survivors, however, are convinced that gacaca will contribute to healing. The same NURC survey that shows that many survivors are motivated to participate in gacaca by a need for peace of mind also shows that 91 per cent of survivors (as opposed to 59 per cent of the general population) believe that gacaca will intensify levels of trauma.[20] Fifty-five per cent of survivors (as opposed to 39 per cent of the general population) claim that they have already suffered too much to want to participate in gacaca.[21] Many survivors doubt the healing capacity of gacaca and view it instead as a forum in which they are likely to experience further turmoil. For some survivors, discussing their experiences publicly will reawaken painful memories that will increase their sense of grief, particularly if the public reception during gacaca is not entirely favourable. Nathan, the Pentecostal pastor in Nyamata quoted earlier, said, 'There are no easy solutions for survivors. Gacaca is not designed for healing. Only God can heal our wounds ... Gacaca will not bring back the dead.'[22] Survivors often believe that their wounds are too deep and that gacaca will either leave those wounds untouched or even deepen them through public exposure.[23] As discussed in previous chapters, gacaca's capacity to retraumatise the population by unearthing unsettling details of the past is a key reason that many people refuse to attend gacaca hearings.

[20] NURC, 'Opinion Survey on Participation in Gacaca', Annexe 3, p.18.
[21] Ibid., Annexe 4, p.10.
[22] Author's survivor interviews, Nathan, Butare (author's translation). Nathan's perspective echoes a common view within Pentecostal theology, to which many Rwandans subscribe, which holds that humans do not facilitate healing but rather healing comes only from God in the form of miracles or 'signs and wonders' (see, for example, A. Anderson, 'Pentecostal Approaches to Faith and Healing', *International Review of Mission*, 91, 363, 2002, pp.523–34; R. Menzies, 'A Pentecostal Perspective on "Signs and Wonders"', *Pneuma*, 17, 2, 1995, pp.265–78). Most Pentecostals therefore would consider it theologically unsound to suggest that gacaca aids individuals' healing after the genocide.
[23] Research conducted by IRDP also raises this concern about the possible retraumatisating effects of public deliberations at gacaca, especially the 'brutality of some confessions' (IRDP, *Building Lasting Peace in Rwanda: Voices of the People*, Kigali: IRDP, November 2003, pp.147–9). See also Dauge-Roth, 'Testimonial Encounter', pp.171–2.

Overall, genocide suspects discuss healing through gacaca much more extensively than survivors. In some cases, suspects believe that they themselves have experienced trauma and require healing through gacaca. Suspects' families also describe their trauma as a result of their loved ones being accused of genocide crimes and imprisoned for so many years. 'I am sick of answering my neighbours' questions about why my men are in jail', said Céleste, a forty-seven-year-old widow in Butare whose son, brother and two uncles were accused of genocide crimes. 'Life will only start for me again when my family returns home.'[24]

When discussing healing at gacaca, most genocide suspects describe types of healing as liberation and employ similar language to survivors when talking of their need for 'peace of mind'. This phrase means something very different depending on whether suspects believe they are guilty of committing genocide crimes. The discussion here focuses on those who have confessed to committing crimes because I conducted the majority of my interviews with genocide suspects in the ingando and in their home communities after they had been released from jail as a result of their confessions. For those who do not believe they are guilty and who are often still in jail – I also conducted interviews with many of these individuals – 'peace of mind' usually refers to their overcoming feelings of paranoia, anomie and oppression as a result of allegations against them. Many suspects who proclaim their innocence express a fear that their communities will refuse to accept them back because of these accusations. Daniel, a detainee in the ingando at Butare who claimed that he was innocent of the charges of murder levelled against him, said,

> The community is informed about my situation and they know that I am innocent, so I will be exonerated at gacaca … Some people have told lies about me already and there may be more lies at gacaca … But I'm sure that eventually I will be exonerated and that will bring me great peace of mind.[25]

For some suspects, a sense of liberation may come at gacaca when they are able to refute the accusations made against them and, if their denials prove convincing, when they are released into their communities.

---

[24] Author's general population interviews, Céleste, Butare, Kibingo, 14 May 2003 (author's translation).

[25] Author's solidarity camp interviews, Butare (no. 2), 29 April 2003 (author's translation).

Stronger sentiments concerning 'liberation' and 'release' are expressed by suspects who have accepted their guilt and confessed to committing genocide crimes. As Justine, a detainee in the ingando at Gashora, said,

> I didn't kill anyone during the genocide but I was present when others killed. Why did I confess to being present when others committed crimes? When you confess, you unburden yourself of the past.[26]

Among suspects who have confessed, views regarding the potential for gacaca to bring healing are very different from those of suspects who plead their innocence. Those who have confessed often wish to experience the healing of their consciences and a release from guilt and shame. Many suspects claim that their religious faith persuaded them to confess, either through personal reflection upon their own beliefs and the gradual realisation that confession was necessary, or through the encouragement of clergy or confession teams who visited them in jail. 'It is not an easy thing to confess unless you are pushed by the Bible', said Maurice, a detainee in the ingando at Kigali Ville. He explained that in 1998 several pastors from nearby churches visited him in prison. After conversations with them over a long period, Maurice converted to Christianity and later became part of a confession team, encouraging other detainees to confess to their crimes.

> I was converted while I was in prison. Because I wanted to live in peace with myself, I decided to confess to being part of a group that killed a man during the genocide ... Now I have nothing to fear at gacaca. Gacaca is only a threat to those who have not yet confessed.[27]

Jean d'Amour, a detainee in the ingando at Ruhengeri, claimed that he did not need clergy to convince him to confess to his crimes. 'It was easy to confess', he said. 'No one else assisted me in confessing. It was only my own conscience. The word of God teaches that unless we confess we cannot have freedom within ourselves.'[28]

In keeping with these religious influences, when discussing healing at gacaca, suspects often employ highly metaphorical, theological language to describe the forms that they believe healing will take. Many suspects employ the metaphor of the body and express a desire for 'cleansing' through confession. They often feel that their crimes have polluted their souls and that they therefore require some form of purification:

[26] Author's solidarity camp interviews, Gashora (no. 15), 18 April 2003 (author's translation).
[27] Author's solidarity camp interviews, Kigali Ville (no. 5) (author's translation).
[28] Author's solidarity camp interviews, Ruhengeri (no. 11) (author's translation).

> I was forced to kill during the genocide, against my will ... Before I confessed to what I did ... I felt dirty and needed cleansing. Being a Christian, I knew that I needed to confess to feel clean again.[29]

> I have confessed to assisting in the killing of a man. After the genocide, I fled to Congo but returned soon after ... I was converted [to Christianity] in Congo. The conditions there were very bad but ... God helped me find the courage to come back. Now I will tell the truth about my crimes at gacaca. Confessing is important for the truth, for my faith and for my own cleanness.[30]

These views invoke the Judaeo-Christian notion of washing away a person's sins after he or she has confessed: "'Come now, and let us reason together," says the Lord. "Though your sins are as scarlet, they will be as white as snow. Though they are red like crimson, they will be like wool."'[31] Some detainees describe the act of confession as taking 'medicine', providing a cure for the emotional, psychological and spiritual malaise caused by their crimes. Célestin, the detainee in the ingando at Butare quoted earlier, said, 'Confession is like medicine. It doesn't taste good and it takes courage to swallow it. But if we tell the truth to the families of our victims, then we will be cured.'[32] Athanase, a provisionally released suspect in Bugesera district, said, 'Confession is the cure for the bad things we have done. When you confess to these things, you feel like a new person.'[33] The overall emphasis of these statements concerning personal freedom, cleansing and cure is on healing as liberation, expressed as a method of redemption and renewal, an opportunity for detainees to be made whole again. Wholeness may be interpreted as internal when it refers to detainees' desire to overcome their guilt (in essence, to regain the wholeness of the individual psyche) or external when it refers to their desire to regain a standing in the communities where they committed their crimes (to regain their place in the wholeness of the community, which in turn contributes to their sense of inner well-being).

Commentators' perspectives on healing through gacaca

Finally, the existing commentary on healing at gacaca comes primarily from Rwandan academic writers and NGO psychosocial workers.

---

[29] Author's solidarity camp interviews, Gashora (no. 12) (author's translation).
[30] Author's solidarity camp interviews, Kigali Ville (no. 8), 12 April 2003 (author's translation).
[31] *The Holy Bible (New International Version)*, Isaiah 1:18.
[32] Author's solidarity camp interviews, Butare (no. 21) (author's translation).
[33] Author's detainee follow-up interviews, Athanase, Kigali Ngali, Bugesera, 9 September 2008.

A small number of non-Rwandan commentators and NGO personnel highlight the immense need for personal healing in Rwanda in a way which, for example, the Rwandan government rarely does. These observers, however, provide few details of how this healing may occur and they rarely view gacaca as a potential forum for that healing. Laurie Anne Pearlman and Ervin Staub, two psychologists who have conducted long-term trauma analysis and recovery programmes in Rwanda since 1999, discuss methods of healing in Rwanda. Their work highlights the need for systematic counselling programmes across the country to aid individuals suffering from post-genocide trauma. Pearlman and Staub argue that gacaca may assist some traumatised survivors and perpetrators, although they offer little explanation of how it will contribute in this regard, stating only, 'The involvement of the community in the process of punishment [as in gacaca] can be both healing and empowering.'[34] For these psychologists, general counselling is necessary for survivors and perpetrators to experience healing, and gacaca may at best augment the work of trauma-recovery workshops and other forms of counselling.

Other psychologists such as Karen Brounéus echo Rutinburana's concerns above, warning against the dangers of further traumatisation through processes such as gacaca that require public engagement on highly emotional and often divisive issues. On the basis of interviews with sixteen women participants in gacaca, Brounéus argues,

> In the case of gacaca, the judges are not professionally trained in giving psychological support. Furthermore, the proceedings are held in a schoolroom or most often outdoors, with a panel of nine judges, the accused perpetrator, and the assembled villagers as audience, including the family and friends of the accused. These factors are likely to increase the feeling of vulnerability in comparison with a therapeutic setting and be an additional discomfort to the witness.[35]

More elaborate interpretations of healing at gacaca come from Rwandan academics and NGO practitioners. When Rwandan commentators explore individual healing in the context of gacaca, they generally emphasise – like Pearlman and Staub – the need for both survivors and perpetrators of the genocide to experience healing. Solomon Nsabiyera, whose work with World Vision has included conducting healing

---

[34] E. Staub and L.A. Pearlman, 'Healing, Reconciliation, and Forgiving after Genocide and Other Collective Violence', in Helmick and Petersen, *Forgiveness and Reconciliation*, p.209.

[35] K. Brounéus, 'Truth-Telling as Talking Cure? Insecurity and Retraumatization in the Rwandan Gacaca Courts', *Security Dialogue*, 39, 1, 2008, p.63.

workshops for genocide suspects still in prison, emphasises the importance for personal healing of the reflective time that many suspects spend
in jail.[36] Reflection here is important for healing as liberation, as perpetrators deal with feelings of guilt resulting from their crimes. 'Detainees
have had many years in jail to ponder what they have done', Nsabiyera
explains, 'and to deal with the guilt that many of them feel because of
their crimes. This time to think is very important for healing.'[37] In this
interpretation, suspects' healing is a personal process that occurs primarily in jail, rather than at gacaca, although Nsabiyera adds that public
confession at gacaca may 'confirm to detainees the importance of their
private decisions' and help facilitate their reintegration into the community, which will enhance their sense of personal liberation by increasing their feeling of communal acceptance.[38] Again, such views underline
the extent to which healing as liberation, particularly where liberation is
understood as empowering individuals to participate once again in the
community, is closely linked to healing as belonging.

Nsabiyera further stresses the connection between healing as liberation and healing as belonging when he argues that, for survivors, sharing painful experiences with the community is important in two separate
stages: in its articulation, giving survivors a sense of freedom from the
thoughts and feelings that they have harboured silently for years; and
in its reception, as others in the community acknowledge survivors'
pain and share similar experiences with them. 'There will be no clos-
ing without disclosing', Nsabiyera argues, echoing Rutinburana's view
that traumatised individuals will not experience the healing of their
psychological and emotional wounds unless they first publicly express
their anger, sorrow and fear.[39] Such a process, according to Nsabiyera, is
'necessarily painful' but it is also likely to produce 'unity in the healing
process' as many individuals come to realise that others have suffered
similar pain and loss to their own.[40]

[36] For detailed descriptions of these workshops, see, S. Nsabiyera Gasana, 'Confronting Conflict
and Poverty through Trauma Healing: Integrating Peace-Building and Development Processes
in Rwanda', in Clark and Kaufman, *After Genocide*, pp.145–70; and J. Steward, 'Only Healing
Heals: Concepts and Methods of Psycho-Social Healing in Post-Genocide Rwanda', in Clark
and Kaufman, *After Genocide*, pp.171–90.

[37] Author's observer interviews, Nsabiyera, 20 January 2003.

[38] *Ibid.*

[39] *Ibid.*

[40] *Ibid.*

Critique of sources' perspectives on healing through gacaca

It is necessary now to critically analyse the official, popular and observer interpretations of healing through gacaca, taking a thematic approach. Some sources rely on problematic assumptions that require either significant alterations or outright rejection, particularly when they are compared to the practical reality of healing through gacaca. In most instances, problems with the expressed views centre on the tensions inherent in gacaca's attempt to balance elements of truth and healing as shown in the gacaca jurisdiction at Ruhengenge on 6 April 2003. After discussing the problems with these sources' interpretations, this section outlines several important elements of healing through gacaca that they neglect.

First, some official, popular and critical sources emphasise the importance of public dialogue at gacaca for suspects' and survivors' healing. Public discussion, they argue, contributes both to healing as liberation, for example in Rutinburana's and some survivors' view that discovering key historical facts will free individuals from their ignorance, and to healing as belonging, as they argue that engagement and sharing personal experiences in a communal environment will increase individuals' sense of connection to the community, which in turn will help facilitate personal healing. These sources are undoubtedly correct to emphasise the importance of public dialogue in facilitating healing as liberation and healing as belonging. However, they assume that such forms of conversation will lead straightforwardly to healing. They argue that survivors will discover the facts of the past and experience a relatively immediate sense of release from their uncertainty. They also assume that survivors' sharing personal experiences at gacaca will automatically generate a greater sense of belonging, thus overcoming their feelings of isolation and loneliness.

Public discussion at gacaca, however, is much more complex than these views suggest. As Rutinburana recognises, 'opening wounds' publicly at gacaca is a complicated, often fraught process that risks retraumatising many participants. Nsabiyera is right to argue that opening these wounds will be 'necessarily painful'. Public engagement at gacaca may in fact prove to be entirely detrimental to healing, for example – as Ndangiza mentions above – for rape victims who face the prospect of discussing traumatising personal experiences in front of gacaca judges. Therefore, what most sources neglect is the extent to which it is not *knowledge* at gacaca – either discovered through the expression of historical facts or shared when participants in gacaca compare and contrast personal experiences of the genocide – but *acknowledgement* that contributes most significantly to healing. When the general assembly fails to acknowledge the personal experiences that participants describe at gacaca – if it displays insufficient understanding or empathy towards those describing their pain – then such dialogue does not contribute to healing as belonging. Dauge-Roth also observes the importance of communal acknowledgement in the Rwandan context:

> By refusing to remain silent or silenced, survivors aim not only to keep the memory of those who died alive, but to also gain social recognition and legitimacy within the ongoing dialogues through which social memory and belonging are shaped. Their testimony, then, aims not only to represent the past as it has been witnessed, but at the same time symbolises a social performance of the survivors' agency within their community … [T]he testimonial impulse … signals a desire for connectedness that requires survivors to forge the social recognition of their disconnection so that their alterity does not amount to their exclusion.[41]

Regarding healing as liberation, the discovery of salient historical facts often produces further trauma, as suggested by the exhumation of mass graves in Ruhengenge, unless survivors receive communal acknowledgement of their experiences. The community must assist survivors in coming to terms with the new information they have received. In all of these respects, mediators such as gacaca judges and other community leaders play a vital role in shaping the public discourse at gacaca in ways that facilitate healing rather than producing further trauma.[42]

Second, many genocide suspects argue, similarly to those who equate public engagement with relatively immediate forms of healing, that their confessions in front of the general assembly will lead automatically to healing as liberation from feelings of guilt. Many suspects argue that confession will naturally gain the community's acceptance and that they will be able to participate again in the 'family' of the community. This is the ideal notion of suspects' healing at gacaca, as first private then public confession leads ultimately to integration into, and greater participation in, communal life. Healing, however, will not always take this course, as many survivors express scepticism regarding detainees' motivations for confessing in light of the reduced prison sentences afforded to those who confess early. If the community does not accept detainees' confessions

---

[41] Dauge-Roth, 'Testimonial Encounter', pp.166–7.
[42] For similar findings from interviews with gacaca participants, see Brounéus, 'Truth-Telling as Talking Cure?', pp.68–73.

or help them reintegrate, then private confession becomes detainees' only source of healing, though this would entail only personal release from guilt rather than an increased sense of belonging and capacity for communal participation. Thus, suspects' healing is affected greatly by private and public experiences both within, and outside of, gacaca. Mediators again play an important role in preparing the general assembly to respond to detainees when they appear before gacaca.

Third, while some sources neglect the difficulties inherent in public dialogue and confession at gacaca, they also underestimate the extent to which post-genocide healing will inevitably entail long-term processes. Detainees who describe gacaca as a 'cure' for their emotional or psychological torment after the genocide suggest that gacaca will provide almost immediate healing. The nature of people's pain and their feelings of loss of self are immense and highly complex. Their negative feelings have become deeply entrenched over many years and will not be resolved without significant reflection and discussion. It is questionable whether it is even valid to discuss 'resolving' or 'curing' people's feelings of trauma after conflict, as survivors will live forever with the emotional and psychological impact of the genocide. Martha Minow rightly argues, 'Survivors of mass atrocity often feel as though they themselves died, or are living among the dead. Then endurance, not healing, is what survivors come to seek.'[43] Survivors may never feel that they have completely overcome their trauma. Successfully enduring the pain of the past may therefore be the best they can hope for, and we should view healing after conflict, as Karl Dortzbach proposes, as 'simply a step on the journey to wholeness'.[44]

Gacaca may begin the process of healing, allowing individuals to publicly discuss personal experiences, which, for various reasons, may have been previously impossible. The sources examined here often neglect the extent to which healing is an ongoing process. Guilty suspects will continue to regret their crimes and survivors will continue to grieve the deaths of their friends and family for years after gacaca, perhaps indefinitely. These participants will require ongoing assistance, particularly if they have experienced retraumatisation during gacaca hearings. Furthermore, because forms of engagement and communal participation

[43] M. Minow, 'The Hope for Healing: What Can Truth Commissions Do?' in Rotberg and Thompson, Truth v. Justice, p.242.

[44] K. Dortzbach, 'Wholeness and Healing in Community: Toward Understanding Effective African Church Interventions Following Community Violence', unpublished PhD thesis, Faculty of Theology, University of Pretoria, June 2002, p.63.

are key processes in facilitating healing as belonging, sustained participation in communal activities outside of gacaca will be crucial for individuals' long-term healing. Negative experiences outside of gacaca can easily undermine many of the gains in healing made during gacaca.

One practical way in which gacaca may provide an initial step on survivors' journey towards wholeness is through reparations and restitution. As argued in Chapter 8 concerning restorative justice, the sources analysed here rarely discuss reparations after the genocide. The types of compensation and reparation that the Gacaca Law requires, though, display a marked capacity for facilitating initial forms of healing. A key factor that exacerbates survivors' feelings of emotional and psychological trauma after the genocide is extreme levels of material deprivation. Survivors often cannot engage in the reflective and communal participatory processes necessary for healing because overwhelming poverty drastically reduces the time that they can spend on activities other than subsistence employment. Compensation may therefore alleviate some of the financial burden on survivors, freeing up time for more healing-related processes. Reparations may also contribute directly to survivors' healing as belonging because reparations constitute a direct form of acknowledgement of survivors' experiences and subsequent pain and loss. State compensation, such as through the government's Compensation Fund, constitutes official recognition of survivors' experiences, although, as discussed earlier, to date the Fund has lain almost entirely dormant since gacaca's inception. More importantly, when reparations come directly from perpetrators, they represent offenders' acknowledgement of the anguish that they have inflicted on survivors. Much of the benefit of reparations in this regard relies on the spirit with which perpetrators provide them. Compensation accompanied by a begrudging attitude will simply inflame tensions between suspects and survivors and thus exacerbate survivors' feelings of trauma. Alphonse's description of divisive arguments surrounding compensation in his community highlight that this process is far from inherently restorative or healing. Nonetheless, reparations through gacaca can help facilitate healing in an integrated, holistic manner.

In conclusion, while the various processes of healing as liberation and healing as belonging show gacaca's capacity to deal with trauma, doubts must be raised over the extent to which gacaca alone can assist in this regard. Within gacaca, we have seen the difficulties that mediators face in trying to pursue objectives such as truth while simultaneously minimising their traumatising side effects. It is impossible to completely avoid short-term trauma at gacaca, as participants must confront parties with whom they have previously been in conflict and fraught truths about the past. Such immediate trauma can only be justified by emphasising gacaca's potential for facilitating long-term healing, such as through the processes of healing as belonging embodied in survivors' finding commonality with others through public dialogue and engagement. My observations of gacaca hearings suggest that many people are willing to participate in gacaca, in order to discover the truth about the past or to see justice delivered to genocide perpetrators. However, many participants argue that they will have to forfeit a crucial degree of healing in order to pursue these other aims. Therefore, without careful mediation, questions remain over how effectively gacaca can pursue healing alongside other objectives such as truth and reconciliation.

More importantly, given the deep personal, psychological and emotional issues involved, healing is by nature a long-term process that individuals cannot complete solely within gacaca. Healing for many Rwandans will be a life-long pursuit. Furthermore, many individuals are likely to suffer retraumatisation after gacaca, as external events in the wider social, cultural and political realms affect their journey toward wholeness. There is a significant risk that external events will eventually undermine many of the gains made at gacaca. Gacaca may help initiate the healing process but it will bring very few Rwandans a sense of 'finality' or 'closure'. While gacaca displays an undeniable capacity to facilitate healing as liberation and healing as belonging, it alone cannot achieve final results in these regards.

Gacaca embodies various processes that contribute to healing as liberation and healing as belonging, deploying methods of confession, discovery of historical facts, public and private memorial, communal acknowledgement and material restitution that assist individuals holistically in overcoming trauma. A key feature of these processes is their focus on healing individuals' identities, which have been badly damaged during the genocide. Aiding individuals in regaining a sense of the coherence of the self, and of the connections between the self and the community, requires deep reflection on the part of the individual and sustained engagement with others. Healing is therefore both an internal and a communal pursuit. Gacaca creates a space in which internal and external processes of healing are possible, while emphasising the need for individuals to express themselves emotionally, to make themselves vulnerable to others, which may cause further anguish. Such initially traumatic processes, however, are necessary if individuals are to ultimately

experience healing. Gacaca displays a marked capacity to facilitate healing as liberation and healing as belonging for both survivors and suspects, although we must also recognise the severe limitations of gacaca
in this pursuit. Healing will inevitably take much longer than the dur-
ation of gacaca and will rely heavily on external emotional, psychological
and material influences. Within these limitations, however, gacaca has
to date displayed an important practical capacity to facilitate healing,
emphasising the need to rebuild Rwandan society from the level of the
individual upward, in concert with gacaca's more community-wide and
nationwide objectives.

GACACA AND FORGIVENESS

Forgiveness is a theme rarely discussed in the context of post-conflict
societies because, for many people, it connotes amnesty for perpetrators or religious beliefs to which they may not subscribe. In the context
of gacaca, however, all three groups of sources analysed argue that forgiveness is possible through gacaca. This may reflect a harking back to
traditional gacaca, in which forgiveness was an explicit principle. My
research shows that people's religious persuasion is the primary influence
on their views of post-genocide forgiveness, as well as their experiences of
the genocide, either as perpetrators, survivors or members of the broader
community.

   This section explores forgiveness through gacaca by asking four questions: first, what *form* do sources believe forgiveness should take after
the genocide? The issue of form centres on who is expected to participate in forgiveness processes and what forgiveness entails. Regarding the
actors involved, the sources analysed here describe four different forms
of forgiveness through gacaca: forgiveness between individual perpetrators and survivors, which I call 'inter-personal forgiveness'; forgiveness
between an individual perpetrator and his or her community, or 'individual–group forgiveness'; forgiveness between an individual perpetrator
and God, which constitutes 'divine forgiveness'; and forgiveness between
an individual perpetrator and the state, which I call 'official forgiveness'.
Once we determine whom forgiveness should involve, does forgiveness
entail parties' forgoing direct, personal revenge against perpetrators, forgetting crimes committed, or some other action?

   Second, this section investigates how different sources interpret the
processes by which forgiveness occurs at gacaca. This question relates
both to the general processes of forgiveness, asking whether forgiveness

entails a one-off transaction between parties or a long-term process, and more specific issues, such as who should initiate forgiveness. A key component of this analysis of forgiveness processes is the *conditions* that different sources believe are necessary for forgiveness to be granted, for example whether apology and a request for forgiveness from perpetrators are necessary or whether survivors or others may meaningfully grant it before perpetrators initiate the process.

Third, what *motivations* are considered crucial for inspiring people to ask for, or to grant, forgiveness? Does forgiveness stem from a sense of religious or moral duty or a desire to achieve certain pragmatic outcomes, such as perpetrators' healing as liberation, which releases them from feelings of guilt and shame when survivors forgive them of their crimes?

Finally, this section explores the *outcomes* that these sources expect from forgiveness through gacaca. Does forgiveness contribute to rebuilding long-term relationships between perpetrators and survivors or will it simply act as a circuit-breaker to survivors' desire for personal revenge, thus leading to a more peaceful coexistence? In analysing different sources' interpretations, this section distinguishes between two main types of outcomes of forgiveness: a fundamentally pragmatic response that requires only that survivors forgo resentment and direct, personal retribution against perpetrators and does not require significant rebuilding of relationships between them, an outcome that I call 'basic forgiveness'; and a more expansive view that expects forgiveness to facilitate the restoration of broken relationships, which I call 'profound forgiveness'.

Analysing the official, popular and critical views of the form, processes, motivations and outcomes of forgiveness at gacaca, this section argues that forgiveness is an important aim of gacaca but that it is necessary to refute a common perception of post-genocide forgiveness as an obligated, immediate action that necessarily precludes any form of punishment. This section argues instead that forgiveness through gacaca should be understood as a gift that survivors bestow upon perpetrators. Furthermore, the inevitably long-term nature of forgiveness processes, as well as many survivors' deep sense of anger and resentment that must be managed for forgiveness to occur, mean that we should interpret gacaca's pursuit of forgiveness as successful only within significant limitations.

Government's perspectives on forgiveness through gacaca
Before 2008, all government discussions of forgiveness emanated from public pronouncements by state officials, and even these were disparate, undoubtedly reflecting the government's fear of being perceived

as forcing forgiveness on traumatised survivors. Unlike all of the other expressed aims examined in this book, there is no mention of forgiveness in the Organic Law, Gacaca Manual or Gacaca Law, until the latter was revised in 2008. This version of the Gacaca Law for the first time includes 'a request for forgiveness' (along with a guilty plea and repentance) as essential for any suspect's confession to be considered legitimate and to enable plea-bargaining.[45] The Gacaca Law states that the request for forgiveness must be made to 'a duly constituted bench, a judicial police officer or a public prosecutor investigating the case'.[46] It is unclear why forgiveness has so recently emerged in the Gacaca Law. This development may reflect the regularity of discussions of forgiveness among everyday participants in gacaca, as explored in greater detail below, thus representing an important example of popular impulse driving state action. Alternatively, the inclusion of forgiveness as an essential criterion for a legitimate confession may constitute a recognition that many suspects confess falsely to crimes and display minimal remorse for their actions.

Given the scarcity of official comment on forgiveness at gacaca, it is difficult to interpret how the government understands it. The form of forgiveness represented in the Gacaca Law appears to be official forgiveness or forgiveness between the individual suspect and the state. Potentially different interpretations emerge from pronouncements by state officials. At the National Summit on Unity and Reconciliation in 2000, then-Executive Secretary of the NURC, Aloysea Inyumba, outlined a long list of steps which 'Rwandans should go through in order to achieve unity and reconciliation'.[47]Although she did not claim that this pertained specifically to gacaca, she argued that a vital step towards unity and reconciliation was to 'sensitise and encourage those who have committed crimes to tell the truth and openly ask for forgiveness [from] those they committed them against', adding, 'those who were offended should also be courageous enough to forgive their offenders'.[48] Rutinburana argues that encouraging genocide suspects to 'tell the truth and to ask for forgiveness' is a key component of the NURC's gacaca sensitisation programme.[49] The Rwandan government website records two occasions, immediately before and after the inauguration of the gacaca jurisdictions in 2002, in

---

[45] Gacaca Law (Modified 2008), Articles 15–20.
[46] Ibid., Article 12.
[47] NURC, Report on the National Summit of Unity and Reconciliation, 2000, p.47.
[48] Ibid., p.47.
[49] Author's government interviews, Rutinburana, 2003.

which President Kagame connects gacaca with the pursuit of forgiveness. In the first instance, Kagame argues, '[Gacaca] will allow us to bring some suspects to justice, to have those who were falsely implicated to be freed, and also to allow for those with much lesser charges to be freed. This will be a way of rebuilding the society, of reconciling people and encouraging forgiveness.'[50] The second article reports, 'President Kagame … called upon those who committed crimes to be courageous enough to confess the crimes they committed and ask for forgiveness.'[51]

From such views, there is little sense of exactly how the government defines forgiveness, either generally speaking or in the context of gacaca, nor the factors that should motivate forgiveness after the genocide. Regarding the form that forgiveness should take through gacaca, the government argues that forgiveness is essentially an interpersonal process between individual perpetrators and survivors whom Kagame and Inyumba argue will have to show courage in pursuing forgiveness. Kagame's close linkage of reconciliation, rebuilding society and forgiveness, however, suggests an element of individual–group forgiveness in which individual suspects seek forgiveness from their communities. It is not clear exactly what the government believes forgiveness would entail, for example whether survivors or the community should forgo direct, personal retribution or feelings of resentment towards perpetrators, or something greater such as forgetting the crimes committed.

Regarding the modalities of forgiveness, Inyumba and Rutinburana interpret it as a two-way process in which, they argue, perpetrators must be willing to confess their crimes and to ask for forgiveness, and in response survivors must be ready to grant forgiveness to perpetrators. These comments suggest that perpetrators should initiate any moves towards forgiveness by first apologising, and asking for forgiveness, for their crimes. Libérata, a detainee in the ingando in Butare, recorded in her notes from the government's lessons in the camp that 'the community will forgive us if we tell them the truth.'[52] The government recognises, though, that many survivors will need to receive more than perpetrators' confessions and apologies before they are ready to forgive.

---

[50] Republic of Rwanda, 'President Kagame Allays Concerns about Gacaca', Department of Information, Government of Rwanda, 14 April 2002, www.gov.rw/government/07_11_01_genoconcern.htm.

[51] Republic of Rwanda, 'Gacaca Judicial System Launched in Kigali', Department of Information, Government of Rwanda, 18 June 2002, www.gov.rw/government/061802.html.

[52] Author's solidarity camp lesson notes, Mukaruranewa, Butare, 29 April 2003 (author's translation).

'[F]or families of victims to believe that the offending party seeking forgiveness is genuinely contrite', argues Cyanzayire, 'there must in addition [to guilty pleas and requests for mercy] be certain concrete and tangible actions, through which Gacaca can build confidence among populations and achieve reconciliation.'[53]

In terms of motivations, the state does not appear to view forgiveness as survivors' duty. Inyumba and Kagame both argue instead that those who grant forgiveness will need to be 'courageous'. As Kagame argues, gacaca should simply 'encourage' forgiveness, suggesting that it is an arduous process that may begin at gacaca but is likely to involve ongoing discussions between perpetrators and survivors long afterwards.

Finally, government sources do not indicate clearly the outcomes they expect from forgiveness through gacaca. Kagame's linkage of 'rebuilding society', 'reconciling people' and 'encouraging forgiveness' implies that he interprets forgiveness in a profound sense as contributing to the sorts of restorative processes examined in relation to the themes of justice and reconciliation in other chapters. In this sense, forgiveness of individuals will contribute to rebuilding relationships in the wider community. As increasing numbers of survivors grant forgiveness to perpetrators, they may feel increasingly ready to engage in wider reconciliatory processes, in the same way that personal healing contributes to reconciliation from the level of the individual upward.

Population's perspectives on forgiveness through gacaca

How does the population interpret the role of gacaca in encouraging forgiveness? Particularly within suspects' and survivors' collective interpretations of forgiveness, there is significant disagreement and ambiguity. The population's views are myriad and reflect a wide range of social and cultural influences. Generally speaking, survivors express greater scepticism than suspects about the idea that gacaca should pursue forgiveness. Many suspects, and a minority of survivors, claim that forgiveness is possible after the genocide. Many survivors, though, argue that they are unable to forgive perpetrators, especially those who killed their loved ones, and that it would be unjust for the government or anyone else to ask them to do so. 'I can never forgive that man', said Agnès, a survivor in Ruhengeri Ville, referring to a close friend's brother whom she watched hack her husband to death with a machete outside of her house. 'When I go to gacaca, I will tell the judges who this man is because I know him

[53] Cyanzayire, 'The Gacaca Tribunals: Reconciliatory Justice', p.45.

and I saw with my own eyes what he did. I will never be able to forgive him.'[54] For other survivors, forgiveness is necessary but nonetheless secondary to more pressing concerns. As we saw in the section on healing, Patience, a survivor from Gisenyi whose three children were killed during the genocide, said that the fact that her children's bodies had never been found precluded her for the time being from forgiving those guilty of their murder.[55]

First, how do popular sources interpret the form that forgiveness should take at gacaca? Even when it is encouraged in interviews to elaborate on what forgiveness entails, the population rarely offers more than general definitions. It is possible, however, to discern within popular interpretations each of the four forms of forgiveness outlined above: inter-personal, individual–group, divine and official forgiveness. First, many detainees and nearly all survivors who believe that some form of forgiveness is possible through gacaca argue that it is necessarily an interpersonal issue between individual survivors and perpetrators. Most of the population interprets interpersonal forgiveness as requiring survivors to forgo direct, personal reprisals against convicted perpetrators, which many survivors may see as their right given the extreme violence they have suffered. In this view, forgiveness at gacaca will not nullify all attempts at punishment against perpetrators but only direct, personal forms of punishment. As Marie-Claire, a survivor in Nyamata whose husband and five children were murdered during the genocide, said,

> I won't go to gacaca unless I am forced to go. I have already forgiven the killers ... Gacaca is still necessary because it will expose the truth of what the killers did ... The guilty will still receive justice even though we forgive them.[56]

For some survivors, forgiveness not only entails their forgoing personal retribution but also their forgetting the crimes committed against them. Forgetting is sometimes described as occurring after survivors agree to forgive perpetrators. Some survivors, however, interpret forgetting as a prerequisite for forgiveness. Romain, a survivor from Butare, said, for example,

---

[54] Author's survivor interviews, Agnès, Ruhengeri, Ruhengeri Ville, 4 May 2003 (author's translation).
[55] Author's survivor interviews, Patience, Gisenyi.
[56] Author's survivor interviews, Marie-Claire, Kigali Ngali (author's translation).

I am able to forgive those who killed my brother and my best friend but not now. I am too angry ... When I forget what happened, I will be able to forgive. Forgetting though will take a very long time.[57]

A minority of popular sources, usually detainees, interprets forgiveness as an individual–group transaction in which they confess to, and apologise for, their crimes and ask for forgiveness from their community. The community may then choose to offer or withhold forgiveness depending on how it judges the sincerity of suspects' confessions. These sources hold that such interactions will take place solely within the confines of gacaca when suspects confess publicly and ask for forgiveness from the general assembly. Most sources in this regard interpret forgiveness as requiring the community to forgo direct reprisals and resentment against convicted *génocidaires*. Serestini, a twenty-five-year-old detainee in the ingando at Gashora, who confessed to prison authorities and later to survivors at a pre-gacaca hearing that he murdered a man during the genocide, said,

I have no fear about facing my community at gacaca ... They already know everything I did during the genocide because I have already told them ... I will go to gacaca and the community will forgive me straight away, right there and then.[58]

Peter Uvin and Charles Mironko cite several suspects' expectation of individual–group forgiveness on the basis of their positive interactions with survivors during prison gacaca hearings in 1998 and 2000.[59] Similarly, as quoted in the gacaca journey narratives in Chapter 4, Alphonse said in 2006, 'Gacaca will start after the [Constitutional] referendum ... I will tell the truth and the victims will forgive me. There is no question about that.'

A third interpretation of forgiveness comes from a small group of detainees who argue that the most important form of forgiveness comes not from their victims but from God. Some detainees express uncertainty regarding whether survivors will forgive them; they therefore view divine forgiveness as the likeliest means of atonement for their crimes. Many detainees argue, like Sylvestre, a detainee in the ingando at Ruhengeri, that 'the community may refuse to forgive me but God always forgives.'[60]

[57] Author's survivor interviews, Romain, Butare (author's translation).
[58] Author's solidarity camp interviews, Gashora (no. 10) (author's translation).
[59] P. Uvin and C. Mironko, 'Western and Local Approaches to Justice in Rwanda', *Global Governance*, 9, 2003, pp.227–8.
[60] Author's solidarity camp interviews, Ruhengeri (no. 4) (author's translation).

Jean Damascène, a provisionally released suspect in Gisenyi, said, 'I'm not sure if the survivors will forgive me. Many of them are still very angry. But I have confessed and I know that God has forgiven me.'[61] In such cases, forgiveness takes a divine form and concerns rebuilding a fractured relationship with God rather than with survivors. Many Protestants in particular view forgiveness as an immediate process in which God automatically forgives those who confess their sins to him and ask for his forgiveness. It is not always clear what suspects believe divine forgiveness will entail. However, as discussed below concerning motivations behind divine forgiveness, most suspects expect that God's forgiveness will involve his absolution of their sins and a willingness to rebuild a relationship with them.

The final popular interpretation of the form of forgiveness through gacaca constitutes a one-off, official transaction in which suspects seek forgiveness from the state. Emmanuel, a detainee in the ingando in Butare, argued that he expected to receive forgiveness not only from God and the families of his victims but also 'forgiveness from the government' after confessing his crimes at gacaca.[62] It is unclear from such expressions what official forgiveness entails, except for the state's foregoing any punishment of convicted génocidaires. Notably, Martin, a detainee in the ingando in Gashora, claimed, 'The government has already forgiven me, so now the community will forgive me too.'[63] Martin did not elaborate on how he knew that the government had forgiven him. However, he seemed to interpret his release from prison into the ingando, and the prospect of soon returning to his home community, as signs of official forgiveness.[64]

Much of the population views forgiveness after the genocide as a two-way process that occurs primarily during gacaca hearings. The most common expression of this process involves detainees' initiation of forgiveness by confessing to their crimes, followed by an apology and a request for their victims to forgive them. The next step, according to the majority of detainees and survivors, involves survivors' acceptance or rejection of this apology, depending on the level of sincerity that the confessor has displayed, and their granting of, or refusal to grant,

---

[61] Author's gacaca interviews, Jean Damascène, Gisenyi, Nyabihu, 14 June 2006.
[62] Author's solidarity camp interviews, Butare (no. 16) (author's translation).
[63] Author's solidarity camp interviews, Gashora (no. 5), 18 April 2003 (author's translation).
[64] PRI notes that many convicted perpetrators increasingly view the relatively lenient punishment of community service in TIG camps as an 'expression of forgiveness by the State' (PRI, Report IX, p.27).

forgiveness. As Juliene, the survivor in Butare quoted above, argued, full confession and a genuine display of remorse are common preconditions for granting forgiveness. Only one of my interviewees described a process of forgiveness substantially different from this. Marie-Claire, the survivor in Nyamata who said earlier, 'I won't go to gacaca unless I am forced to go', claimed that she had forgiven the murderers of her husband and five children without ever having confronted them about their crimes. She claimed that it was not necessary for the perpetrators to ask for forgiveness, explaining instead, 'God forgives so we must forgive.'[65]

The most common component of processes of forgiveness described by the population is an emphasis on victims' willingness to accept the contrition of perpetrators who confess and to forgo any assumed claim to direct, personal revenge against the guilty. In essence, this definition of forgiveness equates to victims giving perpetrators a 'second chance' by dispelling any desire for personal revenge and by allowing perpetrators to begin a new life in their home communities. This view describes forgiveness as a long-term process, involving an ongoing dialogue between survivors and perpetrators long after gacaca is complete. Gacaca may provide the forum in which perpetrators initially confess to their crimes, apologise and ask for forgiveness, but many survivors claim that they will find it difficult to forgive perpetrators immediately. Robert, a thirty-eight-year-old farmer in Butare, whose brother and two uncles were still in jail, accused of genocide crimes, said, 'The community will forgive those who are guilty, but it will depend on how bad their crimes were. The worst crimes are very hard to forgive.'[66] Survivors will often need to reflect on the confessions and apologies they have heard and to judge the sincerity of perpetrators' words.

What then do popular sources believe will motivate suspects and survivors to engage in forgiveness processes at gacaca? In popular interpretations, two expressed motivations for forgiveness predominate: a sense of Christian duty that requires individuals to ask for, and to grant, forgiveness; and anticipated instrumental advantages of forgiveness. Neither of these explanations – forgiveness as an obligation or as the facilitator of certain pragmatic outcomes – necessarily incorporates the intuitive notion that detainees should ask for forgiveness foremost as an expression of remorse for their crimes. This is not to suggest that those accused of genocide crimes on the whole lack remorse, although many do. On

---

[65] Ibid.
[66] Author's general population interviews, Robert, Butare (author's translation).

numerous occasions during my interviews, detainees expressed sorrow for their crimes and claimed that they wished to express contrition directly to their victims. For example, Fabien, a detainee in the ingando at Butare, was twelve years old when he murdered two children during the genocide and participated in a group killing of a man at a roadblock. During his time in prison, where he was detained alongside both genocide and common-law suspects, he claimed that he realised the wrongness of his crimes and confessed to the prison authorities:

> During the genocide I believed that all Tutsi were bad ... But when I was in prison, I lived with many Tutsi and they were just like my parents ... Before I used to think that all Tutsi were rich ... Now I want to go to gacaca and tell the survivors that I am sorry for what I did. And I know they will forgive me when I tell them the truth.[67]

Such a sense of remorse is not always an instantaneous response to the crimes that many detainees have committed. In one instance, Issa, a suspect in the ingando at Ruhengeri, said that while he had always felt sorry for his crimes, he felt the deepest sense of remorse and the need to ask for forgiveness after he himself became the victim of injustice when his wife committed adultery while he was in prison. It was only after his wife visited him in jail, confessed her infidelity and begged for his forgiveness, Issa explained, that he fully realised his need to express his remorse directly to the family of his victims and to beg for their forgiveness.[68] At the same time, many suspects, such as Cypriet, whom I interviewed along the gacaca journey as discussed in Chapter 4, display little remorse for their crimes and instead blame their actions on manipulation by government officials or offer more nebulous explanations such as their having been 'caught up' in the general atmosphere of lawlessness and murder during the genocide. These circumstances, some detainees argue, made it impossible for them to refuse to participate in the killings.

Christian notions of atonement and redemption are important influences on the popular interpretation of forgiveness as motivated by a sense of religious duty. The most common explanation from both survivors and detainees of why forgiveness is necessary after the genocide is that, because God has forgiven his children for the sins that they have confessed, they must ask for forgiveness from, and be willing to

---

[67] Author's solidarity camp interviews, Butare (no. 8), 29 April 2003 (author's translation).
[68] Author's solidarity camp interviews, Ruhengeri (no. 12), 3 May 2003 (author's translation).

forgive, each other. Forgiveness therefore is a sign of gratitude for the grace and mercy believers have received from God. Such an interpretation stems from biblical passages such as this central one in the Gospel according to Matthew: 'For if you forgive men when they sin against you, your heavenly Father will also forgive you. But if you do not forgive men their sins, your Father will not forgive your sins.'[69] On this basis, Vedaste, a detainee in Butare, explained that he did not fear returning to his home community from the ingando because 'the people who live there are Christians and they will forgive me.'[70] Jean-Baptiste, a survivor in Nyamata, said after a gacaca hearing that 'we must forgive because God forgives', adding, 'it is our Christian duty and if we do not forgive then we become the sinners.'[71] In this sense, individuals' religious convictions are viewed as transcending any personal reticence towards asking for, or granting, forgiveness. In many Christian interpretations, the commandment to forgive in turn characterises as a sinner any person who refuses to forgive a confessed and remorseful transgressor. Survivors' participation in Christian gacaca hearings reinforces these views, as clergy exhort parishioners to publicly confess the sins they have committed against one another. At Christian gacaca, church leaders commonly preach that it is every Christian's duty to forgive anyone who has wronged them and that anyone who refuses to forgive displays ingratitude for the mercy they have received from God.[72]

Regarding the second popular expression of motivations for seeking forgiveness through gacaca, community leaders and the wider population describe different types of pragmatic considerations. Church leaders and gacaca judges in particular argue that survivors should forgive confessed perpetrators in order to achieve community-wide benefits. The most common pragmatic reason why forgiveness is necessary, according to these leaders, is to encourage detainees who appear before gacaca to tell the truth about their crimes. If detainees believe that survivors and the wider community will forgive them, the argument goes, then they will be more willing to divulge what they have done. During a gacaca hearing I attended in Save district of Butare province, a local pastor gave a short talk at the beginning of the meeting, in which he exhorted the general assembly to tell the truth and to be ready to forgive because 'truth

[69] The Holy Bible (New International Version), Matthew 6:14–15.
[70] Author's solidarity camp interviews, Butare (no. 19) (author's translation).
[71] Author's gacaca interviews, Jean-Baptiste, Kigali Ngali (author's translation).
[72] Karekezi, 'Juridictions gacaca', p.34.

287

is the liberator and we must help detainees to confess their crimes.'[73] He continued: 'We won't hurt them with lies and we will welcome them home, ready to forgive them, so they will tell the truth about what they have done.'[74]

Some suspects reverse this process and argue that, by telling the truth, they will encourage survivors to forgive them. 'It is not easy to confess to crimes like mine', said Alexis, a detainee in the ingando at Gashora, who confessed to participating in the group killing of a woman during the genocide when he was eleven years old. 'But I want to help the community forgive me at gacaca ... One day I hope the community will let me go back to my farm and let me start my life again.'[75] In this view, truth is a token that can be traded for forgiveness.

Another popular explanation of the pragmatic motivations behind forgiveness through gacaca, which comes from suspects rather than survivors or other sections of the population, relates to their perceived need to rebuild fractured relationships in the community. Many detainees believe that their asking for forgiveness will encourage survivors and the broader community to accept them back. As Julbert, a detainee in the ingando at Butare who confessed to being part of a group of murderers during the genocide, claimed, 'It was the word of God that told me to confess to my crimes. Now it will be possible to live together with the genocide survivors again. We will be able to live together after they forgive me.'[76] This argument expresses a key motivation for detainees when they confess to crimes and ask for forgiveness, namely a desire to avoid direct reprisals from genocide survivors and to reintegrate smoothly into their home communities.

Detainees who interpret forgiveness in its official form usually argue that asking the government for forgiveness will help them benefit from gacaca's plea-bargaining system. Vedaste, who stated that forgiveness from God and the wider community was necessary for his gaining a sense of inner peace, also said that it would be necessary for him to 'ask for forgiveness from the government which may help decrease my prison sentence'.[77] Suspects' expressed motivations for forgiveness, such as this one, which sometimes appear at first to be influenced largely by religious persuasions, often coincide with more pragmatic considerations.

[73] Author's gacaca observations, Butare, Save (author's translation).
[74] Ibid.
[75] Author's solidarity camp interviews, Gashora (no. 18), 18 April 2003 (author's translation).
[76] Author's solidarity camp interviews, Butare (no. 4) (author's translation).
[77] Author's solidarity camp interviews, Butare (no. 19) (author's translation).

For other detainees and some survivors, a psychological type of pragmatic motivation for asking for forgiveness is to overcome their sense of guilt. As described regarding healing through gacaca, many guilty suspects claim to have experienced great upheaval in their consciences during their time in jail, often as a result of religious meditation or the influence of church leaders who visited them. Again influenced by certain Christian conceptions of atonement, many detainees claim that asking for forgiveness will help them overcome their sense of shame; in essence 'cleaning the slate' of their past and allowing them to move forward with a clearer conscience. Forgiveness is therefore interpreted as one pragmatic means towards healing as liberation.

What outcomes then do popular sources expect from forgiveness through gacaca? Generally speaking, the population argues that forgiveness through gacaca will produce any of three different outcomes. First, popular interpretations focus on the extent to which forgiveness will help rebuild fractured relationships between individuals. On that basis, popular views concerning restorative outcomes from forgiveness divide into two further categories: a basic, pragmatic view which holds that forgiveness will facilitate the peaceful coexistence of individuals previously in conflict; and a profound view which holds that forgiveness will encourage individuals to engage more closely with one another to build deeper relationships in the future. It is not always clear whether the population believes that forgiveness will facilitate basic or profound restorative outcomes. Therefore, it is often necessary to infer popular views in this regard from other statements relating to forgiveness.

The basic interpretation of the restorative outcomes of forgiveness through gacaca generally comes from genocide suspects. According to many suspects, forgiveness means that victims agree to disregard what has taken place in the past to allow perpetrators and victims to coexist peacefully in the future. Elie, a detainee in the ingando at Ruhengeri, expressed a common view among suspects: 'Reconciliation, when we all can live together again, will happen when the guilty ones ask forgiveness at gacaca and the victims agree to forgive them.'[78] During the gacaca journey, as quoted in Chapter 4, the provisionally released suspect Laurent also connected forgiveness with reconciliation, although he put greater onus on suspects to rebuild fractured relationships. 'Reconciliation doesn't come from the sky', he said. 'It means living together, saying sorry, asking for forgiveness. It is much more than words – it is actions.' In

---

[78] Author's solidarity camp interviews, Ruhengeri (no. 9), 3 May 2003 (author's translation).

a twist to survivors' interpretations, some detainees come close to equating forgiving with forgetting, suggesting that, when survivors agree to forgive them, they will also agree to forget the crimes committed against them. This view manifests in many suspects' seemingly unquestioning confidence that they will gain acceptance back into the community after their release from the ingando. Such a perspective is common among suspects who have participated in pre-gacaca hearings and received favourable responses from survivors. As Emmanuel, a detainee in the ingando in Butare, said, 'I have this confidence in my community because I went through the early gacaca while I was still in prison. I can go back home in confidence because I am already forgiven.'[79]

In interpreting many detainees' views, it is often difficult to differentiate between forgiveness and reconciliation. Many suspects use the terms interchangeably because, in their view, each term refers to a renewed sense of togetherness after the genocide. Two external influences have heavily shaped many suspects' connections of forgiveness and reconciliation. First, many detainees claim that confession teams encouraged them to admit to their crimes in jail. According to several detainees in the ingando, one of the main messages of the teams was that confession would secure their early release from prison. Many detainees also claim that the confession teams told them that asking for forgiveness from survivors was the main way to avoid direct, personal reprisals and to enable a smooth reintegration into their home communities. Domatien, a detainee in the ingando in Butare, said, 'The confession teams who visited us in prison told us that it was necessary to confess and to ask for forgiveness. They told us that if we confessed, then we would have no problem with the judgments at gacaca and that our community would accept us back.'[80] This connection between asking for forgiveness and acceptance back into the community was reinforced by many detainees' experiences of pre-gacaca hearings, where they came face to face with survivors while they were still in prison or in the ingando. During these hearings, some detainees, such as Emmanuel in Butare, claimed to have already asked for forgiveness from the families of their victims and to have received survivors' assurances that they would be welcomed home. Emmanuel said, 'I have already met with the family of my victims and told them what I did. The family forgave me at this meeting and I know

[79] Author's solidarity camp interviews, Butare (no. 16), 29 April 2003 (author's translation).
[80] Author's solidarity camp interviews, Butare (no. 12), 29 April 2003 (author's translation).

it will be the same at gacaca … Then I will be allowed to live in the community again.'[81]

From my research, much of the population appears to view forgiveness as an immediate act that occurs solely during gacaca hearings. This no doubt reflects suspects' hope that they will receive immediate forgiveness after confessing at gacaca. Many survivors, however, claim that they will refuse outright at gacaca to forgive those found guilty of crimes. In neither of these two dominant perspectives is there significant scope for a view of forgiveness as a long-term process that may extend outside of gacaca. The population's views appear to draw on certain Christian notions of forgiveness, particularly within Protestantism, according to which a believer receives immediate forgiveness for his or her sins after confessing them to God. Because many believers interpret confession and the request for, and granting of, forgiveness from their sins as a single, immediate act, they view forgiveness at gacaca in the same way.

However, not all detainees are so confident of receiving positive reactions from their communities, particularly if large numbers of survivors still live there. The tense mood of the detainees on the bus on the day of their release from the ingando in Kigali Ville, as they neared the drop-off point near Gashora, indicated the uncertainty and anxiety that many of them felt at the prospect of returning to the places where they committed crimes during the genocide. Any linkage of forgiveness and forgetting appears to be only a minority view; in essence, the most extremely pragmatic interpretation of the likely outcomes of forgiveness.

In my interviews, nearly all survivors describe the need to remember and, where necessary, to bring individuals to account for past crimes. The idea that forgiveness entails forgetting is anathema to most survivors because, as we have already seen concerning healing, forgetting such immense trauma will be impossible for anyone who experienced the genocide at first hand. Most survivors also oppose the idea of forgetting crimes because they are intent on achieving some degree of retributive justice. Augustin, a forty-six-year-old survivor in Gisenyi whose elderly parents were murdered during the genocide, said,

> Gacaca is very dangerous for survivors. Why are these prisoners back here now? It makes me very scared to have them here, so close to my house. Reconciliation won't happen here. The survivors can't forget the past and we will fight for justice.[82]

[81] Author's solidarity camp interviews, Butare (no. 16) (author's translation).
[82] Author's survivor interviews, Marcus, Gisenyi (author's translation).

Rose, the survivor in Nyamata quoted in Chapter 4, echoed these sentiments. One of her sons, Rose explained, was a Hutu whom she adopted after his parents fled to Zaire near the end of the genocide. 'His parents killed some of the children in my household', she said. Rose's parents, her son, three nephews and two nieces were killed during the genocide. She did not know who had killed her parents, but she suspected that the parents of her adopted son were responsible for the murder of the six children. I asked why she had adopted the boy. 'Before the genocide', she said, 'we all lived together. No one cared if you were Hutu or Tutsi – we were like one family. Their children lived with my children. This one has really always been my son.' Rose explained that one of her teenage nieces, murdered because she was a Tutsi, had married a Hutu only months before the genocide began. Her niece's husband was also murdered because the interahamwe accused him of protecting Tutsi. 'I have forgiven [my son's parents] for what they did, even though I will probably never be able to tell them. But I will never forget what happened. Who can forget such horrible things? These things stay in your mind forever ... There is a serious need for justice here but instead we see the perpetrators walking around freely. This is not right.'[83]

Many Rwandans' motivation to rebuild relationships, both personal and communal, through forgiveness at gacaca means that they expect this process to result in more optimistic forms of restoration. Some sources argue that forgiveness will create a new, shared life for survivors and perpetrators, which allows both groups to move forward together, not by forgetting past crimes but by recognising what has occurred and finding new ways to coexist. Particularly when people believe that forgiveness will contribute to personal forms of healing as liberation through gacaca, for example as many detainees view confession as important for overcoming guilt, then they often interpret forgiveness as a means to overcome personal burdens that hinder the rebuilding of relationships. 'The main reason why I confessed', said Thaddée in the ingando at Gashora,

> is because I want to rejoin the survivors. This will happen when I tell them the truth about my crimes and they forgive me. If the truth comes out, gacaca will go well. The government will make sure that people tell the truth.[84]

[83] Author's survivor interviews, Rose, Nyamata.
[84] Author's solidarity camp interviews, Gashora (no. 19), 19 April 2003 (author's translation).

Thus, some popular sources argue that forgiveness enables the re-establishment of relationships and the construction of new forms of community after the genocide.

Commentators' perspectives on forgiveness through gacaca

Finally, how do commentators interpret the role of gacaca in facilitating forgiveness? Generally speaking, few commentators discuss forgiveness in the context of gacaca. Where they do, their views – like the population's – are shaped largely by the degree to which they subscribe to certain religious perspectives. The main source of differences in commentators' interpretations of forgiveness through gacaca is a divide between religious and secular understandings. Most commentators, particularly in the Rwandan academic community, who draw explicitly on Christian doctrine, view forgiveness as one of gacaca's central aims. Most secular commentators, on the other hand, are deeply sceptical of attempts to facilitate post-genocide forgiveness. As with the official and popular interpretations, it is not always clear how critical sources interpret forgiveness through gacaca, necessitating inferences of commentators' interpretations of forgiveness from their more general views.

First, what form do commentators argue forgiveness should take at gacaca? Among commentators who believe that forgiveness is a legitimate objective of gacaca, the majority (both Rwandan and non-Rwandan) argue that forgiveness is essentially an interpersonal act between individual perpetrators and survivors that is likely to begin at gacaca but is also likely to involve difficult, ongoing discussions. Gasibirege describes gacaca as an important 'space for forgiveness' in which judges encourage individuals to pursue this objective.[85] Jean-Paul Mugiraneza, formerly a senior researcher at IRDP, argues that forgiveness is crucial for Rwandans to rebuild personal and communal relationships after the genocide. Forgiveness, though, Mugiraneza argues, must be the 'very final stage of gacaca' and must be the personal choice of those individuals who have committed or suffered particular crimes.[86]

Although they rarely articulate this explicitly, most commentators who support pursuing forgiveness through gacaca interpret forgiveness as entailing survivors forgoing direct, personal retribution and feelings of resentment against perpetrators. Some critics of pursuing forgiveness through gacaca, such as Klaas de Jonge from PRI, argue

[85] Gasibirege, 'Recherche qualitative', p.145 (author's translation).
[86] Author's observer interviews, Mugiraneza.

that forgiveness will also involve survivors forfeiting a significant degree of formal recourse for genocide crimes. De Jonge states, 'It is unfair to expect forgiveness at gacaca because survivors are already burdened with enough pain after the genocide without asking them to forgive those who killed their friends and family.'[87] Jean-Claude Ngendandumwe, Coordinator of the Catholic Peace and Justice Commission, however, denies that there is any pressure from church officials or other leaders during gacaca hearings to seek or offer forgiveness. 'The possibility is always there for survivors to offer forgiveness', he explains, 'but no one forces anyone to forgive. Forgiveness should always be a choice.'[88]

Regarding the processes of forgiveness through gacaca, most advocates of forgiveness emphasise their long-term nature. 'Gacaca's work of repentance', argues Nsabiyera, echoing Dortzbach's view of healing mentioned earlier, 'begins a journey between those asking for forgiveness and those who are forgiving.'[89] This journey, Nsabiyera argues, will be long and arduous, as gacaca begins slowly rebuilding trust between parties previously in conflict. Nsabiyera argues that at gacaca there are two forms of forgiveness, 'official and personal'.[90] Official forgiveness is largely symbolic and is carried out during gacaca hearings in front of the general assembly. The main purpose of official forgiveness, according to Nsabiyera, is to inspire others to ask for, and to grant, forgiveness. Many individuals who participate in the process of official forgiveness, though, he argues, will also need to experience personal forgiveness, which occurs far from the public gaze and through a process of deeper engagement and rebuilding of trust. Such a process takes time and requires more diverse interactions between individuals than are possible at gacaca.

Concerning the motivations behind forgiveness, many critics are sceptical of the intentions behind calls for gacaca to facilitate survivors' forgiveness of perpetrators. Because critics view forgiveness as a process driven more by the judges and leaders in charge of gacaca, rather than by remorse from perpetrators or by survivors' willingness to forgive, they doubt the value of considering forgiveness as an objective of gacaca. PRI argues, '[C]onfessions [of perpetrators of mass crimes] without real or genuine regret are very common. To say, "I was wrong, very sorry", can be done without true acknowledgement of one's guilt, especially if

---

[87] Author's observer interviews, de Jonge.
[88] Author's observer interviews, Ngendandumwe (author's translation).
[89] Author's observer interviews, Nsabiyera, 3 February 2003.
[90] *Ibid.*

it is just a matter of a verbal apology.'[91] Critics view many instances of perpetrators asking for forgiveness as too hasty and lacking the reflection and signs of remorse necessary to convince survivors and others that their requests are sincere. Uvin goes one step further and suggests that genocide suspects are likely to ask for forgiveness in order to benefit from gacaca's plea-bargaining system. Uvin, who generally supports gacaca's system of confession and plea-bargaining because it 'creates ... strong incentives to speak out, to discuss, and to not follow the law of silence',[92] also argues, 'Prisoners who confess and ask for forgiveness can receive dramatic reductions in penalties ... To benefit from the community service provisions, the accused have to ask for forgiveness publicly.'[93]

Some commentators argue that two further motivations underlie individuals' desire to seek or grant forgiveness. First, some observers argue that religious leaders force their congregations to request and grant forgiveness. John Prendergast and David Smock, two critics of forgiveness through gacaca, argue that pressure from Catholic church leaders heavily influences suspects and survivors in this regard. Religious coercion, they argue, will be 'emasculating' of the gacaca process and will lead to 'a sort of religiously sanctioned impunity'.[94]

Second, some commentators argue that many Rwandans consider forgiveness as a central aim of gacaca because, regardless of their personal experiences of the genocide, forgiveness will help them throw off the burdens of the past and release them to live more vibrantly. Nsabiyera, for example, argues,

> Holding grudges blocks better thinking ... We [as survivors] must separate out and clarify our emotions so that we realise that forgiveness at gacaca can be a process of healing. First we must forgive ourselves for not forgiving others in the past. Then we will be ready to forgive others and to experience healing.[95]

Nsabiyera argues that many survivors carry an immense burden of fear and pain after the genocide. They express hatred towards those who killed their loved ones, which, Nsabiyera argues, can become debilitating, affecting all facets of their lives. Forgiving perpetrators for their crimes is therefore vital for survivors' release from these negative

---

[91] PRI, 'PRI Research Team on Gacaca', p.16.
[92] Uvin, 'The Introduction of a Modernized Gacaca', p.9.
[93] Uvin, 'Gacaca Tribunals in Rwanda', pp.117–18.
[94] Prendergast and Smock, 'Postgenocidal Reconstruction'.
[95] Author's observer interviews, Nsabiyera, 3 February 2003.

emotions, offering an opportunity to start life afresh, with a renewed sense of inner peace and improved relations with others. As we have already seen regarding healing at gacaca, perpetrators often express a need to be liberated from feelings of guilt. Some commentators argue that many perpetrators will experience release from guilt when their victims forgive them.

Inevitably, commentators' different interpretations of the processes and motivations of forgiveness at gacaca influence their views on its likely outcomes. Critical views of forgiveness, such as de Jonge's, assume that forcing survivors to forgive perpetrators will simply increase survivors' resentment and anger. Most advocates of forgiveness through gacaca meanwhile argue that forfeiting direct, personal vengeance, as basic forgiveness entails, will result in more peaceful cohabitation between parties previously in conflict. Some advocates of forgiveness argue that something more profound than mere cohabitation is also possible. For example, Nsabiyera argues that forgiveness should involve fostering a deeper, more profound engagement between perpetrators and survivors. If forgiveness at gacaca is to be truly meaningful, according to Nsabiyera, forgoing personal vengeance is insufficient because it will leave in place many of the sources of pain, anxiety and hatred. Only through deeper engagement can perpetrators and survivors overcome these emotions that have made closer relationships impossible in the past. In particular, Nsabiyera argues that processes of truth-telling inherent in forgiveness will help rebuild relationships between parties previously in conflict. 'Truth-telling', he argues, 'can bring healing and makes repentance possible.'[96] When perpetrators trust the general assembly to listen calmly and peacefully to their expressions of guilt and explanations of their actions, then they will be more likely to confess to their crimes, to ask for forgiveness and to engage closely with survivors in order to help rebuild relationships.

Critique of sources' perspectives on forgiveness through gacaca

The striking combination of religious and pragmatic, personal and communal elements renders forgiveness through gacaca a highly complicated theme. It is necessary now to support some of the views expressed by the three groups of sources examined, and to reject, modify or supplement others. This section critiques the official, popular and critical interpretations of forgiveness through gacaca according to questions of form,

[96] *Ibid.*

processes, motivations and outcomes. In many instances, this analysis draws on a broader philosophical and theological literature in order to illuminate the views of the sources analysed here.

In sources' interpretations of the form that forgiveness should take at gacaca, there are significant tensions between its private and public dimensions. In particular, the question of who can forgive is crucial but often answered unsatisfactorily. First, the individual–group and official forms of forgiveness expressed by some detainees propose a morally unjustified interpretation of who can forgive. These forms assume that either the community as a whole or the state may forgive a perpetrator, even though the perpetrator committed crimes against individual victims. The Gacaca Law encourages such a view by only requiring suspects to confess publicly in front of the general assembly but not privately to victims. It is not even clear whether the specific victims are required to be present when suspects make public confessions at gacaca.[97] Furthermore, as stated earlier, for a confession to be considered legitimate according to the revised Gacaca Law, suspects need only request forgiveness from 'a duly constituted bench, a judicial police officer or a public prosecutor investigating the case', rather than from their victims.

In turn, the view expressed by a minority of suspects that they should seek forgiveness from the government is also probably influenced by facets of Catholic doctrine that emphasise the Church's authority over forgiving sins. During the sacrament of Penance, Catholic believers confess their wrongdoings to bishops and priests who absolve confessors in the name of Christ. Some detainees appear to substitute the authority of the Church for that of the government when seeking forgiveness for their genocide crimes. The individual–group and official forms of forgiveness, however, are flawed because only individual victims, who have directly suffered a crime, may forgive those who have injured them. In cases where victims are dead or severely incapacitated, then their loved ones, who have suffered immense trauma as a result of these crimes, may forgive on their behalf. In all other cases, no external individual, group or institution may forgive perpetrators of these crimes.

The divine form of forgiveness that some detainees advocate is problematic for similar reasons. According to this view, genocide perpetrators may ask for forgiveness from God. This form of forgiveness is important for many Christians who believe that their genocide crimes damaged their relationship with God and that asking for divine forgiveness

---

[97] Gacaca Law (Modified 2004), Article 54.

is necessary for rebuilding it. This interpretation is popular among Protestant detainees who tend to take a more privatised approach to forgiveness, viewing it as a matter solely between the individual believer and God, occurring within the believer's conscience without mediation by a priest or another external party. Such a view becomes problematic when some detainees interpret this as a substitute for interpersonal forgiveness from their victims. While committing crimes may be seen as breaking God's commandments, for example the biblical commandment not to murder, perpetrators have committed these crimes against other individuals. Therefore, if they seek forgiveness from God, then they are morally obligated to also request it from their victims. The problem with divine forgiveness in the context of gacaca is not with this form of forgiveness per se but with some suspects' view that it substitutes for forgiveness from survivors.

The final category of problems concerning the form of forgiveness refers to what various sources argue forgiveness should entail. Both supporters and critics of pursuing forgiveness through gacaca offer unconvincing interpretations of the requirements of forgiveness. Unsatisfactory interpretations here centre around two issues: amnesty and amnesia. First, some non-Rwandan critics such as de Jonge, Prendergast and Smock mistakenly argue that forgiveness entails forgoing any attempt to punish the guilty. As a result, de Jonge argues that the amnesty resulting from forgiveness will generate greater anger and resentment among survivors. Implicit in de Jonge's criticisms is the view that forgiveness leads to condoning crimes and therefore fosters impunity. Forgiveness, however, is not inherently incompatible with punishment but rather only with direct, personal retribution. Forgiveness requires only that survivors forgo personal vengeance against perpetrators. The role of punishing those found guilty is instead handed over to the state. Forgiveness also does not entail condoning crimes but rather requires full acknowledgement of wrongdoing as perpetrators openly confess to, apologise and ask for forgiveness of, their crimes. Implicit in perpetrators' request for, and survivors' granting of, forgiveness is a mutual remembrance of the crimes committed; a recognition that the crimes were morally wrong and that some form of response is now required.[98]

---

[98] For a more detailed discussion of how forgiveness is compatible with certain forms of punishment, see M. Volf, 'Forgiveness, Reconciliation and Justice: A Christian Contribution to a More Peaceful Social Environment', in Helmick and Petersen, *Forgiveness and Reconciliation*, pp.44–7.

Another flawed interpretation claims that forgiveness will inherently require survivors to forget the crimes committed against them. Some detainees documented above argue that forgiveness entails amnesia, while some survivors argue that they will first have to forget the crimes against them before they can forgive the perpetrators. Such a view manifests psychological and philosophical flaws. At the outset, it is psychologically impossible for survivors to forget what has happened to them and their loved ones. Individuals cannot simply choose amnesia, although, as Susanne Buckley-Zistel argues based on fieldwork in rural Rwanda, many individuals try to do so.[99] Céleste, the Hutu widow quoted earlier, whose son, brother and two uncles were still in jail, accused of perpetrating genocide crimes, said, 'No one will ever forget what has happened. Even our children know all the stories now because we have told them.'[100] Innocent Rwiliza, a survivor interviewed by journalist Jean Hatzfeld, said:

> We forget nothing. For me, I can go several weeks without seeing my late wife and children's faces, though until then I had dreamed of them every night. But never a single day do I forget that they are here no longer, that they were chopped down, that they wanted to exterminate us, that neighbours of long-standing turned in a matter of hours into beasts. Every day I pronounce the word 'genocide'.[101]

Given the extreme violence of the genocide and the fact that most crimes were committed by individuals whom the victims knew intimately, most survivors will never forget the deep anguish of these events.

More importantly, nothing in the concept of forgiveness necessitates forgetting. It is commonplace in quotidian discourse to connect forgiveness with forgetting; such a linkage, however, probably stems more from the alliteration of the two words than from any reasoned philosophical connection. Rather than requiring amnesia, forgiveness necessitates acknowledgement of the past. Expecting survivors to forget the events of the genocide constitutes an unjust imposition; an imposition, however, to which forgiveness through gacaca is also opposed. Sources who link forgiveness with forgetting misinterpret what forgiveness entails, both

---

[99] S. Buckley-Zistel, 'We are Pretending Peace: Local Memory and the Absence of Social Transformation and Reconciliation in Rwanda', in Clark and Kaufman, *After Genocide*, pp.129–31.

[100] Author's general population interviews, Céleste, Butare (author's translation).

[101] Quoted in J. Hatzfeld, *Into the Quick of Life: The Rwandan Genocide – The Survivors Speak*, London: Serpent's Tail, 2008, p.83.

generally and in the context of gacaca. By advocating amnesia, these sources also risk increasing survivors' feelings of anger and resentment at the lack of acknowledgement of past crimes, when forgiveness in fact entails encouraging survivors to overcome these negative sentiments.

Regarding the motivations behind parties' desire for forgiveness through gacaca, some suspects' reasons for requesting forgiveness and some survivors' reasons for granting forgiveness are flawed. Four expressed motivations from the sources analysed in particular display crucial problems: forgiveness as motivated by the supposed benefits for suspects from gacaca's plea-bargaining system; more broadly, forgiveness sought or granted in order to each achieve personal, pragmatic outcomes; forgiveness motivated by the belief that suspects deserve to be forgiven; and forgiveness motivated by suspects' or survivors' sense of moral or religious duty.

First, the view expressed by several popular and critical sources that suspects may seek forgiveness in order to benefit from gacaca's plea-bargaining system is misinformed. Uvin's argument for example that '[t]o benefit from the community service provisions, the accused have to ask for forgiveness publicly' is technically mistaken.[102] At the time of Uvin's writing in 2003, none of the legal documents governing gacaca made explicit reference to forgiveness. In the current context, the 2008 revision of the Gacaca Law does not require suspects to ask for forgiveness publicly but rather from a range of state officials, possibly behind closed doors.

Second, following closely from the problem of linking forgiveness with plea-bargaining, there are both practical and moral problems with the wider motivation of seeking, or granting, forgiveness in order to achieve certain pragmatic ends. Especially when detainees seek forgiveness in order to reduce their sentences or to hasten their reintegration into the community, pragmatic motivations for forgiveness will often prove counter-productive. Many detainees openly emphasise these pragmatic motivations for their requests for forgiveness, rather than expressing genuine remorse for their crimes. In response, without sincere, complete confessions, apologies and requests for forgiveness from detainees, most survivors will refuse to forgive them. Detainees' optimism concerning the ease with which survivors will forgive them and welcome them back into the community, sometimes encouraged by detainees' experiences at pre-gacaca hearings, neglects the negative feelings that many survivors

---

[102] Uvin, 'Gacaca Tribunals in Rwanda', pp.117–18.

must negotiate in order to forgive. In practical terms, such motivations will deter many survivors from forgiving suspects whose confessions prove unconvincing.

In moral terms, detainees' requests for forgiveness that are driven by pragmatic motivations, rather than by sincere remorse for their crimes, are illegitimate. Regardless of whether or not survivors find suspects' confessions and requests for forgiveness convincing, suspects should seek forgiveness foremost because they wish to express remorse to their victims. The desire to achieve pragmatic benefits of forgiveness, such as reduced sentences or hastier reintegration into the community, should, if anything, be a secondary motivation. Not only suspects, however, express pragmatic motivations for seeking forgiveness; survivors also describe similar benefits of forgiving perpetrators, particularly their desire to overcome debilitating forms of anger and resentment, employing forgiveness as what Robert Enright describes as a 'self-healing strategy'.[103] Enright argues that a key reason why some victims of mass crimes forgive their transgressors is because, in doing so, they will experience healing from anger and a desire for revenge and thus a form of rehumanisation as a result of achieving greater social harmony with perpetrators.

How legitimate are survivors', rather than suspects', pragmatic motivations for forgiveness? Certainly survivors' personal motivations for granting forgiveness are more justified than guilty suspects'. Survivors are morally entitled to pursue personal healing after the genocide, and forgiving perpetrators for many survivors will aid this objective. However, forgiveness loses much of its meaning when survivors pursue it solely for their own gain. As the philosopher Aurel Kolnai argues, forgiveness is best viewed as an 'exquisite act of charity or benevolence', in which the forgiver is motivated primarily by a spirit of magnanimity.[104] Forgiveness is a gift that the forgiver bestows upon the perpetrator out of feelings of compassion and generosity, rather than for personal gain, regardless of how legitimate the forgiver's benefits from forgiving may be. Therefore, while it is perhaps inevitable that pragmatic calculations enter into forgiveness, such motivations devalue it in moral terms.

Third, the notion of forgiveness as a gift is important for countering a view implied by some detainees that survivors should grant them

---

[103] R. Enright and the Human Development Study Group, 'The Moral Development of Forgiveness', in W. Kurtines and W. Gewirtz (eds.), *Handbook of Moral Behavior and Development*, vol. I, London: Lawrence Erlbaum, 1991, p.31.

[104] A. Kolnai, 'Forgiveness', *Proceedings of the Aristotelian Society*, 74, 1973–4, p.104.

forgiveness because they deserve it. Some detainees suggest they have earned forgiveness by offering complete confessions, sincere apologies and requests for forgiveness or committing other favourable acts towards survivors. The problem with such a view is that, by definition, forgiveness can never be deserved. Jacques Derrida makes this point convincingly when he describes the 'paradox' of forgiveness: forgiveness is paradoxical, Derrida argues, because 'forgiveness forgives only the unforgivable.'[105] If forgiveness entailed forgiving only the forgivable, then forgiveness would be rendered meaningless; it would imply that, by its very nature, a certain wrongdoing could deserve or justify forgiveness, thus rendering forgiveness superfluous. Forgiveness only retains its meaning and power as a supererogatory virtue. Derrida recognises, and is sympathetic to the notion, that pragmatic considerations often motivate forgiveness, especially for victims who seek release from anger and hatred. However, in its purest sense, Derrida argues, forgiveness is 'hyperbolic, mad'; a 'plunge … into the night of the unintelligible'.[106] Therefore, detainees cannot justifiably argue that they warrant forgiveness.

Fourth, the notion of forgiveness as a gift illuminates problems with another commonly expressed motivation for forgiveness, namely the view that survivors have a Christian obligation to forgive perpetrators. Problems with the view of forgiveness as a duty echo problems with the notion of forgiveness as desert. Some survivors argue that they must forgive perpetrators, regardless of the latter's motivations for requesting forgiveness, because their Christian faith requires them to forgive out of gratitude for God's mercy. According to a common doctrine in many Christian denominations, an individual's forgiveness from God is contingent upon the fulfilment of two criteria: the repentance of sins and, in turn, his or her forgiveness of others for their sins. Some denominations, particularly within Protestantism, contest this doctrine and emphasise only the first of these criteria, arguing that believers will receive immediate, divine forgiveness when they confess their sins to God and ask for his forgiveness. In this second view, forgiving fellow humans is an act separate from receiving forgiveness from God. Nevertheless, the view that forgiveness from God is contingent upon granting forgiveness to others is a

---

[105] J. Derrida, *On Cosmopolitanism and Forgiveness*, trans. M. Dooley and M. Hughes, London: Routledge, 2001, p.32.
[106] *Ibid.*, p.49.

likely motivation for many Rwandans' view that survivors should forgive perpetrators out of a sense of Christian duty.

The notion, though, that individuals 'must forgive because God forgives', with its implication of an unconditional obligation to forgive perpetrators, is problematic on both theological and practical grounds. On a theological level, absent from some suspects' and survivors' descriptions of a supposed duty to grant forgiveness in response to God's gift of grace is the fact that, even in biblical accounts of forgiveness, God only forgives sinners after they have confessed their sins. Furthermore, within the scope of God's mercy, forgiveness is still conditional upon the spirit of sincerity in which individuals confess and express remorse. In the Gospel according to Luke, Jesus tells a parable of a Pharisee and a tax collector who come to the temple to pray. The Pharisee stands in the centre of the temple where the crowds can hear him and prays pompously: 'God, I thank you that I am not like other men – robbers, evildoers, adulterers – or even like this tax collector. I fast twice a week and give a tenth of all I get.'[107] The tax collector in contrast expresses profound humility and remorse for his sins, laying on his chest and praying, 'God, have mercy on me, a sinner.'[108] Jesus concludes, 'I tell you that this [tax collector], rather than the other, went home justified before God. For everyone who exalts himself will be humbled, and he who humbles himself will be exalted.'[109] God rejected the Pharisee's prayer because it lacked humility and sincerity. The tax collector's prayer, on the other hand, found divine favour because it expressed genuine remorse and a sincere desire for forgiveness. In the context of gacaca, therefore, even survivors who feel that their Christian faith requires them to forgive genocide perpetrators are free to refuse to forgive perpetrators if they doubt the honesty and sincerity of their confessions. On theological grounds, survivors retain a crucial degree of personal judgment; on occasions, they may discern that it would be unjustified to forgive perpetrators whose confessions seem contrived. In essence, the Christian obligation is not to forgive always but to demonstrate a *readiness* to forgive when perpetrators display genuine remorse. While forgiveness does not incorporate any element of desert, it retains a crucial element of conditionality.

On practical grounds, the interpretation of a biblical commandment to forgive unconditionally amounts to a damaging level of coercion.

---

[107] *The Holy Bible (New International Version)*, Luke 18:11–12.
[108] *Ibid.*, Luke 18:13.
[109] *Ibid.*, Luke 18:14.

This view entails forcing survivors to forgive perpetrators even when they doubt the sincerity of perpetrators' confessions or simply when they do not feel ready to forgive because of continuing feelings of anger and pain. If survivors feel that they are being coerced to forgive, their feelings of anger and resentment towards those whom they forgive and those who force them to forgive will increase. Therefore, regardless of the key influence of Christian ideals on popular interpretations of forgiveness through gacaca, we must reject the argument that survivors should forgive *unconditionally* out of a sense of Christian obligation.

Regarding processes of forgiveness through gacaca, one component of the sources' interpretations requires further consideration: the time frame in which some sources claim that forgiveness occurs. In particular, the view expressed, often implicitly, by some popular and critical sources of forgiveness as a one-off transaction between individuals is highly problematic. For forgiveness to be truly meaningful, it may constitute more than a single act during gacaca hearings. The view of forgiveness as a one-off transaction between perpetrators and survivors implies a form of cheap absolution of the guilty. Implicit in some religious interpretations, forgiveness constitutes a relatively straightforward sequence of confession, penance and absolution in Catholic doctrine or private confession and atonement in Protestant theology. Most interpretations of forgiveness through gacaca involve a two-way dialogue between the guilty party and the individual from whom he or she is requesting forgiveness, similar to the dialogue that occurs between a confessor and a priest in a religious setting. Most sources analysed here assume that the priest in the religious context – or the survivor at gacaca – may then decide to grant or deny forgiveness to the confessor directly after the transgressor has confessed.

Forgiveness through gacaca, however, will often take much longer than the immediate forgiveness represented in the religious setting. Many survivors will find it difficult or even impossible to forgive perpetrators because of the degree of their personal suffering. They may wish to reflect further on the confessions and apologies that they hear at gacaca before forgiving perpetrators much later. The precise timing and the amount of time necessary for survivors to forgive are important considerations. Viewing forgiveness as a one-off act undermines the possibility that some survivors may only in time, after experiencing personal healing through other components of gacaca or through other positive interactions with perpetrators in daily life, feel that they are ready to forgive. Gacaca may simply begin this longer-term process, recognising that forgiveness is arduous, involving different stages of emotional transition, and requires great courage from those who confess and ask for forgiveness, but particularly from those who grant it. As Brian Frost argues, forgiveness is a process, 'rather than something to be applied temporarily, like a poultice'.[110]

Finally, how convincing are the official, popular and critical interpretations of the likely outcomes of forgiveness through gacaca? The key to answering this question is to recall the distinction at the beginning of this section between basic and profound forgiveness. Basic forgiveness stems largely from single acts at gacaca and requires survivors' forgoing direct, personal revenge and feelings of resentment towards perpetrators. In this outcome, forgiveness requires that survivors vow to forgo attempts to mete out direct retribution against those found guilty of genocide crimes and to allow the state instead to punish perpetrators. Many Rwandans will undoubtedly consider basic forgiveness a remarkable achievement if gacaca is able to facilitate such an outcome, given the degree of hatred and desire for revenge that characterises many survivors after the genocide.

From several of the sources examined above, however, it is evident that many perpetrators and survivors expect that something more than basic forgiveness is necessary after the genocide and that profound forgiveness may be possible through gacaca. Several sources argue that forgiveness will result in improved relations between individuals. In this view, gacaca facilitates a deeper sense of trust between parties previously in conflict as survivors come to view perpetrators' remorse as genuine and deeper engagement becomes possible. There is no reason to believe that participants in gacaca should automatically resign themselves to pursuing only basic forgiveness. Certainly in some communities, local conditions will dictate that only basic forgiveness is possible. In contrast to the negative views of critics such as de Jonge, however, my interviews indicate that in some communities the population desires the sort of profound forgiveness that paves the way for healing as positive liberation, deeper forms of engagement and ultimately reconciliation. Missing from de Jonge's argument is a recognition that some survivors, usually those inspired by a religious perspective, are willing to forgive voluntarily and to try to rebuild relationships with perpetrators. In such circumstances it is unjustified to encourage only basic forgiveness.

---

[110] B. Frost, quoted in M. Henderson, *Forgiveness: Breaking the Chain of Hate*, Wilsonville, Oreg.: Book Partners, 1999, p.4.

There are unquestionably major obstacles to achieving forgiveness after the genocide, not least the immense pain and anger that survivors must manage in order to forgive the guilty. Gacaca judges must create an open environment that is conducive to survivors' dealing with these sentiments. No one can force survivors to forgive. Many detainees also offer incomplete confessions and insincere apologies, increasing survivors' suspicions and feelings of resentment, and scuppering any hopes of facilitating forgiveness. The most crucial issue in considering forgiveness through gacaca is the long-term dialogue between survivors and perpetrators that forgiveness entails. For many individuals, forgiveness will take months or years, ensuring that the process extends far beyond gacaca. While gacaca displays an unquestionable capacity for encouraging suspects to confess to, and to ask forgiveness for, their crimes and survivors to grant forgiveness, often drawing on Christian principles shared by much of the population, in most cases gacaca at best provides a starting point for forgiveness.

This section has argued that forgiveness through gacaca may legitimately be pursued in two forms – interpersonal (between an individual perpetrator and victim) and divine (between a perpetrator and God) – but that the latter is only legitimate when combined with the former. Some detainees in particular argue that they wish to pursue individual–group forgiveness, in which they seek forgiveness from their entire community, or official forgiveness, in which they request forgiveness from the government. Such views erroneously assume that external bodies may forgive on behalf of the individual victims of crimes.

Forgiveness, as the only objective of gacaca that garners no mention in the Gacaca Law until very recently, best embodies the popular spirit of gacaca and highlights the crucial ways in which the population shapes gacaca to its own ends and according to its own beliefs. This theme underscores popular ownership of gacaca and the dynamism of the process. Rather than representing centralised state control, as some human-rights critics have argued, gacaca often embodies major social and cultural influences drawn from the population that find little expression in official discourse. People's religious convictions in particular are largely responsible for the widespread view that gacaca should help facilitate forgiveness. Some advocates of forgiveness, informed by Christian doctrine, mischaracterise forgiveness as a moral or religious duty. We should view forgiveness only as an undeserved gift, which in its truest form is given in a spirit of charity and generosity, but which victims may choose or refuse to give. In opposing the notion of forgiveness as an obligation, we should recognise that forgiveness often entails arduous, long-term processes, particularly as many survivors must negotiate feelings of anger, hatred and resentment in order to forgive perpetrators. Forgiveness is an immensely costly pursuit, particularly after an event as divisive and violently destructive as genocide, and many survivors may justifiably decide that they are unwilling to forgive. As with healing, forgiveness is likely to entail deep and continued interactions between suspects and survivors long after gacaca is complete.

CHAPTER 10

(RE)FUSING SOCIAL BONDS: GACACA AND RECONCILIATION

INTRODUCTION

Reconciliation, the final objective of gacaca explored in this book, is among its most commonly and variably discussed aims. Without prompting during interviews, most Rwandan respondents express some view on reconciliation, including many who describe it as gacaca's central objective. This chapter analyses official, popular and critical interpretations of reconciliation through gacaca according to the following taxonomy: first, what *form* do these sources argue reconciliation should take? This question relates to the actors involved, asking whether reconciliation entails rebuilding relationships between individuals, between individuals and groups or on a group-to-group basis. Second, to what *degree* should reconciliation be pursued? Does reconciliation constitute a fundamentally pragmatic outcome such as the peaceful cohabitation of previously antagonistic parties, something more ambitious such as the creation of a new dynamic between parties that generates a more meaningful engagement between them than in the past, or an intermediary, retrospective outcome such as a reversion to a form of unity that has been forfeited during conflict? Third, this chapter explores what *types of methods* these groups believe are necessary to achieve reconciliation. For example, is reconciliation a short- or long-term process, which occurs solely through gacaca or in conjunction with other social processes? In the concluding chapter, I draw together the strands of argument from Chapters 5–10 to show that gacaca pursues reconciliation by first facilitating the other profound objectives and generally by fostering greater engagement, which is the bridge to reconciliation.

Similar to the exploration of popular participation in Chapter 5, this chapter argues that the government's rhetoric of national unity – a concept that several sources conflate with reconciliation – damages the pursuit of reconciliation. In contrast, a boon for gacaca's prospects of facilitating reconciliation is the extent to which many Rwandans' religious beliefs shape their views concerning the need for rebuilding broken relationships and the capacity of gacaca to help in this regard. Many communities subsume Christian ideals into their interpretations and practices of gacaca and draw from these substantial energy and motivation for reconciliation. One important consequence of the linkage of theological principles and gacaca is that, on the basis of their religious beliefs, many Rwandans express optimism that gacaca will facilitate reconciliation after the genocide and they actively engage in this pursuit. Nevertheless, empirical evidence from gacaca hearings and interviews in communities around Rwanda highlights that reconciliation is at best a distant result in most of the country, although gacaca constitutes an important starting point in this process.

Government's perspectives on reconciliation through gacaca

Official pronouncements on the theme of reconciliation generally, and on reconciliation as an outcome of gacaca specifically, are increasingly common but usually vaguely defined. Sarkin argues that the term 'reconciliation' is new to the government's vocabulary and that post-genocide necessities have forced the government to consider for the first time the meaning and requirements of reconciliation.[1] The introduction to the Gacaca Law lists 'justice and reconciliation in Rwanda'[2] as one of gacaca's main aims, while the Gacaca Manual states that a primary objective of gacaca is to facilitate 'the reconciliation of the Rwandan people and the reinforcing of their unity through the creation of an environment favourable to dialogue and to collaboration in the search for a concerted solution to the problems of justice'.[3] Drawing on the traditional practice of gacaca, the post-genocide institution is, according to the NURC, 'designed to be reconciliatory, restorative as well as

---

[1] Sarkin, 'Gacaca Courts and Genocide', p.69.
[2] Gacaca Law (Modified 2004), Introduction.
[3] Gacaca Manual, p.8 (author's translation).

community participatory'.[4] The form of reconciliation described in the NURC document is group-to-group, focusing on mending relationships between groups of genocide perpetrators and survivors who are assumed to have lived in a previous state of 'unity'. Because the government banned the use of ethnic labels on national identity cards in 2003[5] and has often used laws criminalising 'divisionism' to curtail public discussions of ethnicity, the groups involved in this process are never described as Tutsi or Hutu but rather as 'victims ... and suspects'[6] or 'survivors and perpetrators'.[7]

Echoing the view that unity can be regained in Rwanda, the government interprets the degree of reconciliation necessary after the genocide in retrospective terms, emphasising the need to *restore* a lost sense of social cohesion. According to this view, Rwandan history comprises identifiable periods when different groups in society formed a unified, national whole which provides a template for how these groups should live together today. The government claims that social harmony is a dynamic innate in Rwandan society that can be rediscovered in the current context by instituting practices, such as those embodied in gacaca, that reinforce or 'strengthen ... unity'.[8] Implicit in the government's perspective is a belief that certain modes of public participation – expressed in its regular linkage of 'collaboration' and 'reconciliation' – are necessary if groups in conflict wish to relearn how to coexist.

Regarding the official interpretation of the types of methods for achieving reconciliation through gacaca, communal action, such as public participation in gacaca, is the key to reinforcing unity or achieving reconciliation; two concepts that, despite their apparent separation in the title of the NURC, are largely synonymous in the government's discourse. While reconciliation is generally interpreted as an outcome of gacaca, the government also emphasises the extent to which the processes of gacaca are reconciliatory, seeking a consistency of philosophy in gacaca's methods and outcomes. The government argues that gacaca's processes are collaborative: the population, rather than state or

[4] Ndangiza, 'Transitional Justice and Reconciliation', p.4. See also Rusagara, *Resilience of a Nation*, p.190.
[5] See, for example, M. Lacey, 'A Decade after Massacres, Rwanda Outlaws Ethnicity', *New York Times*, 9 April 2004, www.nytimes.com/2004/04/09/international/africa/09RWAN.html?hp=& pagewanted=all&position=.
[6] Gacaca Manual, pp.10–11.
[7] Ndangiza, 'Transitional Justice and Reconciliation', p.3.
[8] *Ibid.*, p.7.

community leaders, constitutes the main agent, and communal dialogue is the primary mode of deliberation.[9] In short, the government argues that popular participation and a greater sense of togetherness during the process of gacaca will produce a greater sense of togetherness, or reconciliation in the group-to-group sense, outside of gacaca.

In the official discourse, this connection between reconciliatory processes within and beyond gacaca is relatively straightforward, with the former leading naturally to the latter. The government does not explain whether other mediating processes or institutions are necessary to achieve this translation of localised to wider reconciliatory outcomes. Gacaca is thus seen as a test run of reconciliation, a chance for different groups in the community to experience in a closed setting how they may interact more harmoniously in daily life. According to Augustin Nkusi, former chief adviser to the Gacaca Commission and current spokesperson of the Office of the Prosecutor General,

> Gacaca contributes to reconciliation in a very general way but very quickly ... It gets the community to say who is responsible for committing crimes and it gets those who are guilty to tell the people what they did and to explain their actions ... Because people talk together so much at gacaca, it will not take us many years to experience reconciliation in Rwanda.[10]

Nkusi's view assumes that reconciliation is a short-term process, functioning as a *reminder* of the unity that he argues characterised Rwandan society before it was undermined by external political forces.

Recently, some state officials have spoken more cautiously about gacaca's capacity to facilitate reconciliation, reflecting practical challenges observed in gacaca's daily operation. 'Gacaca has contributed greatly to justice but reconciliation to a much lesser extent', said Ndangiza in 2008.

> Perhaps there will be reconciliation after gacaca ... Probably there will be more reconciliation when the perpetrators return home from TIG. Gacaca helps start to rebuild trust, beginning a process of reconciliation ... The government has also been organising reconciliation associations between perpetrators and victims, for example income-generating activities that are important for trust-building between these groups and their families. You have to remember that we also need to achieve

[9] Mucyo, 'Gacaca Courts and Genocide', p.53.
[10] Author's government interviews, Augustin Nkusi, Chief Adviser, Supreme Court of Rwanda, 6th Chamber (Gacaca Commission), Kigali, 2 February 2003 (author's translation).

reconciliation between the confessors and their own families. Many of these perpetrators have been rejected by their own families and many of them now say that the victims are their best friends. We have a very complicated situation in this country.[11]

Here Ndangiza emphasises the role of gacaca in 'beginning a process of reconciliation'; a more cautious assessment than Nkusi's bold statement above regarding gacaca's rapid contribution to reconciliation.

Population's perspectives on reconciliation through gacaca

The popular perspective of reconciliation through gacaca echoes much of the government's discourse, in particular the rediscovery of a lost sense of unity, which is generally equated with achieving reconciliation. Ciprien, a trader in Kacyiru district of Kigali Ville, several of whose cousins were accused of genocide crimes and had been recently provisionally released, said, 'Of course we can all live together after gacaca. Hutu and Tutsi have always lived together. Soon it will be just like before.'[12] There is a stronger sense among everyday Rwandans, however, that reconciliation will require much more than a simple reversion to an assumed forfeited sense of social cohesion. Much of the population argues that gacaca will need to facilitate new interactions between groups previously in conflict to achieve reconciliation. Boniface, a survivor in Kigali Ville said, 'By talking to each other at gacaca we can learn to live together again. But this will take time. These things aren't easy for us because of the genocide.'[13] At the same time, there is much scepticism, not surprisingly among survivors in particular, about the prospects of achieving reconciliation in Rwanda generally and achieving it through gacaca specifically. Augustin, a survivor in Gisenyi, said, 'Reconciliation will never happen in Rwanda because we can't forget what happened in the past. Gacaca won't change any of this. People are still too hurt and people are still too angry.'[14] The NURC perceptions survey in 2003 found that 37 per cent of the general population, and 57 per cent of genocide survivors, believe that after gacaca survivors and released detainees would have

---

[11] Author's government interviews, Ndangiza, 2008. For an analysis of the NURC's use of local associations, especially theatre groups that have been subsumed into government sensitisation programmes surrounding gacaca, see A. Breed, 'Performing Reconciliation in Rwanda', *Peace Review: A Journal of Social Justice*, 18, 4, 2006, pp.507–13.

[12] Author's general population interviews, Ciprien, Kigali Ville, Kacyiru, 22 May 2003 (author's translation).

[13] Author's survivor interviews, Boniface, Kigali Ville (author's translation).

[14] Author's survivor interviews, Augustin, Gisenyi (author's translation).

difficulty living together.[15] According to the same survey, 72 per cent of the general population, but only 47 per cent of genocide survivors, believe that families of convicted perpetrators and families of victims would be able to reconcile after gacaca.[16] As with most of the objectives of gacaca examined in this book, there is no homogeneous public interpretation of reconciliation through gacaca or of the prospects for achieving it. Different groups interpret reconciliation as a post-genocide aim in very different ways, though some elements of this theme are consistent across large sections of Rwandan society.

In contrast to the government's interpretation of reconciliation through gacaca as primarily group-to-group, genocide suspects, survivors, gacaca leaders and the general population all describe reconciliation on an individual basis. More than any other source, the population articulates the crucial personal, emotional issues involved in reconciliation. For many Rwandans, reconciliation is less an issue of community-wide or national importance than a question of rebuilding relationships with other individuals, many of whom were their neighbours before the genocide. For much of the population, the nature of the face-to-face interactions that occur at gacaca indicates the likelihood of achieving reconciliation in the future. As Eugene, a detainee in the ingando in Kigali Ville, said, 'At gacaca I will tell the family members of those I killed what I did during the genocide. They will listen and respond to what I tell them. These will be the first steps toward our living together again.'[17] When asked what sort of reception he expected upon returning to his original community, Eugene gave a mixed response, saying initially, 'I have no reason to be scared of my community', then admitting, 'I am not too sure about how my neighbours will react when I go home.'[18] In my interviews, most genocide suspects argue that they will need to be reconciled to the friends and families of their victims but that this will not be easy, given the feelings of anger and resentment that pervade communities of survivors. As described in Chapter 4, as the gacaca journey progressed for Cypriet and Alphonse, they expressed increasing doubts over their ability to reconcile with survivors, especially as they had experienced intimidation and discord with survivors following their return from prison and ingando.

[15] NURC, 'Opinion Survey on Participation in Gacaca', Annexe 4, p.25.
[16] Ibid., Annexe 4, p.34.
[17] Author's solidarity camp interviews, Kigali Ville (no. 9), 12 April 2003 (author's translation).
[18] Ibid.

Survivors and inyangamugayo also emphasise the importance of rec-onciliation between individuals, stressing the need to rebuild fractured relationships on a personal rather than a group basis, though they also mention the latter form of reconciliation to a lesser extent. As quoted in Chapter 7, Michel, the president of a judges' panel in Butamwa district of Kigali Ville, described reconciliation through gacaca as occurring pri-marily on an individual-to-individual basis. 'Gacaca is important for rec-onciliation', he said, 'because what happens here is real justice where we are all together, criminals and the innocent, and people can talk to one another face to face'.[19] After the same hearing, Solomon, a survivor who had lost the majority of his family during the genocide, expressed disap-pointment that those suspected of killing his family were not brought to the hearing to give evidence as the gacaca judges had promised the week before. 'The reason I came to gacaca today is because I want to speak to the killers', Solomon said. 'Talking to them face to face is important for our reconciliation. How can I live with them again unless I can talk to them first?'[20] Solomon said that he wished to engage the suspects indi-vidually, to hear them describe what they had done during the genocide and to answer his questions regarding their actions and motives. He con-ceded, however, that

> it is very hard to talk to the killers because they usually lie about what they have done ... They tell many kinds of lies to try and make us believe they are innocent – 'I was sick at the time [of the genocide]', 'I was in a different community', 'I didn't kill'. The truth may come one day but we will have to wait.[21]

This difficulty in convincing suspects to tell the truth about their crimes, Solomon said, made it hard to countenance living with them in the future. Benoit Kaboyi, then-Senior Legal Adviser to (and now Executive Secretary of) Ibuka, argued that many survivors felt that they would never be able to completely trust those accused of committing genocide crimes and that this was the biggest barrier to reconciliation:

> As an organisation, we encourage survivors to participate in gacaca, but some survivors simply don't want gacaca. They don't trust the detainees to

---

[19] Author's gacaca interviews, Michel, Kigali Ville, Butamwa, 21 May 2003 (author's translation).

[20] Author's gacaca interviews, Solomon, Kigali Ville, Butamwa, 21 May 2003 (author's translation).

[21] Ibid.

tell the truth ... In reality, reconciliation is maybe only possible between survivors and family members of the killers, not for the killers themselves. And even then reconciliation is the ideal. Maybe only peaceful cohabitation is possible. There may be cohabitation first, then a period of détente. It will probably take several generations for reconciliation to be possible.[22]

While members of all groups within Rwandan society discussed here emphasise the individual nature of reconciliation through gacaca, the population also describes two other forms of reconciliation: between groups and between individuals and groups. Many survivors and gacaca leaders echo the government's interpretation of reconciliation as a group-to-group process. As in the official discourse, the population rarely defines group-to-group reconciliation in terms of building better relations between Hutu and Tutsi but rather between genocide perpetrators and survivors. The popular discourse surrounding group-to-group reconciliation also regularly slips into a discussion of the need to regain a lost sense of unity. A common description of the main aim of gacaca was expressed by Edouard, a member of the general population in Kigali Ville, who said that gacaca was important for 'helping us learn to live side by side again'.[23] Faustin, a gacaca judge in Nyamata, argued, 'Gacaca is vital for us because it will help us live together again, both the guilty and the survivors of the genocide.'[24] These views express a fundamentally community-oriented perspective of reconciliation, founded on the assumption that the community previously displayed a sense of wholeness that the genocide destroyed but gacaca can restore.

Many detainees describe a third form of reconciliation through gacaca, arguing that individuals need to reconcile with groups, and more specifically they as suspects need to reconcile with the communities in which they are accused of committing genocide crimes. Similar to popular interpretations of individual-to-individual reconciliation, this perspective takes an essentially personal view of reconciliation, with the key exception that in individual-to-group reconciliation suspects appear more concerned with their ability to *reintegrate peacefully* into their

---

[22] Author's observer interviews, Benoit Kiboyi, Legal Officer, Ibuka, Kigali, 20 May 2003 (author's translation).

[23] Author's general population interviews, Edouard, Kigali Ville, Kacyiru, 22 May 2003 (author's translation).

[24] Author's gacaca interviews, Faustin, Kigali Ngali, Nyamata, 19 May 2003 (author's translation)

previous communities, rather than with rebuilding broken relationships with certain individuals.

A common articulation of suspects' desire for individual-to-group reconciliation connects reintegration with confession. In the ingando in Gashora, for example, a detainee named Serestini said that he wanted to confess in front of his community during a gacaca hearing so that he could 'live peacefully with others' in the future.[25] Many detainees whom I interviewed expressed a hope that they would be able to regain a sense of belonging, which they felt they had forfeited as a result of committing (or having been accused of) genocide crimes. As quoted in Chapter 4, Alphonse said several weeks after returning to his home community after prison and ingando, 'I will tell the truth and the victims will forgive me. There is no question about that. I expect only good things at gacaca, no more punishment, just cohabitation.'

For most detainees, however, discussions of individual-to-group reconciliation reflect their desire to avoid direct reprisals from genocide survivors when they return to their home communities, rather than a genuine desire to reintegrate fully into – or to *belong to* – these communities. Their main motivation is fear rather than a sense of loss of meaningful relationships. It is not always possible to discern which of these two motivations lies behind detainees' expressed desire to experience individual-to-group reconciliation. However, it is evident that fear motivates many detainees' hopes of achieving reconciliation with their previous communities.

The four groups within the population – genocide suspects, survivors, gacaca leaders and the remainder of the general population – also articulate different interpretations of the *degree* of reconciliation that they believe is desirable or possible through gacaca. It is crucial to observe that of the four groups only some suspects, and a small minority of survivors, describe the degree of reconciliation as a reversion to, or a restoration of, a pre-existing unity in Rwandan society. As discussed in previous chapters, some survivors claim that gacaca is important for 'making us all like family again'.[26] This view is more common among detainees, who usually echo the sentiment expressed by Célestin, a detainee in the ingando in Butare, who said,

> The most important thing about gacaca is that it will bring reconciliation ... It will help us all [suspects and survivors] return to the family.

[25] Author's solidarity camp interviews, Gashora (no. 10), 18 April 2003 (author's translation).
[26] Author's survivor interviews, Romain, Butare, Kibingo, 14 May 2003 (author's translation).

Survivors have the right not to forgive us [suspects], but we can hope that the family will be brought together again.[27]

Most survivors, gacaca leaders and the wider population, though, rarely speak of restoring unity (and are sometimes deeply sceptical of this rhetoric) and express instead, to varying degrees, the view that gacaca must facilitate the creation of a new dynamic between groups previously in conflict. They argue that reconciliation must be forward-looking rather than seeking to reinstate a lost sense of social cohesion. Survivors generally describe more cautiously than gacaca leaders how forward-looking they should be in predicting the degree of reconciliation that is possible through gacaca. Many survivors express a pragmatic view of reconciliation as peaceful cohabitation, in which deep engagement between genocide perpetrators and survivors may not be possible but where nonetheless gacaca may help facilitate a more peaceful coexistence between these groups. Patrice, a genocide survivor in Ruhengeri, expressed this pragmatic version of reconciliation when he argued, 'Gacaca may help us live side by side one day, but not now. There is still too much pain and anger in the community. We won't be able to live together for a very long time.'[28]

Most gacaca judges are more optimistic about achieving forward-looking reconciliation through gacaca, emphasising the ways in which popular participation in gacaca fosters a new form of group dialogue in Rwandan society, thus providing a new means of conflict resolution which these groups may employ outside of gacaca. Alice, a gacaca judge in Ruhengeri, argued, 'Gacaca gets people to talk together, often for the first time. We are building the unity of our people by getting them to come together in this place and to solve problems together. This is how gacaca is able to help us achieve reconciliation.'[29] Oscar, a gacaca judge in Musanze district, said, 'Gacaca's main contribution has been to build new relations between people. It has shown that not all Hutu are implicated in crimes and that they can now live with survivors, resolve problems with them and eat at the same table. Now you're seeing real reconciliation happening here.'[30] These views hold both that a reversion to a pre-existing unity is not viable, hence the emphasis on *building* unity or new relations, but nevertheless that something more than mere coexistence

---

[27] Author's solidarity camp interviews, Butare (no. 21), 29 April 2003 (author's translation).
[28] Author's survivor interviews, Patrice, Ruhengeri (author's translation).
[29] Author's gacaca interviews, Alice, Ruhengeri (author's translation).
[30] Author's inyangamugayo interviews, Oscar, Northern Province, Musanze, 2 September 2008.

may be possible. Therefore, according to this perspective, it is necessary to pursue the creation of a new social dynamic through gacaca, hoping that the more open, collaborative processes of gacaca will allow different groups to discuss their tensions and conflicts in a more constructive fashion than they have in the past.

Although different groups in Rwandan society interpret the degree of reconciliation through gacaca in very different ways, their interpretations draw on a similar understanding of the types of reconciliation processes employed in gacaca. The population generally views these methods in a similar fashion to the government, emphasising the importance of internal collaborative processes at gacaca which encourage a more constructive dialogue between groups and thus facilitate reconciliation outside of gacaca. These notions of collaboration constitute important forms of engagement, emphasising the need for parties to work closely together on common goals, such as resolving disputes or verifying the facts of legal cases heard at gacaca. This engagement is often highly confrontational. Participants regularly debate deeply emotional issues face to face in a public forum. This level of personal engagement concerns many suspects and survivors, who worry that they will be forced to make themselves too vulnerable. 'I have already experienced so much pain', said Augustin, a survivor in Gisenyi whose parents were killed during the genocide.

> The government has given us no explanation for why the prisoners have been released. Why are they back here now? Gacaca will be dangerous for us survivors because we will have to see them face to face. This scares me.[31]

Not all participants, though, express concern over the demanding forms of engagement that gacaca requires. Eugene, the detainee in the Kigali Ville ingando quoted earlier, said,

> There is no reason for any of us [detainees] to be scared at gacaca ... I don't know how my neighbours will respond to me when I return to my community. But I know that for us gacaca will be like taking our first steps towards reconciliation. We will have to take many steps if we are going to learn to live together again.[32]

In my interviews, it is not always clear how genuinely suspects express this level of confidence in gacaca. It is possible that some detainees, for

---

[31] Author's survivor interviews, Augustin, Gisenyi (author's translation).
[32] Author's solidarity camp interviews, Kigali Ville (no. 9) (author's translation).

example, express confidence in gacaca because they wish to please the officials who oversee the ingando or other state officials, or because they wish to convince themselves that they will receive a warm welcome from the community.

The popular interpretation of gacaca's reconciliatory processes differs from the government's by contending that gacaca will incorporate fundamentally long-term processes, involving a difficult, protracted dialogue between suspects and survivors. This view of gacaca's methods is consistent with the population's overall belief that there is little 'unity' to which it can revert and that reconciliation will require the creation of new dynamics between individuals and groups. In particular, individuals who have been in conflict cannot simply return to more harmonious relationships which they are assumed to have shared in the past. In many cases, these relationships never existed and, where they did, they have been so damaged by the genocide that it will be impossible to ever rebuild them to their previous shape and depth. Viewing reconciliation as a largely individual-to-individual dynamic ensures that the process towards reconciliation appears more arduous, making concrete and more visceral what – in the state's discourse – appears abstract and detached from the personal lives of everyday Rwandans. According to the popular perspective, reconciliation is an ongoing process, as expressed in the view above of gacaca representing the first steps in a long series towards reconciliation. This process may find its genesis at gacaca but it will require further positive engagement between parties to restore relationships in a meaningful and sustainable manner.

Two crucial dynamics that heavily influence the population's views on both the degree and methods of reconciliation through gacaca are almost entirely neglected in the literature on gacaca: first, people's religious beliefs and, second, their involvement in unofficial versions of gacaca heavily influence how they interpret gacaca generally and reconciliation as an objective of gacaca specifically. In my interviews with suspects and survivors, religious believers regularly describe gacaca and its objectives in theological terms, despite this language never appearing in gacaca's governing legal documents. Individuals who subscribe to a particular religious worldview, especially one founded on Christian principles, usually speak more positively about the need for, and the level of, reconciliation they believe is possible through gacaca.

The basis of their optimistic expressions regarding reconciliation, however, varies greatly, underlining the different ways in which different individuals interpret the same religious principles and in turn how they deploy these principles in interpreting gacaca. For some Christian adherents, optimism about achieving reconciliation through gacaca stems from their feelings of solidarity with other believers. 'Because the people at gacaca are Christians, they will forgive us, and we will be able to live together again', said Vedaste, a detainee who, before arriving in the ingando in Butare, had confessed to committing murder during the genocide.[33] Some detainees assume that others in their community will subscribe to their Christian values and therefore the community will be ready first to forgive, and second to reconcile with, them when they appear at gacaca.

Some survivors also argue, on the basis of their Christian principles, that reconciliation is an important and likely outcome of gacaca. It is not always clear, however, what degree of reconciliation they believe is possible after the genocide. Some survivors agree with Vedaste's perspective and invoke a perceived religious obligation to forgive, and subsequently to reconcile with, those who have committed crimes against them and their loved ones. Marie-Claire, a survivor in Nyamata quoted earlier, said,

> I have already forgiven the killers. God forgives, therefore we must forgive … There is no one pressuring me to forgive the people who killed my family. It is only the word of God that tells me to forgive.[34]

Marie-Claire argued that she did not need to attend gacaca in order to forgive those who had murdered her family. However, she said that at gacaca there would be a 'chain of revelation' that meant that 'the guilty will receive their justice', after which she could countenance living with the convicted criminals again in the community.[35] Similarly, Jean-Michel, a university student from Nyamirambo district in Kigali Ville, whose older brother and three younger sisters were killed during the genocide, said, 'I can forgive because God forgives. Gacaca is like a classroom where the judges will show us how to forgive and how to live together again.'[36] Because God has forgiven, and reconciled with, them after they have sinned, many Christian believers argue that they must be willing to display grace and mercy to genocide perpetrators as a sign of gratitude for the mercy they have received from God.

---

[33] Author's solidarity camp interviews, Butare (no. 19), 29 April 2003 (author's translation).
[34] Author's survivor interviews, Marie-Claire, Kigali Ngali (author's translation).
[35] Ibid.
[36] Author's survivor interviews, Jean-Michel, Kigali Ville (author's translation).

It is not clear what degree of reconciliation is implied in Marie-Claire's and Jean-Michel's idea that forgiveness will allow survivors and perpetrators to one day 'live together again'. That forgiveness is at all considered a part of the reconciliation process suggests that a deep sense of engagement between survivors and perpetrators is necessary at gacaca. Implicit in this view is the understanding that a survivor will not forgive a perpetrator without an intense interaction first occurring between them. However, whether the reconciliation that follows from this is assumed to be of equal meaning and intensity, or whether it implies that survivors and perpetrators are likely to accept coexisting peacefully rather than engaging with one another at a deeper level after gacaca, is uncertain.

Some survivors who claim that their Christian beliefs are the primary motivation for their willingness to reconcile with suspects argue that Christian gacaca hearings in their churches encouraged them to adopt this positive attitude. In particular, some survivors argue that Christian gacaca teaches them that they have an obligation to forgive, and to reconcile with, those who have caused them harm in the past. Missionary organisations such as African Enterprise have also encouraged many Christian survivors to participate in gacaca and to seek reconciliation with genocide perpetrators.[37] Simon, the survivor in Nyamata quoted in the previous chapter who found his wife dead in his house but never recovered the bodies of his two children, said, 'God helped me keep my mind and heart intact. It wasn't easy to stay calm or sane.'[38] He said that after the genocide he attended regular Christian gacaca sessions after morning mass at his church, where the priest told those in attendance that 'God forgives us, so we must forgive one another.'[39] Simon claimed Christian gacaca convinced him that it was necessary to reconcile with the murderers of his wife and children.

As suggested by Simon's experiences of Christian gacaca, the second key influence on the population's views on reconciliation is its participation in unofficial versions of gacaca. Many detainees claim that their experiences during pre-gacaca hearings, in which they have come face to face with survivors in the community in a test run of official gacaca before they are released from the ingando, reinforced their confidence about achieving reconciliation. Vedaste said that attending pre-gacaca

[37] Morgan, 'Healing Genocide'.
[38] Author's survivor interviews, Simon, Kigali Ngali, Nyamata, 19 May 2003 (author's translation).
[39] Ibid.

hearings in his home village increased his confidence in being able to engage meaningfully with his community during official gacaca:

> When I was allowed to leave [ingando] to visit the people in my village, it was very good. I have visited my community five times now and each time I talked with the families there as we had before the war ... This is why gacaca is important: it brings all the people together again ... There is no doubt that gacaca will punish me but it will also reconcile us.[40]

Some detainees express greater confidence on the basis that at pre-gacaca hearings they were able to prove their innocence to survivors and government officials. Five detainees interviewed in the ingando at Ruhengeri argued that they had been exonerated at pre-gacaca hearings and that this gave them confidence concerning their welcome upon returning to their communities and their ability to engage meaningfully with survivors during official gacaca hearings.[41] Matiyasi, a detainee in the ingando at Butare, derived an even greater sense of confidence from the pre-gacaca hearings he attended. While in prison, he had confessed to being present for, though not directly involved in, a murder during the genocide. At the pre-gacaca hearings, he argued, he had 'already been judged', which meant that he would not have to appear at official gacaca after his release from the ingando because his was considered a 'completed case'.[42] This conclusion is in fact legally incorrect, as all detainees who are found guilty of genocide crimes at pre-gacaca hearings must still face official gacaca; only detainees who can prove their innocence at pre-gacaca can avoid appearing at official gacaca.[43]

Some detainees express similar attitudes concerning their experiences during prison gacaca hearings. Antoine, a fifty-two-year-old detainee in the ingando at Gashora, who confessed while in prison to being in a group of men who committed murder, though he denied being directly involved in any killings, said that he expected 'a warm welcome back in the village after I am released' because he had already met the families of some of his victims when they attended prison gacaca hearings.[44] 'My crimes are in the open', Antoine said, 'so I already know how I will be received when I go back to the village. Some of the victims' families even

---

[40] Ibid.
[41] Author's solidarity camp interviews, Ruhengeri (no. 5); Ruhengeri (no. 6); Ruhengeri (no. 10); Ruhengeri (no. 14); Ruhengeri (no. 16), 3 May 2003.
[42] Author's solidarity camp interviews, Butare (no. 14), 29 April 2003 (author's translation).
[43] Gacaca Law (Modified 2004), Articles 46–50, 59–63.
[44] Author's solidarity camp interviews, Gashora (no. 6), 18 April 2003 (author's translation).

brought me gifts after I came to the ingando because I had confessed to them what I did during the genocide.[45] During the gacaca journey described in Chapter 4, Alphonse also stated that his experience as an urumuri during prison gacaca would allow him to more easily negotiate the official gacaca process.

Not all detainees who have attended pre- or prison gacaca, though, express this confidence. Cypriet, whose personal experience of the gacaca journey was also described in Chapter 4, initially expressed optimism about the community's welcome upon his release from the camp on the basis of positive experiences at pre-gacaca. When interviewed after his release from the ingando, however, he expressed doubts about meeting survivors in his community, saying, 'it is difficult to know the state of survivors' hearts.'

Some survivors also argue that pre-gacaca hearings encouraged them to pursue reconciliation with perpetrators. Simon, the survivor quoted above, claimed that – along with Christian gacaca – his participation in a pre-gacaca meeting encouraged him to begin reconciling with the murderer of his wife: 'I am not worried about detainees coming back from the camps because I have already met the man who killed my wife when the authorities brought him to my house', Simon explained.[46] During this pre-gacaca meeting, the man who killed Simon's wife was brought from the ingando at Gashora to confess his crime directly to Simon, to apologise and to ask for his forgiveness.[47] Simon said that he had forgiven the detainee because the man expressed contrition for his crimes and because he believed that God wanted him to forgive. He asked the detainee whether he had also killed his two children, to which the man responded that he had not. 'There were two officials from the camp who came with the man to my house', Simon said. 'But this was only about two men talking – the guilty man and me.'[48] Simon said that this pre-gacaca meeting made him more confident about participating during official gacaca hearings after detainees were eventually released from the ingando. In such cases, direct contact between the parties concerned beyond the confines of official gacaca appear crucial for the improved relationships between them.

---

[45] Ibid.

[46] Ibid.

[47] I attempted to find this detainee during my research in the Gashora solidarity camp, to discuss his visit to Simon's home, but I was unable to locate him.

[48] Ibid.

It is clear that the rhetoric of duty and obligation, first discussed regarding the theme of popular participation in Chapter 5, is important for encouraging different groups in Rwandan society to participate in gacaca and to pursue outcomes such as reconciliation. Furthermore, unofficial versions of gacaca are important for increasing many individuals' sense of duty. As argued concerning popular participation, some groups in society – usually suspects – claim that, by participating in gacaca, they are fulfilling a duty to the government and thus helping it achieve certain social and political outcomes after the genocide. Similarly, other sources – usually survivors – view reconciliation as a Christian duty, an obligation to God that manifests in a readiness to reconcile with others. Parallel practices of gacaca, particularly pre- and Christian gacaca, crucially influence popular interpretations of gacaca and cultivate a sense of obligation to pursue reconciliation through gacaca. State and church leaders advise participants more readily in these unofficial versions of gacaca than in the official version, where elites are excluded from running gacaca, although as previously discussed they also play an important role in the latter. My interviews with suspects and survivors suggest that church leaders have been particularly effective at inculcating in participants in Christian gacaca a rhetoric of the obligation to forgive and reconcile, which consequently heavily shapes their understandings of official gacaca.

Despite legal restrictions upon their involvement in gacaca, church leaders also wield a significant influence over the running of official gacaca hearings. On occasions, church leaders have intervened in these hearings to impart Christian principles to the general assembly. During a gacaca hearing I attended in Butare province, a local pastor stood at the beginning of the hearing and exhorted the general assembly to 'welcome all the detainees home when they are released and show them that we are ready to forgive and that we can live together again'.[49] The methods of reconciliation that many church leaders advocate in the context of gacaca involve intense engagement between participants during hearings. Their emphasis on survivors' need to forgive their transgressors, in particular, requires parties to engage in a difficult, protracted dialogue at gacaca, with a view towards interacting meaningfully with one another outside of gacaca.

It is not clear from official and popular sources' discussions of parallel practices of gacaca whether there is a deliberate, simultaneous

---

[49] Author's gacaca observations, Butare, Save (author's translation).

campaign by state and church officials to communicate a rhetoric of the population's obligation to participate in gacaca and to pursue outcomes such as reconciliation. Interviews with Ndangiza and Rutinburana at the NURC suggest that the government and churches encourage reconciliation through gacaca for different – though ultimately mutually reinforcing – reasons.[50] As noted in the Introduction to this book, many historians argue that in the past Rwandan culture has displayed clear and worrying signs of systematic social and political control by elites. The state and church have been instrumental in creating this culture of control, sometimes acting separately, at other times in concert. The Catholic Church in particular closely aligned itself, both socially and politically, with Hutu governments after the middle of the twentieth century.[51] Without clearer evidence of deliberate coordination between the government and church leaders concerning gacaca, it is possible only to conclude that the rhetoric of gacaca as a duty expressed by these two groups of elites is largely coincidental. Nevertheless, the government is acutely aware of the important role that the churches play in encouraging their members to participate in gacaca. Aloysie Cyanzayire, Deputy Chief Justice of the Supreme Court, speaking at the National Summit on Unity and Reconciliation in 2002, highlighted the work of church leaders visiting detainees in prison: 'Considering that religious organizations have been encouraging their faithful to plead guilty', she argued, '[my workshop] group recommended that religious organizations should have it on their agenda to help Government sensitize people on the need to be responsive to, and supportive of, the Gacaca tribunals and to say the truth.'[52]

Commentators' perspectives on reconciliation through gacaca

Finally, the widest-ranging interpretations of the form, degree and types of methods of reconciliation through gacaca come from commentators. Most Rwandan observers view reconciliation as a central – if not *the* central – objective of gacaca, while most non-Rwandans do not discuss reconciliation in this context, emphasising instead the deterrent elements of the system in keeping with the dominant discourse on gacaca.

---

[50] Author's government interviews, Ndangiza, 2006 and 2008; Rutinburana, 2008.
[51] See, for example, Prunier, *The Rwanda Crisis*, ch. 2; T. Gatwa, *Rwanda: eglises – victimes ou coupables?: Les églises et l'idéologie ethnique au Rwanda, 1900–1994*, Yaoundé: Éditions Clé, 2001, chs. 2–5.
[52] Cyanzayire, 'The Gacaca Tribunals: Reconciliatory Justice', p.44.

Regarding the form of reconciliation that gacaca facilitates, commentators describe, with varying degrees of clarity and precision, all three forms expressed in the official and popular views: reconciliation on group-to-group, individual-to-individual and individual-to-group bases. Commentators on gacaca rarely connect multiple forms of reconciliation in a philosophical or programmatic way, describing them instead as separate processes that often appear to have little impact on one another. Both Rwandan and non-Rwandan observers emphasise the importance of gacaca for facilitating reconciliation, which is described variously as 'community-rebuilding',[53] 'reviving communal life',[54] 'mending the social fabric',[55] 'negotiating a new social contract',[56] 'recovering the culture of solidarity'[57] and 'restoring social equilibrium'.[58] It is not clear exactly what these terms mean, for example whether community rebuilding or reviving communal life entail the restoration of relationships between groups or between individuals or something entirely different.

Few commentators elaborate on who exactly is supposed to be reconciling with whom through gacaca. We may assume, however, that the form of reconciliation to which observers of gacaca usually refer is group-to-group because these descriptions take a largely top-down view of reconciliation that emphasises the need to restore a community-wide dynamic rather than relationships between individuals. For example, Helena Cobban argues, 'Building on an essentially communitarian view of the relationship between the individual and society ... systems [like gacaca] pursue the restoration of harmony within the community as the main goal, rather than the examination and punishment of individual wrongdoers.'[59] Whether this 'restoration of harmony' will occur between individuals or between groups in society is unclear. In Cobban's case, her main aim appears to be to contrast the reconciliatory functions of gacaca with more exclusively punitive measures, rather than fleshing out what form of reconciliation may result from gacaca. However, in this attempt to contrast reconciliation with strictly punitive processes, which concern individual perpetrators, commentators such as Cobban often

---

[53] Daly, 'Between Punitive Justice and Reconstructive Justice', p.378.
[54] Gasibirege, 'L'Élection des juges inyangamugayo', p.101 (author's translation).
[55] Karekezi, 'Juridictions gacaca', p.55 (author's translation).
[56] Gasibirege, 'Recherche qualitative sur les attitudes des Rwandais', p.124 (author's translation).
[57] Author's observer interviews, Nsabiyera, 3 February 2003.
[58] Karekezi, 'Juridictions gacaca', p.34 (author's translation).
[59] Cobban, 'The Legacies of Collective Violence', pp.12–13.

describe reconciliation (usually implicitly) as a positive outcome experienced by the entire community. As cited in Chapter 8, Bert Ingelaere and Lars Waldorf also focus on gacaca's potential for group-to-group reconciliation, defined explicitly as between Hutu and Tutsi. They argue that gacaca has generally failed to facilitate reconciliation; for Ingelaere, this is because gacaca has been overly punitive and allowed for only minimal dialogue among participants; for Waldorf, gacaca falls short in this regard because the state has politicised gacaca in an attempt to collectivise the guilt of the Hutu population.

Most commentators are more explicit when describing reconciliation through gacaca as an individual-to-individual process, though they rarely discuss this form of reconciliation. In this instance, commentators focus on the potential for gacaca to reconcile individual genocide suspects and survivors. As with popular views of reconciliation through gacaca, when questions become more personal, moving away from generalities concerning reconciliation at the community level to focus on difficult issues of restoring individual relations, arguments regarding what reconciliation may look like and what processes it entails become more explicit and detailed. Peter Harrell, for example, who like Cobban rarely defines the nature or processes of community-wide reconciliation – in one rare instance, he argues, 'Seeing the "strong men" currently in prison out working to rebuild the country they tried to destroy should certainly have a reconciliatory effect on communities' – is clearer about what reconciliation will entail and who should be involved in the process when discussing individual-to-individual reconciliation.[60] Employing similar language to Cobban in describing gacaca as a system of 'communitarian restorative justice', Harrell argues,

> Gacaca's requirement that offenders apologize publicly as a precondition for their confessions' acceptance may further facilitate reconciliation … [Apologies] backed by real remorse … will promote both the victim's sense of security, by assuring him that his attacker will not strike again, and a reconciliation between the two.[61]

In this instance, Harrell is unequivocal that reconciliation involves rebuilding relationships between individual perpetrators and survivors and that apology and remorse are important means to this outcome.

[60] Harrell, *Rwanda's Gamble*, p.87.
[61] *Ibid.*, p.87. For a detailed critique of Harrell's version of communitarian restorative justice through gacaca, see P. Clark, 'Judging Genocide on the Grass', *Oxonian Review of Books*, 3, 2, 2004, www.oxonianreview.org/issues/3-2/3-2-4.htm.

No non-Rwandan commentators and only a small minority of Rwandan observers discuss the importance of gacaca for individual-to-group reconciliation. Commentators who discuss individual-to-group reconciliation mostly equate this form of reconciliation with reintegrating detainees into their home communities.[62] Harrell, however, argues that not only the reintegration of detainees may facilitate this form of reconciliation but, more importantly, also the involvement of those detainees in community service. By engaging those found guilty of genocide crimes in activities that provide material benefits for survivors, Harrell argues, community service as a punishment also has 'the potential to reconcile a wrongdoer with the larger community' by changing the way in which the community views his or her motives and actions.[63] PRI argues similarly that using community service as a form of punishment is partly intended 'to repair the social tissue and promote reconciliation'[64] while contributing to 'the social rehabilitation of detainees'.[65]

Both Harrell and PRI imply that the engagement of detainees with survivors through community service promotes reconciliation: convicted perpetrators must participate actively in work programmes, sometimes working side by side with survivors, such as in rebuilding houses or tending communal gardens. This interpretation of reconciliatory processes on an individual-to-group basis is more robust than detainees' descriptions of this form of reconciliation solely as their peaceful reintegration into their previous communities. Harrell's interpretation shows one way in which the reconciliation of returned detainees to their communities may be possible (e.g. through community service) rather than the mere reintegration of detainees, which may entail little more than detainees' avoidance of reprisals after they return home.

This distinction between reintegration of suspects and the reconciliation of suspects and survivors is especially important for questions concerning the *degree* to which reconciliation may occur through gacaca. Not only do commentators note all three forms of reconciliation through gacaca examined so far but they also interpret the degree of reconciliation according to the three variations already described: reconciliation as cohabitation, as restoring a lost sense of unity and as creating a new dynamic between parties previously in conflict. There is a gulf between

---

[62] Karekezi, 'Juridictions Gacaca', pp.87–9.
[63] Harrell, *Rwanda's Gamble*, p.87.
[64] PRI, 'Interim Report', p.9.
[65] *Ibid.*, p.10.

the views of non-Rwandan and Rwandan commentators in this regard. The former group expresses greater scepticism than the latter about the level of reconciliation that is possible after the genocide. From my interviews with observers of gacaca and from the critical literature, a minority of non-Rwandan commentators views mere cohabitation – a largely pragmatic arrangement similar to the peaceful reintegration for which many detainees hope – as the degree of reconciliation that is possible or preferable through gacaca. Klaas de Jonge of PRI, for example, argues that the highest degree of reconciliation that gacaca can achieve is one in which 'Rwandans are able to live together without fear'.[66] Gacaca, he argues, should aim only to achieve peaceful coexistence between genocide perpetrators and survivors, which would still be a remarkable outcome given the traumatic legacies of the genocide and the numerous institutional constraints upon gacaca. Concomitantly, to expect any more than facilitating the non-violent cohabitation of perpetrators and survivors would be unrealistic and may even result in the imposition on survivors of an expressed obligation to live with those who have wronged them. Given survivors' traumatic experiences, de Jonge argues, it is unjust to expect them to engage with perpetrators in any deep and taxing way.[67]

For most commentators, however, and particularly for Rwandan observers, the peaceful cohabitation of survivors and perpetrators is too low an expectation of gacaca.[68] Gacaca, they argue, can foster – and, according to many commentators, *should* actively foster – more meaningful interactions and relationships between parties previously in conflict. Rwandan commentators place greater store than non-Rwandans in the engagement between participants in gacaca. In turn, the majority of Rwandan commentators interpret the degree of reconciliation that is possible or desirable through gacaca as a reversion to a lost state of social cohesion. Karekezi argues that a constant element of the gacaca process is an 'effort toward the restoration of social equilibrium'.[69] Nsabiyera argues that gacaca helps Rwandans 'recover … a culture of solidarity which we lost during the genocide'.[70] Both Karekezi's and Nsabiyera's

---

[66] Author's observer interviews, Klaas de Jonge, Research Coordinator, PRI, Kigali, 29 January 2003.

[67] *Ibid.*

[68] For a Rwandan commentator's (and survivor's) sceptical view of the possibility of reconciliation after the genocide, see J.-B. Kayigamba, 'Without Justice, No Reconciliation: A Survivor's Experience of Genocide', in Clark and Kaufman, *After Genocide*, pp.33–42.

[69] Karekezi, 'Juridictions Gacaca', p.34 (author's translation).

[70] *Ibid.*

interpretations of reconciliation assume that a desirable form of social interaction previously existed in Rwanda and can be regained. Nsabiyera argues, however, that the recent past also displays decidedly undesirable elements, such as a lack of genuine dialogue between different groups in Rwandan society, which gacaca must overcome in order to achieve reconciliation. This view emphasises the need for engagement between parties to resolve past conflicts. According to Nsabiyera, the past offers lessons on how Rwandans may live together again in the present, but they will not learn these lessons without genuine, long-term dialogue during, and outside of, gacaca.

What distinguishes most commentators', and especially Rwandan commentators', interpretations of reconciliation from the government's rhetoric of regaining a sense of unity is the more rigorous processes that they believe reconciliation requires. Most commentators offer a forward-looking interpretation of the processes of reconciliation through gacaca, in contrast to the retrospective emphasis of the official discourse. Unity, most commentators imply, is not something that can simply be remembered and easily regained; it must be fought for, as parties at gacaca wrestle with difficult issues concerning the nature, and causes, of their conflicts. Karekezi, for example, quotes Kader Asmal's assertion that reconciliation is not 'the manufacture of a cheap and easy bonhomie' but instead requires 'facing unwelcome truth in order to harmonise incommensurable world views'.[71] Reconciliation, Karekezi argues, will be difficult to achieve and will require protracted, often painful engagement between individuals and groups in order to restore broken relationships. Nonetheless, these Rwandan commentators argue, such a degree of reconciliation is possible through gacaca and should constitute one of its main objectives.[72]

Concerning the types of methods for achieving reconciliation, most commentators argue that engagement between parties at gacaca is only the beginning of a long-term dialogue that is necessary for individuals and groups to be truly reconciled. Gacaca creates a forum in which individuals and groups can discuss the nature of, and possible solutions to, their conflicts. This dialogue, however, must continue in the future, outside of gacaca, to achieve a deeper sense of engagement and thus reconciliation. Therefore, most commentators, mainly Rwandan but also the few non-Rwandan authors who explicitly discuss reconciliation in

[71] K. Asmal, quoted in Karekezi, 'Juridictions Gacaca', p.85.
[72] Ibid., pp.83–90.

this context, view gacaca as the beginning of a much longer, deeper process of rebuilding individual and communal relationships. Gasibirege emphasises the need for gacaca to instil important values in the population if gacaca is to succeed in 'creating a meeting place ... for reviving communal life'.[73] Other processes and institutions separate from gacaca, he argues, will then largely determine whether Rwandans can reconcile after gacaca's initiation of restorative processes.

Critique of sources' perspectives on reconciliation through gacaca

How convincing then are the official, popular and critical perspectives regarding the form, degree and types of methods of reconciliation through gacaca? In general, some components of the three groups' views on these issues constitute useful interpretations of gacaca's pursuit of reconciliation. These views, however, provide only a basic structure for understanding reconciliation in this context and it is necessary to add much more substance to it and to evaluate it on the basis of empirical evidence gathered from communities around Rwanda. In this analysis, I propose a more detailed view of what reconciliation means generally and specifically in the context of gacaca. In particular, I argue that the connection between engagement and reconciliation is important for understanding what form, degree and types of methods reconciliation through gacaca entails and that reconciliation requires more of individuals and groups involved in gacaca than the sources here usually suggest.

Regarding the form of reconciliation that gacaca facilitates, a synthesis of the official, popular and critical perspectives offers a more convincing account than any of these views taken separately. A key virtue of the popular interpretation of the form of reconciliation that gacaca encourages is its emphasis on the need for reconciliation between individuals. Greater engagement and dialogue in the general assembly are important for individuals to come to terms with the sources of, and solutions to, their conflicts. With their focus on reconciliation between groups previously in conflict and in a national sense, some government and observer sources neglect the crucial ways in which large-scale events such as genocide also constitute a series of personal conflicts that produce long-term acrimony and mistrust between individuals. Reconciliation must therefore occur on a personal level, between survivors, perpetrators and their families, to convince these individuals that they can live meaningfully with one another. Examples such as the one above involving Simon, the

---

[73] Gasibirege, 'L'élection des juges Inyangamugayo', p.101.

survivor in Nyamata, and the man who killed his wife, highlight the importance of this individual dimension, as well as the remarkable capacity of some survivors to reconcile with perpetrators.

Similarly, state officials and commentators who focus solely on reconciliation in the form of a group-to-group dynamic neglect the vital ways in which individuals also need to experience reconciliation with entire groups, particularly in the case of detainees who seek reconciliation with their home communities. Nevertheless, many detainees' arguments concerning the importance of reconciliation are problematic because they often equate reconciliation with reintegration. A peaceful re-entry into the community is very different from rebuilding relationships. Some detainees' conflation of reconciliation and reintegration suggests their reluctance to engage fully with the community when they return. Many suspects hope that avoiding reprisals will constitute a successful and meaningful transition back into their communities. As described in Chapter 4, regarding Laurent's, Cypriet's and Alphonse's experiences of the gacaca journey, many provisionally released detainees returned to live in houses on the outskirts of their communities as they awaited their trials at gacaca. These suspects succeeded for lengthy periods in avoiding reprisals by genocide survivors, but they also avoided any form of genuine engagement with survivors, thus scuppering any chances of interacting meaningfully with their communities and of achieving individual-to-individual or individual-to-group reconciliation. Of the three former detainees, only Alphonse stated that he had over time renewed contact with some survivors, while continuing to actively avoid others. The transition from reintegration to reconciliation takes substantially longer than some sources suggest and involves further interactions between detainees and their communities beyond the initial interactions immediately after detainees return home and during gacaca. Reintegration should only be connected to ideas of reconciliation if it is interpreted in a long-term sense in which to reintegrate means enabling individuals to engage with those around them and thus to cooperate long after gacaca is over. Without ongoing engagement and cooperation, reintegration relates solely to re-entry, a short-term action that bears little resemblance to the long-term engagement necessary for reconciliation.

That reconciliation should be interpreted as a group-to-group process is perhaps inevitable in a context such as post-genocide Rwanda where conflict has resulted primarily from antagonisms between Hutu and Tutsi. All of the sources analysed here to some extent interpret reconciliation through gacaca as occurring on a group-to-group basis. In the government's interpretation, the form of reconciliation that gacaca may facilitate is defined exclusively in this sense. However, what stands out from the various sources' interpretations of group-to-group reconciliation is the general absence (with the exception of Ingelaere's and Waldorf's analyses) of an explicit discussion of ethnicity and particularly the role of ethnicity in fomenting conflict in Rwanda. Reconciliation requires a discussion of the sources of conflict, if parties are to resolve their problems and build stronger relationships. Most sources discuss group-to-group reconciliation as necessary between perpetrators and survivors rather than between Hutu and Tutsi. There are very good reasons for emphasising 'perpetrators' and 'survivors' in this regard, to avoid employing an absolutist discourse whereby all Hutu are considered perpetrators and all Tutsi survivors. As Nigel Eltringham argues persuasively, neither of these absolutist categories holds because many Hutu and individuals of mixed heritage were victims of crimes during the genocide and many Tutsi committed crimes.[74] Nevertheless, it is necessary to recognise the fundamental role of ethnicity in motivating the perpetration of the genocide. Despite the government's clampdown on the use of ethnic labels, many of my interviewees discuss ethnicity explicitly – for example, Alphonse's discussion of gacaca's neglect of RPF crimes in Chapter 4 – and the subject arises regularly during gacaca hearings.[75]

Crucially missing from official, popular and critical interpretations of the form of reconciliation through gacaca is the need to view individual-to-individual, individual-to-group and group-to-group reconciliation as necessarily interconnected processes. Attempts to facilitate reconciliation between different groups are likely to falter if individuals within those groups still feel enmity towards individuals in other groups. If I hate my neighbour because of his or her membership of a particular collective, for example an ethnic group, then I will find it near impossible to participate in wider processes of reconciliation between my own group and that of the person whom I hate. Conversely, an experience of personal reconciliation between myself and a member of a perceived rival group may aid my participation in processes of group-to-group reconciliation.

Humans function within different layers of identity, viewing themselves as individuals who have crucial relations with other individuals

[74] Eltringham, *Accounting for Horror*, ch.4.
[75] For example, author's gacaca observations, Ruhengeri, Cyeru, 6 May 2003; Gisenyi, Rubavu, 23 May 2003; Gisenyi, Rubavu, 14 June 2006.

around them, while all the time feeling embedded within deep communal identities. These layers of self-understanding mean that events that affect the community to which individuals feel deep attachments will also resonate in the individuals concerned. Genocide as an event or process that is intended to destroy an entire people group such as the Tutsi affects the emotional and psychological conditions of members of the targeted group qua individuals, as they suffer personal injury at the hands of other individuals (and particularly in the Rwandan context, where so many victims know the perpetrators intimately), and qua members of the group, as their communal consciousness is afflicted by the destruction wrought on the collective. Processes of reconciliation therefore must address this multi-layered sense of affliction and the combination of individual and group relations which must be rebuilt simultaneously if individuals and communities are to live together and cooperate meaningfully in the future.

To what degree then should Rwandans pursue reconciliation and what degree of reconciliation is possible through gacaca? As they did regarding popular participation in gacaca, both the official and some popular sources analysed here regularly define reconciliation in a retrospective sense as restoring unity. For reasons already expressed elsewhere in this book, we should be sceptical of any discourse that conflates reconciliation and national unity or that holds that the response to the fractured nature of Rwandan society after the genocide should be to restore an assumed lost sense of social harmony. In all likelihood, this past unity never existed or, if it did, those who have experienced mass violence on the scale of the genocide cannot easily reimagine it. An additional argument against defining reconciliation as unity is that unity as the government and some genocide suspects define it emphasises the need to rebuild relationships at a group level, whether in separate communities or in the nation as a whole, thus neglecting the need for individual-to-individual reconciliation. An interpretation of the necessary degree of reconciliation after the genocide as retrospective, in the form of restoring unity, is therefore unconvincing.

Instead, an interpretation of reconciliation that lies somewhere between the optimistic and pragmatic interpretations articulated by various sources is more compelling. The problem with exclusively pragmatic views of reconciliation, such as those expressed by de Jonge and some genocide survivors, which holds that peaceful cohabitation is the best that Rwandans can hope for after the genocide, is their questionable fatalism. Certainly we should be realistic about the extent to which the three forms of reconciliation are possible after an event as devastating as genocide. It is unjustified, however, to dismiss at the outset the possibility of achieving a more optimistic level of reconciliation. Different individuals and different groups previously in conflict have experienced this conflict in different ways, some more deeply than others. As a result, some individuals and groups will find it easier than others to reconcile with one another, as highlighted by the highly variable popular interpretations of reconciliation cited above. For a survivor such as Simon in Nyamata, forgiveness and reconciliation were perhaps possible because of his religious convictions and his experiences of unofficial forms of gacaca, which took place out of the public eye and allowed more intimate engagement with his wife's murderer. During the gacaca journey narrated in Chapter 4, Alphonse described experiencing positive relationships with some survivors in his community, including those he met regularly for drinks, and negative relationships with others. In the case of a survivor who was directly affected by Alphonse's crimes – Muteteli, the mother of several of his victims – their relationship was tense but functional, to the point that they could farm the same plot of land. Alphonse's case therefore captures the full spectrum of reconciliation, from pragmatic coexistence through to a more profound building of relations.

On this basis, it is judicious to aim for the highest degree of reconciliation possible: the optimistic interpretation outlined above, which emphasises the creation of a new sense of engagement and new forms of discourse and active cooperation. A core assumption of the optimistic interpretation of reconciliation proposed here is that, in most instances of broken relationships in the three forms discussed above, the damage wrought during conflict will have been so great as to require rebuilding these relationships from the foundations. People's memories of crimes during the genocide, whether they have been a victim or perpetrator, will be so overwhelming that these recollections will override any of a time (if ever there were such a time) when their relationships with members of other groups were more harmonious. Therefore, if parties previously in conflict wish to learn to live together again, they will need to engage closely with one another at gacaca and create a dialogue on the root causes of the conflicts between them in order to build effective relationships after gacaca. They will also need to be creative rather than retrospective in their methods, seeking to build new relationships rather than reverting to old ones.

Reconciliation at the optimistic level requires a two-stage process: one by which parties engage directly with one another on the root causes of their conflicts, in order to find solutions to these problems, and a second by which they then seek to generate a discourse and modes of active cooperation that produce more meaningful interactions in the future. These stages are admittedly broad: the first is essentially one of conflict resolution and the second of relationship transformation, seeking to take the relationship beyond being defined solely by the conflict and emphasising instead a deeper, long-term engagement. Completion of the first stage constitutes achieving the pragmatic level of reconciliation that commentators such as de Jonge argue is the best for which Rwandans can hope after the genocide. The second stage is motivated by a hope that something more than mere cohabitation – itself unquestionably an impressive achievement after such destructive conflict – may be possible. The second stage also assumes that parties will cultivate principles and methods of conflict resolution or, in the government's language, 'problem-solving', so that they are able to deal peacefully and effectively with conflicts as they arise in the future. This need for the development of long-term problem-solving mechanisms underscores the need for reconciliation to be sustainable and assumes that some degree of conflict in the future is inevitable. The evidence displayed in this book, from the statements of participants in gacaca and observations of hearings and people's interactions in daily life, suggests that a minority of Rwandans may have reached the second stage of a deeper engagement than merely peaceful coexistence. For most Rwandans, however, even the first stage of addressing root causes of their conflicts has proven difficult, although as the discussions of popular participation and truth in this book highlight in particular, gacaca has enabled substantial progress in these regards, despite the manifest challenges.

Both stages of reconciliation are likely to take a long time and will require the sorts of difficult discussions to which several of the Rwandan critical and popular sources analysed above allude, particularly in the context of individual-to-individual reconciliation. In some communities, only stage one may be possible; in others, there may be scope for pursuing a more ambitious outcome. Those in charge of facilitating reconciliatory processes must discern the extent to which it is possible to achieve the second, transformative stage of reconciliation and when it is more prudent to aim solely for a more pragmatic result. Nevertheless, to aim solely for a pragmatic degree of reconciliation is to deny some individuals and groups, for whom reconciliation may prove to be a more viable pursuit if localised conditions are conducive, the opportunity to strive for the highest degree of reconciliation of which they are capable.

One of the most important localised factors that increases the likelihood that genocide perpetrators and survivors will engage meaningfully at gacaca in order to achieve reconciliation is people's religious beliefs, particularly when principles of grace, mercy and forgiveness constitute key elements of their faith. Many survivors' statements that, on the basis of their religious convictions, they are ready to forgive, and to reconcile with, genocide perpetrators are vital for gacaca's ability to facilitate reconciliation. As my interviews with genocide suspects and survivors show, people's deeply rooted religious beliefs regularly influence their interpretations of gacaca and its objectives to such an extent that they feel compelled to apply these principles in their engagement with others at gacaca. Christian gacaca hearings crucially reinforce many survivors' belief that they have a divine duty to reconcile with perpetrators. Pre-gacaca hearings have also allowed many suspects and survivors to engage in a quieter, more private environment before they interact more publicly during official gacaca hearings. These interactions have increased many parties' confidence in official gacaca's chances of facilitating their reconciliation in the future.

At the same time, we should be wary of some of the ways in which people's religious beliefs have so far shaped their views on gacaca and on reconciliation. As with the dangers noted earlier regarding viewing involvement of gacaca as fulfilling a duty to the state, there are dangers associated with the expressed duty to forgive or to reconcile, which stems from some people's religious beliefs and which is reinforced by practices such as Christian gacaca. In this case, the danger is that this religious sense of duty will lead participants in gacaca to simply go through the motions at official gacaca. Believers may engage in processes of reconciliation not because they genuinely view these processes as personally valuable but because they wish to obey, and thus to win favour with, their religious leaders. Highlighting the general theme of civic education and coercion throughout this book, Irénée Bugingo, Senior Researcher at IRDP, said, 'Reconciliation has become one of the key pillars of the RPF philosophy, and many of the churches share this view ... Reconciliation and forgiveness should take time but instead reconciliation has often been taught.'[76]

---

[76] Author's observer interviews, Irénée Bugingo, Senior Researcher, IRDP, Kigali, 22 August 2008 (interview conducted jointly with Nicola Palmer).

A religious sense of duty does not always equate, however, to simply wishing to obey church leaders: as we have seen, some survivors argue that obedience to God, rather than to their leaders, motivates them to display grace to the guilty in the form of participation in processes of reconciliation through gacaca. This sense of duty may prove advantageous to gacaca's chances of facilitating reconciliation because a divine obligation may truly inspire believers to engage wholeheartedly in gacaca, as opposed to the debilitating sense of duty to the government that some sources express. It is not always clear from my interviews with survivors whether obedience to God or to church leaders motivates their expressed sense of duty to forgive and reconcile. However, duty to the former may inspire some participants to contribute to processes of forgiveness and reconciliation at gacaca.

Blind obedience to political leaders also ensures that participants in the gacaca process will not engage genuinely with others, increasing distrust between different parties and forfeiting any long-term benefits of their dialogue at gacaca. Ruth, the detainee in the ingando at Kigali Ville quoted earlier, who had been a high-school teacher before the genocide and claimed that she had been falsely accused of murder, said she was concerned that some of her fellow detainees had the wrong motivations for wanting to reconcile with their victims:

> Reconciliation, in the end, really comes from the authorities. These people in the camp like to obey ... They obey like animals. What we really need is reconciliation from the heart. People need to reflect on their actions during the genocide, then they will be ready to reconcile with the survivors.[77]

Ruth's views echo those of Laurent, the detainee interviewed along the gacaca journey, who claimed, 'We need reconciliation without sentimentality. Reconciliation doesn't come from the sky.'

This section has argued so far that we must view reconciliation as necessarily incorporating the simultaneous rebuilding of relationships in individual–individual, individual–group and group–group forms. Because the individuals engaged in reconciliation processes inevitably experience these forms of reconciliation as interconnected, to fail to facilitate reconciliation in one of these forms is to undermine reconciliation in the others. The critical literature has generally neglected the personal dimension of reconciliation. This section has also argued that it

---

[77] Author's solidarity camp interviews, Kigali Ville (no. 12) (author's translation).

is justified to aim for the highest degree of reconciliation that is possible given localised conditions in communities after the genocide. For various reasons, some individuals and some groups will find it easier to pursue reconciliation than others. Gacaca therefore must be sufficiently flexible as to gauge the appropriate level of reconciliation, be it the optimistic or the pragmatic interpretation of reconciliation outlined above, that may be pursued given local constraints. The readiness for reconciliation that many suspects and survivors express as a result of their religious beliefs is a key indicator that a more optimistic level of reconciliation is possible in some communities.

With this view of the forms and degrees of reconciliation that gacaca is justified in pursuing, what types of methods is it capable of deploying in pursuit of reconciliation? Again we can draw much of our response to this question from the official, popular and critical sources analysed above. In some instances it is necessary to go beyond the views of these sources. In the concluding chapter, I recall the exact methods that gacaca deploys in pursuit of reconciliation, via the pursuit of earlier profound objectives such as truth, healing and forgiveness, but for now it is necessary only to draw the broad contours of the types of methods of reconciliation that are required, and that gacaca displays a capacity to facilitate.

Of the three sources analysed here, the government's view of the types of methods necessary to achieve reconciliation through gacaca is the most problematic. The official view that reconciliation is a short-term process that occurs during gacaca hearings and is likely to produce relatively fast results is unsustainable and does not reflect most Rwandans' experience. The conception of reconciliation as a relatively short-term process occurring almost exclusively within gacaca carries weight only if we accept that reconciliation equates to restoring a sense of unity which is latent within Rwandan culture. As already argued, the government's rhetoric concerning restoring unity is highly flawed. The balancing of pragmatic and optimistic interpretations of the degree of reconciliation possible generally and through gacaca specifically entails long-term processes, involving difficult discussions that take participants in gacaca to the root causes of their conflicts. The evidence from communities such as those observed during the gacaca journey and elsewhere suggests that some individuals may have begun experiencing reconciliation – even if they are predominantly in the early phases of meaningful relationship transformation – but most communities still find themselves heavily divided, particularly between Hutu and Tutsi and between Tutsi who lived through the genocide and those who have subsequently returned to Rwanda. In this context, processes of reconciliation will unavoidably take many years.

Gacaca creates a space in which individuals have begun discussing genocide-related issues, especially the sources of their conflicts, with a view towards rebuilding their fractured relations. As suspects are encouraged to confess their crimes publicly and to apologise to their victims, survivors who often feel great anger and resentment towards suspects may now feel that they are ready to engage with them. Given the public setting of gacaca and its cacophony of voices, individuals may find that the most crucial discourse between them will occur outside of gacaca, in a more private space. However, gacaca is an important starting point, as suspects and survivors meet face to face and the entire community may engage in, and benefit from, their dialogue.

We must see reconciliation through gacaca as a long-term process that relies on meaningful engagement occurring during gacaca hearings but continuing outside of this immediate context. There are no easy solutions, no ready-made historical templates to which Rwandans can revert in order to achieve reconciliation after the genocide. As Norman Porter was quoted in Chapter 5, engagement requires individuals to make themselves vulnerable to one another, often discussing and debating as they have not done previously. The risks involved in such a process, and the uncertainty over the results of such intimate interactions, are immense. Particularly if communities choose to pursue more ambitious degrees of reconciliation, the level of engagement between parties previously in conflict must increase as well as the possibility that people's vulnerability will lead them to act unpredictably and sometimes in ways that are counter-productive to the pursuit of reconciliation through engagement at gacaca. Gacaca judges must be aware of the risks involved in the intense engagement required of participants in gacaca and must ensure that such engagement is productive in terms of pursuing gacaca's stated objectives.

This chapter has argued that we can identify a need in post-genocide Rwanda for reconciliation in three forms – individual–individual, individual–group and group–group – and that gacaca displays a marked capacity to facilitate reconciliation in each of these forms, especially in the individual–individual case that all of the sources analysed here, except for some genocide survivors, have largely ignored. Gacaca displays an observed capacity to facilitate these three forms of reconciliation to either an optimistic or pragmatic degree, depending on local circumstances that shape the extent to which reconciliation is possible in particular communities. In practice, some individuals and some groups are closer to achieving reconciliation than others. This chapter has shown that people's religious beliefs, especially concerning Christian principles of grace, mercy and atonement, are a crucial local influence on communities' chances of successfully facilitating reconciliation. The current literature almost completely ignores the effect of people's religious convictions on their interpretations of, and readiness to participate in, gacaca. Overall, there is greater optimism concerning the chances of achieving reconciliation after the genocide among segments of the population who, on the basis of their Christian beliefs, view these ideals as valuable responses to past crimes. Some religious views are detrimental to the cause of facilitating reconciliation, particularly when certain Christian leaders and their followers define it as a moral duty to be fulfilled for the sake of the Church and its hierarchy or as a process that will be completed quickly and relatively painlessly. Nevertheless, most commentators', particularly non-Rwandan authors', interpretations of gacaca are inadequate due to their neglect of the effects of religious interpretations on people's understandings of gacaca, especially on themes such as reconciliation.

Finally, this chapter has shown that reconciliation through gacaca entails both short- and long-term methods and processes that involve immediate engagement between parties previously in conflict during gacaca hearings that then must flow forth into further engagement between these parties after gacaca. Gacaca constitutes an important starting point for reconciliation. It has already reaped significant restorative dividends in some communities. If engagement between parties ceases at gacaca, however, then there is little chance of reconciliation occurring. Reconciliation, and the engagement that is the bridge to facilitating it, are arduous, long-term processes. The evidence from communities around Rwanda suggests that gacaca has at best aided some individuals and groups in embarking on the road to reconciliation.

CONCLUSION

INTRODUCTION

To summarise, gacaca is a dynamic, hybrid institution, borne out of
heady ideals, political necessity and compromise, whose complex evolution since 2001 stems from a wide range of popular and state-run factors. All Rwandan sources analysed here express a discernible ethos
of popular ownership over gacaca and underline the crucial agency of
Rwandans in addressing the legacies of the genocide, articulated foremost through the concept of popular participation as the modus operandi of gacaca. Of the nine expressed objectives of gacaca analysed
in this book – clearing the backlog of genocide cases, improving the
conditions in the prisons, economic development, truth, peace, justice,
healing, forgiveness and reconciliation – only economic development is
entirely unfeasible through gacaca. Regarding the remaining themes,
based on empirical observations, gacaca has produced highly variable
results.

Evidence from jurisdictions around Rwanda highlights gacaca's suc-
cesses in handling the backlog of cases and delivering retributive justice, facilitating crucial processes of truth-telling and truth-hearing,
and providing for positive peace by creating a dialogical space for the
resolution of people's past conflicts, which is critical to sustaining more
cohesive relations in the long-term. Gacaca has also proven effective in
many communities at initiating processes of restorative justice, healing, forgiveness and reconciliation, although these objectives inevitably
stretch beyond the time frame of gacaca, given the slow, emotional and

interpersonal dynamics concerned. In other communities, however, these objectives are very distant prospects or have in fact been undermined by people's experiences of gacaca. The analysis in Chapters 5–10 indicates that most commentators have grossly overstated the predicted or observed problems with gacaca: it has not degenerated into mob justice nor constituted a form of state-sanctioned collective condemnation of the entire Hutu population. Countering such criticisms, the hybridity of gacaca's methods has facilitated both legal protection of individual suspects and a high degree of popular participation and moulding of the institution over time according to localised needs and beliefs. In short, gacaca has been more diverse, responsive and kinetic than most critics contend.

This final chapter comprises three sections: first, it draws together the strands of argument in Chapters 6–10, namely the analysis of gacaca's pragmatic and profound aims and formal and negotiated methods, to show that gacaca represents a radical, comprehensive approach to transitional justice. In displaying the galaxy of gacaca's eight feasible objectives, which so far have been treated predominantly as discrete, this section briefly explores the compatibilities and tensions manifest in this simultaneous pursuit of different (and different types of) aims. This analysis of multiple objectives suggests that we should be sober about gacaca's attempt at a holistic response to the genocide, while recognising its substantial achievements.

Second, on the basis of this interpretation of gacaca's galaxy of aims, this chapter critiques the dominant discourse of gacaca, principally its misinterpretation of gacaca's hybrid aims and methods. This section argues that the prevailing view of gacaca is flawed for various methodological reasons and for reasons stemming from its narrow interpretation of gacaca's objectives, namely its sole focus on deterrent justice. In countering this view, this section also defends gacaca against several human-rights criticisms raised by proponents of that perspective.

Finally, this chapter distils some immediate implications from the findings in this book regarding the nature and efficacy of gacaca. These implications concern two main areas: the use of community-level transitional processes in other contexts in Africa and further afield; and the social and political future of Rwanda. Together, these elements highlight the importance of gacaca in aiding Rwanda's recovery after the genocide and in contexts far beyond.

HOLISM: CONNECTING GACACA'S PRAGMATIC AND PROFOUND OBJECTIVES

As argued in Chapter 2, the primary purpose of hybrid systems of transitional justice institutions is to facilitate holism, seeking to respond to the range of physical, psychological and psychosocial needs of individuals and groups after conflict. Gacaca's internal hybridity, particularly its combination of pragmatic and profound objectives, similarly seeks to respond to the Rwandan population's broad spectrum of post-genocide needs. The breadth of the objectives analysed in this book, from the practical need to return hundreds of thousands of able-bodied detainees to their communities to healing survivors' deep psychological wounds, underscores the enormous scope of gacaca, reflecting the ambitions, hopes and desires of its creators and participants. This section assembles the arguments from Chapters 6–10 to highlight gacaca's complex galaxy of objectives. Evaluating the normative and empirical claims from those chapters shows that gacaca's simultaneous pursuit of different objectives has rarely been straightforward. In some cases, these aims have been mutually reinforcing; in others, they have caused significant tensions, suggesting that a major challenge for gacaca has been handling overly lofty expectations about what it can achieve in the post-genocide environment.

This section does not discuss all of the possible connections among gacaca's various objectives, only the most important for highlighting the complexity of its hybrid approach to transitional justice. Regarding gacaca's most compatible aims, several objectives function symbiotically in practice, exemplifying gacaca's quest for holism. In particular, the pursuit of forgiveness is deeply entwined with that of healing. As many suspects and survivors claim, receiving or offering forgiveness is important for healing as liberation; for suspects through their release from guilt and shame by confessing to, and being forgiven for, their crimes; and for survivors through freedom from feelings of anger and resentment which they may experience after forgiving perpetrators. In turn, individuals who experience healing may feel more disposed to forgive others, particularly if they define healing as liberation in the positive sense, which encourages them to engage more closely with others, including those who have wronged them. Forgiveness and truth also function symbiotically, in that most survivors view truth in the form of a complete and sincere confession as a prerequisite for forgiveness. Sensing a more forgiving environment at gacaca, suspects often feel encouraged to tell the truth about their crimes, in the hope that they will gain a favourable reception from their audience.

Overall, a series of four objectives in particular is mutually reinforcing: reconciliation, peace, forgiveness and healing. First, positive peace, with its emphasis on educating the population to identify the root causes of its conflicts and to discover effective remedies, is crucial for overcoming discord and rebuilding relationships, as reconciliation entails. In turn, reconciliation reinforces positive peace by encouraging the ongoing engagement between parties that is necessary for the maintenance of peace in the long term. Second, by its very nature, profound forgiveness holds that parties who participate in forgiveness processes should seek to rebuild their relationships. In this way, profound forgiveness helps facilitate reconciliation by overcoming parties' respective feelings of guilt and resentment, thus helping facilitate renewed relations. Reconciliation then provides the basis of a strengthened relationship from which parties are more likely to seek, and to offer, forgiveness, when conflicts inevitably arise in the future. Third, healing as positive liberation, as individuals feel free to engage with other individuals and their community, helps facilitate reconciliation by unburdening individuals and encouraging greater engagement. Reconciliation may in turn encourage healing as belonging, as reconciled individuals feel welcomed in their rebuilt relationships and thus may begin overcoming feelings of alienation and loneliness after conflict.

While gacaca's pursuit of some profound objectives is mutually reinforcing, the combination of other objectives proves more problematic. In particular, tensions between pursuing truth and healing, and between retributive or deterrent justice and restorative justice or reconciliation, highlight the main tensions in gacaca as a whole. First, we have already seen the problems associated with the simultaneous pursuit of truth and healing in the gacaca hearing at Ruhengenge, described in Chapter 3. While truth-hearing about the past may contribute to healing by providing the necessary facts about the fate of people's loved ones, and truth-telling may facilitate healing by allowing survivors to receive public acknowledgement of their anguish, truth-hearing and truth-telling at gacaca can also retraumatise many individuals, thus undermining healing. Retraumatised individuals in turn are unlikely to engage meaningfully with others, ensuring that a lack of healing also entails a reluctance to seek reconciliation.

Second, as argued earlier, gacaca represents a deliberate attempt to shape the punishment of perpetrators towards more restorative and reconciliatory ends. In particular, gacaca's use of community service and compensation as punishment encourages convicted perpetrators to engage meaningfully with survivors, either by working on labour programmes that benefit, or may even involve, survivors directly, or by providing personal restitution to survivors. However, neither community service nor compensation is inherently reconciliatory. For example, compensation demanded unfairly or given grudgingly may in fact inflame existing tensions, as Alphonse suggested during the gacaca journey in Chapter 4. The greater problem for reconciliation, however, concerns the reimprisonment of many suspects who are convicted of serious genocide crimes. Reimprisonment as an outcome of retributive or deterrent justice, while a justified response to crimes committed, also damages attempts at restoration or reconciliation. By removing perpetrators from the community, reimprisonment renders impossible any meaningful engagement between perpetrators and survivors. That a percentage of suspects tried at gacaca have returned to prison for lengthy periods raises the question of how effectively retributive or deterrent justice at gacaca can facilitate long-term engagement and in turn reconciliation. It is clear that community service and compensation constitute important punitive measures that can contribute to rebuilding relationships. Reimprisonment, however – which affects many individuals convicted of Category 1 and 2 crimes – jeopardises the engagement that begins at gacaca but needs to continue in the long-term for reconciliation to occur.

The two main tensions explored here – between truth and healing and between forms of justice and reconciliation – affect both the daily running of gacaca and its overall pursuit of society-wide objectives. As argued in Chapter 3, the population expresses confusion over whether, and how, these concurrent objectives should be pursued. As exemplified by the hearing at Ruhengenge, this confusion negatively influences how gacaca functions from day to day. The tension between truth and healing generally derives from popular interpretations of gacaca and its aims, because the population describes healing as an objective of gacaca much more readily than the government. The tension between different forms of justice and reconciliation results largely from the statutes of the Gacaca Law, which enshrine all of these objectives as key aims of gacaca.

Despite these problems, there is no reason to assume that the tensions inherent in gacaca's simultaneous pursuit of pragmatic and profound objectives render these entirely unfeasible objectives of gacaca. Judges often mediate these tensions, for example by explaining to the population that it is possible to pursue both truth and healing, provided healing is seen as a long-term objective that may require initial retraumatisation. As we saw above, several profound objectives are also mutually reinforcing, affording gacaca a sense of coherence in its pursuit of different aims. Nonetheless, beyond the practical challenges for gacaca as identified in earlier chapters regarding discrete objectives, this analysis of gacaca's pursuit of hybrid, simultaneous objectives shows the difficulties inherent in such a comprehensive attempt at holism.

CRITIQUE OF THE DOMINANT DISCOURSE ON GACACA

Most interpretations of gacaca and its objectives in the existing literature, particularly from non-Rwandan human-rights critics such as AI and HRW, are highly unsatisfactory. My critique of the dominant discourse takes two forms, one methodological and one focused on the particular objectives of gacaca that the discourse advocates. First, the methodology according to which most commentators interpret gacaca displays two problems: (1) a flawed approach whereby most commentators focus solely on the legal statutes governing gacaca when interpreting its objectives, thus neglecting the ways in which gacaca operates as a dynamic socio-legal institution and often diverges from the principles and methods outlined in the legal documents; and, (2) most commentators' neglect of the vital impact of external social and political developments elsewhere in Rwandan culture on the ways in which the community interprets, and participates in, gacaca. Part (1) of the methodological critique focuses on the evolutionary nature of gacaca as a whole, while part (2) concerns specific, external social, cultural and political factors that influence popular interpretations of gacaca.

Second, largely on the basis of their flawed methodology for interpreting gacaca, most commentators interpret gacaca too narrowly and neglect aims other than the form of deterrent justice that constitutes their sole lens of analysis. The objectives-based critique identifies two problems with the dominant discourse on gacaca: (1) the unconvincing view held by its proponents that justice, which is determined formally to facilitate exclusively deterrent outcomes, is an adequate response to the legacies of the genocide, thus ignoring the other aims of gacaca explored above, which respond more fully to the population's needs; and (2) these commentators' mistaken assumption that gacaca fails to provide for impartial decision-making and to guarantee important legal safeguards;

virtues which they claim result solely from a strict due process approach to justice.

Regarding part (1) of the methodological critique, the discussion of several objectives in this book highlights the flawed analytical methodology behind the dominant discourse on gacaca. Focusing exclusively on gacaca's legal statutes, the prevailing view belies the importance of concepts of public collaboration, negotiation and engagement throughout the daily running of gacaca. The often unpredictable outcomes of popular participation in gacaca, and consequently the dynamic nature of the institution as a whole and its effect on the public's evolving interpretations of, and involvement in, gacaca, cannot be captured in its legal documents alone. For example, the idea expressed in Chapter 10 of gacaca as a test run of reconciliation, where collaboration and engagement during hearings help facilitate meaningful interactions in the future, stresses the openness of discussions at gacaca. Notions of building peace through collaboration, communally negotiating justice and truth and achieving healing as belonging all rely heavily on the idea of gacaca as a participatory process. The important (though not entirely) undirected method by which the population pursues these objectives necessitates an exploration of the population's practices and subsequent reinterpretations of gacaca and its objectives. By not only ignoring the effects of popular involvement in gacaca, in terms of the population's shaping of the institution according to local needs and beliefs, but – as we saw in Chapter 5 regarding gacaca's modus operandi of popular participation – by also viewing popular involvement as anathema to impartial justice, proponents of the dominant discourse fail to recognise the kinetic nature of gacaca. They assume that gacaca operates in practice as it appears on paper. Most human-rights critics therefore fail to analyse gacaca on its own terms.

Furthermore, even if we agree that gacaca should be analysed solely through its legal statutes, the dominant discourse remains unconvincing. The problem here is that, even on the basis of gacaca's legal statutes, we should not interpret formal, deterrent justice as gacaca's sole objective. The Gacaca Law states that gacaca has been established 'to achieve justice and reconciliation in Rwanda' and is designed 'not only with the aim of providing punishment, but also reconstituting the Rwandan Society that had been destroyed by bad leaders'.[1] The Gacaca Law thus enshrines reconciliation and restorative justice as key objectives of gacaca. These

[1] Gacaca Law (Modified 2004), Introduction.

aims are glaringly absent from the orthodox interpretation of gacaca, even when they appear in the same documents on which proponents of this view base their analyses. We must conclude therefore that the dominant discourse is founded on a highly selective reading of gacaca's legal statutes and that, as a result, it provides an inadequate view of gacaca's aims.

Part (2) of the methodological critique shows that, because the dominant discourse ignores the importance of popular interpretations of gacaca, it inevitably overlooks the influence of external social, cultural and political factors on the daily running of gacaca. Human-rights critics neglect three factors in particular that heavily shape the population's interpretations of gacaca's objectives: many Rwandans' worldview; religious principles; and parallel, unofficial practices of gacaca. First, as my exploration of truth and healing through gacaca shows clearly, a discernible Rwandan worldview influences popular interpretations and expectations of gacaca. When women brought framed photographs to the gacaca hearing at Nyarufunzo, in search of communal recognition and a sense of healing as belonging, they underlined the importance of communal identity. Because personal attachments to the community are so crucial in shaping Rwandans' sense of their own identity – as expressed in some sources' descriptions of engaging as a 'family' at gacaca – overcoming feelings of estrangement resulting from trauma is crucial for participants' sense of restoring their own humanity and regaining the unity of the self. Similarly, many survivors' pursuit of therapeutic truth-hearing and truth-hearing, which often involve the community's provision of historical facts (to fill gaps in survivors' personal and collective memories) and acknowledgement of survivors' pain, display the importance of communal identities for the population's participation in gacaca. To ignore the cosmology within which participants comprehend their agency in gacaca is to overlook an essential aspect of their involvement in the process.

Second, this book has shown that people's religious, particularly Christian, principles influence their interpretations of gacaca and that this observation finds almost no mention in the existing literature. Christian conceptions of grace, mercy, redemption and atonement in particular manifest in much of the population's connection of gacaca with the pursuit of reconciliation, healing, forgiveness and truth. The most enthusiastic expressions of a desire to pursue reconciliation and forgiveness, among suspects, survivors and the general population, come from those who subscribe to Christian beliefs. The language with which many detainees describe the importance of confession at gacaca for their sense of healing or with which survivors describe the 'cure' of discovering the precise fate of their loved ones during the genocide, with emphases on notions of 'release' and 'cleansing', appropriates Christian concepts of redemption and renewal. Exploring the population's use of religious concepts in gacaca is vital to understanding some of the major social and cultural influences on the institution.

Third, many of the population's views about official gacaca draw on its participation in unofficial, parallel practices, especially traditional, pre-, prison and Christian gacaca. The population's expectation that gacaca will constitute open, participatory hearings and pursue reconciliation and modes of punishment that facilitate restoration all draw heavily on the methods and objectives of the traditional institution. Much of the population also derives its views on reconciliation and restorative justice from its experiences of pre- (and, to a lesser extent, prison) gacaca, in which suspects and survivors come face to face in preparation for their interactions at official gacaca. The dialogue that ensues during pre-gacaca meetings influences many Rwandans' confidence in, or distrust of, official gacaca's ability to foster meaningful dialogue and improved relations. Finally, the importance of religious concepts for the population's interpretations of gacaca is increased by many Rwandans' participation in Christian gacaca hearings. In particular, many survivors cite their involvement in Christian gacaca – where church leaders often claim that believers have a religious duty to forgive, and to reconcile with, those who have transgressed them – as motivating their readiness to forgive perpetrators and to pursue reconciliation. Many of the concepts and practices of these unofficial versions of gacaca, in which the population participates concurrently with official gacaca, are subsumed into the official institution. The dominant discourse on gacaca is lacking for its neglect of the impact of parallel practices on the population's expectations of, and participation in, official gacaca.

I turn now to the objectives-based critique of the dominant discourse on gacaca. Part (1) of the objectives-based critique argues that the sole objective that proponents of the dominant discourse ascribe to gacaca – formal, deterrent justice – is, on its own, an inadequate response to the problems and challenges facing Rwanda after the genocide. Part (1) of this critique deals separately with the inadequacies of only taking a formal approach to transitional justice and only pursuing deterrent outcomes. I have already explored in detail the deficiencies of an exclusively formal approach to justice in my response to human-rights critics in

Chapter 6. To summarise those earlier arguments, the formal approach is inadequate in political and operational terms, because it defies the spirit of gacaca by severely limiting the population's participation in the sorts of open, largely undirected dialogue that most Rwandans expect from gacaca. The view of gacaca implicit in the dominant discourse would therefore undermine the population's discursive understanding of gacaca. Moreover, by seeking to incorporate lawyers into gacaca, this view would alter the power dynamics and the tone of hearings and stymie discussions of non-legal matters concerning participants' personal, emotional experiences of the genocide. These actions would negatively influence the content that participants may discuss at gacaca and in the process alienate the population.

The view central to the dominant discourse, which holds that non-legal pursuits are inappropriate at gacaca, in turn assumes that deterrent justice is an adequate response to the legacies of the genocide. It is clear, though, that punishment of perpetrators alone will not fulfil the needs identified in gacaca's profound objectives. The key problem with a singular focus on punishment is that this response amounts to the physical separation of perpetrators and survivors, thus undermining the potential for their meaningful engagement. As we have seen, engagement – and its related processes of negotiation and collaboration – is crucial for the pursuit of positive peace, restorative justice, forgiveness and reconciliation. By failing to assemble perpetrators and survivors to discuss face to face the causes of, and solutions to, their conflicts, deterrent justice, on its own, fails to provide the benefits that the pursuit of profound objectives through gacaca can facilitate.

Proponents of the dominant discourse imply, for example, that punishment contributes to peace by deterring future criminals. As argued earlier, however, it is not only doubtful that punishment will deter future perpetrators but, more importantly, something much more than deterrence is necessary to produce lasting peace. Positive peace requires that parties deal with the root causes of their conflicts; a process that requires lengthy, messy discussions. Such interactions are impossible without the sense of engagement that gacaca facilitates. More importantly, gacaca shows how punishment can be shaped towards wider, reconciliatory ends, fulfilling survivors' need (and many human-rights critics' desire) to see perpetrators punished while also contributing to rebuilding fractured personal and communal relationships. Focusing solely on deterrent justice, as proponents of the dominant discourse advocate, is therefore an insufficient response to the needs of the population after the genocide.

Finally, part (2) of the objectives-based critique of the dominant view of gacaca maintains that its proponents mischaracterise gacaca as a form of mob justice, which fails to protect innocent suspects. Human-rights critics ignore the important legal safeguards enshrined in the Gacaca Law, for example the need for nine judges to meet *in camera* and to reach a consensus about the evidence presented before passing judgments, and the ability of those found guilty at gacaca to appeal any decisions to a higher jurisdiction. Such provisions afford suspects a vital layer of legal protection at gacaca. The Gacaca Law also affords judges significant powers to control the content and tenor of evidence during hearings. Judges may halt individual testimony, banish destructive participants or stop hearings altogether if any participants are threatened with violence. Proponents of the dominant discourse, while basing their interpretations of gacaca solely on its legal documents, again offer a selective reading of these texts by failing to recognise the substantial legal safeguards which they enshrine and which resulted principally from government concessions to international concerns during the Urugwiro negotiations. Consequently, these critics ignore gacaca's formal boundaries, which limit the negotiated aspects of hearings, and protect the rights of suspects.

IMPLICATIONS OF THE FINDINGS OF THIS BOOK

I conclude by outlining two main categories of the implications of my findings. First, the use of community-based transitional processes – especially those that derive from traditional conflict resolution mechanisms – is becoming increasingly widespread in societies recovering from mass atrocity. The experience of gacaca therefore provides important lessons for the formulation, practice and study of localised transitional justice elsewhere. A central debate regarding responses to the northern Ugandan conflict – and a principal point of contention between the Ugandan government and the Lord's Resistance Army (LRA) during the Juba peace negotiations between 2006 and 2008 – concerns the possible use of community-based rituals to reintegrate former LRA combatants and to reconcile them with their victims and affected communities. The LRA delegation to the Juba talks, along with various northern Ugandan civil-society leaders, advocated the use of local practices to address crimes committed during the conflict. These parties argued that local (especially Acholi) rituals constituted a vital alternative to prosecutions of atrocity perpetrators by the ICC, which they characterised as a neo-colonialist imposition by external actors and a form of punitive justice that would deter the LRA from further negotiations and ultimately jeopardise peace.[2] As mentioned in Chapter 2, gacaca has become an explicit touchstone for discussions of localised transitional justice in Uganda, with Ugandan officials regularly citing the virtues of gacaca in their advocacy of community-based rituals. As with gacaca, AI, HRW and other legal observers criticised the proposed use of the rituals on the grounds of a lack of due process and a preference for more formal modes of justice, particularly through the ICC.

Other countries in Africa and beyond have enacted or considered similar localised responses to mass atrocity. Between 1999 and 2004, the Barza Inter-Communautaire – a community-level conflict-resolution mechanism in the eastern DRC – assembled the cultural leaders of the nine major ethnic groups in North Kivu to mediate ethnic-based disputes. Over those five years, the Barza ensured there was no major outbreak of violence in its sphere of influence.[3] In Sudan, provincial leaders have discussed the potential modernisation of 'idara ahlia' or native administration tribunals in Darfur to deal with disputes stemming from the current conflict in the region.[4] Meanwhile, in Timor-Leste, local village elders and other community leaders have conducted hearings to address mass violence in the country since 1999, including overseeing compensation ceremonies. Echoing aspects of the gacaca experience, community-based practices in Timor-Leste have over time attracted involvement by national and international elites, who have attempted

[2] LRA Delegation to the Juba Talks, 'LRA Position Paper on Accountability and Reconciliation in the Context of Alternative Justice System for Resolving the Northern Ugandan and Southern Sudan Conflicts', Juba, Southern Sudan, August 2006, p.1. For further discussion of the Ugandan experience of local transitional justice, see P. Clark, 'Recreating Tradition: Lessons from Rwanda for Community-Based Transitional Justice in Uganda', in K. Vlassenroot and T. Allen (eds.), The Lord's Resistance Army: War, Peace and Reconciliation Northern Uganda, Oxford: James Currey, forthcoming; P. Clark, 'Beyond Polarisation: Debating Local Accountability and Reconciliation Rituals in Northern Uganda', in P. Wrange and J.F. Onyango (eds.), The International Criminal Court and the Juba Peace Process, Kampala: Fountain Publishers, forthcoming; T. Allen, 'Ritual (Ab)use? Problems with Traditional Justice in Northern Uganda', in Waddell and Clark, Courting Conflict?, pp.47–54.
[3] P. Clark, 'Ethnicity, Leadership and Conflict Mediation in Eastern Democratic Republic: The Case of the Barza Inter-Communautaire', Journal of Eastern African Studies, 2, 1, March 2008, pp.1–17.
[4] J. Morton, 'Conflict in Darfur: A Different Perspective', Resource Paper, Hempstead: HTSPE, June 2004.

to shape local hearings towards ends substantially different from those intended by the local population.[5]

The experience of gacaca is useful for foreign contexts such as these in several respects. Community-based processes in Uganda, the DRC, Sudan and Timor-Leste display many of the same features as gacaca, including the transformation of traditional practices, the involvement of state and provincial leaders, opposition from international human-rights observers and similar tensions between pragmatic considerations – not least dealing with thousands of criminal cases and thousands of victims in the context of judicial breakdown – and more profound concerns, including the pursuit of peace, healing and reconciliation. The gacaca experience highlights that major innovation, including melding customary and modern law, can yield substantial benefits for the population, provided those who create and oversee such processes can navigate inevitable tensions between issues of elite control and popular ownership, and between punitive and reconciliatory objects. Gacaca may therefore inspire further innovation in transitional societies, although the challenges of gacaca's hybridity must also be recognised in this regard.

For the creators and observers of such localised practices, the methodology adopted in this book may prove useful in coming to terms with the internal hybridity of such mechanisms and establishing appropriate conceptual frameworks in which to assess their effectiveness. Rwanda will not be the last transitional society to reform traditional, community-based processes in order to address mass atrocity. Rwanda's experience of gacaca may therefore prove educative for other societies that adopt such an approach.

Finally, the gacaca experience bears considerable implications for the Rwandan population. As highlighted in this book, gacaca has had mixed success in pursuing most of its objectives. Some communities are already reaping the benefits of gacaca, following constructive engagement between parties during hearings that have allowed all social groups to discuss their experiences of the genocide and fruitful interactions beyond gacaca. In such places, profound results including healing, forgiveness and reconciliation are certainly possible. Elsewhere, however, gacaca has had either minimal impact, because of piecemeal community participation during hearings, or has aggravated people's circumstances through a lack of justice, inadequate degrees of truth and increased trauma. These

---

[5] T. Hohe, 'Justice without Judiciary in East Timor', *Conflict, Security and Development*, 3, 3, 2003, pp.335–57.

experiences pose serious challenges for the individuals and communities concerned and, more broadly, for justice and the rule of law in Rwanda, as it is likely that gacaca will remain in some form to address everyday community infractions in the future. The reverberations from gacaca will therefore be felt for many years to come.

Gacaca constitutes the heart of Rwanda's attempts at personal and communal reconstruction after the genocide and one of the most revolutionary transitional justice approaches pursued anywhere in the world. It also represents an immense risk, handing the reins of reconstruction to a heavily traumatised, divided society. Nonetheless, it is a risk Rwanda had to take, given the enormity of the genocide and its societal impact, as well as the severe constraints on the nation's resources. Gacaca's success in facilitating pragmatic and profound outcomes in many communities must be lauded, but we must also recognise its major limitations and the problems it has produced. The same innovation and endurance displayed by Rwandans who created, guided and participated in gacaca, often in the face of substantial international criticism, will be needed to navigate a highly uncertain future.

GLOSSARY

abunzi	mediation committees
chaka-mchaka	a form of indoctrination camp used during the Ugandan bush war for military cadres
gacaca	literally, grass or lawn; name also given to community-level dispute resolution mechanism and court system designed to prosecute genocide cases (pronounced ga-CHA-cha)
gacaca nkiristu	Christian gacaca; a dispute resolution mechanism used in some Rwandan churches
Ibuka	literally, 'to remember'; name of the largest organisation of Rwandan genocide survivors
ingando	literally, an encampment or assembly area; a Rwandan military space used for briefing troops; more recently, a civic education camp
interahamwe	'those who work together'; name given to genocidal militias
inyangamugayo	literally, a person of integrity; a gacaca judge
mwami	a chief
nyumbakumi	the head of ten households
uburere buruta ubuvuke	Rwandan proverb, 'people are not born with values'
urumuri	literally, 'the light'; name given to judges during prison gacaca

BIBLIOGRAPHY

Books

African Rights, *Rwanda: Death, Despair and Defiance* (revised edition), London: African Rights, 1995.

Amaza, O.O., *Museveni's Long March: From FRELIMO to the National Resistance Movement*, London: Pluto Press, 1996.

Amis, M., *Experience: A Memoir*, Toronto: Alfred A. Knopf Canada, 2000.

Arendt, H., *The Human Condition*, Chicago, Ill.: University of Chicago Press, 1958.

Barnett, M., *Eyewitness to a Genocide: The United Nations and Rwanda*, Ithaca, NY: Cornell University Press, 2002.

Berkeley, B., *The Graves Are Not Yet Full: Race, Tribe and Power in the Heart of Africa*, New York: Basic Books, 2001.

Berry, J. and C. Berry (eds.), *Genocide in Rwanda: A Collective Memory*, Washington, DC: Howard University Press, 1999.

Braeckman, C., *Rwanda: histoire d'un génocide*, Paris: Fayard, 1994.

Braithwaite, J., *Crime, Shame and Reintegration*, Cambridge: Cambridge University Press, 1989.

  Restorative Justice and Responsive Regulation, Oxford: Oxford University Press, 2002.

Bronkhorst, D., *Truth and Reconciliation: Obstacles and Opportunities for Human Rights*, Amsterdam: Amnesty International, 1995.

Charny, I., *How Can We Commit the Unthinkable? Genocide: The Human Cancer*, Boulder, Col.: Westview Press, 1992.

Chrétien, J.-P., *Le Défi de l'ethnisme: Rwanda et Burundi – 1990–1996*, Paris: Karthala, 1997.

Chrétien, J.-P., J.-F. Dupaquier, M. Kabanda and J. Ngarame (eds.), *Rwanda: les médias du génocide*, Paris: Éditions Karthala, 1995.

Clark, P. and Z.D. Kaufman (eds.), *After Genocide: Transitional Justice, Post-Conflict Reconstruction and Reconciliation in Rwanda and Beyond*, London: Hurst & Co., 2009.

Crawford, B. and R. Lipschutz (eds.), *The Myth of 'Ethnic Conflict': Politics, Economics and 'Cultural' Violence*, Berkeley, Calif.: University of California–Berkeley International and Area Studies Press, 1998.

Dallaire, R., *Shake Hands with the Devil: The Failure of Humanity in Rwanda*, Toronto: Random House, 2003.

de Lame, D., *A Hill among a Thousand: Transformation and Ruptures in Rural Rwanda*, Madison, Wisc.: University of Wisconsin Press, 2005.

Derrida, J., *On Cosmopolitanism and Forgiveness*, trans. M. Dooley and M. Hughes, London: Routledge, 2001.

Des Forges, A., *Leave None to Tell the Story: Genocide in Rwanda*, New York: Human Rights Watch, 1999.

Destexhe, A., *Rwanda and Genocide in the Twentieth Century*, trans. A. Marschner, New York: New York University Press, 1995.

Drumbl, M., *Atrocity, Punishment, and International Law*, Cambridge: Cambridge University Press, 2007.

Ehrenreich, B., *Blood Rites: Origins and History of the Passions of War*, New York: Henry Holt, 1998.

Ellis, S., *The Mask of Anarchy: The Destruction of Liberia and the Religious Dimension of an African Civil War*, London: Hurst & Co., 1999.

Eltringham, N., *Accounting for Horror: Post-Genocide Debates in Rwanda*, London: Pluto Press, 2004.

Fujii, L.A., *Killing Neighbors: Webs of Violence in Rwanda*, Ithaca, NY Cornell University Press, 2009.

Gaita, R., *A Common Humanity: Thinking about Love and Truth and Justice*, Melbourne: Text Publishing, 1999.

Gatwa, T., *Rwanda – Églises: victimes ou coupables? les églises et l'idéologie ethnique au Rwanda 1990–1994*, Yaoundé: Cle, 2001.

Gourevitch, P., *We Wish to Inform You that Tomorrow We Will be Killed with Our Families: Stories from Rwanda*, New York: Farrar, Straus, and Giroux, 1998.

Harrell, P., *Rwanda's Gamble: Gacaca and a New Model of Transitional Justice*, New York: Writers Club Press, 2003.

Hatzfeld, J., *A Time for Machetes: The Rwandan Genocide – The Killers Speak*, trans. Linda Coverdale, London: Serpent's Tail, 2008.

Into the Quick of Life: The Rwandan Genocide – The Survivors Speak, trans. Gerry Feehily, London: Serpent's Tail, 2008.

The Strategy of Antelopes: Rwanda after the Genocide, trans. Linda Coverdale, London: Serpent's Tail, 2009.

Hayner, P., *Unspeakable Truths: Facing the Challenge of Truth Commissions*, New York: Routledge, 2002.

Henderson, M., *Forgiveness: Breaking the Chain of Hate*, Wilsonville, Oreg.: Book Partners, 1999.

Jennings, C., *Across the Red River: Rwanda, Burundi and the Heart of Darkness*, London: V. Gollancz, 2000.

Johnstone, G., *Restorative Justice: Ideas, Values, Debates*, Uffculme: Willan Publishing, 2002.

Keane, F., *Season of Blood: A Rwandan Journey*, London: Viking, 1995.

Khan, S., *The Shallow Graves of Rwanda*, London: I.B. Tauris, 2000.

Kimonyo, J.-P., *Revue critique des interpretations du conflit Rwandais*, Cahiers du Centre de Gestion des Conflits (no. 1), Butare: Université Nationale du Rwanda, 2000.

Klinghoffer, A., *The International Dimension of Genocide in Rwanda*, New York: New York University Press, 1998.

Kuperman, A., *The Limits of Humanitarian Intervention: Genocide in Rwanda*, Washington, DC: Brookings Institution Press, 2001.

Lemarchand, R., *Burundi: Ethnic Conflict and Genocide*, New York: Wilson Center, 1996.

Lemarchand, R., *Burundi: Ethnocide as Discourse and Practice*, New York: Wilson Center, 1994.

MacIntyre, A., *Three Rival Versions of Moral Enquiry: Encyclopedia, Genealogy and Tradition*, London: Duckworth, 1990.

Magnarella, P., *Justice in Africa: Rwanda's Genocide, Its Courts, and the UN Criminal Tribunal*, Aldershot: Ashgate, 2000.

Mamdani, M., *When Victims Become Killers: Colonialism, Nativism, and the Genocide in Rwanda*, Princeton, NJ: Princeton University Press, 2001.

McCullum, H., *The Angels Have Left Us: The Rwanda Tragedy and the Churches*, Geneva: WCC Publications, 1996.

Melvern, L., *A People Betrayed: The Role of the West in Rwanda's Genocide*, London: Zed Books, 2000.

Conspiracy to Murder: The Rwandan Genocide, New York: Verso, 2004.

Minow, M., *Between Vengeance and Forgiveness: Facing History after Genocide and Mass Violence*, Boston, Mass.: Beacon Press, 1998.

Misser, F., *Vers un nouveau Rwanda? Entretiens avec Paul Kagame*, Brussels: Karthala, 1995.

Mujawayo, E. and S. Belhaddad, *La Fleur de Stéphanie: Rwanda entre réconciliation et déni*, Paris: Flammarion, 2006.

Munyandamutsa, N., *Question du sens et des repères dans le traumatisme psychique: réflexions autour de l'observation clinique d'enfants et d'adolescents survivants du génocide Rwandais de 1994*, Geneva: Éditions Médecine et Hygiène, 2001.

Museveni, Y., *Sowing the Mustard Seed: The Struggle for Freedom and Democracy in Uganda*, London: Macmillan, 1997.

Neuffer, E., *The Key to My Neighbor's House: Seeking Justice in Bosnia and Rwanda*, London: Bloomsbury, 2000.

Off, C., *The Lion, the Fox and the Eagle: A Story of Generals and Justice in Rwanda and Yugoslavia*, Toronto: Vintage Canada, 2000.

Overdulve, C., *Rwanda: un peuple avec une histoire*, Paris: Harmattan, 1997.

Peskin, V., *International Justice in Rwanda and the Balkans: Virtual Trials and the Struggle for State Cooperation*, Cambridge: Cambridge University Press, 2008.

Porter, N., *The Elusive Quest: Reconciliation in Northern Ireland*, Belfast: The Blackstaff Press, 2003.

Prunier, G., *Rwanda in Zaire: From Genocide to Continental War*, London: Hurst, 1999.

The Rwanda Crisis, 1959–1994: History of a Genocide, London: Hurst, 1998.

Rawls, J., *A Theory of Justice*, Oxford: Clarendon Press, 1972.

Rudasingwa, T., *Rwanda: Background to Genocide*, Dar es Salaam: Thackers Publishers, 1994.

Rusagara, F., *Resilience of a Nation: A History of the Military in Rwanda*, Kigali: Fountain Publishers Rwanda, 2009.

Sartre, J.-P., *Nausea*, trans. L. Alexander, New York: New Directions Publishing, 1964.

Shutte, A., *Philosophy for Africa*, Rondebosch: University of Cape Town Press, 1993.

Simpson, K., *Truth Recovery in Northern Ireland: Critically Interpreting the Past*, Manchester: Manchester University Press, 2009.

Staub, E., *The Roots of Evil: The Origins of Genocide and Other Group Violence*, Cambridge: Cambridge University Press, 1989.

Straus, S., *The Order of Genocide: Race, Power, and War in Rwanda*, Ithaca, NY: Cornell University Press, 2006.

Taylor, C., *Sources of the Self: The Making of the Modern Identity*, Cambridge, Mass.: Harvard University Press, 1989.

Tertsakian, C., *Le Château: The Lives of Prisoners in Rwanda*, London: Arves Books, 2008.

Tutu, D., *No Future without Forgiveness*, New York: Doubleday, 1999.

United Nations, *The United Nations and Rwanda: 1993–1996*, Geneva: United Nations, 1996.

United States Institute for Peace, *Special Report: Rwanda: Accountability for War Crimes and Genocide*, Washington, DC: United States Institute of Peace Library, January 1995.

Uvin, P., *Aiding Violence: The Development Enterprise in Rwanda*, West Hartford, Conn.: Kumarian Press, 1998.

Waddell, N. and P. Clark (eds.), *Courting Conflict? Justice, Peace and the ICC in Africa*, London: Royal African Society, 2008.

Wallis, A., *Silent Accomplice: The Untold Story of France's Role in the Rwandan Genocide*, London: I.B. Tauris, 2007.

Chapters in edited collections
Abu-Nimer, M., A. A. Said and L. S. Prelis, 'Conclusion: The Long Road to Reconciliation', in M. Abu-Nimer (ed.), *Reconciliation, Justice and Coexistence: Theory and Practice*, Lanham, Md.: Lexington Books, 2001, pp.339–48.

Allen, T., 'Ritual (Ab)use? Problems with Traditional Justice in Northern Uganda', in N. Waddell and P. Clark (eds.), *Courting Conflict? Justice, Peace and the ICC in Africa*, London: Royal African Society, pp.47–54.

Babalola, S., 'Perceptions about the Gacaca Law in Rwanda: Evidence from a Multi-Method Study', in E. Ntaganda (ed.), *Les Juridictions gacaca et les processus de réconciliation nationale*, Cahiers du Centre de Gestion des Conflits (no. 3), Butare: Université Nationale du Rwanda, May 2001, pp.97–120.

Bloomfield, D. 'Reconciliation: An Introduction', in D. Bloomfield, T. Barnes and L. Huyse (eds.), *Reconciliation after Violent Conflict: A Handbook*, Stockholm: International Institute for Democracy and Electoral Assistance, 2003, pp.10–18.

Buckley-Zistel, S., 'We are Pretending Peace: Local Memory and the Absence of Social Transformation and Reconciliation in Rwanda', in P. Clark and Z.D. Kaufman (eds.), *After Genocide: Transitional Justice, Post-Conflict Reconstruction and Reconciliation in Rwanda and Beyond*, London: Hurst & Co., 2009, pp.125–43.

Chalk, F., 'Hate Radio in Rwanda', in H. Adelman and A. Suhrke (eds.), *The Path of a Genocide: The Rwanda Crisis from Uganda to Zaire*, New Brunswick, NJ: Transaction Publishers, 1999, pp.93–107.

Chrétien, J.-P., 'Un génocide africain: de l'idéologie à la propagande', in R. Verdier, E. Decaux and J.-P. Chrétien (eds.), *Rwanda: un génocide du XXème siècle*, Paris: L'Harmattan, 1995, pp.45–55.

Clark, P., 'Beyond Polarisation: Debating Local Accountability and Reconciliation Rituals in Northern Uganda', in P. Wrange and J.F. Onyango (eds.), *The International Criminal Court and the Juba Peace Process*, Kampala: Fountain Publishers, forthcoming.

'Recreating Tradition: Lessons from Rwanda for Community-Based Transitional Justice in Uganda', in K. Vlassenroot and T. Allen (eds.), *The Lord's Resistance Army: War, Peace and Reconciliation Northern Uganda*, Oxford: James Currey, forthcoming.

'The Rules (and Politics) of Engagement: The Gacaca Courts and Post-Genocide Justice, Healing and Reconciliation in Rwanda', in P. Clark and Z.D. Kaufman (eds.), *After Genocide: Transitional Justice, Post-Conflict Reconstruction and Reconciliation in Rwanda and Beyond*, London: Hurst & Co., 2009, pp.297–320.

Crocker, D., 'Truth Commissions, Transitional Justice and Civil Society', in R. Rotberg and D. Thompson (eds.), *Truth v. Justice: The Morality of Truth Commissions*, Princeton, NJ: Princeton University Press, 2000, pp.99–121.

Dallaire, R., 'Text of the January 11, 1994 Cable', in H. Adelman and A. Suhrke (eds.), *The Path of a Genocide: The Rwanda Crisis from Uganda to Zaire*, New Brunswick, NJ: Transaction Publishers, 1999, p.xxi.

Des Forges, A. and T. Longman, 'Legal Responses to the Genocide in Rwanda', in E. Stover and H. Weinstein (eds.), *My Neighbor, My Enemy: Justice and Community in the Aftermath of Mass Atrocity*, Cambridge: Cambridge University Press, 2004, pp.49–68.

Enright, R. and the Human Development Study Group, 'The Moral Development of Forgiveness', in W. Kurtines and W. Gewirtz (eds.), *Handbook of Moral Behavior and Development*, vol. I, London: Lawrence Erlbaum, 1991, pp.123–52.

Estrada-Hollenbeck, M., 'The Attainment of Justice through Restoration, Not Litigation: The Subjective Road to Reconciliation', in M. Abu-Nimer (ed.), *Reconciliation, Justice and Coexistence: Theory and Practice*, Lanham, Md.: Lexington Books, 2001, pp.65–85.

Galtung, J., 'After Violence, Reconstruction, Reconciliation, and Resolution: Coping with Visible and Invisible Effects of War and Violence', in M. Abu-Nimer (ed.), *Reconciliation, Justice and Coexistence: Theory and Practice*, Lanham, Md.: Lexington Books, 2001, pp. 3–23.

Gasibirege, S., 'L'Élection des juges *inyangamugayo*: rupture ou continuité', in E. Ntaganda (ed.), *De la paix à la justice: les enjeux de la réconciliation nationale*, Cahiers de Centre de Gestion des Conflits (no. 6), Butare: Université Nationale du Rwanda, November 2002, pp.93–127.

'Recherche qualitative sur les attitudes des Rwandais vis-à-vis des juridictions-gacaca', in E. Ntaganda (ed.), *Les Juridictions gacaca et les processus de réconciliation nationale*, Cahiers du Centre de Gestion des Conflits (no. 3), Butare: Université Nationale du Rwanda, May 2001, pp.121–73.

'Résultats définitifs de l'enquête quantitative sur les attitudes des Rwandais vis-à-vis des juridictions-gacaca', in E. Ntaganda (ed.), *De la paix à la justice: les enjeux de la réconciliation nationale*, Cahiers de Centre de Gestion des Conflits (no. 6), Butare: Université Nationale du Rwanda, November 2002, pp.38–92.

Gnamo, A., 'The Rwandan Genocide and the Collapse of Mobutu's Kleptocracy', in H. Adelman and A. Suhrke (eds.), *The Path of a Genocide: The Rwanda Crisis from Uganda to Zaire*, New Brunswick, NJ: Transaction Publishers, 1999, pp.321–49.

Gopin, M., 'Forgiveness as an Element of Conflict Resolution in Religious Cultures: Walking the Tightrope of Reconciliation and Justice', in M. Abu-Nimer (ed.), *Reconciliation, Justice and Coexistence: Theory and Practice*, Lanham, Md.: Lexington Books, 2001, pp.87–99.

Gutmann, A. and D. Thompson, 'The Moral Foundations of Truth Commissions', in R. Rotberg and D. Thompson (eds.), *Truth v. Justice: The Morality of Truth Commissions*, Princeton, NJ: Princeton University Press, 2000, pp.22–44.

Halvorsen, K., 'Protection and Humanitarian Assistance in the Refugee Camps in Zaire: The Problem of Security', in H. Adelman and A. Suhrke (eds.), *The Path to a Genocide: The Rwanda Crisis from Uganda to Zaire*, New Brunswick, NJ: Transaction Publishers, 1999, pp.307–20.

Hicks, D., 'The Role of Identity Reconstruction in Promoting Reconciliation', in R. Helmick and S. Petersen (eds.), *Forgiveness and Reconciliation: Religion, Public Policy, and Conflict Transformation*, Philadelphia, Pa.: Templeton Foundation Press, 2001, pp.129–49.

Holiday, A., 'Forgiving and Forgetting: The Truth and Reconciliation Commission', in S. Nuttall and C. Coetzee (eds.), *Negotiating the Past: The Making of Memory in South Africa*, Oxford: Oxford University Press, 2000, pp.43–56.

Ingelaere, B., 'The Gacaca Courts in Rwanda', in L. Huyse and M. Salter (eds.), *Traditional Justice and Reconciliation after Violent Conflict: Learning from African Experiences*, Stockholm: IDEA, 2008, pp.24–59.

Kakwenzire, J. and D. Kamukama, 'The Development and Consolidation of Extremist Forces in Rwanda, 1990–1994', in H. Adelman and A. Suhrke (eds.), *The Path to a Genocide: The Rwanda Crisis from Uganda to Zaire*, New Brunswick, NJ: Transaction Publishers, 1999, pp.61–91.

Karekezi, A., 'Juridictions gacaca: lutte contre l'impunité et promotion de la réconciliation nationale', in E. Ntaganda (ed.), *Les Juridictions gacaca et les processus de réconciliation nationale*, Cahiers du Centre de Gestion des Conflits (no. 3), Butare: Université Nationale du Rwanda, May 2001, pp.9–96.

Karekezi, A., A. Nshimiyimana and B. Mutamba, 'Localizing Justice: Gacaca Courts in Post-Genocide Rwanda', in E. Stover and H. Weinstein (eds.), *My Neighbor, My Enemy: Justice and Community in the Aftermath of Mass Atrocity*, Cambridge: Cambridge University Press, 2004.

Katumanga, M., 'Folk Poetry as a Weapon of Struggle: An Analysis of the Chaka Mchaka Resistance Songs of the National Resistance Movement/Army of Uganda', in K. Njogu and H. Maupeu (eds.), *Songs and Politics in Eastern Africa*, Dar es Salaam: Mkuki na Nyota Publishers, 2007, pp.129–55.

Kayigamba, J.-B. 'Without Justice, No Reconciliation: A Survivor's Experience of Genocide', in P. Clark and Z.D. Kaufman (eds.), *After Genocide: Transitional Justice, Post-Conflict Reconstruction and Reconciliation in Rwanda and Beyond*, London: Hurst & Co., 2009, pp.33–42.

Kiss, E., 'Moral Ambition within and beyond Political Constraints: Reflections on Restorative Justice', in R. Rotberg and D. Thompson (eds.), *Truth v. Justice: The Morality of Truth Commissions*, Princeton, NJ: Princeton University Press, 2000, pp.68–98.

Lederach, J., 'Five Qualities of Practice in Support of Reconciliation Processes', in R. Helmick and R. Petersen (eds.), *Forgiveness and Reconciliation: Religion, Public Policy, and Conflict Transformation*, Philadelphia, Pa.: Templeton Foundation Press, 2001, pp.183–93.

Longman, T. 'Justice at the Grassroots? Gacaca Trials in Rwanda', in N. Roht-Arriaza and J. Mariezcurrena (eds.), *Transitional Justice in the Twenty-First*

Century: Beyond Truth versus Justice, Cambridge: Cambridge University Press, 2006, pp.206–28.

Meier, C., 'Doing History, Doing Justice: The Narrative of the Historian and of the Truth Commission', in R. Rotberg and D. Thompson (eds.), *Truth v. Justice: The Morality of Truth Commissions*, Princeton, NJ: Princeton University Press, 2000, pp.261–78.

McNulty, M., 'The Militarization of Ethnicity and the Emergence of Warlordism in Rwanda', in P. Rich (ed.), *Warlords in International Relations*, Basingstoke: Macmillan Press, 1999, pp.81–102.

Mertus, J., 'Truth in a Box: The Limits of Justice through Judicial Mechanisms', in I. Amadiume and A. An-Na'Im (eds.), *The Politics of Memory: Truth, Healing and Social Justice*, London: Zed Books, 2000, pp.142–61.

Minow, M., 'The Hope for Healing: What Can Truth Commissions Do?' in R. Rotberg and D. Thompson (eds.), *Truth v. Justice: The Morality of Truth Commissions*, Princeton, NJ: Princeton University Press, 2000, pp.235–60.

Montville, J., 'Justice and the Burdens of History', in M. Abu-Nimer (ed.), *Reconciliation, Justice and Coexistence: Theory and Practice*, Lanham, Md.: Lexington Books, 2001, pp.129–43.

Mucyo, J., 'Gacaca Courts and Genocide', in C. Villa-Vicencio and T. Savage (eds.), *Rwanda and South Africa in Dialogue: Addressing the Legacies of Genocide and a Crime against Humanity*, Cape Town: Institute for Justice and Reconciliation, 2001, pp.49–54.

Mutagwera, F., 'Détentions et poursuites judiciaires au Rwanda', in J.-F. Dupaquier (ed.), *La Justice internationale face au drame Rwandais*, Paris: Karthala, 1996, pp.17–36.

Ngesi, S. and C. Villa-Vicencio, 'Rwanda: Balancing the Weight of History', in E. Doxtader and C. Villa-Vicencio (eds.), *Through Fire with Water: The Roots of Division and the Potential for Reconciliation in Africa*, Claremont: Institute for Justice and Reconciliation, 2003, pp.1–34.

Nsabiyera Gasana, S., 'Confronting Conflict and Poverty through Trauma Healing: Integrating Peace-Building and Development Processes in Rwanda', in P. Clark and Z.D. Kaufman (eds.), *After Genocide: Transitional Justice, Post-Conflict Reconstruction and Reconciliation in Rwanda and Beyond*, London: Hurst & Co., 2009, pp.145–70.

Petersen, R., 'A Theology of Forgiveness: Terminology, Rhetoric, and the Dialectic of Interfaith Relationships', in R. Helmick and R. Petersen (eds.), *Forgiveness and Reconciliation: Religion, Public Policy, and Conflict Transformation*, Philadelphia, Pa.: Templeton Foundation Press, 2001, pp.3–25.

Prunier, G., 'Opération Turquoise: A Humanitarian Escape from a Political Dead End', in H. Adelman and A. Suhrke (eds.), *The Path of a Genocide: The Rwanda Crisis from Uganda to Zaire*, New Brunswick, NJ: Transaction Publishers, 1999, pp.281–305.

Rotberg, R., 'Truth Commissions and the Provision of Truth, Justice and Reconciliation', in R. Rotberg and D. Thompson (eds.), *Truth v. Justice: The Morality of Truth Commissions*, Princeton, NJ: Princeton University Press, 2000, pp.3–21.

Rutembesa, F., 'Ruptures culturelles et génocide au Rwanda', in J.-P. Kimonyo (ed.), *Ruptures socioculturelles et conflit au Rwanda*, Cahiers du Centre de Gestion des Conflits (no. 2), Butare: Université Nationale du Rwanda, April 2001, pp.93–123.

Sarkin, J., 'Gacaca Courts and Genocide', in C. Villa-Vicencio and T. Savage (eds.), *Rwanda and South Africa in Dialogue: Addressing the Legacies of Genocide and a Crime against Humanity*, Cape Town: Institute for Justice and Reconciliation, 2001, pp.54–91.

Schabas, W., 'Le Rwanda, le Burundi, et la maladie d'impunité', in R. Verdier, E. Decaux and J.-P. Chrétien (eds.), *Rwanda: un génocide du XXème siècle*, Paris: Harmattan, 1995, pp.115–23.

Schirch, L., 'Ritual Reconciliation: Transforming Identity/Reframing Conflict', in M. Abu-Nimer (ed.), *Reconciliation, Justice and Coexistence: Theory and Practice*, Lanham, Md.: Lexington Books, 2001, pp.145–61.

Shriver, D., 'What is Forgiveness in a Secular Political Form?' in R. Helmick and R. Petersen (eds.), *Forgiveness and Reconciliation: Religion, Public Policy, and Conflict Transformation*, Philadelphia, Pa.: Templeton Foundation Press, 2001, pp.151–7.

Soyinka, W., 'Memory, Truth and Healing', in I. Amadiume and A. An-Na'im (eds.), *The Politics of Memory: Truth, Healing and Social Justice*, London: Zed Books, 2000, pp.21–37.

Staub, E. and L. Pearlman, 'Healing, Reconciliation, and Forgiving after Genocide and Other Collective Violence', in R. Helmick and R. Petersen (eds.), *Forgiveness and Reconciliation: Religion, Public Policy, and Conflict Transformation*, Philadelphia, Pa.: Templeton Foundation Press, 2001, pp.195–217.

Steward, J., 'Only Healing Heals: Concepts and Methods of Psycho-Social Healing in Post-Genocide Rwanda', in P. Clark and Z.D. Kaufman (eds.), *After Genocide: Transitional Justice, Post-Conflict Reconstruction and Reconciliation in Rwanda and Beyond*, London: Hurst & Co., 2009, pp.171–90.

Tutu, D., 'Foreword', in R. Helmick and R. Petersen (eds.), *Forgiveness and Reconciliation: Religion, Public Policy, and Conflict Transformation*, Philadelphia, Pa.: Templeton Foundation Press, 2001, pp.ix–xiii.

Uvin, P., 'The Gacaca Tribunals in Rwanda (Case Study)', in D. Bloomfield, T. Barnes and L. Huyse (eds.), *Reconciliation after Violent Conflict: A Handbook*, Stockholm: International Institute for Democracy and Electoral Assistance, 2003, pp.116–21.

Vandeginste, S., 'Les Juridictions gacaca et la poursuite des suspects auteurs du génocide et des crimes contre l'humanité au Rwanda', in F. Reyntjens and S. Marysee (eds.), *L'Afrique des Grands Lacs (Annuaire 1999–2000)*, Paris: L'Harmattan, 2000, pp.75–93.

Volf, M., 'Forgiveness, Reconciliation, and Justice: A Christian Contribution to a More Peaceful Social Environment', in R. Helmick and R. Petersen (eds.), *Forgiveness and Reconciliation: Religion, Public Policy, and Conflict Transformation*, Philadelphia, Pa.: Templeton Foundation Press, 2001, pp.27–49.

Journal articles

Adelman, H., 'Genocidists and Saviours in Rwanda', *Other Voices*, 2, 1, February 2000, pp.1–13.

Akhavan, P., 'Justice and Reconciliation in the Great Lakes Region of Africa: The Contribution of the International Criminal Tribunal for Rwanda', *Duke Journal of Comparative and International Law*, 7, 325, 1997, pp.325–48.

Allen, J., 'Balancing Justice and Social Unity: Political Theory and the Idea of a Truth and Reconciliation Commission', *University of Toronto Law Journal*, 49, 3, summer 1999, pp.318–37.

Anderson, A., 'Pentecostal Approaches to Faith and Healing', *International Review of Mission*, 91, 363, 2002, pp.523–34.

Andrews, M., 'Forgiveness in Context', *Journal of Moral Education*, March 2000, pp.75–86.

Apuuli, K.P., 'Procedural Due Process and the Prosecution of Genocide Suspects in Rwanda', *Journal of Genocide Research*, 11, 1, March 2009, pp.11–30.

Babic, J., 'Justifying Forgiveness', *Peace Review*, 12, 1, March 2000, pp.87–93.

Baker, B., 'Popular Justice and Policing from Bush War to Democracy: Uganda, 1981–2004', *International Journal of the Sociology of Law*, 32, 4, 2004.

Bhavnani, R. and D. Backer, 'Localized Ethnic Conflict into Conflict and Genocide: Accounting for Differences in Rwanda and Burundi', *The Journal of Conflict Resolution*, 44, 3, 2000, pp.283–307.

Bolocan, M.G., 'Rwandan Gacaca: An Experiment in Transitional Justice', *Journal of Dispute Resolution*, 2004, pp.355–400.

Botman, R., 'Justice that Restores: How Reparation Must be Made', *Track Two*, 6, 3 and 4, December 1997.

Braeckman, C., 'New York and Kigali', *New Left Review*, 9, May–June 2001, pp.141–7.

Breed, A., 'Performing Reconciliation in Rwanda', *Peace Review: A Journal of Social Justice*, 18, 4, 2006, pp.507–13.

Brittain, V. 'The Arusha Tribunal Costs Too Much for Very Few Results', *African Geopolitics*, 11, summer 2003, www.african-geopolitics.org/show.aspx?ArticleId=3537.

Brounéus, K., 'Truth-Telling as Talking Cure? Insecurity and Retraumatization in the Rwandan Gacaca Courts', *Security Dialogue*, 39, 1, 2008, pp.55–76.

Burke-White, W., 'A Community of Courts: Toward a System of International Criminal Law Enforcement', *Michigan Journal of International Law*, 24, 1, autumn 2002, pp.54–61.

Calhoun, C., 'Changing One's Heart', *Ethics*, 103, 1, October 1992, pp.76–96.

Clark, P., 'Ethnicity, Leadership and Conflict Mediation in Eastern Democratic Republic: The Case of the *Barza Inter-Communautaire*', *Journal of Eastern African Studies*, 2, 1, March 2008, pp.1–17.

'Hybridity, Holism and "Traditional" Justice: The Case of the Gacaca Courts in Post-Genocide Rwanda', *George Washington International Law Review*, 39, 4, 2007, pp.765–837.

'Judging Genocide on the Grass', *Oxonian Review of Books*, 3, 2, 2004, www. oxonianreview.org/issues/3-2/3-2-4.htm.

'When the Killers Go Home: Local Justice in Rwanda', *Dissent*, summer 2005, pp.14–21.

Cobban, H., 'The Legacies of Collective Violence: The Rwandan Genocide and the Limits of Law', *Boston Review*, April/May 2002, www.bostonreview.net/BR27.2/cobban.html.

Coghlan, B., R. Brennan, P. Ngoy, D. Dofara, B. Offo, M. Clements and T. Stewart, 'Mortality in the Democratic Republic of Congo: A Nationwide Survey', *The Lancet*, 367, 7 January 2006, pp.44–51.

Corey, A. and S. Joireman, 'Retributive Justice: The Gacaca Courts in Rwanda', *African Affairs*, 103, 2004, pp.73–89.

Crocker, D., 'Transitional Justice and International Civil Society: Toward a Normative Framework', *Constellations*, 5, 4, 1998, pp.492–517.

Daly, E., 'Between Punitive Justice and Reconstructive Justice: The Gacaca Courts in Rwanda', *New York University Journal of International Law and Politics*, 34, 2002, pp.355–96.

Dauge-Roth, A., 'Testimonial Encounter: Esther Mujawayo's Dialogic Art of Witnessing', *French Cultural Studies*, 20, 2009, pp.165–80.

Des Forges, A., 'Shame: Reply to Kuperman and His Response', *Foreign Affairs*, May–June 2000, pp.141–4.

'The Ideology of Genocide', *ISSUE: A Journal of Opinion*, 23, 2, 1995, pp.44–7.

Des Forges, A. and K. Roth, 'Justice or Therapy? A Discussion on Helena Cobban's Essay on Crime and Punishment in Rwanda', *Boston Review*, summer 2002, www.bostonreview.net/BR27.3/rothdesForges.html.

Drew, P., 'Dealing with Mass Atrocities and Ethnic Violence: Can Alternative Forms of Justice Be Effective? A Case Study of Rwanda', *Canadian Forum on Civil Justice*, 2000.

Drumbl, M., 'Punishment, Postgenocide: From Guilt to Shame to Civis in Rwanda', *New York University Law Review*, 75, November 2000, pp.1221–326.

'Sclerosis: Retributive Justice and the Rwandan Genocide', *Punishment and Society*, 2, 3, 2000, pp.287–308.

Fierens, J., 'Gacaca Courts: Between Fantasy and Reality', *Journal of International Criminal Justice*, 3, 2005, pp.896–919.

Gourevitch, P., 'Letter from Rwanda: After the Genocide', *The New Yorker*, 71, December 1995, pp.78–95.

Haile, D., 'Rwanda's Experiment with People's Courts (Gacaca) and the Tragedy of Unexamined Humanitarianism', Institute of Development Policy and Management Discussion Paper, Antwerp: University of Antwerp, January 2008.

Harel, Z., B. Kahana and E. Kahana, 'The Effects of the Holocaust: Psychiatric, Behavioral, and Survivor Perspective', *Journal of Sociology and Social Welfare*, 11, 1984, pp.915–29.

Hartwell, M., 'The Role of Forgiveness in Reconstructing Society after Conflict', *Journal of Humanitarian Assistance*, June 2000.

Hayner, P., 'Fifteen Truth Commissions: 1974–1994 – A Comparative Study', *Human Rights Quarterly*, 16, 4, November 1994, pp.597–655.

Heller, K.J. 'What Happens to the Acquitted?', *Leiden Journal of International Law*, 21, 2008, pp.663–80.

Hintjens, H., 'Explaining the 1994 Genocide in Rwanda', *The Journal of Modern African Studies*, 37, 2, 1999, pp.241–86.

Hohe, T., 'Justice without Judiciary in East Timor', *Conflict, Security and Development*, 3, 3, 2003, pp.335–57.

Joireman, S., 'Justice for a Genocide?', *Global Review of Ethnopolitics*, 2, 2, January 2003, pp.65–6.

Kamatali, J.-M., 'The Challenge of Linking International Criminal Justice and National Reconciliation: The Case of the ICTR', *Leiden Journal of International Law*, 16, 2003, pp.115–33.

Kolnai, A., 'Forgiveness', *Proceedings of the Aristotelian Society*, 74, 1973–4, pp.91–106.

Kuperman, A., 'Rwanda in Retrospect', *Foreign Affairs*, 79, 1, January/February 2000, pp.94–118.

Lambourne, W., 'The Pursuit of Justice and Reconciliation: Responding to Genocide in Cambodia and Rwanda', *Columbia International Affairs Online*, June 1999, www.ciaonet.org/isa/law01.

Landsman, S., 'Alternative Responses to Serious Human Rights Abuses: Of Prosecution and Truth Commissions', *Law and Contemporary Problems*, 59, 4, autumn 1996, pp.81–92.

Lemarchand, R., 'Rwanda: The Rationality of Genocide', *ISSUE: A Journal of Opinion*, 23, 2, 1995, pp.8–11.

Linfield, S., 'Trading Truth for Justice? Reflections on South Africa's Truth and Reconciliation Commission,' *Boston Review*, summer 2000, www.boston-review.mit.edu/br25.3/linfield.html.

Longman, T., 'An Assessment of Rwanda's Gacaca Courts', *Peace Review: A Journal of Social Justice*, 21, 3, 2009, pp.304–12.

'Genocide and Socio-Political Change: Massacres in Two Rwandan Villages', *ISSUE: A Journal of Opinion*, 23, 2, 1995, pp.18–21.

Lumsden, M., 'Breaking the Cycle of Violence', *Journal of Peace Research*, 34, 4, November 1997, pp.377–83.

Mamdani, M., 'A Brief History of Genocide', *Transition*, 87, 2000, pp.26–47.

'From Conquest to Consent as the Basis of State-Formation: Reflections on Rwanda', *New Left Review*, 216, 1996, pp.3–36.

Martin, D., 'Retribution Revisited: A Reconsideration of Feminist Criminal Law Reform Strategies', *Orgoode Hall Law Journal*, 36, 1, 1998, pp.151–88.

McNulty, M., 'French Arms, War and Genocide in Rwanda', *Crime, Law and Social Change*, 33, 1/2, 2000, pp.105–29.

Menzies, R., 'A Pentecostal Perspective on "Signs and Wonders"', *Pneuma*, 17, 2, 1995, pp.265–78.

Merry, S., 'Legal Pluralism', *Law and Society Review*, 22, 1988.

Meyerstein, A., 'Between Law and Culture: Rwanda's Gacaca and Postcolonial Legacy', *Law and Social Inquiry*, 32, 2, spring 2007, pp.467–508.

Miller, S., 'Collective Responsibility, Armed Intervention and the Rwandan Genocide', *International Journal of Applied Philosophy*, 12, 1998, pp.223–47.

Morris, M., 'The Trials of Concurrent Jurisdiction: The Case of Rwanda', *Duke Journal of Comparative and International Law*, 7, 1997, pp.349–72.

Newbury, C., 'Background to Genocide in Rwanda', *ISSUE: A Journal of Opinion*, 23, 2, 1995, pp.12–17.

Ntampaka, C., 'Le Gacaca Rwandais: une justice répressive participative', *Dossiers de la Revue de Droit Pénal et de Criminologie*, 2001, pp.211–25.

Odendaal, A., 'For All its Flaws: The TRC as a Peacebuilding Tool', *Track Two*, 6, 3 and 4, December 1997.

Oomen, B., 'Donor-Driven Justice and its Discontents: The Case of Rwanda', *Development and Change*, 36, 5, 2005, pp.887–910.

Orentlicher, D., 'Settling Accounts: The Duty to Prosecute Human Rights Violations of a Prior Regime', *New York Law Journal*, 100, 8, June 1991, pp.2562–8.

Packer, G., 'Justice on a Hill: Genocide Trials in Rwanda', *Dissent*, 49, 2, spring 2002, pp.59–72.

Power, S., 'Bystanders to Genocide: Why the United States Let the Rwandan Tragedy Happen', *The Atlantic Monthly*, September 2001, pp.84–108.

Rettig, M., 'Gacaca: Truth, Justice, and Reconciliation in Postconflict Rwanda', *African Studies Review*, 51, 3, December 2008, pp.25–50.

Reyntjens, F., 'Le *Gacaca* ou la justice du gazon au Rwanda', *Politique Africaine*, 40, December 1990, pp.31–41.

'Rwanda, Ten Years On: From Genocide to Dictatorship', *African Affairs*, 103, 2004, pp.177–210.

Sarkin, J., 'The Necessity and Challenges of Establishing a Truth and Reconciliation Commission in Rwanda', *Human Rights Quarterly*, 21, 3, 1999, pp.767–823.

'The Tension between Justice and Reconciliation in Rwanda: Politics, Human Rights, Due Process and the Role of the Gacaca Courts in Dealing with the Genocide', *Journal of African Law*, 45, 2, 2001, pp.143–72.

'The Trials and Tribulations of South Africa's Truth and Reconciliation Commission', *South African Journal on Human Rights*, 12, 4, 1996, pp.617–40.

Scherrer, C., 'Towards a Theory of Modern Genocide: Comparative Genocide Research: Definitions, Criteria, Typologies, Causes, Key Elements, Patterns and Voids', *Journal of Genocide Research*, 1, 1999, pp.13–23.

Shalom, S., 'The Rwanda Genocide: The Nightmare that Happened', *Zed Magazine*, April 1996, pp.1–25.

Smith, D., 'The Genesis of Genocide in Rwanda: The Fatal Dialectic of Class and Ethnicity', *Humanity and Society*, 19, 4, 1995, pp.57–71.

Smith, N., 'The Psychocultural Roots of Genocide', *American Psychologist*, 53, 1998, pp.743–53.

Sosnov, M., 'The Adjudication of Genocide: Gacaca and the Road to Reconciliation in Rwanda', *Denver Journal of International Law and Policy*, 125, 2007–8, pp.125–54.

Soyinka, W., 'Hearts of Darkness: Review of Gourevitch', *New York Times Books*, 4 October 1998, pp.11–15.

Staub, E., 'Genocide and Mass Killing: Origins, Prevention, Healing and Reconciliation', *Political Psychology*, 21, 2, 2000, pp.367–82.

'Justice, Healing, and Reconciliation: How the People's Courts in Rwanda Can Promote Them', *Peace and Conflict: Journal of Peace Psychology*, 10, 1, 2004, pp.25–32.

Teitel, R., 'Transitional Jurisprudence: The Role of Law in Political Transformation', *Yale Law Journal*, 106, 7, May 1997, pp.2009–80.

Tully, L.D., 'Human Rights Compliance and the Gacaca Jurisdictions in Rwanda', *Boston College International and Comparative Law Review*, 26, 2, 2003, pp.385–414.

Uvin, P., 'Difficult Choices in the New Post-Conflict Agenda: The International Community in Rwanda after the Genocide', *Third World Quarterly*, 2001, 22, 2, pp.177–89.

Uvin, P. and C. Mironko, 'Western and Local Approaches to Justice in Rwanda', *Global Governance*, 9, 2003, pp.219–32.

von Hoyweghen, S., 'The Disintegration of the Catholic Church in Rwanda: A Study of the Fragmentation of Political and Religious Authority', *African Affairs*, 95, 380, July 1996, pp.379–401.

Waldorf, L., 'Mass Justice for Mass Atrocity: Rethinking Local Justice as Transitional Justice', *Temple Law Review*, 79, spring 2006, pp.1–92.

Werchick, L., 'Prospects for Justice in Rwanda's Citizen Tribunals', *Human Rights Brief*, 8, 3, 2001, pp.15–18.

Zehr, H., 'Restorative Justice: When Justice and Healing Go Together', *Track Two*, 6, 3 and 4, December 1997.

United Nations, government and non-governmental organisation reports and legal documents

African Rights, 'Gacaca Justice: A Shared Responsibility', Kigali: African Rights, January 2003.

'Prisoner Releases: A Risk for the Gacaca System', Kigali: African Rights, 16 January 2003.

Amnesty International, 'Namibia: Caprivi Treason Trial – Justice Delayed is Justice Denied!', AI Index AFR 42/002/2003, 4 August 2003.

'Rwanda: Gacaca – A Question of Justice', AI Index AFR 47/007/2002, December 2002.

'Rwanda: Gacaca – Gambling with Justice', Press Release, AI Index AFR 47/003/2002, 19 June 2002.

'Rwanda: Human Rights Organisation Forced to Close Down', AI Index AFR 47/001/2005, 10 January 2005.

'Rwanda: Reports of Killings and Abductions by the Rwandan Patriotic Army, April – August 1994', AI Index AFR 47/016/1994, 20 October 1994.

'Rwanda: The Troubled Course of Justice', AI Index AFR 47/10/00, April 2000.

'Rwanda: Two Years after the Genocide – Rights in the Balance (Open Letter to President Pasteur Bizimungu)', AI Index AFR 47/02/96, 4 April 1996.

Avocats Sans Frontières, 'Les 'Juridictions Gacaca' au Jour le Jour', ASF, 19 June 2002–27 July 2003, www.asf.be/FR/Frameset.htm.

'Monitoring of the Gacaca Courts, Judgement Phase, Analytical Report, March–September 2005', Brussels: ASF, 2005.

Babalola, S. and J. Karambizi, 'Evaluation of the Gacaca Promotional Campaign in Rwanda: Report of Main Findings', Baltimore, Md. Johns Hopkins University, Population Communication Services, 2003.

Bugingo, S., 'Gacaca Courts Prepare for Trials', Press Release, Kigali: NURC, 9 July 2004.

Gasibirege, S. and S. Babalola, 'Perceptions about the Gacaca Law in Rwanda: Evidence from a Multi-Method Study', Special Publication (no.

19), Baltimore, Md.: Johns Hopkins University School of Public Health, Center for Communication Programs, April 2001.

Harvard Law School, 'Gacaca Jurisdictions: Interim Report of Observations, June 10–August 8 2002', Cambridge, Mass.: Harvard Law School, 2002.

Human Rights Watch, 'Ituri "Covered in Blood": Ethnically Targeted Violence in Northeastern DR Congo', Washington, DC: HRW, April 2003.

'Law and Reality: Progress in Judicial Reform in Rwanda', New York: HRW, 25 July 2008.

'Preparing for Elections: Tightening Control in the Name of Unity', HRW Briefing Paper, Kigali: HRW, May 2003.

'Rwanda: Human Rights Developments', *World Report 2001*, HRW, December 2001.

'Shattered Lives: Sexual Violence during the Rwandan Genocide and its Aftermath', New York: HRW, September 1996.

'Struggling to Survive: Barriers to Justice for Rape Victims in Rwanda', New York: HRW, September 2004.

'The Rwandan Patriotic Front', New York: HRW, 1999.

'US: Revival of Guantanamo Military Commissions a Blow to Justice', New York: HRW, 15 May 2009.

'What Kabila is Hiding: Civilian Killings and Impunity in Congo', New York: HRW, October 1997.

Institut de Recherche et de Dialogue pour la Paix, *A Time for Peace: Canvassing the Views of Rwanda's People in the Search for Lasting Peace*, Kigali: IRDP, August 2008.

Building Lasting Peace in Rwanda: Voices of the People, Kigali: IRDP, November 2003.

'IRDP Bulletin No. 2', Kigali: IRDP, December 2007.

International Centre for Prison Studies, 'Prison Brief for Rwanda', King's College, London: ICPS, 2002.

International Criminal Tribunal for Rwanda, 'Minutes of Proceedings: Nyiramasuhuko, Case No. ICTR-98-42-T', ICTR Trial Minutes, 15 April 2004, www.ictr.org/ENGLISH/cases/Nyira/minutes/2004/040415.pdf.

'Statute of the ICTR', United Nations, 1995.

'The Prosecutor vs. Fulgence Kayishema: Brief of Human Rights Watch as *Amicus Curiae* in Opposition to Rule 11 *bis* Transfer', Case No. ICTR-2001-67-I, 3 January 2008.

'The Prosecutor vs. Ildephonse Hategekimana: Decision on Prosecutor's Request for the Referral of the Case of Ildephonse Hategekimana to Rwanda, Rule 11 *bis* of the Rules of Procedure and Evidence', Case No. ICTR-00-55B-R11 *bis*, 19 June 2008.

International Crisis Group, 'Congo Crisis: Military Intervention in Ituri', ICG, 13 June 2003.

'"Consensual Democracy in Post Genocide Rwanda": Evaluating the March 2001 District Elections', Nairobi/Brussels: ICG, 9 October 2001.

'International Criminal Tribunal for Rwanda: Justice Delayed', New York: ICG, 7 June 2001.

'Scramble for the Congo: Anatomy of an Ugly War', ICG, 20 December 2000.

International Panel of Eminent Personalities to Investigate the 1994 Genocide in Rwanda and the Surrounding Events, Organization of African Unity, 'Report of International Panel', Nairobi: OAU, 2000.

International Rescue Committee, 'Mortality in the Democratic Republic of the Congo', New York: IRC, December 2004.

Kagame, P., 'Kagame Speaks on Eve of the Launch of Gacaca Trials', excerpt of radio interview with BBC, reprinted on official government website, Republic of Rwanda, 5 October 2001, www.rwanda1.com/government/president/interviews/2001/gacaca.html.

Ligue Rwandaise pour la Promotion et la Defense des Droits de l'Homme, 'Juridictions gacaca au Rwanda: résultats de la recherch sur les attitudes et opinions de la population Rwandaise', Kigali: LIRPODHOR, August 2000.

'Problematique de la preuve dans les procès de génocide: l'institution imminente des juridictions gacaca constituerait-elle une panacée?', Kigali: LIPRODHOR, June 2000.

'Situation des droits de la personne au Rwanda en 2002: rapport annuel de la LIPRODHOR', Kigali: LIPRODHOR, June 2003.

Lord's Resistance Army Delegation to the Juba Talks, 'LRA Position Paper on Accountability and Reconciliation in the Context of Alternative Justice System for Resolving the Northern Ugandan and Southern Sudan Conflicts', Juba, Southern Sudan, August 2006.

National Unity and Reconciliation Commission, 'Nationwide Grassroots Consultations Report: Unity and Reconciliation Initiatives in Rwanda', Kigali: NURC, January 2001.

'Opinion Survey on Participation in Gacaca and National Reconciliation', Kigali: NURC, January 2003.

'Reconciliation and Democratization: Experiences and Lessons Learned in Reconciliation and Democratization from Germany, South Africa, Namibia and Rwanda', Kigali: NURC, October 2003.

'Report on the National Summit on Unity and Reconciliation', Kigali: NURC, 18–20 October 2000.

'Report of the National Summit on Unity and Reconciliation', Kigali: NURC, 26–28 October 2002.

'Training Manual on Conflict Management', Kigali: NURC, February 2006.

National University of Rwanda, *Proceedings of the Workshop on 'Rethinking Peace, Coexistence and Human Security in the Great Lakes'*, Butare: Center for Conflict Management, National University of Rwanda, April 2002.

Norwegian Helsinki Committee for Human Rights, 'Prosecuting Genocide in Rwanda: The Gacaca System and the International Criminal Tribunal for Rwanda', Oslo: NHCHR, September 2002.

Oxford Policy Management, 'The Impact of Increases in Public Expenditure on Poverty in Rwanda', Oxford: OPM, March 2003.

Penal Reform International, 'Gacaca Courts in Rwanda', Kigali: PRI, 2003.

'Interim Report on Research on Gacaca Jurisdictions and its Preparations (July–December 2001)', Kigali: PRI, January 2002.

'Monitoring and Research Report No. IX on the Gacaca: Community Service (TIG) – Areas of Reflection', Kigali: PRI, March 2007.

'PRI Research Team on Gacaca (Report III: April–June 2002)', Kigali: PRI, July 2002.

'PRI Research on Gacaca Report (Report IV): The Guilty Plea Procedure, Cornerstone of the Rwandan Justice System', Kigali: PRI, January 2003.

'Research on the Gacaca [Report V]', Kigali: PRI, September 2003.

'Research Report on the Gacaca, Report VI: From Camp to Hill, the Reintegration of Released Prisoners', Kigali: PRI, May 2004.

Prendergast, J. and D. Smock, 'Postgenocidal Reconstruction: Building Peace in Rwanda and Burundi', United States Institute of Peace Special Report, USIP, September 1999.

Republic of Rwanda, 'Annex II.6: State Expenditure by Budget Agency – 2009–2012', Ministry of Finance, July 2009.

'Communiqué (Summary, Original in Kinyarwanda)', 7 January 2003, www.gov.rw/government/070103.html.

'Gacaca Judicial System Launched in Kigali', Department of Information, 18 June 2002, www.gov.rw/government/061802.html.

'Imfashanyigisho Y'Ingando N'Andi Mahugurwa', Kigali: NURC, October 2006.

'La Situation actuelle des juridictions gacaca', Kigali: Supreme Court of Rwanda, 6th Chamber (Gacaca Commission), 25 June 2003.

'Les Parténaires du processus gacaca', official rwandan government website, www.inkiko-gacaca.gov.rw/fr/partenaires.html.

'Loi Organique No. 33/2001 du 22/6/2001 modifiant et completant Loi Organique No. 40/2000 du 26 Janvier 2001 portant creation des "juridictions gacaca" et organisation des poursuite des infractions constitutives du crime de génocide ou de crimes contre l'humanité, commises entre le 1 Octobre 1990 et 31 Decembre 1994', Official Gazette of the Republic of Rwanda, Kigali, 22 June 2001.

'Loi Organique No. 8196 du 30/8/96 sur l'organisation des poursuites des infractions constitutives du crime de genocide ou de crimes contre l'humanité, commises à partir de 1er octobre 1990', Official Gazette of the Republic of Rwanda, Kigali, 1 September 1996.

'Manuel explicatif sur la Loi Organique portant création des juridictions gacaca', Kigali: Cour Suprème, Département des Juridictions Gacaca, 2001.

'Ministry of Finance and Economic Planning Budgets, 2002–9', Ministry of Finance and Economic Planning, www.minecofin.gov.rw/en/inno-file_galleries.php.

'Minutes of the Symposium on Gacaca', Hotel Umubano, Kigali, 6–7 March 2000.

'Organic Law No. 10/2007 of 01/03/2007 Modifying and Complementing Organic Law No. 16/2004 of 19/6/2004 Establishing the Organisation, Competence and Functioning of Gacaca Courts Charged with Prosecuting and Trying the Perpetrators of the Crime of Genocide and Other Crimes against Humanity, Committed between October 1, 1990 and December 31, 1994, as Modified and Complemented to Date', *Official Gazette of the Republic of Rwanda*, 3 January 2007.

'Organic Law No. 13/2008 of 19/05/2008 Modifying and Complementing Organic Law No. 16/2004 of 19/6/2004 Establishing the Organisation, Competence and Functioning of Gacaca Courts Charged with Prosecuting and Trying the Perpetrators of the Crime of Genocide and Other Crimes against Humanity, Committed between October 1, 1990 and December 31, 1994, as Modified and Complemented to Date', *Official Gazette of the Republic of Rwanda*, 19 May 2008.

'Organic Law No. 16/2004 of 19/6/2004 Establishing the Organisation, Competence and Functioning of Gacaca Courts Charged with Prosecuting and Trying the Perpetrators of the Crime of Genocide and Other Crimes against Humanity, Committed between 1 October 1990 and 31 December 1994', *Official Gazette of the Republic of Rwanda*, Kigali, 19 June 2004.

'Organic Law No. 28/2006 of 27/06/2006 Modifying and Complementing Organic Law No. 16/2004 of 19/06/2004 Establishing the Organisation, Competence and Functioning of Gacaca Courts Charged with Prosecuting and Trying the Perpetrators of the Crime of Genocide and Other Crimes against Humanity, Committed between October 1, 1990 and December 31, 1994', *Official Gazette of the Republic of Rwanda*, 27 June 2006.

'Organic Law No. 40/2000 of 26/01/2001 Setting Up Gacaca Jurisdictions and Organising Prosecutions for Offences Constituting the Crime of Genocide or Crimes against Humanity Committed between 1 October 1993 and 31 December 1994', *Official Gazette of the Republic of Rwanda*, Kigali, October 2000.

'President Kagame Allays Concerns about Gacaca', Department of Information, Government of Rwanda, 14 April 2002, www.gov.rw/government/07_11_01_genoconcern.htm.

'Report on the Reflection Meetings Held in the Office of the President of the Republic from May 1998 to March 1999', Kigali: Office of the President of the Republic, August 1999.

United Nations, 'Further Promotion and Encouragement of Human Rights and Fundamental Freedoms, Including the Question of the Programme and Methods of the Work of the Commission: Human Rights, Mass Exoduses and Displaced Persons', UNESCO, UN Doc. E/CN.4/1995/50/Add.4, 16 February 1995.

'Glossary of UN Peacekeeping Terms', UN, www.un.org.Depts/dpko/glossary/p.htm.

'Report of the Independent Inquiry into the Actions of the United Nations During the 1994 Genocide in Rwanda', UN, 15 December 1999.

'Report of the Panel on United Nations Peace Operations', UN Doc. A/55/305-S/2000/809, 21 August 2000.

'Report of the Secretary-General Pursuant to Paragraph 2 of Security Council Resolution 808, UN SCOR, 48th session, Annex, article 9(1)', UN Doc. S/25704, 1993.

'Report on the Situation of Human Rights in Rwanda', UN Doc. E/CN.4/1999/33, 8 February 1999.

'Rwanda's History Stained by Massive Human Rights Violations, But Rule of Law System Painstakingly Constructed to Tackle Forces Seeking to Sow Division, Committee Told', UN Human Rights Committee, UN Doc. HR/CT/705, 19 March 2009.

'Security Council Resolution Adjusting UNAMIR's Mandate and Authorizing a Reduction in its Strength', UN Doc. s/RES/918, UN, 21 April 2004.

'Security Council Resolution Establishing the International Criminal Tribunal for Rwanda', UN Doc. s/RES/955, 8 November 1994.

'Security Council Resolution Establishing UNAMIR for a Six-Month Period and Approving the Integration of UNOMUR into UNAMIR', UN, 5 October 1993.

'Situation in Rwanda: International Assistance for a Solution to the Problems of Refugees, the Restoration of Total Peace, Reconstruction and Socio-Economic Development in Rwanda (Report of the Secretary-General)', UN Doc. A/51/353, 12 September 1996.

'Statement by the Secretary-General Expressing Grief over the Deaths of the Presidents of Burundi and Rwanda and Condemning All Acts of Violence in Rwanda, Particularly the Deaths of 10 Belgian Peacekeepers', UN Doc. SG/SM/5259, UN, 7 April 1994.

USAID (Rwanda), 'Annual Report FY 2003', Kigali/New York: USAID, 10 May 2004.

Print Journalism

Bernault, F., 'Summary: The French Africanist Community and the Rwanda Crisis', *Africa Today*, January–March 1998, 45, 1, pp.59–62.

Bisika, A., 'Otunnu Is Not Obama Because Uganda Is Not USA', *The New Vision*, 2 September 2009.

Blomfield, A., 'Village Courts Will Try Thousands over Rwandan Genocide', *Daily Telegraph*, 5 October 2001, news.telegraph.co.uk/news/main.jhtml?xml=/news/2001/10/05/wrwan05.xml.

British Broadcasting Corporation, 'From Butchery to Executions in Rwanda', 27 April 1998, news.bbc.co.uk/1/hi/programmes/from_our_own_correspondent/84120.stm.

Brittain, V., 'Letter from Rwanda', *The Nation*, 1 September 2003, www.thenation.com/doc.mhtml?i=20030901&s=brittain.

Carroll, R., 'Rwandans Face Village Justice', *Guardian*, 5 July 2004, www.guardian.co.uk/international/story/0,3604,1253924,00.html.

Evêques Catholiques du Rwanda, 'Juridictions gacaca: pour une justice qui reconcilie', *Dialogue*, 230, September–October 2002, pp.3–13.

Gourevitch, P., 'Justice in Exile', *New York Times*, 24 June 1996, A15.

Helsingin Sanomat, 'Prosecutor in Genocide Case Takes Court on Tour of Rwanda Village', 17 September 2009, www.hs.fi/english/article/Prosecutor+in+genocide+case+takes+court+on+tour+of+Rwanda+village/ 1135249393557.

Kanuma, S., 'Local Justice', *Developments*, 24, 2003, www.developments.org.uk/templates/display/text.cfm.

Lacey, M., 'A Decade after Massacres, Rwanda Outlaws Ethnicity', *New York Times*, 9 April 2004, www.nytimes.com/2004/04/09/international/africa/09RWAN.html?hp=&pagewanted=all&position=.

Morgan, T., 'Healing Genocide', *Christianity Today*, 31 March 2004, www.christianitytoday.com/ct/2004/004/4.76.html.

Neuffer, E., 'It Takes a Village', *New Republic*, 222, 15, 10 April 2000, pp.18–20.

Newbury, C., 'Ethnicity and the Politics of History in Rwanda', *Africa Today*, 45, 1, January–March 1998, pp.7–24.

Ntampaka, C., 'Le Gacaca devenu une justice aux mains des victimes', *Umubano*, March 1999, www.umubano.be/02_fr/magazine/s_gacaca.htm.

Sezibera, R., 'The Only Way to Bring Justice to Rwanda', *Washington Post*, 7 April 2002.

Smith, A., 'Rwanda Warns of Hutus Preparing Second Genocide', *Independent*, 4 August 2001, p.13.

Vansina, J., 'The Politics of History and the Crisis in the Great Lakes', *Africa Today*, 45, 1, January–March 1998, pp.37–44.

Wagner, M., 'All the 'Bourgmestre's' Men: Making Sense of Genocide in Rwanda', *Africa Today*, 45, 1, January–March 1998, pp.25–36.

Weisbord, N., 'Traditional Justice for a Genocide', *International Herald Tribune*, 26 September 2003, www.iht.com/articles/111291.html.

Internet sources

Ciabattari, J., 'Rwanda Gambles on Renewal, Not Revenge', *Women's E-News*, 9 October 2000, www.womensenews.org/article.cfm/dyn/aid/301/context.

Fondation Hirondelle, 'Training of Gacaca Judges Starts 8 April 2002', 3 April 2002, www.hirondelle.org/hirondelle.nsf/0/192d793b82d9b481c1256cb80 0591075?OpenDocument.

Gabiro, G., 'Rwanda Genocide: Paying for Reconciliation', Fondation Hirondelle, 19 December 2002, www.hirondelle.org/hirondelle.nsf/0/192 d793b82d9b481c1256cb800591075?OpenDocument.

Goodman, D., 'Justice Drowns in Political Quagmire', *Mail and Guardian Online* (Archives), 31 January 1997, www.mg.co.za.

Hirondelle News Agency, 'Cost of the ICTR to Reach $1 Billion by the End of 2007', 12 May 2006, www.allafrica.com/stories/200605120745.html.

Inyumba, A., 'Restoring Human Dignity and Reconciling the People of Rwanda', *Media Development Index*, 4, 2001, www.wacc.org.uk/modules.php? name=News&file=print&sid=714.

IRIN News, 'Gacaca Judges Undergo "Solidarity Training"', 24 November 2003, www.irinnews.info/report.asp?ReportID=38065&SelectRegion=Gr eat_Lakes&SelectCountry=RWANDA.

'More Genocide Suspects Rearrested', 11 June 2003, www.irinnews.org/print. asp?ReportID=34679.

'Rwanda: Del Ponte Addresses Alleged RPF Massacres with Kagame', 14 December 2000, www.irinnews.org/report.asp?ReportID=7752&SelectRe gion=Great_Lakes&SelectCountry=RWANDA.

'Rwanda: Gacaca Courts Begin Operations', 10 March 2005, www. irinnews.org/report.asp?ReportID=46037&SelectRegion=Grea t_Lakes&SelectCountry=RWANDA.

'Rwanda: Genocide Survivor Group Denounces Killings, Harassment', 16 December 2003, www.irinnews.org/report.asp?ReportID=38445&SelectR egion=Great_LakesSelectCountry=RWANDA.

'Rwanda: ICTR Preparing to Indict First Tutsis', 12 April 2002, www. irinnews.org/report.asp?ReportID=27252&SelectRegion=Grea t_Lakes&SelectCountry=RWANDA.

'Rwanda: Plans to Reform Traditional Courts', 16 June 2004, www.irinnews. org/print.asp?ReportID=41693.

'Rwanda: Release of Thousands of Prisoners Begins', 1 August 2005, www. irinnews.org/report.asp?ReportID=48373&SelectRegion=Great_ Lakes&SelectCountry=RWANDA.

'Special Report on Hopes for Reconciliation under Gacaca Court System', IRIN, 4 December 2002, www.irinnews.org/report.asp?ReportID=31241& SelectRegion=Great_Lakes&SelectCountry=RWANDA.

'Traditional Courts Inaugurated', 24 June 2004, www.irinnews.info/ report.asp?ReportID=41860&SelectRegion=Great_Lakes& SelectCountry=RWANDA.

'Trauma Counsellors Trained', 16 January 2004, www.irin-news.org/report.asp?ReportID=38977&SelectRegion=Grea t_Lakes&SelectCountry=RWANDA.

'Uganda: Forgiveness as an Instrument of Peace', 9 June 2005, www.irinnews. org/S_report.asp?ReportID=47575.

Lerche, C., 'Truth Commissions and National Reconciliation: Some Reflections on Theory and Practice', www.gmu.edu/academic/pcs/lerche71pcs.html.

Morgan, T., 'Healing Genocide', *Christianity Today*, 31 March 2004, www. christianitytoday.com/ct/2004/004/4.76.html.

Ntampaka, C., 'Le *Gacaca*: une juridiction pénale populaire', Agence intergouvernementale de la francophonie, 2001, www.droit.francophonie.org/acct/ rjf/actu/13Ntampa.htm.

Porter, T., 'Restorative Justice: Justice as Peacebuilding', Eastern Mennonite University, 2001, www.emu.edu/ctp/footpaths/vol1no1/page2.html.

Radio Netherlands, 'The Gacaca Fiasco', *Radio Netherlands Wereldomroep*, 14 January 2004, www.rnw.nl/hotspots/html/rwa040114.html.

Reuters, 'Sierra Leone Court Sends Convicts to Rwandan Prison', 31 October 2009, www.reuters.com/article/latestCrisis/idUSLV126612.

Rinaldo, R., 'Can the Gacaca Courts Deliver Justice?', Inter Press Service, 8 April 2004, ipsnews.net/new_nota.asp?idnews=23234.

Vespereni, H., 'Rwandans Back People's Courts', BBC News, 5 October 2001, news.bbc.co.uk/1/hi/world/africa/1581236.stm.

Walker, R., 'Rwanda Still Searching for Justice', BBC, Kigali, 30 March 2004, news.bbc.co.uk/2/hi/africa/3557753.stm.

Conference papers, films, unpublished theses and miscellaneous sources

Aghion, A. (director), *Gacaca: Living Together Again in Rwanda?*, film produced by P. Brooks, L. Bouchard and A. Aghion, New York: First Run Films, 2002.

(director), *In Rwanda We Say ... the Family that Does Not Speak Dies*, film produced by L. Bouchard and A. Aghion, New York: First Run Films, 2004.

Clark, P. and N. Palmer, 'The International Community Fails Rwanda Again', Oxford Transitional Justice Research Working Paper Series, 5 May 2009, www.csls.ox.ac.uk/documents/ClarkandPalmer_Rwanda_Final.pdf.

Cronin, J., 'A Luta Dis-Continue: The TRC Final Report and the Nation Building Project', paper delivered at the University of the Witwatersrand, Johannesburg, June 1999, www.trcresearch.org.za/ papers99/cronin.pdf.

Dortzbach, K., 'Wholeness and Healing in Community: Toward Understanding Effective African Church Interventions Following Community Violence', unpublished PhD thesis, Faculty of Theology, University of Pretoria, June 2002, copy on file with author.

Feil, S., 'Preventing Genocide: How the Early Use of Force Might Have Succeeded in Rwanda', report to the Carnegie Commission on Preventing Deadly Conflict, New York: Carnegie Corporation, 1998.

Fujii, L.A., 'Origins of Power and Identity in Rwanda', paper delivered at the Annual Conference of the International Studies Association, 20–4 February 2001, Chicago, Ill., pp.1–17, www.isanet.org/archive/fujii.html.

Gahima, G., 'What is Understood by Justice in Rwanda Today?', paper delivered at the Newick Park Initiative Conference, 'The Role of the Churches in the Restoration of Justice in Rwanda', Kigali, 19–21 August 1997.

Ingelaere, B., '"Does the Truth Pass across the Fire without Burning?" Transitional Justice and its Discontents in Rwanda's Gacaca Courts', Institute of Development Policy and Management Discussion Paper, University of Antwerp, November 2007.

Institute for Contextual Theology 'The Kairos Document: Challenge to the Church', Cape Town, 1985, www.bethel.edu/~letnie/AfricanChristianity/SAKairos.html.

Kagame, P., 'Preventing Genocide: Threats and Responsibilities', paper delivered at the Stockholm International Forum, 26 January 2004.

Kerrigan, F., 'Some Issues of Truth, Justice and Reconciliation in Genocide Trials before Gacaca Tribunals in Rwanda', Copenhagen: Danish Centre for Human Rights, April 2002.

Molenaar, A., 'Gacaca: Grassroots Justice after Genocide – The Key to Reconciliation in Rwanda?', Research Report 77/2005, Leiden: African Studies Centre, 2005.

Morton, J., 'Conflict in Darfur: A Different Perspective', Resource Paper, Hempstead: HTSPE, June 2004.

Munyeli, J., 'Gacaca comme voie oblige de la reconciliation: cas des prisonniers libérés par le communiqué présidentiel du 01 Janvier 2003 – District de Kanombe', unpublished BA thesis, Department of Sociology, Université Libre de Kigali, June 2004, copy on file with author.

Ndangiza, F., 'Transitional Justice and Reconciliation', paper delivered at the Conference on Policy Research, Ottawa, 21 November 2002.

Pearlman, L.A., 'Psychological Trauma', paper prepared for the 'Healing, Forgiving, and Reconciliation' project, John Templeton Foundation, West Conshohocken, Pa., 13 March 2000, www-unix.oit.umass.edu/%7egubin/rwanda/lec4.htm.

Straus, S., 'Letter from Rwanda: Gacaca Begins', report for the Institute for the Study of Genocide, 26 June 2002.

Tuzinde, I., 'Justice and Social Reconstruction in the Aftermath of Genocide in Rwanda: An Evaluation of the Possible Role of the Gacaca Tribunals', unpublished LLM thesis, Bellville: University of the Western Cape, November 2000, copy on file with author.

Uvin, P., 'The Introduction of a Modernized Gacaca for Judging Suspects of Participation in the Genocide and the Massacres of 1994 in Rwanda', discussion paper prepared for the Belgian Secretary of State for Development Cooperation, 2000.

Vandeginste, S., 'A Truth and Reconciliation Approach to the Genocide and Crimes against Humanity in Rwanda', Antwerp: Centre for the Study of the Great Lakes Region of Africa, May 1998.

'Justice, Reconciliation and Reparation after Genocide and Crimes against Humanity: The Proposed Establishment of Popular Gacaca Tribunals in Rwanda', paper delivered at the All-Africa Conference on African Principles of Conflict Resolution and Reconciliation, Addis Ababa, 8–12 November 1999.

Various, 'The Rwandan Genocide and Transitional Justice: Commemorating the 10th Anniversary of the Genocide', conference at St Antony's College, University of Oxford, 15 May 2004, notes on file with author.

Woodstock Theological Center, 'An Ethic for Enemies: Forgiveness in Politics', Forum Transcript, *Woodstock Report*, 45, March 1996, www.georgetown.edu/centers/woodstock/report/r-fea45.htm.

INDEX

Lightning Source UK Ltd.
Milton Keynes UK
UKOW031227090112

185014UK00013B/116/P